Windows NT Workstation 4 ...

Though Windows NT uses a mouse-driven graphical user int[...]
shortcuts for common tasks. Below you'll find several alternati[...]

Working in Windows Explorer

The procedures described below for files also work with folders.

Sort files

You can sort, or change the list order of the files in a folder in various ways by clicking the column titles in the right-hand pane in the Details view. To sort files by filename, file size, file type, or when modified, click Name, Size, Type, or Modified, respectively. Click once to sort in ascending order, and click again to sort in descending order.

Select multiple files

If you have the standard Windows NT user interface or have installed IE4 and have your Active Desktop set to single-click mode, simply hold the mouse cursor momentarily over the file or folder instead of clicking in the procedures described below.

Click the first file or folder in the right pane. Then do one of the following:

- To select a range of contiguous files, click the last file while pressing the Shift key; or
- Drag your mouse (hold down the primary key and move the mouse) to create a marquee around the files; or
- To select several non-contiguous files, click each additional file while pressing the Control key; or
- To select multiple sets of contiguous files, click the first file of the new range while pressing the Control key. Then click the last file of the range while pressing both Control and Shift. Repeat this procedure for each additional range.

Delete files, first select then

- Press Shift + Del to delete without sending to the Recycle Bin; or
- Drag the selected files to the Recycle Bin; or
- Open a command line session using either command.com or cmd.exe and use the Del or Erase command from the CLI; or
- Right-click the file or selected files, then choose Delete from the context menu. To delete without sending to the Recycle Bin, press the Shift key while choosing Delete; or
- Select the file(s), then click the Delete button on the toolbar.

Move files, first select then

- Drag the file or selected files to the destination folder icon in the same drive. If moving to another drive, hold down the Shift key while dragging; or
- Right-click the selected files, and choose Move from the object menu. Then right-click within or over the destination folder, and choose Paste; or
- Right-drag the file(s) from the destination folder, then choose Move Here from the object menu that appears.

Copy files, first select then

- Drag the file or selected files to the destination folder icon in a different drive. If copying to the same drive, drag while holding down the Shift key. You'll see a + sign next to the mouse cursor when it's over a destination folder you're copying to; or
- Right-click the selected files, and choose Copy from the object menu. Then right-click within or over the destination folder, and choose Paste; or
- Right-drag the file(s) from the destination folder, then choose Copy Here from the object menu that appears.

- Right-click on the Start button then choose Explore All Users from the context menu. Locate the shortcut you wish to remove press the Del key. You must be logged on with administrator level rights to do this.

Adding a shortcut to a program or document

1. Click Add… on the Start Menu Program tab, then type the path and filename of the program or document in the command line field. Or, if you don't know the full path, click the Browse… button instead. If you are adding a shortcut to a document, select All Files (instead of Programs) in the Files of Type field. Navigate your hard drive or network to the desired program or document file and select it. Click Open, so that the filename now appears in the command line field of the Create Shortcut dialog.

2. Click the Next… button to get to the Select Program Folder dialog, and select the folder in which you want to place the shortcut. If you want to create a subfolder for the shortcut, click the New Folder… button, and type in the name for it.

3. Click the Next… button to get to the Select a Title for the Program dialog. Type in a readily recognizable name for the program or document.

Adding a shortcut to a folder

Click Add… on the Start Menu Program tab, then click the Browse… button and navigate your hard drive or network to the desired folder and select it. Now drag the folder with the left or right mouse button to the Start button so that the Start menu pops up. Continue dragging the folder to its desired location in the menu hierarchy before you release the button.

Working directly with shortcuts in the Start menu folder

This is the most efficient method when you are reorganizing your Start menu and adding new folders (submenus) to it at the same time.

1. Right-click the Start button and choose Open…. Or click the Advanced… button on the Start Menu Programs tab of the Taskbar Properties dialog. This opens an Explorer window with the Start Menu folder hierarchy in the left pane and the files in the right pane. The directory tree corresponds exactly to the Start menu hierarchy.

2. Create, rename, move, copy, or delete folders. Move or copy shortcuts to other locations in the tree. Create new data files for registered programs by right-clicking on an empty spot to open the object menu.

To add a new user, log on with administrator level rights then

1. Launch the User Manager by choosing Start | Programs | Administrative Tools (Common) | User Manager.
2. Choose User | New User from the menu.
3. Fill in the blanks.
4. Assign the user to a User Group and give him a profile (if desired).

To recover a user's lost password, log on with administrator level rights then

1. Open the User Manager by choosing Start | Programs | Administrative Tools (Common) | User Manager.
2. Locate the user with the missing password.
3. Delete the user account and create a new one with the same characteristics; or
4. Double-click on the user and alter the password in the resulting dialog box.

To locate your saved files (in their default location)

1. Log on with your rights or with administrator level rights.
2. Locate your folder structure under [%winnt%]\Profiles.
3. Highlight your logged on name folder and press the plus key on the numeric keypad to expand the folder structure.

Key Combination	Purpose
Plus (keypad)	Expand the selected folder.
Minus (keypad)	Collapse an expanded folder or, if it's already collapsed, select its parent folder.
Alt+F4	Close the active program. You can also use it to exit Windows NT if you're at the desktop.
Alt+Tab	Switch to the next window. Keep the Alt key down while tabbing to cycle through open windows until you get to the one you want to activate.
Alt+Shift+Tab	Switch to the previous window.
Backspace	Move one level up in the directory structure (same as clicking the Up tool).
Ctrl+A	Select all files and folders.
Alt+Enter or Alt+double-click	View properties of the selected object.
Ctrl+Esc	Select applications in the order they were opened.
PrintScreen	Copy the screen to the Clipboard.
Alt+PrintScreen	Copy current window to the Clipboard.
Ctrl+Esc	Open the Start menu. Use the arrow keys to select program, and press Enter to start it.
Alt+Enter	Toggle full and window mode (if supported).
Alt+Spacebar	Drop down System menu.
Esc	Cancel the last action in most cases.
Shift+F1	Display context-sensitive help when the application supports it.
Shift+F10	Display the object menu for the selected object.
Tab	Use this key while at the desktop to switch between the desktop, taskbar (Quick Launch), and Start menu.

Adding and (Re-)Arranging Shortcuts on Your Start Menu

Personalize your Start menu by adding shortcuts to your most frequently used folders, programs, and documents.

Moving or copying a shortcut to a new location

1. Click on the Start button, then navigate the Start menu so as to highlight a folder, or a shortcut to a folder, program, or document.
2. Drag the folder or shortcut with the left or right mouse button to the new location indicated by the moving horizontal bar. To navigate into a subfolder, hold the bar over it until it exposes its contents.
3. Release the button to move the folder or shortcut to the current location of the moving bar. To copy the item instead, press the Control key while releasing the button; or
4. Right-click on the Start button then choose Explore All Users from the context menu. Locate the shortcut you wish to move and move it to a new folder. You can also copy the shortcut using the same techniques shown in "Copy files, first select then." You must be logged on with administrator level rights to do this.

Getting to the Start Menu Program dialog

- From the Start menu, select Settings | Taskbar & Start Menu... Or right-click outside any button on the taskbar and choose Properties. Choose the Start Menu Program tab of the Taskbar Properties dialog box.

Removing shortcuts from the Start menu

- Click Remove... on the Start Menu Program tab. Navigate the hierarchy to select the folder or shortcut you want to remove, and click the Remove button. Repeat the last procedure for each item you want to remove; or

Rename a file

- Right-click the file or folder, and choose Rename from the object menu. Type over the existing filename in the rectangular editing box that appears; or

- If you are in double-click (Classic if you have the Active Desktop) mode, you can simply click the filename (and not the file icon) in order to edit the filename; or

- Press F2 while the file icon is highlighted, then edit the filename.

Create a new folder

- Right-click in the parent folder, and choose New | Folder from the context menu. Rename New Folder (the default name) as desired; or

- Choose File | New | Folder from the Explorer's main menu.

Create a shortcut to a file

- Right-click the destination folder, and choose New | Shortcut from the object menu. Provide the path to the file in the Create Shortcut Wizard; or

- Choose File | New | Shortcut from the Explorer main menu and follow the prompts; or

- Right-drag the file(s) to the destination then choose Create Shortcut(s) Here from the context menu that appears.

Starting Programs Quickly

Windows NT provides many ways to start your applications. Here are the easiest ways to do so:

- Double-click a data file associated with the program while in Explorer (for this to work there must already be a file association to the program; otherwise Windows NT will prompt you to create one for that file extension); or

- Double-click the program icon in Explorer; or

- Right-click the program icon while in Explorer, and then click Open in the context menu; or

- Select the program's entry from the Start menu; or

- Create a shortcut to the program on the desktop. Start it by right-clicking or double-clicking the Shortcut icon; or

- Choose Start | Run and then type the application's path and filename. Click OK to start the program; or

- Choose Start | Run and then drag-and-drop the program's icon into the Run dialog box. Click OK to start the application; or

- Use the Find dialog on the Start menu (or press F3) to find your program, and then right-click or double-click it; or

- Place the program icon or its associated data file in the Startup folder in the Start menu. It will run automatically the next time you start Windows NT; or

- Assign a shortcut key to the program, and then start it by using the keyboard shortcut. (You must create a .LNK file to do this).

Windows NT Shortcut Keys

Some of these keys or key combinations can also be used within an application with the same or similar results.

Key Combination	Purpose
F1	Display online help.
F2	When an icon is highlighted, lets you rename the object.
F3	Access the Find dialog.
F5	Refresh a window (useful after saving files to an already open window).
Asterisk (keypad)	Expand all subfolders.

continues...

Using

Windows NT Workstation

Second Edition 4

Paul Cassel

que®

A Division of Macmillan Computer Publishing, USA
201 W. 103rd Street
Indianapolis, Indiana 46290

Contents at a Glance

Using Windows NT Workstation 4, Second Edition

International Standard Book Number: 0-7897-1648-8

Library of Congress Catalog Card Number: 98-84510

Printed in the United States of America

First Printing: August 1998

00   99   98   4   3   2   1

Executive Editor
Grace Buechlein

Managing Editor
Patrick Kanouse

Senior Editor
Elizabeth A. Bruns

Copy Editor
Keith Cline

Indexers
Christine Nelsen
Ginny Bess

Technical Editor
Jeff Perkins

Production
Mona Brown
Michael Dietsch
Ayanna Lacey
Gene Redding

Trademarks

Warning and Disclaimer

Contents

Appendixes

About the Author

Paul Cassel has been working with small computers since the late 1970s. His interest in Microsoft Windows NT dates back to his sneak preview of it in the early 1990s. He has worked with Microsoft on Windows NT since the first release and has been evangelical for the system since the beginning. He worked with Microsoft in developing the first certification specification for Windows NT—what today has become the Microsoft Certification series of programs. Paul is part of a consulting business where he acts as a Windows NT system administrator and network designer for several large and medium sized companies. He has worked with Microsoft's development teams on many projects, including MS-DOS, Windows for Workgroups, Windows 95, Windows 98, Windows NT, and many application programs. He has won numerous MVP awards from Microsoft and similar awards and recognition from other software companies.

Dedication

This book is dedicated to my daughter Tirilee Cassel, the golden champion.

Acknowledgments

This book sports a new, and initially unfamiliar for me, format. This format now forms the basis of the Using series of books from Macmillan Computer Publishing. Both Grace Buechlein and Dean Miller helped me adapt to this new format. I have high hopes that this new format will make books written this way significantly easier for readers to locate the information they buy such books for.

My name appears as sole author of this book, but that's only part of the story. Jeff Schmidt, Jason vanValkenburgh, Anthony Steven, and Frank Battison contributed significant portions to the text. Without their expert additions, this book would not have achieved the level of technical excellence I demanded of it.

No book arrives at the bookstore or book club directly from the author. All books are, by the nature of the beast, a collaborative effort between an author and several editors. Due to the newness of this format, this book required more work from its editors than most do, so these people deserve special mention. I'd like to single out Grace Buechlein (her again!), Tom Lamoureux, and Elizabeth Bruns for their efforts in taking my manuscript and delivering this book.

Finally, I'd like to thank my daughter, Tirilee, who filled in as consultant for me at various Indian nations thus freeing me up enough to get this writing done.

Paul Cassel, New Mexico 1998

Tell Us What You Think!

As the reader of this book, *you* are our most important critic and commentator. We value your opinion and want to know what we're doing right, what we could do better, what areas you'd like to see us publish in, and any other words of wisdom you're willing to pass our way.

As the Executive Editor for the Desktop Operating Systems team at Macmillan Computer Publishing, I welcome your comments. You can fax, email, or write me directly to let me know what you did or didn't like about this book—as well as what we can do to make our books stronger.

Please note that I cannot help you with technical problems related to the topic of this book, and that due to the high volume of mail I receive, I might not be able to reply to every message.

When you write, please be sure to include this book's title and author as well as your name and phone or fax number. I will carefully review your comments and share them with the author and editors who worked on the book.

Fax: 317-581-4663

E-mail: opsys@mcp.com

Mail: Executive Editor
          Desktop Operating Systems
          Macmillan Computer Publishing
          201 West 103rd Street
          Indianapolis, IN 46290 USA

INTRODUCTION

THERE ARE QUITE A FEW COMPUTER BOOKS on the market, many of which discuss Windows NT in some manner or another. During early discussions about this book with the Executive Editor, Grace Buechlein, I decided that none of them addressed the user needs I daily encountered in my consulting business. These user needs stemmed from several situations.

- Experienced Windows users moving to Windows NT
- Experienced UNIX users migrating to Windows NT
- Experienced MS-DOS users migrating to Windows NT
- People new to computing given Windows NT as their first operating system

In each case, the differences or the newness of Windows NT caused people to misuse or underuse their operating systems. However, while each situation stemmed from a different cause, the end result was the same. I decided that any book worth its cost must address the needs of each of the users described above so they can get the most benefit from Windows NT.

People Were Tired

Most Windows NT books go into tiring long discussions about the operating system's theoretical issues rather than just giving people the information they need to use Windows NT.

A Field Report

Most people want to first learn how to use their computer and only afterward, in some cases, the vendor's reasoning about why it implemented features in any particular way. In the world of small computers, practice rules over theory.

Operations of a Feather

Each chapter includes step-by-step instructions functionally grouped together.

Sidenotes by the Dozen

This is a sidenote. There are dozens of them throughout the book loaded with expert tips, tricks and traps for Windows NT.

Finding It in the Index

I learned early on that most books contain good information, but fail by not having a way for the reader to find that information.

This isn't my first book or my first Windows NT book. My field experience showed that the existing books, including mine, weren't always meeting the needs of those who bought them. People didn't want long theoretical explanations of why Microsoft designed Windows NT like it did. They also weren't interested in windy historical digressions about operating systems in general.

I learned that what people wanted was a concise and direct set of instructions covering all the major operational aspects of Windows NT. In other words, people wanted a clear step-by-step guide about how to use Windows NT. That's what this book is.

You will find those step-by-steps by the dozen in this book. I've compiled a list of tasks people using Windows NT need to know how to do. I then classified those tasks into functional areas. Those functional areas make up the chapter organization of this book. This clusters related operations together.

For example, if you want to know how to copy a file or files, you'll find the steps to do so grouped within file operations that include not only copying, but moving, deleting, and renaming files and folders.

In some cases, operations won't classify as belonging only in a single chapter, but span two in slightly different contexts. In these instances, both chapters will cover that operation, but in a contextually valid manner.

By way of analogy, this book is a cookbook rather than a discussion about the theory of cuisine. It gets down in the trenches, giving you no-nonsense instructions about how to use Windows NT. In addition, you'll find dozens of sidenotes. These notes give you short tips, warnings, and neat tricks experts in Windows NT have compiled over time.

You'll also find cross-references and terms defined on their own and by use of related words. The reason for these entries is the recognition that a book isn't of use if it contains information the reader can't locate. I've done my best to make sure that you can find the answers to your questions—even if you don't know the precise way to ask these questions.

Now you know what I've tried to do as the writer of this book. Look it over and decide if I've succeeded. I hope that if you take the time to browse through this book, you'll find a step-by-step or a few sidenotes of value enough that you'll want to buy the whole thing. If so, I've done my job the way I hoped I could.

Browse This Book

Ultimately you have to decide if this book is for you. I hope your browse through the sidenotes and step-by-steps will convince you that this is the right Windows NT book for you.

Using Windows NT Workstation 4

Using and Understanding Windows NT Workstation 4

Using Windows Explorer

Using Files and Folders

The Desktop and Its Organization

Windows NT for Short

Users often refer to Windows NT Workstation as just "Windows NT" or "NT." You will see the product referred to as Windows NT throughout this book. Microsoft also has a companion NT product for computers that act as "servers"—computers on a network that hold files or printers that users share. The server product is called Windows NT Server.

Windows NT History

In 1991, I first saw what would evolve into Windows NT Workstation 4—a very early build back then. The "NT" in the product name stands for "new technology." At the time Windows NT was released, Windows 3.1 and 3.11 dominated the market. These two products carried similar interfaces. Microsoft marketed Windows NT as a more robust platform for corporate environments, with enhanced networking and security features. Subsequently, Microsoft released Windows 95 with a new Windows interface. Soon after, the company released Windows NT 4, much enhanced and also with the new 95-inspired user interface. Today, Windows NT 4 and the other Microsoft Windows product, Windows 98, can be tough to differentiate at a glance, although their architecture is utterly different.

The Windows Explorer Old and New

The Windows Explorer replaces the old File Manager from earlier releases of Windows and Windows NT. For those who like the older way of doing things, Microsoft ships Windows NT 4 with the early style File Manager. This file is named winfile.exe and lives in the main Windows NT folder.

Using Windows Explorer

Much of the work you will do with Windows NT involves working with various files or groups of files that reside on your computer drives. Windows NT comes with a file management feature known as Windows Explorer (often called just "the Explorer"). You will use Windows Explorer to browse your drives, folders, and files. Because working with these elements is at the heart of most of the tasks you will do with Windows NT, this chapter covers Windows Explorer first and then moves on to a discussion of files and folders and the Windows NT desktop.

The best way to learn about the Explorer is to use it. To get started, open the Explorer by clicking on the Start button that by default is at the bottom left side of your screen. The Start button is part of the taskbar, the gray bar at the bottom of your screen.

After you click on the Start button, slide your mouse up to the Programs entry at the top of the menu, and then choose Windows Explorer from the submenu that "flies out" to the right (hence, the name "fly-out menu").

Figure 1.1 shows the menu steps necessary to find the Windows Explorer entry on the Start menu system.

Figure 1.2 shows the open Windows Explorer maximized to fill the entire desktop. To maximize any window under Windows NT, locate the three buttons at the upper right of the window, and if the middle button shows a single square (supposed to be a window icon), click on it. The button's icon will change to a double square, indicating the window has been maximized. If you look closely at Figure 1.2, you can see the window's middle right button set has a double square; this indicates that the application is maximized.

It is normal and expected that your Windows Explorer should appear different from the one shown in the book. Before learning why, let me give you a short tour of the parts of the Windows Explorer.

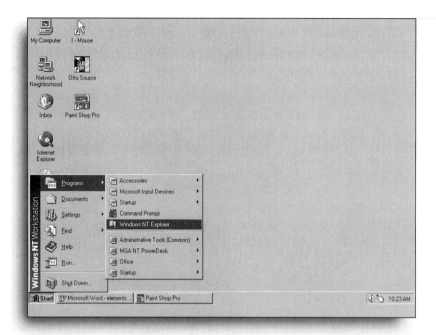

FIGURE 1.1.

By default, the Windows Explorer is on the fly-out menu of the Programs entry in the Start menu.

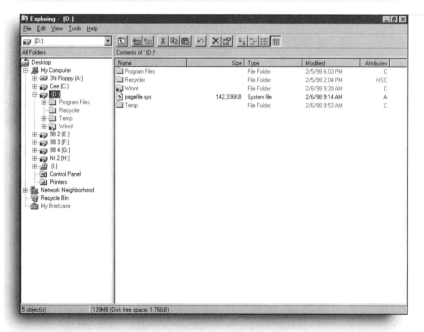

FIGURE 1.2.

The Windows Explorer's function is to explore your computer's files and folders as well as other computers on your network. The Windows Explorer is significantly improved over the older File Manager.

Arranging the Start Menu

((Holding down the primary mouse button (usually the left button) in the Programs section of the Start menu enables you to drag and drop any highlighted entry. This trick only works in user-changeable menus such as Programs, Documents, and Favorites.))

Active Right Buttons

Starting with Windows 95, all Microsoft operating systems became right-button active. Windows NT is no exception.

The Parts of the Windows Explorer

Starting from the top of Figure 1.2, the parts of the Windows Explorer are follows:

- The title bar where the name of the application and, in some cases the names of documents, appears. Your Windows Explorer should have the word *Exploring* along with the place on your computer or network you have open. In the case of the book's example, this is D:, the name of the second volume on this workstation (the first is C:).

- The menu bar with the entries File, Edit, View, Tools, Help. These function like a typical menu system. Click on the entry and you will see a pull-down menu in context of the first entry (on the menu bar). Many entries on the pull-down menu also have fly-out or submenus of their own.

- The toolbar with its various buttons. If your Windows Explorer doesn't show a toolbar, you can view it by clicking on the View entry in the menu bar and choosing Toolbar, the first entry on the pull down.

- Moving down, the left and right panes of the main body of the Windows Explorer are next. This is the main working area of the Windows Explorer. On the left pane appears the uppermost hierarchy of your computer's resources.

- The status bar is at the very bottom part of the Windows Explorer. This is the gray bar at the very bottom of the screen in Figure 1.2 showing the words 5 object(s) and 139MB (Disk free space 1.76GB). You will need sharp eyes to see the entries on the figure's status bar. If your screen doesn't have a status bar, you can make it appear by choosing the View menu and the Status bar entry from the pull-down.

Clicking around with the right mouse button will bring up a context menu, so named because the contents of the menu change depending on the context of the application. Although you never need to use the right button to effectively use Windows Explorer, doing so will save time and menu commands. Keep the right button in mind at all times while moving around in Windows NT—especially in its Windows Explorer.

The Views of Windows Explorer

Windows Explorer allows the following four views of a computer's files and folders in the right pane:

- **Large icons**, where the icons accompanying the files' and folders' names take up about 1/4 square inch each.

- **Small icons**, where the icon accompanying each file or folder name is a little larger than a letter in the filename (using the default font of about 8 points). The files in Small icon view are sorted across and then down the right pane.

- **List**, which is very similar to Small icons, but the files and folders are sorted down columns and then across rows.

- **Details**, where each file or folder's full information (or Properties) is displayed in its respective column. Each column has a head describing the property it displays. These columns are sizable, but not movable within the right pane. You can ask Windows Explorer to sort (arrange or list by) any column by clicking on its head.

Altering the Views of Windows Explorer

I have spent quite a few hours with people as they learn the elements of Windows NT and the Windows Explorer. Overall the best way to gain familiarity with them is by executing tasks. The following steps will give you a quick tour of some of the parts of Windows Explorer.

Examining the right pane of Windows Explorer

1. Open the Windows Explorer if it's not already open. Maximize it to give yourself some working room.

2. Right-click in the right pane away from any file or folder names. Locate the View entry in the context menu. It should be the first entry. Hold the cursor over the View entry for a second and a fly-out menu will appear with four entries corresponding to the various views available in the standard Windows Explorer.

3. Choose each view in any order to see their effects on the right pane. The more files and folders available in the right pane, the more apparent the effect.

Right or Left?

The left button references in this and subsequent chapters refer to the primary mouse button–by default, the left one. If you have swapped mouse button functions, likewise swap the left and right button references in this book.

4. Return to or leave the View as Details. Your screen should resemble Figure 1.2. Place your cursor on the gray bar separating the right and left panes of Windows Explorer. The cursor will change to a vertical bar with left and right arrows. Click and hold the left mouse button and drag the bar to the right or left. This sizes the two panes of the Windows Explorer.

5. Move the mouse cursor to the dark space between any two columns, such as between Name and Size in Figure 1.3. Again click to change the cursor to one indicating that you can size, and then drag the columns left or right. Figure 1.3 shows this operation. The vertical ghost line shows your progress.

FIGURE 1.3.

Click in the right place and your cursor will indicate that it is ready to resize elements of the Windows Explorer.

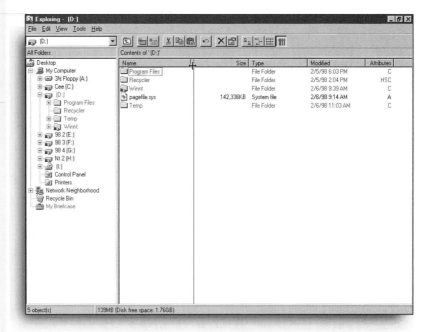

6. Click in any right-pane column other than Name. Note the sorting of the files and folders according to the data in that column. Click in the column again to reverse the sort on the same data. Click on any column head to sort on that column's data. To return to the default sort order, click on the Name column.

7. Locate a folder with a plus sign (+) next to it in the left column. Click on the plus sign. This will open up or expand the left pane's display tree. An expanded branch will have a minus sign (–) next to it. Clicking on the minus sign will collapse the branch. Figure 1.4 shows the first-level collapsed branches from Figure 1.3 expanded one branch deep. Note that plenty of plus signs are left in the partly expanded tree, indicating more branches still collapsed.

One Way or Another

You can also change right-pane Views through the View menu or the various Views buttons on the toolbar. Windows NT doesn't care, but most people prefer the right-click method because they find it faster.

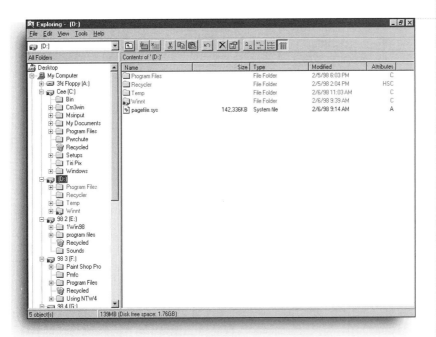

FIGURE 1.4.

You can expand and collapse branches of the volume and folder tree to show or hide detail. Expanding trees eats up a lot of desktop space.

Extensions and Files Shown

Microsoft chose, by default, to hide certain files and file extensions from users. In a moment, we will take a look at how to display and hide these files and extensions. I have seen more people confused over the lack of display of the hidden files and the mysterious disappearance of their file extensions than not. I leave it up to you whether you wish to see the file extensions of so-called known file types, and whether you wish to take a walk on the wild side by displaying all files, including system ones.

Why Hidden Files and Extensions?

I have never gotten a good explanation out of Microsoft as to why it chose, by default, to hide certain files and file extensions from users. The only indication I have gotten is some vague references to people getting themselves into trouble if they can see the files left hidden (by deleting them, perhaps) and confused if they see file extensions.

Rumors, Mac Style

Macintosh enthusiasts claim that behind Microsoft's default hiding of file extensions lies a yearning to make Microsoft's new user interface Mac-like. If so, Microsoft isn't talking.

Known File Types

A known file type is one where the extension is associated with a particular application. The file extension .XLS is usually associated with Excel, for example, and .MDB is associated with Access.

Here's how to show or hide system files as well as files with known extensions.

Showing or hiding system files, hidden files, or files with known extensions

1. Open the Windows Explorer if it is not already open.

2. Pull down the View menu. Choose Options, the final entry. Figure 1.5 shows the dialog box that will appear.

3. Experiment with checking and unchecking the two option buttons and four check boxes in the View tab of this dialog box. Click OK to close the dialog box and review the results of your changes.

FIGURE 1.5.

The Options | View dialog box is where you set global display options for system and known file types.

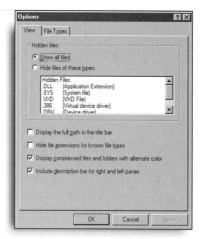

4. To have your screens most resemble this book's screens and to use the views most users prefer, set your View tab in the dialog box identically to the one shown in Figure 1.5.

Using the Windows Explorer to Find Files

Windows Explorer has a good search engine—a good thing. Given the sizes of disks today, it is easy to lose track of where you placed certain files. Here's how to use Windows Explorer to find a file.

Using Windows Explorer to find a file

1. Open the Windows Explorer if necessary. Navigate to the volume where you have installed Windows NT. This is usually where Windows Explorer will start anyway. In the example, this is volume D:. Most Windows NT installs are on volume C:.

2. Choose the menu options Tools | Find | Files or Folders. Your screen should resemble Figure 1.6.

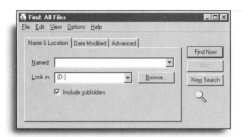

FIGURE 1.6.

Windows Explorer's handy dandy file and folder Find dialog box.

3. Enter xcopy.exe in the Named text box. Make sure the Include Subfolders check box is checked. Click OK to start the search. Figure 1.7 shows the results of the search. Your results should be substantially the same, although your volume will differ in most cases.

4. Click on the two remaining tabs in the Find: All Files dialog box. As you can see, you can also enter date, age, and time criteria to your searches on the middle tab. The third tab, Advanced, enables you to specify the file type from a pull-down list, to specify file size as a search criterion, and to enter a full-scale text search. The text search within files is similar to the GREP utility familiar to generations of UNIX users.

Remember that the Named text box where you entered xcopy.exe will also accept wild cards such as the * and ?. The * allows anything after the asterisk but before the dot in a filename to pass; the ? allows any character in that place. Entering xcopy.* in the Named text box will return files named xcopy.exe, xcopy.com, xcopy.kdk, and so forth.

Local Computer Versus Network

The term "local computer" is used to refer to your personal hard drive (containing at least one drive or volume, usually C:). If your computer is part of a network, your nonlocal drives are those that you need to access through the network.

Entering ?copy.exe in the Named text box will return xcopy.exe, ycopy.exe, zcopy.exe, and so forth, assuming they exist within your computer's grasp. ⟩⟩⟩

FIGURE 1.7.

The Find files and folders routine can dig through layers of nested folders in search of your files.

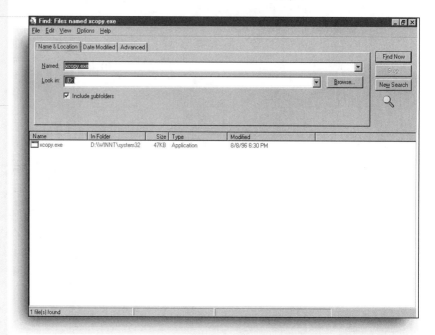

Logical Volumes

A *volume* is a logical device from which a particular user can select files, such as a drive accessed through a networked computer. A logical device doesn't have to be actually present in one location in the physical sense that a personal hard drive is. Users on a network may have access to the same files, for example, but those files may appear on different volumes to the different users—kind of like different ways to slice the same pie. Which volume a user sees the files on depends on the way the drives are set up by the network administrator and the access afforded to the different network users. ⟩⟩⟩

Here's a practical example of how to use the Find utility. I know I have a file regarding a client named Plotsky somewhere on volume (or drive) C:, but I have forgotten the name of the file and its location. I'm not even sure if it's on volume C:, but I'm sure it's on the local computer (My Computer).

Here's how I can go about finding it.

Finding a file based on file contents

1. I open Windows Explorer and start the Find Files and Folders utility. Because I've forgotten the name of the file, I enter *.* for all files in the Named text box. Because I don't know the volume for sure, I pull down the Look in: combo box by clicking on its down-facing arrow, and then select Local Hard Drives. You can see my progress at this stage in Figure 1.8.

2. I don't remember the age or the date of the file, so I ignore the middle tab of the Find dialog box.

3. Clicking on the Advanced tab, I enter `plotsky` in the Containing Text text box. I also pull down the Options menu and make sure the Case Sensitive option isn't checked because I'm unsure if I used the name in all caps or not. Figure 1.9 shows my final settings for this search. I click the Find Now button to start the search. If you want to try this, be prepared for a long search time if your disk is larger than a gigabyte or so.

4. Success! I found the file in My Documents in volume C: within the Plotsky folder in a file Griegos 10,9,97.doc, as you can see from the Search Results dialog box in Figure 1.10.

5. A double-click on the filename in the Find dialog box will bring up the associated application, in this case Microsoft Word. As you can see in Figure 1.11, the file really does contain the word Plotsky.

.?

The user interface for Windows NT Workstation 4 allows the use of the old MS-DOS "wildcards" in filename searches. A wildcard is a character that matches (lets pass) more than one other character. Using a question mark (?) in the search name lets any character pass in place of the question mark. If the files mem.doc and _mom.doc exist on your drive, a search using m?m.doc would retrieve both files.

An asterisk (*) in the search name lets all characters pass up to the point that another specific (literal) character or the dot or the end of the filename appears. For example, mem*.doc will retrieve all files with a .doc extension that are named with files whose first three characters are mem—without regard to what follows those first three characters. »

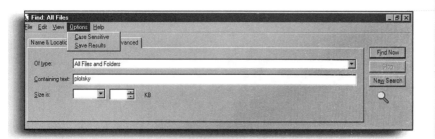

FIGURE 1.10.

Brute force searches like this one take some time, but they, like the mills of the gods, grind (and find) all.

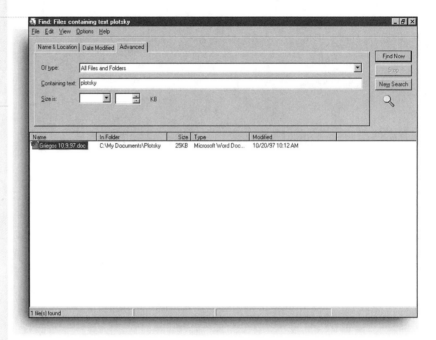

FIGURE 1.11.

A sanity check does reveal the word Plotsky in the file Greigos 10,9,97.doc.

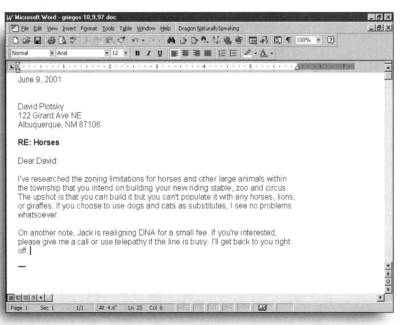

Using Files and Folders

As you can likely infer from the views of Explorer and from your own experience (if any) using personal computers, the file structure of Windows NT is a tree-like affair with folders containing files and other folders. The analogy Microsoft likes to use is that of a filing cabinet. The disk volume (or drive) is like the cabinet, the folders like the drawers, other folders act like hanging files (within other folders), and the files are like the documents.

The relationship between computer volumes, files, and folders is similar to a filing cabinet. Take a cabinet: You can have many drawers in a cabinet, each of which might have many hanging folders, each of which can hold many documents. A computer might have many volumes that can be local or on a network. Each volume can have many folders, each of which can contain more folders. Each folder can contain files (documents) as well as folders. Figure 1.12 shows a simplified tree scheme showing the relationship of volumes (disks), folders, and files.

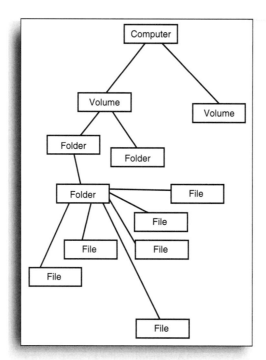

FIGURE 1.12.

The structure of files and folders is analogous to a filing cabinet.

((Just as with a regular filing cabinet, you need to decide on a filing strategy. Here are a few popular schemes:

- *Applications above their documents*. In such a scheme, the application folder contains one or more document folders holding documents specific to that application.

- *Classified documents*. Documents are stored in a separate folder structure according to a classification scheme appropriate to your work or preferences. You might, for example, classify documents according to folders bearing the names Invoices, Letters, Collections, and so forth.

- *Customer or client*. Documents are stored in a separate folder structure according to target. Thus you might have folders called Acme Glassblowing, Bludget Cleaners, Comet Rocketships, and so forth.

- *Date classification*. This just puts all documents having the same date or date range together.

Many people combine two or more schemes, such as having a client (target) folder with subfolders containing specific types of documents such as invoices or letters. How you choose to proceed depends on your preferences and your business needs. That's why these are called "personal" computers.))

Making Folders

You can make folders using the Explorer File | New | Folder menu choices, but this example uses the right-click method.

Creating a new folder using the right-click method

1. Open Explorer if necessary. Navigate to a volume or folder where you wish to locate a subfolder. A subfolder is a folder within a folder or a volume.

2. Right-click in the right pane of Explorer. Choose New from the context menu. Choose Folder from the fly-out menu. This will result in a New Folder entry in Explorer. Your screen should resemble Figure 1.13.

3. Enter any name you think appropriate for your new folder. This example uses Practice and locates the new folder directly under a volume.

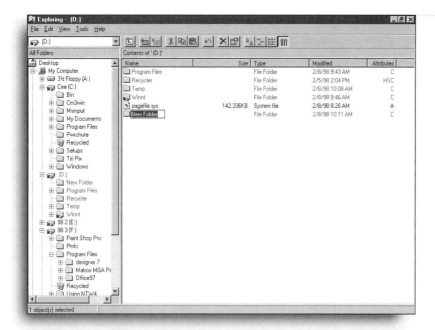

FIGURE 1.13.

This example places a new folder in volume D:, the Windows NT host volume. The new folder is ready for a specific name.

Renaming Files and Folders

You can rename files and folders willy-nilly, but keep in mind a few things. Old applications such as those made for MS-DOS and older versions of Windows can't see long filenames (longer than 8 characters followed by a 3-character extension). Also, altering the extension will, if that extension is associated with an application, disable the association. If you have the extension .WPG associated with WordPerfect and you rename a file called `my fine letter.wpg` to `my fine letter today.wr1`, for example, WordPerfect will not launch upon a double-click on the file unless it's also associated with the .WR1 extension. WordPerfect can still read the file, but the association within Explorer is lost.

With that in mind, let's move on to renaming.

Renaming a file or folder

1. Locate the object you wish to rename in Explorer.

2. Right-click on it and choose Rename from the context menu. The object will enter Edit mode, which is where you were when you made a new folder. Enter the new name or edit the old one. Press Enter or click away from the object

Watch That Name!

When exchanging files or folders with early Microsoft operating systems such as MS-DOS or non-Microsoft systems such as UNIX, you need to keep some limitations in mind. Most UNIX systems can't see the space character, so a filename of `my spiffy files` isn't valid. Instead, use `MySpiffyFiles`.

Windows NT creates an MS-DOS version of filenames that conforms to the 8.3 convention needed by early Microsoft operating systems. In that system, `my spiffy files` will appear as `myspif~1`—usable, but not great.

Click+Pause: A Tricky Fast-Track Technique

Click on any object in Explorer, pause a second (depending on the settings of your double-click), and then click again. If you have got the timing right, which takes some practice, you will enter Edit mode this way.

when done to exit Edit mode and save your work. Press Esc (escape) during the edit to end the edit and restore the old name. Alternatively you can use File | Rename in Explorer to enter Edit mode of a highlighted object.

Copying and Moving Files and Folders

You can copy files and folders by right-clicking, menu entries, or dragging and dropping. Here are the steps. Keep in mind that a file or folder dragged up or down a folder tree (structure) is moved. A file or folder dragged to another volume is copied. A moved file or folder no longer exists in its original location. A copied file or folder does.

Copying or moving files or folders

1. Create a new folder named Practice in any location you think convenient by using the steps in the previous section, "Making Folders." Double-click on the new folder to move into it. Now create two new folders using any names you like. This example uses the names Old and New. Your screen should resemble Figure 1.14.

FIGURE 1.14.

Making folders within folders uses the same procedures as making a folder within the top rank of a volume.

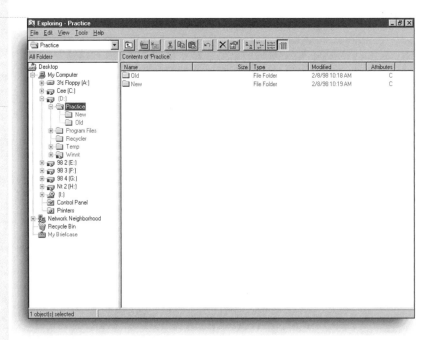

2. You need to find some files appropriate for practicing on to populate your new folders. Locate the System folder under your Windows NT folder. This is usually C:\WINNT, but can be located and named differently. This example's host folder is D:\WINNT. Move down the folder tree by double-clicking or expanding a tree and double-clicking on your final target folder.

3. Click on the first file you see. Hold down the Shift key and click about 10 files down. This will highlight all the files in the range. Your screen should resemble Figure 1.15.

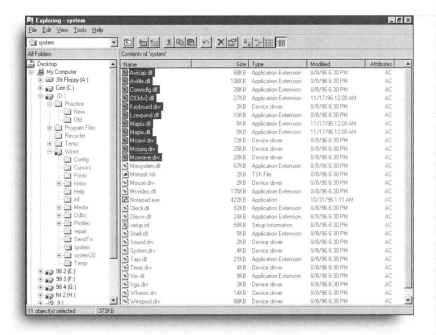

FIGURE 1.15.

Windows NT calls highlighting files and folders "selecting" them. You do this to tell Explorer you have some interest in these files or folders.

4. Choose the menu choices Edit | Copy. Return to the folders you made. This example moves to the folder Old under Practice. Choose the menu choices Edit | Paste. This will paste copies of the selected files into the Old folder. Your screen should resemble Figure 1.16.

FIGURE 1.16.

A copied file remains in its original location while Explorer duplicates it into a new location.

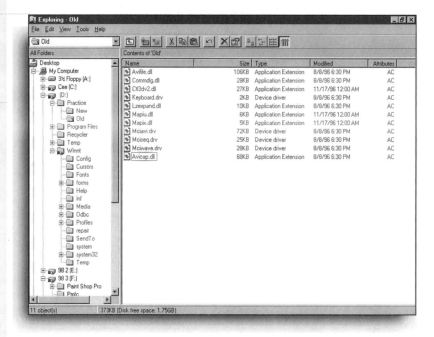

Shifting and Controlling

Holding down the Ctrl (Control) key while dragging up and down a folder tree will copy rather than move a file (or folder). Holding down Shift while dragging to another volume will move rather than copy a file (or folder). How to recover deleted files is covered later in this chapter.

5. Click on any file in Old. This deselects the files other than the one you clicked on. Now hold down the left (primary) mouse button and drag the file to the New folder in the left pane. The file you dragged will now be only in the New folder and not in the Old folder. You can achieve the identical results using the right-click and Cut command in Old and the right-click and Paste in the New folder. Similarly, you can do the identical move by highlighting the file and choosing the menu selection Edit | Cut in Old and Edit | Paste in New. How you work depends on how you prefer; Windows NT doesn't care. This entire operation works identically on files and folders.

Selecting Files

Windows NT, like most graphical user interfaces (GUI), uses the noun-verb metaphor. You first specify which objects (nouns) you have in mind for an operation (for example, you select particular files), and then specify the operation (verb) or action you wish to pursue (for example, you can choose to move or copy the files).

You use the selection process to tell Explorer which objects you wish to take action on.

Here are ways to select files or folders or both. This list uses the word *file*, but it applies to both files and folders.

- Select one file by clicking on it.
- To select a contiguous block of files, click on the first one in the series, hold down the Shift key, and click on the last one.
- To select a noncontiguous block of files, click on the first file, and then hold down Ctrl (Control) while clicking on the rest.
- To select a contiguous block by dragging, click away from a file and then drag through the files you wish to select. You will see an expanding "rubber band," called the marquee, during this process. Figure 1.17 shows this operation in action.

Nouns, Verbs, and NT

Windows NT uses the noun-verb method–selection, and then the action selection. You first select objects (nouns) to apply some action (verb) on and then choose the action. This strikes some people, especially engineers for some reason, as backwards, but that's the way things are and will remain.

Marquee

Literally speaking, a "marquee" is a large tent used for outdoor entertaining. Similarly, a marquee selection throws a "tent" over a group of files.

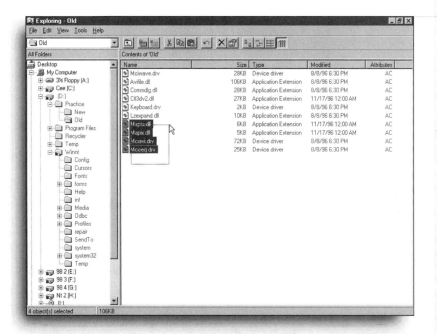

FIGURE 1.17.

A very fast way to copy or move a group of contiguous files is to first marquee select them as shown here and then drag them to their new location.

- You can combine Shift and Ctrl to select several blocks of contiguous files where the blocks themselves aren't contiguous. Here is how. Select the first file of the first block. Press Shift, and then select the last file of the first block. Press Ctrl and select the first file of the second (or subsequent) block. Press Shift and Ctrl and click on the last file of the second block. Figure 1.18 shows the results of these steps.)))

FIGURE 1.18.

You can get fancy by selecting several noncontiguous blocks of contiguous files if that suits your needs.

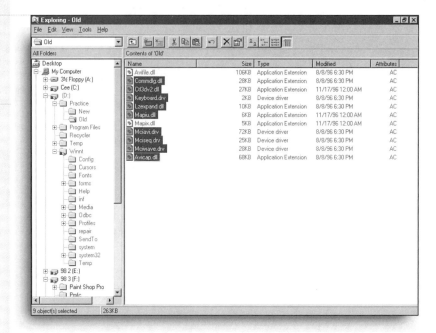

Deleting Files or Folders

(((You can delete files or folders by highlighting them and then doing any of the following:

- Dragging them to the Recycle Bin.
- Clicking on the Delete button in the Explorer toolbar.
- Pressing the Delete (Del) key on your keyboard.

Holding down the Shift key while doing any of these operations permanently deletes the file rather than moving it to the Recycle Bin. Figure 1.19 shows the operation of dragging a group of files to the Recycle Bin.)))

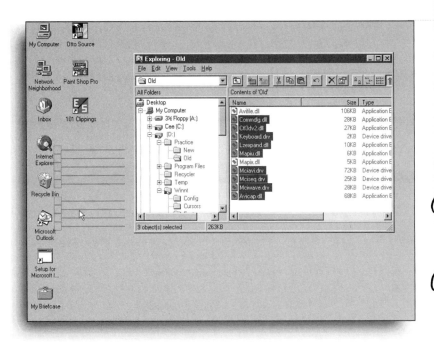

FIGURE 1.19.

These files are taking their first steps to oblivion–the Recycle Bin is their next stop.

Retrieving Deleted Files and Folders

Double-click on the Recycle Bin icon on the desktop or right-click on the icon and choose Open. Locate the file, files, or folder you wish to resurrect. Then follow the procedure outlined in this step by step.

Recovering a deleted file or folder

1. Right-click on the file and choose Restore from the context menu. Figure 1.20 shows this operation.
2. Choose the Recycle Bin menu entries File I Restore.
3. Use Explorer to drag the file or folder out of the Recycle Bin back to its original location.

You can use all your highlighting or selection tricks to get a series or set of files out of the Recycle Bin.

File Folder Complete

Restoring a folder also restores the files it held when it was moved to the Recycle Bin.

File Stopovers

Keep in mind that you can do a drag in more than one step. You might find it easier to move files out of the Recycle Bin onto the desktop and then close the Recycle Bin and open Explorer for the final move from the desktop to the folder where you wish to restore the files. This is a very handy trick in low-resolution video modes where desktop real estate is at a premium.

When Files Disappear

Windows NT moves files that were deleted using the graphical user interface (GUI) into the Recycle Bin. Files deleted at the CLI (command line interface) are gone for good unless you use a third-party undeleter such as Norton's Utilities.

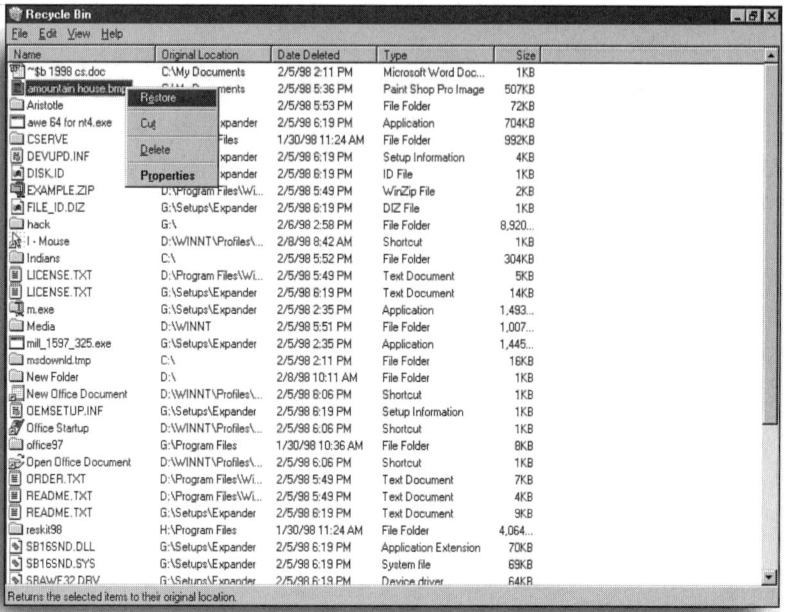

FIGURE 1.20.

You can spring a file or folder from the Recycle Bin by right-clicking and choosing Restore from the menu.

The Emergency Repair Disk, Alias the ERD

An Emergency Repair Disk, commonly referred to as an ERD, is used to repair Windows NT when you encounter certain problems. Make sure you have an ERD, and update it often! ERDs are covered in Chapter 16, "Disaster Prevention" and in Chapter 17, "When Problems Strike."

Putting It Together

File and folder manipulation is central to using Windows NT successfully. If you are not comfortable doing any of the file or folder procedures in this chapter, use the files in the folder named Practice to practice these operations. If you want to get some more files for practice fodder, feel free to do so—just make sure you copy rather than move the files you wish to play with. The files in the Windows NT folder structure are there for a reason. You can move or delete copies of them; if you don't leave the originals behind, however, you risk destabilizing your Windows NT installation.

If you end up doing so, you will need to repair your Windows NT using either a backup or your Emergency Repair Disk.

The Desktop

The desktop, or main working area in the Windows NT graphical user interface (GUI), displays the entries for the Desktop folder for logged on user and all users.

You can have items appear on the desktop by dragging them there from Explorer or placing them directly in the Desktop folder for All Users or for the logged on user. You can also right-click drag items from the Explorer to the desktop and then choose Create Shortcut(s) Here from the context menu that will result when you drop the file or files.

A *shortcut* is a link to a file, folder, or other computer resource. Starting with Windows 95 and continuing in Windows NT 4 and later, the location of resources in the GUI corresponds with the actual location of the resource. A shortcut is an alternative way to access that resource. Although a resource can exist only in one location, it can have an infinite number of shortcuts in an infinite number of locations accessing or "calling" it.

Creating a Desktop File Shortcut

This technique creates a shortcut to a file placed on the desktop. The same procedure works for creating a shortcut anywhere and to anything to which you have permission to travel.

Dragging a shortcut to the desktop

1. Open Explorer. Locate the file to which you wish to create a shortcut.

2. Right-click and drag the file to the desktop. Explorer can't be maximized for this operation.

3. Release the mouse button. Choose Create Shortcut(s) Here from the context menu. Figure 1.21 shows this operation in action.

4. Windows NT will create a shortcut to your file and place it on the desktop. Double-clicking on this shortcut will have the same effect as double-clicking on the file itself within Explorer. You can move or delete the shortcut without affecting the file.

FIGURE 1.21.

Right-click drag has some subtle differences compared to left-click drag.

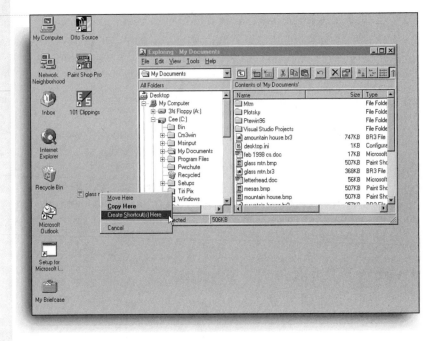

What About Left-Click Drag?

Remember that the desktop is a reflection of what's in folders. A left-click drag onto the desktop will therefore copy a file or folder onto the desktop (from another folder) or move it if you hold down Shift while dragging.

Creating Shortcuts to Resources

Proceed as in the preceding four steps, but this time locate a floppy disk or other drive in Explorer. Again right-click and then drag it to the desktop and again choose Create Shortcut(s) Here from the context menu. Windows NT will create a shortcut to the drive on the desktop. Now anything dragged onto this shortcut will be copied or moved to the disk drive. Figure 1.22 shows the creation of a shortcut to the A: floppy disk drive.

Desktop Properties

If you right-click anywhere away from a resource, file, folder, or shortcut on the desktop, you will get a context menu with Properties as the final entry. Selecting this entry will bring up a tabbed dialog box containing global settings for the desktop. If you have Internet Explorer 4 or later installed on your computer, your entries will vary from the standard ones shown in this section. As the properties for the desktop tend to circle around displays, your properties will also vary depending on the display adapter you have installed. There isn't that much different between all these choices, however. After you get a feel for these properties, you can feel your way around them all.

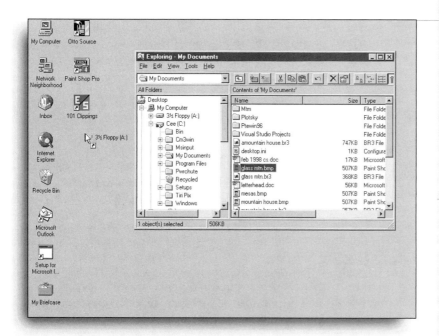

FIGURE 1.22.

Drag any file or folder to this shortcut and it will be copied or moved (depending on the state of Shift and Ctrl) to the floppy disk drive A:. You can create shortcuts to any computer resource this way. Place a few on the desktop and you will see why they're called shortcuts. They save a lot of time.

Changing the Display

The settings for the display fall into several categories. These are as follows (with the tab first and the section second):

- *Settings: (Desktop Area or resolution).* How the amount of information is displayed. Higher resolution means any screen element is smaller, but more elements can exist on the screen at any time. Standard VGA resolution is 640×480. Most people prefer a screen resolution of at least 800×600 or 1024×768. The measurements are in pixels (the dots making up a display). The first number is the horizontal; the second the vertical. The greater the resolution, the greater the RAM requirements for the adapter.

- *Settings: (Color Palette or color depth).* How many colors can be displayed at the same time. This is the same as saying the number of colors available in the palette. The default color depth is only 16. Most modern displays can show up to 16.7 million colors. The greater the color depth, the greater the RAM requirements for the adapter.

What's My Aspect?

All screen resolutions in Microsoft operating systems have an aspect ratio of 4:3, where the 4 is the horizontal measurement. This matches the 4:3 (or 1:1.3333) ratio of your monitor screen. When HDTV arrives in force, we might start seeing screens that have an aspect ratio of 16:9–or like a movie screen.

- *Appearance: (Scheme)*. Which colors and fonts Windows NT uses for its display. Scheme allows the use and saving of pre-defined and user-defined appearance sets or schemes.

- *Screen Saver*. What screen saver, if any, is used by Windows NT.

- *Plus!*. Custom settings for the desktop.

- *Background*. Patterns and bitmaps for use on the desktop.

- *Custom Based on Adapter*. Anything goes here as manufacturers are free to run wild with special adapter features. The way to have users set these features is through custom tabs in Desktop Properties.

Setting Desktop Area

You need a display adapter capable of more than standard resolution for this to work. Almost all modern computers have such a display, but the capacities vary widely.

Setting the desktop area

1. Right-click on the desktop in an empty area. Choose Properties from the context menu. Your screen should resemble Figure 1.23, although it will vary with adapter type.

FIGURE 1.23.

The Properties of the desktop is a tabbed dialog box that varies in content from computer to computer, depending on the display adapter chosen. For example, the MGA tabs come from using a Matrox adapter.

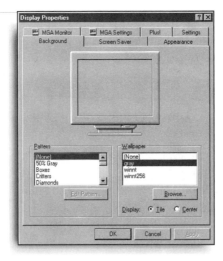

2. Click on the Settings tab. In the example computer, this is renamed the MGA Settings tab. Locate a slider or other device to change the screen area. This should be in the lower right of the tab. The lower left generally contains settings for Color Palette. Choose a new resolution.

3. If there is a Test button, click that. If not, click Apply or OK. Windows NT will offer to test your new resolution. Agree to the test. This will display a bitmap for a few seconds using the new settings and then return you to your old settings, asking for confirmation of the changes. If the test image looked okay, you're free to make the changes. If not, decline. Figure 1.24 shows the test message box offering to do a trial of the new settings.

FIGURE 1.24.

Losing a display is a worrisome event. Windows NT will test your settings before applying them to make sure they will work as you hoped.

Changing Color Depth or Color Palette

Proceed as in "Setting Desktop Area" earlier, but change the Color Palette or Color Depth settings. Some adapters will need to restart Windows NT to apply the new settings. Most won't, however.

Changing the Scheme

You can make your own scheme or choose one made by the color wizards of Redmond if you prefer. Here's how.

Changing your scheme

1. Right-click on the desktop in an empty area. Choose Properties from the context menu. Your screen should resemble Figure 1.23, although it will vary with adapter type.

2. Choose the Appearance tab. To vary the color or font for any element, click on that element or choose it from the Item pull-down combo box in Figure 1.25. After selecting that element, choose the color and font and font size from the two combo boxes with a rectangle around them in the figure.

FIGURE 1.25.

Test your artistic abilities by creating your own custom desktop scheme or choose one supplied by Microsoft.

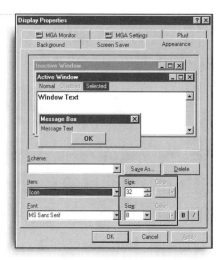

3. If you wish to preserve a scheme of your making, click the Save As button and enter a unique name for your scheme.

4. To try a predefined scheme, pull down the Scheme combo box and choose from the selections offered.

Changing Desktop Options

You can choose several options for the standard desktop, including the icons for such stalwart desktop items as My Computer. Here's how.

Changing options for the desktop

1. Right-click on the desktop in an empty area. Choose Properties from the context menu. Your screen should resemble Figure 1.23, although it will vary with adapter type.

2. Choose the Plus! tab shown in Figure 1.26. The check boxes in the lower section of the tab are self explanatory.

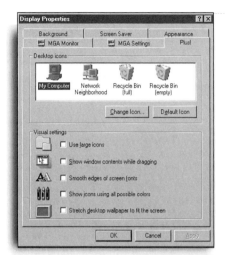

FIGURE 1.26.

The Plus! tab contains little-known, but often appreciated options for the desktop.

3. To change an icon for a desktop item, click on that item, and then choose the Change Icon button. Windows NT will reply with another dialog box. Choose one of the offered icons or choose to browse for another one. You can find icons in icon files, executable files .EXEs, .DLLs, and other files that can contain resources. Figure 1.27 shows the browsing operation in full swing.

4. To restore the default icons, highlight the item you wish to restore and choose the Restore Default button.

Setting the Screen Saver

Screen savers aren't really needed with modern monitors, but some people like them. They can be password protected (password needed to restore screen) to provide some security when you're away from your computer. Setting the screen saver is simple.

Choosing your screen saver

1. Right-click on the desktop in an empty area. Choose Properties from the context menu. Your screen should resemble Figure 1.23, although it will vary with adapter type.

FIGURE 1.27.

You can browse files having icon resources for additional icons to use for standard desktop icons.

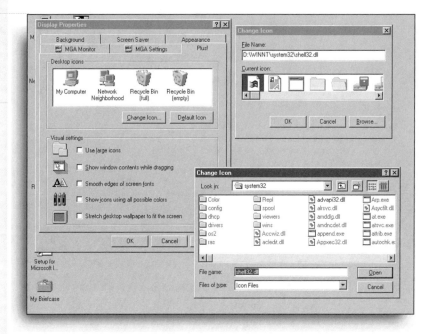

2. Choose the Screen Saver tab. Choose the saver type from the pull-down box labeled Screen Saver.

3. Choose the various settings for some screen savers using the Settings button. Not all savers have settings.

4. Check the Password Protect check box and enter a password if you want to protect your screen from unauthorized viewing while you're away.

5. Enter a time for your saver to launch.

6. If you want, choose Preview to see what your saver will look and act like. Figure 1.28 shows a simple Screen Saver tab. Third-party screen savers are richer in options.

ToolTips

Windows NT is replete with pop-up reminders of what icons, toolbars, and other screen elements are. These reminders, black text on a pale yellow background, are collectively called ToolTips.

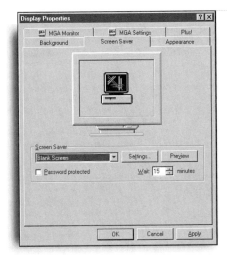

FIGURE 1.28.

Windows NT comes with some screen savers. You can buy more through third-party vendors.

Most ToolTips depend on the application vendor for whether they exist in an application and what they say. Windows NT has some ToolTips of its own. Figure 1.29 shows the taskbar with several applications running. Hold your mouse cursor over the selected (pressed) application and, if its entry is abbreviated—as is usually the case—Windows NT will pop up a ToolTip with the full name of the document.

Note that the entry on the rectangle representing the Exploring - My Documents isn't complete in the rectangle, but is in the ToolTip. The ToolTip is at the very bottom of the screen in Figure 1.29 and has a rectangle drawn around it. Windows NT uses the word *Exploring* to represent the use of the Explorer. Other applications use their real names for taskbar representation.

Try opening Explorer and running your mouse cursor over the buttons on the toolbar. This brings up ToolTips for each button. If you can't see the toolbar, choose View from the menu and click on the Toolbar entry.

ToolTips

ToolTips are pop-up text reminders that appear on your screen when you hold your mouse cursor over certain items. They tell you what the particular item is or does.

ToolTips and Balloons

Some people coming to Windows NT through the Macintosh experience call ToolTips "Balloon Help."

What's a Tray?

The section on the very right of the taskbar is called the System Tray. It contains a volume (speaker) icon and a mouse icon, as well as a clock, seen in Figure 1.29. Windows NT allows entry of running "system"-type applications that might have user-modifiable settings in the Tray. This keeps them handy for quick access.

FIGURE 1.29.

Windows NT is studded throughout with ToolTips. Although mostly used in native applications, Windows NT itself uses them for expansion of abbreviated taskbar entries and Tray icons.

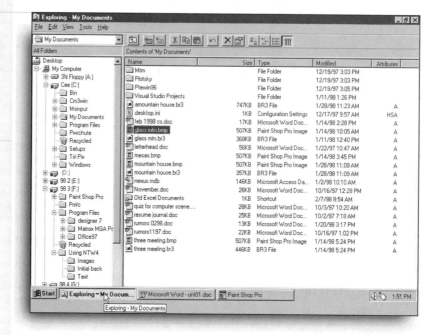

The Taskbar

The taskbar is the gray bar containing the Start button and the System Tray. By default, this object is at the bottom of your screen. The chief purpose of the taskbar is to show and give quick access to the various running applications on your computer. Figure 1.29 shows a taskbar at the bottom of a screen with some running applications. The application with the pressed-in–looking button (Exploring in the figure) is the foremost one. To switch between applications using the taskbar, just click on the application you wish to make foremost. If the machine in Figure 1.29 was yours and you wanted to start working on Microsoft Word, for example, you would click the button immediately to the right of the Exploring button.

Resizing and Moving the Taskbar

You can dock the taskbar on any side of your computer's display. People coming from the Macintosh world often prefer to see their taskbars at the top of the screen. Others prefer the left side.

Most prefer the bottom. An almost universal problem with taskbars is that they get crowded. After you have more than a few applications running, you have a hard time seeing them all on the standard-width taskbar. Figure 1.30 illustrates this problem.

FIGURE 1.30.

It takes only a few applications to fill up the standard-width taskbar. A second of your time will expand the taskbar to a more accommodating size.

Resizing and moving your taskbar

1. To resize the taskbar: Move your cursor to the outer edge of the taskbar. If your taskbar is in the standard location (bottom), this is the top edge. Your cursor will change to a double arrow. Click and drag the taskbar to its new width. The taskbar has a width granularity of one button, so don't try for fine adjustments. Accept the snap to's where they occur.

2. To move the taskbar: Click anywhere on the taskbar away from the System Tray and any button. If necessary, increase the width of the taskbar to find an empty space. Click and drag the taskbar to any edge. You will see a ghost of the taskbar when your cursor arrives in a suitable docking space. You can't float the taskbar as you can most toolbars.

My Icons Are Scrambled!

Events will sometimes scramble Windows NT's brain, making your desktop icons appear incorrectly. The fastest way to fix this is to force a rebuild of the desktop by changing your color palette. You can switch back to your original color palette (depth) after you have retrieved your icons.

Compare Figures 1.30 and 1.31 carefully. Note the lack of the My Computer icon in Figure 1.31—a serious lack. This is because the default setting for the taskbar is Always on Top, or riding over all other screen elements. To see My Computer (and any other hidden icons should this occur to you), right-click on the desktop in an empty area and choose Arrange Icons, using the scheme you prefer. I use By Name in this book unless I'm trying to make a point where that setting is inappropriate. You can also check the Auto Arrange selection in Arrange Icons to automatically shuffle your icons into line.

Other Taskbar Properties

The taskbar has user-configurable properties just like most other items in Windows NT. To see the dialog box with these properties, right-click on the taskbar away from any objects and choose Properties from the context menu. Figure 1.32 shows this dialog box.

FIGURE 1.32.

The taskbar has certain properties useful for fine-tuning its appearance and behavior.

Here are the options on the Taskbar Options tab.

- *Always on Top.* The taskbar floats above all other applications and the desktop.

- *Auto Hide*. The taskbar disappears until you move your cursor over the part of the screen where it will appear. This frees up some screen space. It is almost invaluable when running the taskbar at the top of the screen. If you don't use Always on Top, you can lose the taskbar as it sinks below maximized applications. It's there, but it's not obvious until you remove maximize from your windows. I find people don't like this at all. However, if you have Always on Top selected and Auto Hide not selected, the taskbar eats up status bars. Most veteran Windows NT users put the taskbar at the bottom of the screen with both Auto Hide and Always on Top selected.

- *Show Small Icons in Start Menu*. Adjusts the spacing and appearance of the Start menu. That's the menu that pops up when you click the Start button in the taskbar. This only affects the primary Start menu, not the fly-outs (which are always small).

- *Show Clock*. Sets whether Windows NT shows the time in the System Tray part of the taskbar.

Clearing the Documents Menu and Setting Start Menu Entries

The second tab in the Taskbar Properties dialog box is Start Menu Programs. This has a Clear button to remove all entries from the Documents fly-out menu on Start. This is a valuable feature for some who don't want spies learning which documents they have been working on. This won't clear the MRU (most recently used) from applications. The right way to ensure security is to apply some Windows NT security to your workstation. See Chapter 12, "Managing Users—NT Security."

Because fully securing a workstation is impossible in some situations, clearing the Documents section of Start is the second best option. Just keep in mind those MRUs if you do this. Figure 1.33 shows this tab.

FIGURE 1.33.

The Start Menu Programs tab has a handy way to quickly clear entries from the Documents menu, giving users a modicum of privacy.

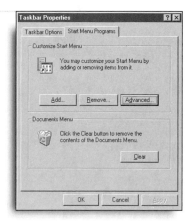

The other three buttons enable you to add, remove, or view the Start menu entries in Explorer mode. You can do the same thing by right-clicking on the Start button. Adding applications this way is somewhat clumsy, because they will all be dumped into Programs. If you choose Advanced, you can edit the Programs folder (Start Menu Programs is a folder just like any other) using the same techniques as with any other Explorer task.

A full discussion of adding, removing, moving, and customizing the Start menu is in Chapter 2 under the heading "Start Menu."

The Windows NT Framework

The Directory Structure of Windows NT

With one fundamental difference, the structure of Windows NT folders (directories) is similar to Windows 95 and Windows 98. The difference is in security. See Chapter 12, "Managing Users—NT Security," for a discussion of how to set up and use Windows NT's security.

The UNIX Superuser

The Windows NT administrator is similar to the UNIX superuser.

Windows NT has strong security compared to other Microsoft operating systems it might superficially resemble. You, the logged on user, have access to common folders (All Users) and to folders specific to you. If you are logged on as administrator, or with the same rights, you have access to all Windows NT folders and services.

The vast majority of Windows NT users log on as administrator or with administrator rights. For the most part, I have written this book with that in mind. The one place that new Windows NT users stumble is the location of their personal files under Windows NT. By default, Windows NT tries to locate your documents in a secured folder structure where others without administrator or other high rights can't get at them. Users familiar with operating systems, such as Windows 95 or 98 with their My Documents folder, often learn to their dismay that they can't find saved files. This is because they're in, by default, a secured location within the Windows NT folder structure.

SEE ALSO

➤ See Chapter 12, "Managing Users—NT Security" and Chapter 13, "Sharing Resources."

Take a look at Figure 2.1. This shows the Explorer with the path D:\WINNT\Profiles\Desktop open. This is my computer and I'm logged on as administrator. There are three shortcuts to the application in \..\Desktop. They are My Briefcase, Otto Source, and PaintShop Pro. Only users logged on as an administrator will see these items. More importantly, files or documents stored in this folder structure won't be available to other users not logged on as administrator.

Now look at Figure 2.2. This shows the items in the administrator's Programs menu structure. These items show up only on the Start|Programs menu when a user is logged on as administrator. Other users won't see or have access to them.

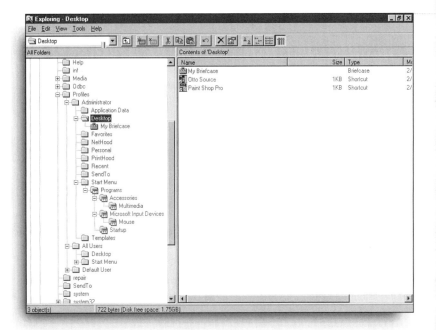

FIGURE 2.1.

Only those logged on as an administrator will see the items within the Administrator folder structure.

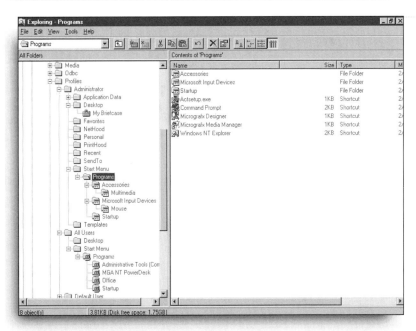

FIGURE 2.2.

The Start menu is likewise protected from unauthorized eyes.

To finish the tour, look at Figure 2.3. This shows the All Users folder structure.

How to Make NT Like 98

Although a slight oversimplification, you can say that always logging on to Windows NT with Administrator-level rights makes it quite similar in behavior to Windows 95/98.

FIGURE 2.3.

The All Users folder structure is the common structure for this Windows NT installation.

Note that there are entries here, but these will be available to all users no matter their security. Compare Figure 2.2 with Figure 2.3. Note that all users will have access to certain Microsoft Office applications, but only the administrator will be able to access the Micrografx ones.

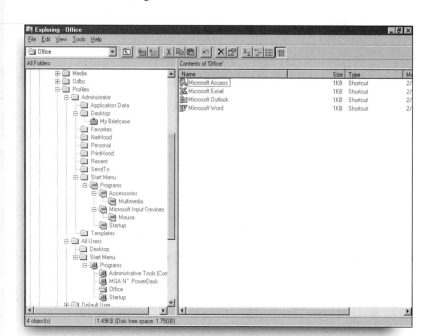

Many Windows NT applications try, by default, to store your documents in the Personal section of the user you're logged on as. If you log on as administrator, store some files in the Personal folder in the Administrator structure, and then log on again with lesser rights, you can't access those files. This is a feature; however, I've learned that to many users it's a panic-causing problem. To avoid being crunched by this, keep in mind a couple of things:

1. Watch carefully where applications running under Windows NT offer to store your files. The Personal folder when logged on as administrator is the Personal folder in the Administrator folder structure. The Personal folder when you're logged on as something else is in the folder structure for that username. If you want to make sure your files are

easily available to all logged on users, store them within the All Users folder structure or in an unsecured place such as My Documents off the root (highest) folder—or right off the volume.

2. Most applications allow you to change their default save paths. If you find yourself always needing to alter the save path under Windows NT, save yourself steps and make the applications behave as you want them to. Just remember that one of the advantages of Windows NT is its security. Bypass this feature only if you're sure you don't need it.

Profiles

A user profile enables users to log on remotely and see a predefined desktop. Consider it a device to manage the look and feel of desktops. You must use Microsoft-brand networking to take advantage of user profiles. Okay, so how do you make another logon identity? Here are the steps to do it manually. A user also creates a profile for himself the first time he logs on.

Making another logon identity

1. Log on with Administrator rights.

2. Choose Start|Settings|Control Panel|System from the Start menu.

3. Click on the User Profiles tab of the resulting dialog box.

4. Choose an existing profile that's closest in identity and rights to the one you wish to create.

5. Click on it to highlight. Click the Copy To button. Enter a name for the new Profile. Figure 2.4 shows the operation at this stage.

6. Click the Change button in the Copy Profile To dialog box if you wish to enter this user in a predefined User Group. Not doing anything with User Groups at this point will create a new profile having the identical rights as the profile you copied from. More on User Groups later in this section.

SEE ALSO

➤ *See Chapter 12, "Managing Users—NT Security," and Chapter 13, "Sharing Resources."*

FIGURE 2.4.

The theme behind making new profiles is to copy an existing profile and then edit the copy to end up where you wish.

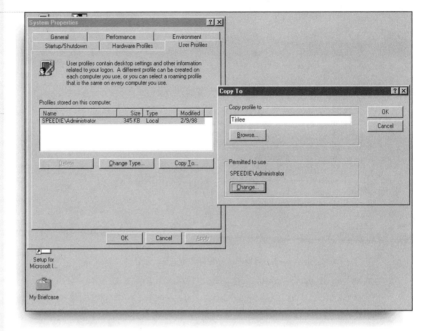

7. Click on OK to exit the dialog boxes. Windows NT will grumble around some and create a new profile. Figure 2.5 shows the results of following the preceding steps, creating a new profile named Tirilee (refer back to Figure 2.4) with administrator rights. Windows NT logically located the new profile in the Administrator folder structure because the new profile has all the rights of an administrator.

Profiles aren't the same as User Accounts. The latter is the heart of Windows NT security; profiles are really just cosmetic or convenience items. For a full discussion of Windows NT security and how to create, delete, and maintain User Accounts, see Chapter 12.

Two Profile Types

Windows NT uses the term "profile" for both user profiles and hardware profiles.

A Quick Tour of the Registry

The Registry is where Windows NT stores information about itself, users, the computer it's running on, and its installed applications. Microsoft emphatically doesn't want users to mess around within the Registry, yet it provides a utility to do so. This is because in some instances a knowledgeable user can enhance Windows NT's performance or fix something that's gone awry.

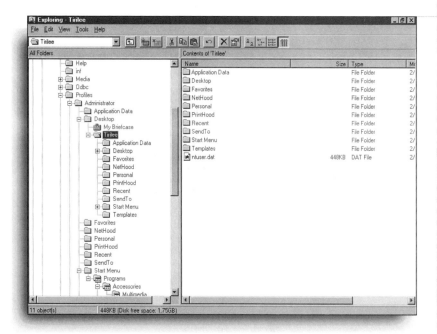

FIGURE 2.5.

Here you have manually created a new profile from an existing one. Note that this folder structure can contain different shortcuts and applications. That's what a profile is all about.

A full discussion of the Registry is worth an entire book of this size, so the amount of coverage devoted here to a Registry discussion is, by necessity, quite abbreviated. Rather than going into great detail, I'll give you an overview of how the Registry's organized and how to locate and edit settings.

SEE ALSO

➤ *See the section titled "Making and Maintaining ERDs" in Chapter 17, "When Problems Strike."*

Structure

To see the structure of the Registry, launch the Registry editor called regedit.exe. To do this, choose the menu selections Start | Run, and then enter regedit in the dialog box. This brings up the standard Registry editor with the Registry loaded. Your screen should resemble Figure 2.6.

You can export the Registry to a text file with the extension .REG by choosing the menu choices Registry | Export Registry File. The reverse operation is to import a Registry in part or entirely by using the menu choices Registry | Import Registry

Danger Ahead

Windows NT will not start with a corrupt or otherwise damaged Registry. Be careful and make sure that you have a current back up of your system before editing Registry entries.

You can export your Registry (Registry | Export Registry in Regedit, for example), but that won't let you restart from a corrupted file.

File. If you wish to browse through the Registry in perfect safety, export the entire Registry and then use a word processor such
as Word or WordPerfect to look through it. You can even edit
the text file and then import the modified file back using the
Import function. Figure 2.7 shows one small Registry exported
in its entirety and read into Word. Note that it is almost 1,300
standard pages long and roughly 2MB in size!

FIGURE 2.6.

The Registry editor isn't on any
menu by default, but Microsoft
does supply it if you choose to
walk on the wild (and risky)
side of life.

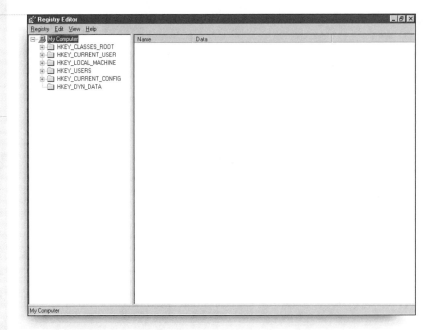

A Tale of Two Editors

Microsoft supplies two Registry editors with Windows NT 4. One is
Regedt32; the other is Regedit.
Regedt32 has a read-only mode
that's handy for browsing, as you
can't inadvertently make changes. It
also shows the Registry classified by
hives (parts of the Registry). It will
not, however, do searches by data
value; Regedit, on the other hand,
will do such searches.

The Registry is divided into five main categories. Each category
has keys, subkeys, and data or values for keys. In a way the organization of a Registry is similar to a disk volume. A computer
can have many volumes, each volume can have many folders,
folders can have subfolders, and the folders contain files. Within
the Registry, your computer has five keys, each of which has
many subkeys (that can have subkeys too), each of which has
entries with data values setting variables for Windows NT's
environment and applications.

You expand the keys just like you do folders in Explorer—by
clicking on the plus signs. Just like Explorer has a Find capacity,
Regedit has a Find utility too. This can search for keys or data

within those keys. Here are the five main keys and their value to Windows NT.

- **HKEY_CLASSES_ROOT**   File extensions, their applications, OLE entries.
- **HKEY_CURRENT_USER**   Console configurations such as user-defined areas of the desktop. Figure 2.8 shows one area of this key, containing color and font information about the desktop. If you wish to see your settings for this key, click on the plus sign next to HKEY_CURRENT_USERS and then click on Console. The full path for this key is HKEY_CURRENT_USER\Console.

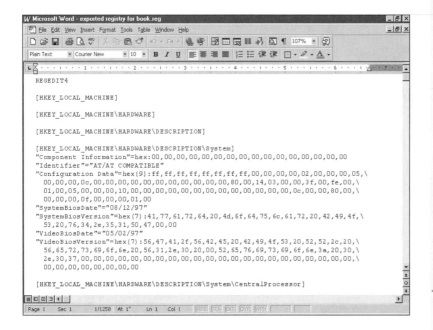

FIGURE 2.7.

Exporting even a modest Registry results in a huge text file.

- **HKEY_LOCAL_MACHINE**   The place for Windows NT to register the hardware it uses. All hardware must register itself or have itself registered before Windows NT will use it. Figure 2.9 shows details about the processor in my machine. The folder labeled 0 means this is information about the first processor (processor 0) in this machine. If this was a dual Pentium II box, there would also be an entry for processor 1. You can tell this is a Pentium II because it is

OLE Entries

OLE stands for object linking and embedding. It is a Microsoft technology for transferring and sharing data between applications. Using OLE, for example, you could link a spreadsheet document to a Word document so that every time you update the spreadsheet, the related spreadsheet data embedded in your Word document would also be updated automatically.

Family 6. A Pentium would be Family 5. This entry also shows the speed of the processor. This key also has a Security key that relates to the network, not to accounts created using the User Manager.

FIGURE 2.8.

The main key, HKEY_CUR-RENT_USER, contains user-alterable configuration settings.

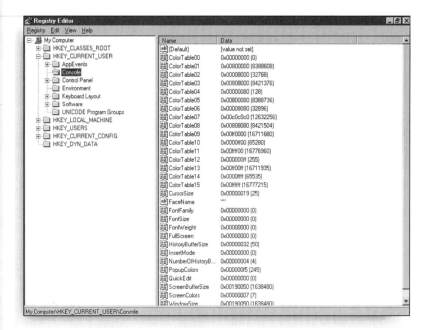

- HKEY_USERS   A key written over each time Windows NT boots. This contains information specific to the logged on users.
- HKEY-CURRENT_CONFIG   Configuration for the display adapter and occasionally other devices requiring special treatment.

Editing the Registry

Here's an example of how to edit a Registry to add function to Windows NT. This example alters the default DOS print output from parallel port 1 to parallel port 2. I don't recommend that you make these changes to your Registry if you choose to follow along unless you're sure that this is the way you wish your computer to operate.

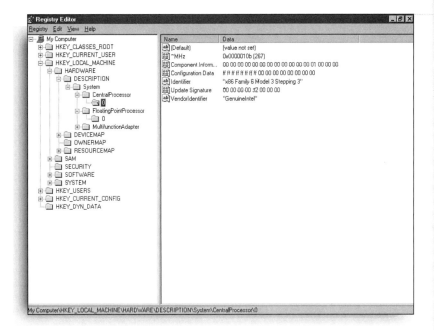

FIGURE 2.9.

HKEY_LOCAL_MACHINE is primarily concerned with hardware.

Editing the Registry to change the default DOS print output from parallel port 1 to parallel port 2

1. Open Regedit. The setting you are looking for is in the HKEY_LOCAL_MACHINE area. The full path to the key you need is HKEY_LOCAL_MACHINE\SYSTEM\ CurrentControlSet\Control\Session Manager\DOS Devices.

2. Navigate to this key and open it. Figure 2.10 shows this stage of the edit.

3. Double-click on the PRN (default printer in DOS) entry in the right pane. Regedit will bring up an edit dialog box as shown in Figure 2.11.

4. Edit the entry LPT1 to read LPT2. Click OK to close the edit dialog box.

5. Exit Regedit.

Regedit Needs Windows NT

Regedit will only run under Windows NT, not DOS. If you munge (that is, "mangle") the Registry to the point it won't start Windows NT, your only solution is to run a repair setup using an ERD and then restoring your backed up Registry using the Import (or Backup / Restore) utility. Chapter 17, "When Problems Strike," has information about these procedures.

FIGURE 2.10.

You can use the Find utility in Regedit to locate keys or data, but after a while you get an idea of where Windows NT stores things.

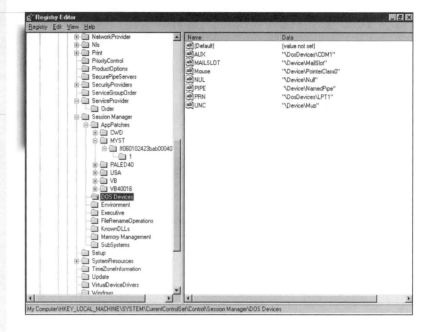

FIGURE 2.11.

Double-clicking opens an edit dialog box. Right-clicking in Regedit brings up a context menu with entries for creating and deleting values and keys.

Hints on the Registry

There are a few books out discussing the subtleties of the Windows NT Registry—for example, *Windows 95 and NT 4.0 Registry & Customization Handbook* (Que Publishing, 1996, ISBN 0-7897-0842-6). There are also several free Web sites with pages dedicated to this esoterica. Just remember to keep your ERD updated when playing.

Note the things you need to successfully do a Registry edit:

- You need to know what you want done.

- You need to have an idea of how Windows NT's Registry handles your goal (such as fooling DOS applications into thinking they're accessing the printer port).

- You need to know where or about where the entry is or you need an idea of what to search for using Regedit's Find utility (Edit | Find or Ctrl+F).

- You need to know the valid entries for the Registry. Entering ABC in the screen shown in Figure 2.11 won't do anything other than damage some Windows NT functionality.

The Start Menu Structure

The Start menu is the menu, along with subsequent submenus, that pops up when you click on the Start button in the taskbar. It has three basic sections that correspond to folders within the Windows NT folder (directory) structure. In an oversimplified sense, they are as follows:

- *The All Users section of Programs.* Applications available to all users who log on to the installed Windows NT.
- *The Middle Section of Programs.* Applications available exclusively to the logged on user or a user with the identical rights (permissions). For more details on permissions and users, see Chapter 12.
- *The Uppermost section of Start.* Where certain setups will install shortcuts to documents or applications to which they wish to draw attention.

Notwithstanding those points, keep in mind that what's available to any logged on user depends on the permissions granted. As most users of Windows NT log on with administrator rights, I'll focus on that situation and leave the security discussions to Chapters 12 and 13.

SEE ALSO

➤ *See Chapters 12, "Managing Users—NT Security," and Chapter 13, "Sharing Resources."*

You can alter the contents of the Start menu by using the same techniques of making, deleting, moving, and copying files and shortcuts you do using the Windows Explorer. Alternatively, you can use the Open command for the Start menu to view the folders in an Icon view similar to the older Program Manager from previous versions of Windows and Windows NT.

To see how the Start menu relates to the folder structure, take a look at Figure 2.12. This shows the Explorer view of the Start menu structure within the Windows NT folder structure.

Note that in Figure 2.12 there is a folder called Office which contains four shortcuts to Microsoft Office applications. You can see the shortcuts in the right pane; the folder is in the left. Now look at Figure 2.13, the Start | Programs menu.

Fast Acting Regedit

After you have clicked OK on any edit within Regedit, the edit is written to the Registry. You don't get a File|Save before exiting to back out entries. This gives you another reason to avoid editing your Registry or making sure you're well backed up before you do.

FIGURE 2.12.

The Start menu exists as a
series of folders within the
Windows NT folder structure.

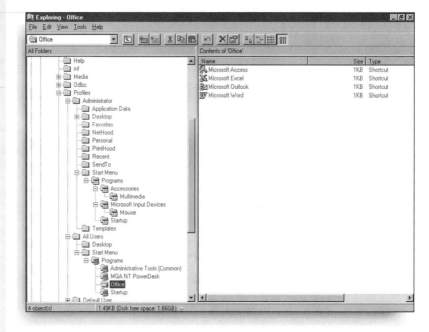

FIGURE 2.13.

Comparing the shortcuts in
Programs|Office with this fig-
ure clearly illustrates the relationship between the Start
folders and the Start menu.

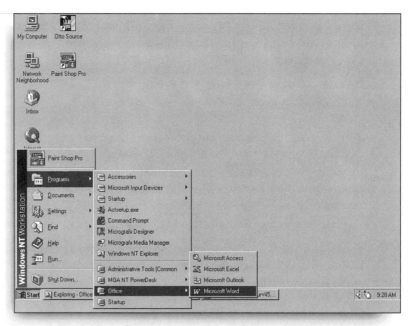

If you look carefully at the top of the menu containing the word
Office in Figure 2.13, you can see the folders and shortcuts

corresponding to the folder structure under the Administrator folder structure from Figure 2.12, too. Moving, copying, deleting, or creating shortcuts (or files themselves) within this folder structure will result in changes to the Start menu structure.

If you right-click on the Start button, you will see the following several options:

- *Open*. Open the Start menu for the logged on user.
- *Explore*. Open the Start menu in Explorer view for the logged on user.
- *Find*. Locate an object in the Start menu structure.
- *Open All Users*. Open the Start menu available for all users.
- *Explore All Users*. Open the Start menu available for all users in Explorer view.

Happily for you, the user of Windows NT, but sadly for authors like me who thrive on complexity and its explanation, there's nothing tricky at all about configuring the Start menu. Here are a few working examples of how it's done. In each example, I will illustrate a slightly different technique. Any of the techniques is satisfactory to do any of the tasks. The reason for showing different ways is so that you can choose the way you prefer.

Assume that you want to add a shortcut to an application and want that shortcut to appear above the Programs entry in Start.

Adding a shortcut that appears above the Programs entry in Start

1. Right-click on the Start button and choose Open All Users. Your screen should resemble Figure 2.14.

Different Explorers or Not?

No functional or cosmetic difference exists between using the Windows Explorer to browse the Start menu structure or opening the Start menu in Explorer view. The latter just starts the Explorer despite the implication that something different is about to happen.

FIGURE 2.14.

Start modifying the Start menu by right-clicking on Start.

2. Locate the application or shortcut you wish to include in Start. In this case it is the PaintShop Pro shortcut already on the desktop. You can use a desktop icon or locate any other available to you using the Explorer.

3. Right-click on the shortcut or file you wish to place in Start and drag it to the open window with the title bar Start Menu. Release the object anywhere in the window other than on the Programs icon and choose Create Shortcut(s) Here from the menu. Figure 2.15 shows this process in action.

FIGURE 2.15.

Most people like to place shortcuts in Start, but you can choose to actually move files here if you prefer.

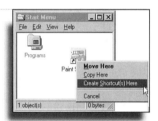

4. Close the Start Menu window by pressing Alt+F4 or clicking on the close window icon (the one with the X) in the upper-right corner of it.

Figure 2.16 shows the results of the operation.

FIGURE 2.16.

Dropping a file or shortcut outside Programs puts the object directly on the Start menu rather than in Start|Programs.

Now assume that you want to place a shortcut within Programs or one of its folders.

Placing a shortcut with Programs or one of its folders

1. Right-click on the Start button and choose Open All Users. Your screen should resemble Figure 2.17.

2. Double-click Programs to open its subfolders. If you wish the shortcut (or other folder) to appear right under Programs, you don't need to open Programs, but just right-click and drag the soon-to-be shortcut onto and drop it on Programs. Figure 2.17 shows the Programs icon opened to show other folders.

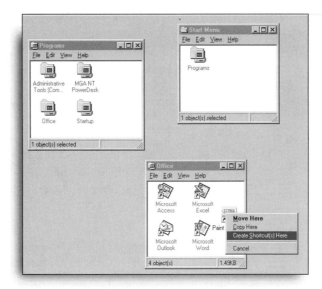

FIGURE 2.17.
The Open of the Start menu launches Explorer in large icon view.

3. You may need to open a series of folders until you find the place you wish to drop your icon. This example drops the shortcut of PaintShop Pro into the Office folder, as you can see in Figure 2.17.

4. Close all the open windows. Click on Start and navigate to where you expect your shortcut to reside. Make sure it's there. Figure 2.18 shows the successful results of the operation in Figure 2.17.

You can also use Explorer view or the Explorer itself (same thing, really) to achieve the identical results. Here's how to use the Explorer to add a shortcut to the Accessories folder. The same technique works for any folder in Start.

Fast Track Closing of Windows

If you have a series of nested windows open and wish to close them all simultaneously, Shift-click on the Close button of the last opened window. Shift-click is Windows talk for "Close All Opened Before Me." Shift+Alt+F4 works identically.

FIGURE 2.18.

The new shortcut is just where you wanted it—deeply nested within the Start menu.

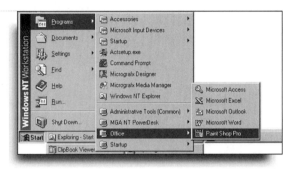

Using Explorer to add a shortcut to the Accessories folder

1. Open the Explorer.

2. Locate the folder to which you wish to add a shortcut (or move a file).

3. Right-click and drag, or use any other Explorer technique you favor to add a file, object, or shortcut to the folder. Figure 2.19 shows the adding of a shortcut to PaintShop Pro in the Accessories folder.

FIGURE 2.19.

Any technique you prefer to use in Explorer will get the job done when modifying the Start menu.

4. After you have dropped or pasted your object, check your work. You can see the results of Figure 2.19 in Figure 2.20.

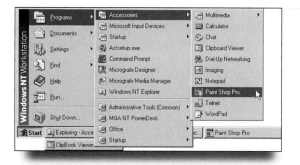

FIGURE 2.20.

There's more than one way to skin a Start cat.

Here's a fast track way to add something to the top of your Start menu. Right-click and drag the object and drop it on the Start button itself. That will place a shortcut to the object above Programs in Start.

You can use identical techniques to edit, rename, delete, or rearrange the objects in Start. The sky's the limit.

Customizing the Active Desktop

Installing the Active Desktop

Windows NT comes in various forms, depending on when the distribution media was pressed. This chapter assumes you have the earliest release of Windows NT 4, which requires a Service Pack (SP) patch and the addition of the Active Desktop from a separate medium. If you have a later version of Windows NT or you have already applied the patch, you can skip over the irrelevant sections.

The *Active Desktop* is the phrase used to describe Internet Explorer 4 (and higher) when used on a local machine. Installing the Active Desktop consists of installing Internet Explorer 4 (if necessary) and setting certain local options.

Before proceeding with any install of the Active Desktop, you need to make sure your version of Windows NT is ready. This requires patching with Service Pack 3 (SP3) or higher if you have a version of Windows NT that lacks the services of the patch.

When you boot up, you will see a version announcement along with the blue screen during the hardware check. This shows the exact version of Windows NT you're booting. If in doubt, you can try to install SP3. If it is superfluous, the Setup program will tell you. Alternatively, you can try to install Internet Explorer 4 (IE4, or the Active Desktop). If you need a patch, that program's setup will tell you too. In other words, you can't make a mistake by trying for an install.

If you need SP3, you can get it from all the usual suspects (including Microsoft's main Web or FTP site). Various subscription services offered by Microsoft such as the Developer Network also offer the SPs on CD. The patch is roughly 18 MB, so be ready for a long download if you're on a dial-up connection and have to go that route.

Once downloaded, fire up Windows NT, navigate to the location were the SP lurks, and launch it.

SEE ALSO

➤ *See Chapter 1, "Using and Understanding Windows NT Workstation 4," and Chapter 2, "The Windows NT Framework," for navigation tips.*

A Time for Backups

Installing either an SP or a new Internet Explorer drastically changes your system. Before proceeding, this is a good time to make a new ERD and perform a full-system backup. This will enable you to return your machine to its running state independent of any uninstall routines packaged with the setup routines. See Chapter 16, "Disaster Prevention," and Chapter 17, "When Problems Strike," for detailed information on ERDs and backups.

There is no need to unZIP; the distribution file is an executable one. Figure 3.1 shows the start of the Service Pack installation.

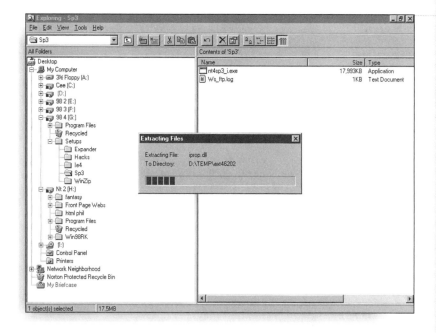

FIGURE 3.1.

The Service Packs are large executables that extract themselves and then proceed with an almost utterly automatic installation.

After a self-verification and extraction of certain files, the Service Pack Setup Wizard will launch. You will note that the Setup Wizard includes an Uninstall option. For this to work, you must opt for an Uninstall directory (folder). This stores all your old files in case you find a need to return to an unpatched version of Windows NT. Keep in mind that uninstalling the SP will also destroy your installation of Internet Explorer 4 (or later) if you have added that to your Windows NT setup. Figure 3.2 shows the dialog box in the SP3 Wizard where you accept or decline an Uninstall directory (folder).

Click through the Next buttons, choosing the Uninstall option you like until you get to the Finish button and Setup runs. After copying files, the setup routine demands a restart of your computer. This is because Setup can't update certain system files while your machine is running and must do so during boot. You should, however, see the change in your blue screen, indicating that you're now running a patched version of Windows NT. You might also be prompted for your distribution CD or its location.

Sites for Sore NTs

Both the Microsoft Web and FTP sites contain quite a bit of valuable information and files for keeping your Windows NT running smoothly or for finding out why it isn't.

Regular visits to these sites will keep you updated on what's new. The Web site, famous for its knowlege base of articles on all Microsoft products including NT, is justifiably the most visited site on the entire Web.

FIGURE 3.2.

If at all in doubt about the performance of an SP, opt to create an Uninstall directory so that you can return your machine to its former state.

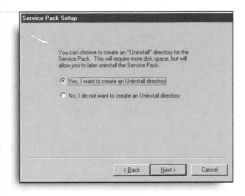

After your machine starts up fully, the screen at Control Panel | System | General won't show any change for the patch. This is inconsistent compared to how Microsoft shows patches and upgrades to Windows 95 and 98.

Internet Explorer 4 and Beyond

Now that your machine is prepped with an SP, it is ready to have Internet Explorer (IE) installed along with its Active Desktop. Again, how you do this depends on your specific situation. Many applications, including all the latest ones from Microsoft, come with the most recent version (as of their release) of Internet Explorer (as do many other programs or suites).

If you don't have any distribution media containing IE, you can download IE from any of dozens of Web or FTP sites (including Microsoft's own sites). Like the SPs, these are large downloads that will take many hours if you are on dial-up connection. This example uses an IE4 distributed along with Microsoft Publisher 98.

Old Internet Explorers

The Active Desktop became reality with Internet Explorer 4. Earlier versions of IE don't have it.

When it ran, Publisher 98's Setup program installed a shortcut to IE4's Setup program on the desktop of Windows NT. Figure 3.3 shows this shortcut. This will launch the IE setup routine if the Publisher 98 CD is inserted. Run your IE setup using whatever method you have chosen. Microsoft has a Web-based setup available for the IE; you just download a small Setup program and run it (IE4SETUP.EXE, in the case of IE4). When run, this program searches the Web for additional setup files, downloads them, and then runs the installation routine.

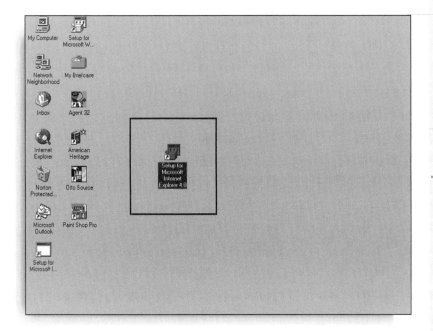

FIGURE 3.3.

Many programs, including just about all of them from Microsoft, include the files needed to add the IE version current when the programs' CDs were pressed.

Run the Setup program. A wizard walks you through this setup, stopping first at a EULA (end user license agreement). You will then be given various options such as a Standard or Full install.

SEE ALSO

➤ *See the section titled "Making and Maintaining ERDs" in Chapter 17.*

Standard install includes the browser, Active Desktop, an email and newsreader, and a few components to make Web and Web-like multimedia possible. Full install includes all that and whatever add-ons Microsoft thinks will ring your chimes. IE4's Full option includes Microsoft Chat, FrontPage Express, and NetMeeting along with some other folderol.

You will also get an option to update your desktop from the dreary old Windows NT look to the shiny new Active Desktop *visage*. You can choose to activate the Active Desktop either now or later. For purposes of this discussion, assume a Full install and

Remember Backups!

I can't stress this enough. Installing Internet Explorer drastically changes your system well beyond just installing a new browser. Make a new ERD and perform a full system backup now to be safe. No change to a system this radical can be 100% foolproof. A backup enables you to return your machine to its running state independent of any uninstall routines packaged with the setup routines. See Chapter 16, "Disaster Prevention," and Chapter 17, "When Problems Strike," for detailed information on ERDs and backups.

Big Changes Ahead

The change to an Active Desktop can mean dramatic changes in the way you interact with Windows NT. You can go fully radical or crank it back quite a bit by opting for the classic desktop. Either way, it's an adventure.

update to the Active Desktop. Figure 3.4 shows the dialog box for the latter.

FIGURE **3.4.**

You can change the look of your desktop to Active either now or after Setup has finished its run.

You need to specify a country for your Channels (more on this later) and a target directory (folder). After making those choices, Setup runs to completion. This takes some time. Before the changes are effective, Setup must restart your machine.

After your machine restarts, note that you now have some additions to your desktop—if you have opted for the Active Desktop option. Figure 3.5 shows one variation.

FIGURE **3.5.**

This is the Active Desktop after Windows NT restarts pursuant to the installation of an Internet Explorer version 4 or higher.

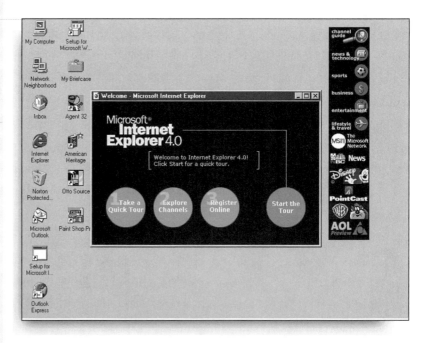

One of the options in the bright dialog box at the forefront is Start the Tour. If you are unfamiliar with how IE operates, this is a good use of some time. You can register your copy of IE now if you wish, but you must be online to do so.

You will also note some changes to items such as the taskbar and the Start menu. These changes are more fully discussed later in this chapter.

Channels

Microsoft is making a big deal out of *Channels* with IE4. Channels are like a subscription to a Web site, but not just any old Web site. Real Channel sites need to contain certain elements that make them work especially well with IE rather than any other browser.

The next several pages go into detail about Channels and the Channel Bar—the most obvious change or addition to your desktop when you go "active." You might prefer to skip ahead to the section titled "The New Active Desktop" for more information on the desktop itself, and then return to this section on Channels after having browsed through that.

Microsoft certainly wants to continue to influence, and even set, Internet standards. Channels represent one particularly minor standard that might have major repercussions. If you add a Channel to your desktop (browser), for example, you will most likely visit that site over and over. Thus, somewhat predictably, you will be exposed to advertising or other sales pitches at that site.

You can set your desktop (browser, really) to update your Channels to see whether there are any changes at a designated site. You can also save time with the Active Desktop by setting it to download a Channel site at a convenient time (say, night), so you can browse it offline later (the next day, maybe).

Figure 3.5 shows a Channel Bar to the right of the Welcome screen. This bar contains several sites and several categories.

To explore the world of Channels, get yourself online if you're not by default. If you need to establish an online connection, the upcoming wizard will step you though the process.

Your ERD Isn't Any Good

An ERD made with a non-Active Desktop version of Windows NT can't be used to restore a system with the Active Desktop. Trying to do so will usually result in a nonbooting system. This is the right time to create another backup and a new ERD. Refer to Chapter 16, "Disaster Prevention," and Chapter 17, "When Problems Strike," for details on these operations.

Don't Like Channels?

You don't need to use Channels to enjoy the benefits of an Active Desktop. You don't need to use the Active Desktop when IE4 is your browser. These are just options available with IE4.

The best place to start is the Channel Guide—the top entry on the bar. Locate the Channel Guide and click on it. You will be offered a quick overview of what Channels are. Accept or decline as you see fit, and then move on to the next area.

You will move into the Connection Wizard stage of the guide. Choose whatever options you need from the wizard's selections. This chapter assumes you already have a connection. If you need details on setting up a dial-up connection, see Chapter 11, "Installing and Configuring Internet Explorer 4 or Netscape Communicator 4." Figure 3.6 shows the option button to choose if you already have a connection. If you don't, you can step through the wizard (assuming that you have your connection details, such as ISP and IPs, at hand).

FIGURE 3.6.

The Connection Wizard exits, depositing you at the Channel Guide page at the Microsoft Web site.

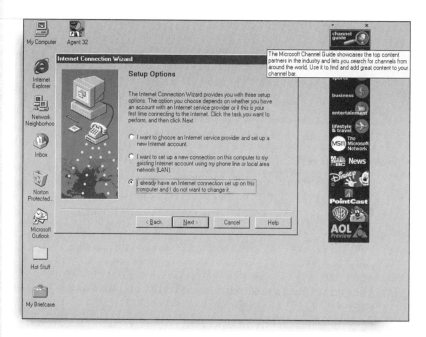

Figure 3.7 shows the Active Channel site as of this writing. Obviously, the site will change from time to time and may look different from what is shown in the figure. Don't be alarmed; it won't be *that* different!

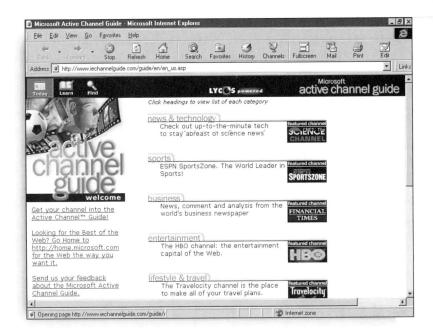

FIGURE 3.7.

This site is the stepping-off point to find Active Channels on the Web.

For this example, I will choose the Entertainment link by clicking on it. This brings up a page with the various Channels classified by Microsoft as belonging in the Entertainment section.

SEE ALSO

➤ *See Chapter 11, "Installing and Configuring Internet Explorer 4 or Netscape Communicator 4."*

Figure 3.8 shows this page. It is divided vertically into three sections. At the far left, you can click on (to select) the various Channels in groups of seven. The second section to the right of this shows the Channels in each group. Figure 3.8 shows the first group, containing the Channels WB, Comics, Happy Puppy, and so forth.

The final section is a search tool that enables you to find a site by name. If you want to see whether MrShowBiz has an Active Channel, for example, you just enter that in the supplied text box and click on Find.

After you have found a Channel you wish to take a closer look at (preview), click on its icon. This example used Happy Puppy. As soon as you click on an icon, you will start a preview and have the option to subscribe by clicking on the Add Active Channel button in the preview. Figure 3.9 shows a preview with the Add Active Channel button circled.

FIGURE 3.8.

There are too many Channels to fit on any page, so Microsoft groups them by number.

Clicking on Add Active Channel brings up a dialog box where you can set the "hotness" of your subscription—all the way from not very hot (the top button) to asking to download the site for offline viewing and seeking updates regularly (the bottom button). This example uses the bottom button.

Click on OK, and you will move to the site to which you have just subscribed. Figure 3.10 shows this for Happy Puppy (at the time of writing). If you actually visit this site, again be aware that what you see might differ from what is shown in this figure.

To end the session, click on File | Close from the Internet Explorer menu or click the Close button in the title bar.

This chapter continues with an exploration of the Active Desktop offline, except for a short trip back online to look at putting an active component on the desktop.

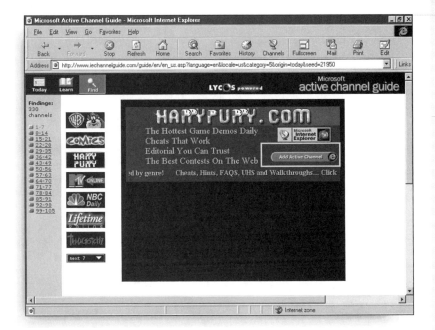

FIGURE 3.9.

Previewing a Channel doesn't subscribe to it. To do that, you must click on the Add Active Channel button highlighted here.

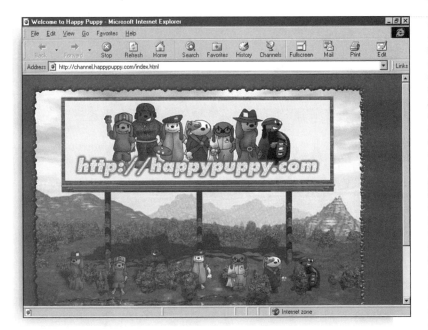

FIGURE 3.10.

This is the Active Desktop after Windows NT restarts pursuant to the installation of Internet Explorer 4 or higher.

SEE ALSO
➤ *See Chapter 7, "Using Internet Explorer 4."*

After you exit from a newly subscribed-to site, notice that Windows NT has added it to your Channel Bar. Figure 3.11 shows the Happy Puppy site added to the Channel Bar shown in Figure 3.5.

FIGURE 3.11.

The new Active Desktop part of Windows NT will add subscribed-to Channels to your Channel Bar automatically.

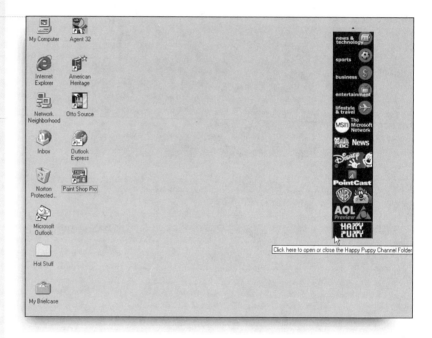

The New Active Desktop

Adding Internet Explorer 4 or higher to your machine not only gives you a suite of Internet tools (good for intranets and extranets, too), it also gives you a new user interface (UI, or GUI for graphical user interface). This section describes some of the options this new interface offers.

The key to options in the modified UI is the right-click on an object. The Properties entry is the place where most options lie, but not all. Clicking on their Close buttons will close the new objects on the desktop, such as the Channel Bar. This button isn't visible in the Channel Bar until the bar has the focus. If your Channel Bar is on the desktop and you don't want it to be, place your mouse cursor on the top entry, the one describing Channels.

This brings up a ToolTip-like entry describing the channel. It will also pop up a title bar-like place at the very top of the Channel Bar. The two entries on this bar are a pull-down menu on the left and a Close button on the right. Click on the Close button to remove the Channel Bar from your desktop. To see the Channel Bar entries again, click on the View Channels entry in the new split taskbar. If you wish to place the Channel Bar back on your desktop, right-click on the desktop, choose Properties, select the Web tab, and then select Show the Internet Explorer Channel Bar. Figure 3.12 shows the Channel Bar with the Close button popped up. Figure 3.13 shows the new taskbar with the View Channels icon circled. Figure 3.14 shows the Web tab in the Properties dialog box.

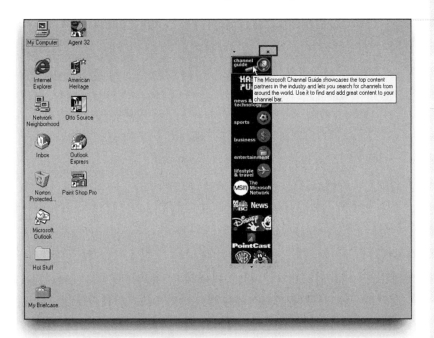

FIGURE 3.12.

The Channel Bar has a hidden title bar that pops up when you move your mouse cursor over the top entry.

FIGURE 3.13.

The new taskbar has four sections by default. One of the default entries in it is an icon to pop up your Channel selections.

FIGURE 3.14.

You can restore your Channel Bar to the desktop through the Properties dialog box.

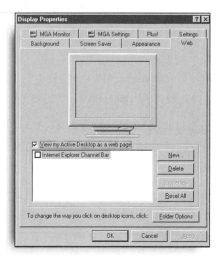

The New Taskbar

As you can see from your own desktop and Figure 3.13, the Active Desktop has an altered taskbar. By default this new taskbar has four sections. The Start button and tray retain the same functions. Depending on which version of Internet Explorer you have installed, however, you might see some cosmetic changes to the Start menu itself.

SEE ALSO

➤ *See the section titled "The Taskbar" in Chapter 1, "Using and Understanding Windows NT Workstation 4."*

Quick Launch

By default, the running applications section remains functionally the same too. The real change is in the addition of a new section to the taskbar, the Quick Launch area. This is the area where the View Channels icon and button appear. Figure 3.13 shows this section.

You can drag and drop to add or remove shortcuts or files from this area. Here's how to add or remove a file, usually a shortcut, from the Quick Launch area of the new taskbar.

SEE ALSO
➤ *See the section titled "The Start Menu Structure" in Chapter 2, "The Windows NT Framework."*

Adding items to the Quick Launch area of the taskbar

1. Locate the object you wish to copy to the Quick Launch area of the taskbar. This can be a shortcut, a file, an application, or a document.

2. Drag the object from its location (such as the Explorer, a folder in Start, or the desktop) to the Quick Launch area of the taskbar. You might find this easier if you uncheck the Auto Hide feature of the taskbar, although this isn't necessary.

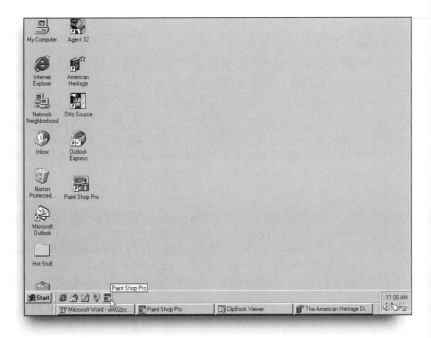

FIGURE 3.15.

The easiest way to add or remove objects from Quick Launch is by dragging and dropping.

3. Release the mouse button to drop the object onto the taskbar. Figure 3.15 shows the dropping of a desktop icon onto the taskbar.

The removal of an object from Quick Launch is similar. Keep in mind that manipulation of a shortcut doesn't affect the underlying application. That is, deletion of a shortcut will not delete the file to which it refers (is linked).

Removing items from the Quick Launch area of the taskbar

1. Select the object you wish to remove.

2. Drag it off the taskbar's Quick Launch area.

3. Drop it anywhere you wish to relocate it.

4. Alternatively, right-click on the icon you wish to remove and choose Delete from the context menu. Figure 3.16 shows this menu.

FIGURE 3.16.

You can remove objects from the Quick Launch area by use of the context menu.

Context Everywhere

Remember to try right-clicking everywhere you can on the desktop. Right-clicking in the Quick Launch area of the taskbar brings up a very useful context menu including an entry to show the title of the Quick Launch area.

As with so many things in Windows NT, you can choose other alternatives for adding and removing things from the Quick Launch. You can right-click on a shortcut (or other object), for example, and then choose Copy from the context menu, right-click on the Quick Launch near existing icons, and choose Paste. By doing so, you paste a copy of an object or shortcut onto Quick Launch.

If that weren't enough, there is yet another option. Quick Launch is a folder (surprise!) that you can manipulate just like any other folder you have rights to. Figure 3.17 shows the location of the folder represented by the Quick Launch shown in Figure 3.16. The logged on user is administrator. This makes the entire path to the Quick Launch folder D:\WINNT\ Profiles\Administrator\Application Data\Microsoft\Internet Explorer\Quick Launch for this install of Windows NT on the D: volume.

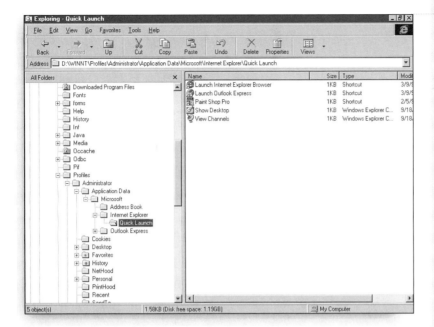

Figure 3.17.

Quick Launch is a folder like just about everything else in the Windows NT GUI.

Toolbars Within the Taskbar

The Quick Launch is only the first of many improvements in the taskbar. You can also add many other toolbars to the taskbar, just like you can in an application. Naturally you have to be somewhat careful when doing so because you can clog up the taskbar with so many toolbars that it becomes less effective.

As with so many things, the route to configuring the taskbar for adding toolbars is the right-click.

Adding and configuring new toolbars within the taskbar

1. Right-click on the taskbar to bring up the context menu.

2. Locate the Toolbars entry. Move your mouse cursor to that entry. This will invoke a flyout menu.

3. From the flyout menu, choose the toolbar you wish to add or choose New Toolbar. If you chose a predefined toolbar, your work is ended, and the new toolbar will be added to your taskbar. Figure 3.18 shows the addition of the Desktop Toolbar to a taskbar. Note how in Figure 3.18 there is an entry in the Desktop Toolbar for every entry on the desktop.

Some of the desktop entries aren't visible on this screen because they're scrolled off to the right on the toolbar.

FIGURE 3.18.

You can add predefined tool-bars to the taskbar with a few simple clicks.

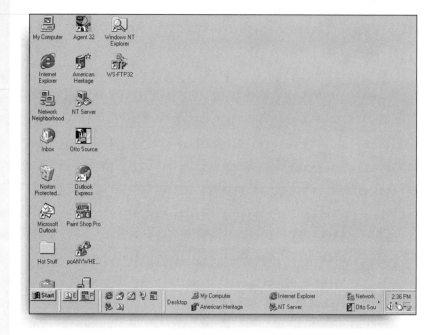

4. If you want to add a toolbar that is not predefined, choose New Toolbar from the flyout. This brings up an Explorer-like folder browser. Choose a folder to add as a toolbar. This example used the Control Panel. Figure 3.19 shows the taskbar with the Control Panel added as a toolbar.

FIGURE 3.19.

You can add folders and ser-vices such as printers and Control Panel to the taskbar as new toolbars.

5. Figure 3.20 shows the results of adding the Control Panel to the taskbar as a toolbar.

FIGURE 3.20.

Applets accessed from the Control Panel on the toolbar will behave just like Control Panel applets accessed in other ways.

Removing added toolbars from the taskbar is even easier than adding them. Here's how to do this.

Removing a toolbar from the taskbar's display

1. Right-click on the toolbar you wish to remove right at the "raised" bar at its extreme left (see Figure 3.21).

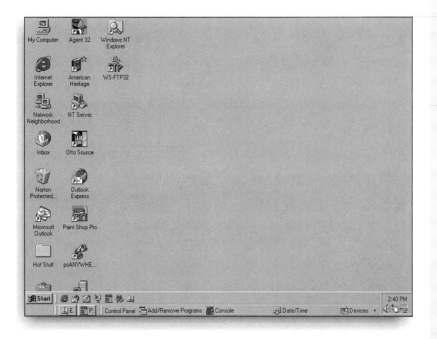

FIGURE 3.21.

Right-click on the bar to open the toolbar's context menu. Click on it to move it around or resize it.

2. Choose Close from the context menu. Figure 3.22 shows the context menu for a toolbar. Windows NT will remove the specific toolbar from the taskbar after receiving your confirmation.

FIGURE 3.22.

The toolbars have familiar context menus if you know where to click on them.

3. You can also choose Toolbars from the context menu and remove the check marks from the entries there. The deselected toolbars will disappear.

Manipulating Toolbars and the Taskbar

You can also change the size and location of the toolbars within the taskbar or the entire taskbar itself. The key to doing this is the raised area to the left of the bars.

SEE ALSO

➤ *See the section titled "The Taskbar" in Chapter 1, "Using and Understanding Windows NT Workstation 4."*

To resize a bar horizontally, complete the following exercise.

Adjusting the display of toolbars within the taskbar

1. Move the cursor over the raised area leftmost on the bar.

2. The cursor changes to a double arrow.

3. Click and drag the bar left or right to expand or shrink the bar to the desired size.

4. Release the mouse button.

You can also adjust the size of the taskbar.

To resize the entire taskbar, follow these steps:

1. Move your cursor to the edge of the taskbar closest to the desktop.
2. The cursor changes to a double arrow.
3. Click and drag the taskbar to resize.
4. Release the mouse button.

You can also alter the location of toolbars within the taskbar.

To move a toolbar within the taskbar, follow these steps:

1. Move the cursor over the raised area leftmost on the bar.
2. The cursor changes to a double arrow.
3. Click the mouse button and drag the toolbar over another toolbar or to another location in the taskbar. This will take some experimentation until you get the hang of it. Try making the taskbar at least double width. (See the resizing steps in the preceding exercise. The single-sized taskbar is difficult for most people to manipulate in this operation.)
4. Release the mouse button.
5. Resize the toolbar as desired. Figure 3.23 shows the taskbar with its toolbars moved and resized into a horizontal array.

FIGURE 3.23.

You can arrange the toolbars within the taskbar to match your needs or desires. Here the Quick Launch bar has been moved to a place between the standard taskbar open area and the tray.

1 The Quick Launch bar has been moved.

You can move the entire taskbar along with its included toolbars, too. Here's how.

Moving the taskbar from its default location

1. To make this easier, widen the taskbar at least double width. (Refer back to the resizing the taskbar steps.)

2. Click on the taskbar directly below the Start button.

3. Drag the taskbar to any screen edge where it will dock itself. Figure 3.24 shows the taskbar at the top of the desktop.

FIGURE **3.24.**

The taskbar demands that it be docked at one of the four sides of the desktop. It won't float.

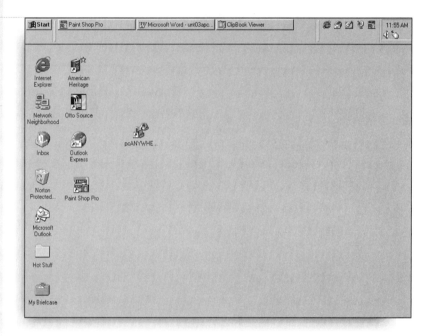

4. You can't float the taskbar as you can some toolbars within applications. Similarly, you can't float the toolbars that belong within the taskbar.

5. To see any icons on the desktop that are covered up by the taskbar, right-click on the desktop and choose any entry on the Arrange Icons flyout. If you select Auto Arrange, the icons will jump around on their own.

Active Elements on the Desktop

You can add a *subscription* to your desktop as an Active Element. This displays like a Web page embedded into your desktop. If the subscription is regularly or even constantly updated, such as a stock ticker, your desktop can display the constant updates, too. In this way to can have items—such as a stock ticker or weather map—as part of your desktop.

Even non-updated items can make good elements if you plan on referring to them regularly. If you work in Human Resources, for example, having the company's Employee Policy Manual as part of your desktop will mean it's always handy. When you add an Active Element to your desktop, you automatically subscribe to it also. Here's how to add an Active Element to a desktop.

Active Doesn't Mean Speedy

Active Elements on your desktop can slow down the entire performance of your computer or just the desktop. This is true, only somewhat less so, for the Active Desktop itself.

Adding an Active Element to a desktop

1. Make sure that you are connected to whatever service required. This example uses the Internet.

2. Right-click on the desktop away from any existing icons or elements.

3. Choose Properties from the context menu.

4. Choose the Web tab from the Properties dialog box.

5. Click the New button. A dialog box asks whether you wish to choose the new element from the Active Desktop Gallery, as shown in Figure 3.25. This is a Microsoft site on the Web. This example uses the gallery.

6. The gallery is a set of links to various sites capable of being elements on the Active Desktop. Click on the category you wish to see the sites for, and then choose the particular site. This brings up a preview of the site along with an icon inviting you to add the element to the Active Desktop. The icon is labeled Add to Active Desktop. You can see a preview and this button in Figure 3.26.

FIGURE 3.25.

The Web tab controls the elements on the Active Desktop.

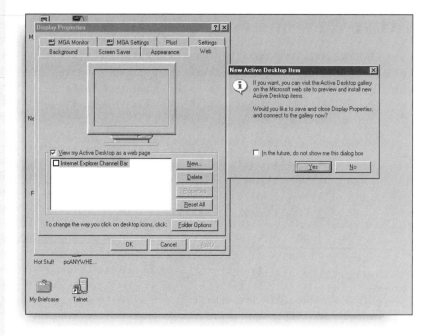

FIGURE 3.26.

You can preview sites for use as Active Desktop elements just as when you are considering subscribing to a site.

7. When you find a site you wish to use on your desktop, click on the Add to Active Desktop icon. After a few confirmation dialog boxes, this will start a download. After the download is finished, Windows NT will add the component to your desktop occasionally along with an icon linking to the site. Figure 3.27 shows these additions.

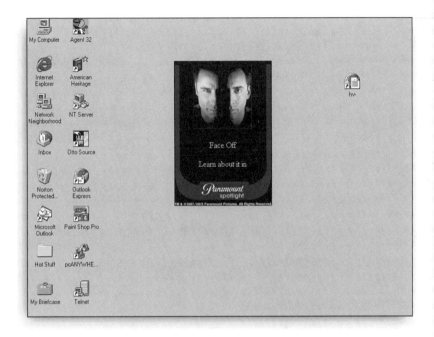

FIGURE 3.27.
The Active Desktop download added two items to a desktop.

8. You can add more elements to an Active Desktop. Figure 3.28 shows the addition of a weather map from MSNBC.

After you have some Active Desktop components, here's what you can do.

Using Active Desktop components

1. Click on the component. This will give it the focus and bring up a subtle title bar. Click on the title bar to move the component around the desktop. Use standard Windows techniques to resize the component.

2. Click on a component. Pull down the System menu on the left of the title bar. Choose Properties from this menu.

Fast Active Desktop Additions

A faster way to add an element to a desktop is to use IE to browse for it, and then right-click and drag it to the desktop. When you release your mouse button, choose Create Active Desktop Item(s) here from the pop-up menu.

This will bring up a dialog box with a component's configurable options. Figure 3.29 shows one tab from the weather map Active Desktop component.

FIGURE 3.28.

You can load a desktop up with Active Desktop components, but it soon gets rather crowded. This weather map, for example, is confusing at the western part of the United States because of the overlay of other desktop items.

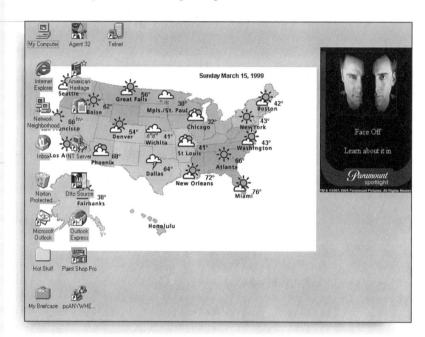

FIGURE 3.29.

The properties of Active Desktop items vary, depending on the purpose of the item.

3. Right-click on a component. Choose Save Picture As to save the component as a graphic file. Choose Set as Wallpaper to set this element as the desktop's wallpaper.

4. Click on the component to give it focus. Click on the Close entry to the right of the title bar to remove this element temporarily from the desktop.

5. Right-click on the desktop away from any existing elements or objects. Choose Properties and then the Web tab from the resulting dialog box. Add or remove installed elements from the desktop by using the exposed check boxes, as shown in Figure 3.30.

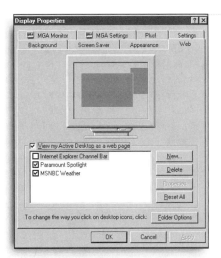

FIGURE 3.30.

The Web tab of Desktop Properties holds information on installed Active Desktop elements.

How the Active Desktop Affects Explorer

The addition of IE4 or higher to Windows NT also changes the way Explorer looks, and in some ways, behaves. For the most part, these changes are self evident. Figure 3.31 shows the new Explorer look, which places a Web-like interface to good old Explorer. The two arrow buttons on the toolbar at the very left, which act as go forward and go backward on the Web, trace and retrace your file and folder navigation when used locally (workstation or LAN).

More Properties

Right-clicking on an Active Desktop component and then choosing Properties from the context menu brings up an informational dialog box different from the one brought up by the System menu.

If you right-click on the desktop away from any existing objects or icons, you will see a new entry, Active Desktop, on the context menu. This enables you to start and stop the Active Desktop and to customize it. Disabling View as Web Page, for example, removes all Active Desktop elements from the desktop in one swoop. Restoring the setting replaces them.

There is a huge addition to the options available after you add IE4 or higher. You can take two paths to see those options.

Exposing folder options

Either

1. Right-click on the desktop away from any existing icons or objects.

2. Choose Properties from the context menu.

3. Choose the Web tab.

4. Choose the Folder Options button. After a confirmation dialog box, Windows NT presents these options.

or

1. Start Explorer.

2. Click on a file or folder (away from a Web link).

3. Choose View|Folder Options.

Either path leads to the dialog box shown in Figure 3.31.

FIGURE 3.31.

This dialog box is the entryway into a veritable blizzard of configuration options for an Active Desktop.

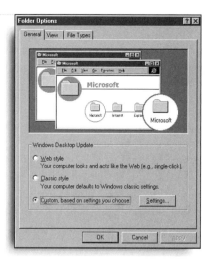

You have three basic ways to view a desktop with IE 4 or higher installed. These are listed in the General tab shown in Figure 3.31. Most people prefer the Custom setting rather than the bland Classic or the overly Web-oriented Web style. You can experiment without penalty among these three to determine where your interest lies.

The meat of customization for your desktop lies in two areas of this dialog box. The Settings button brings up the dialog box shown in Figure 3.32.

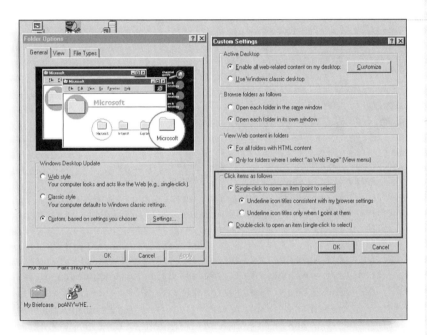

FIGURE 3.32.

The Custom Settings dialog box includes a few items that can confuse operations on the desktop to a very frustrating level.

Most of these settings are obvious or duplicates of other settings, but one isn't. This is the bottom option set. This controls the way your mouse behaves on the Active Desktop. If you find yourself confused over things such as icons launching when you just single-clicked on them, check here to see whether your mouse is set to behave the same way with icons as it is with Web links.

The second meaty area is the View tab on the dialog box, shown in Figure 3.31. This tab is shown in Figure 3.33.

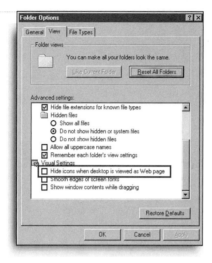

Whose Computer Is It?

Some people really and truly don't like the Web-like navigation when transplanted to their desktops. If you aren't sure, give it try for three days or so. By that time, either you won't want to live without it, or won't want to live with it.

Hiding in Plain Site

You can always create a folder on your desktop and then move all your desktop shortcuts into that. This way you will have a very neat desktop, but also have those icons handy.

Again, some of these items are duplicates of other items, but some aren't. Take a look at the bottom entries, especially stuff like hiding desktop icons when you view the desktop in the Web view. If you don't know this is going on, you might be frustrated to tears over your missing icons.

The reason people like to hide their desktop icons becomes obvious if you look back at Figure 3.28. If those icons that cover the western United States were hidden, the weather map would be more readable. You can restore your view of desktop icons either by unchecking this box or by disabling View as a Web Page from the desktop context menu.

Figure 3.34 shows a desktop with hidden icons and the entry highlighted to bring them back.

Experiment freely with the Folder Options dialog box until you find the right combination to suit your style and workflow.

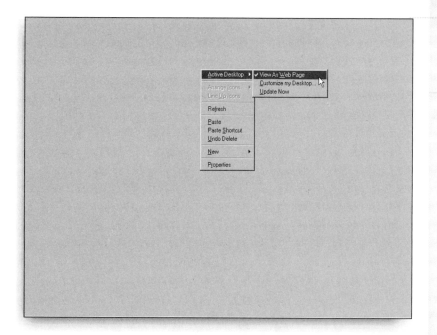

FIGURE 3.34.
You can pop your icons back into view by using the context menu of the desktop.

Using Printers and Fonts

Printer Services

From a user view, printing in Windows NT is the same as printing through any other version of Windows. Here is the process in summary.

Printing a document

1. Decide to print a document.

2. Choose a printer or use the default printer.

3. Set up the printer for a special print job or leave the printer at its default.

4. Tell Windows NT to print.

The behind-the-scenes action after step 4 is a bit complex. Here it is, again in summary.

1. The program the user wants to print from (such as WordPerfect) requests printing services from the graphics device interface (GDI) part of Windows NT. The GDI matches up the requested printing services with the capability of the printer the user has requested to produce the document.

2. A complex communication involving the files winspool.drv, spools.exe, spools.dll, and localspl.dll writes the formatted file to disk to free up the program application. This returns control of his program to the user faster than if the program had to feed the print job to the (usually very slow) printer. Windows NT will feed the printer from this file rather than from the program. At the termination of the print job, Windows NT deletes the disk file of the formatted print job.

3. The print job is fed to the printer with separator pages added if requested. If the printer and port are bidirectional (the printer can talk back to the computer), the print monitor handles the feed job. If the port or device isn't bidirectional, the job is essentially "dumped" to the printer through the port.

4. The printer translates the bitmap fed it by Windows NT and produces the requested patterns (characters and images).

Before any printing takes place, you need to install the printer on your local machine; if you use a remote printer, you also need to set up that remote printer (server).

Setting Up a Printer

There isn't any single method for setting up a printer in Windows NT. Microsoft recommends a generic method, but printer manufacturers are free to vary from that in any way they see fit. The end product of setting up a printer is to create a printer profile within your copy of Windows NT, install the needed support files (drivers), and configure the printer for its defaults. You don't need to do these steps manually because the setup printer programs handle them for you.

Here are the steps for setting up a typical printer under Windows NT.

Setting up a typical printer under Windows NT

1. Open the Printers folder by choosing the Printers entry in the right pane of Explorer or choose Start | Settings | Printers from the main Windows NT menu system. Figure 4.1 shows the Explorer method. The computer used for this screen has no printers currently installed.

2. Double-click on the Add Printer icon. This starts the Add Printer Wizard.

3. The first dialog box is critical. You need to tell the wizard whether the printer you wish to set up will be connected to your computer (the My Computer option also known as a local printer) directly or if you will be connecting to a printer installed and shared over your network. This example will use a local printer and then show you how to share it. The setup process is very similar whether you're setting up a local or a remote printer, but you need to start out telling Windows NT's wizard which it should be.

4. Choose an option button and click Next. You now need to tell the wizard what port it will find the printer on. Most local printers use LPT1:. If in doubt, confer with your

administrator or look at your printer documents. Printer Pooling, the check box at this dialog box, refers to associating two printer devices with one physical printer. Click Next after choosing your port options.

FIGURE 4.1.

Until you set up a printer, the Printers folder contains only a program to install a new printer.

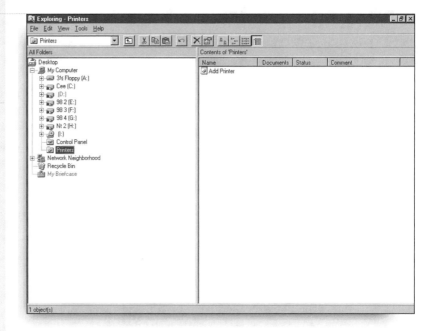

5. The next dialog box, shown in Figure 4.2, is the heart of the wizard. Here is where you tell Windows NT what type of printer you will be using. You will need the printer drivers for any printer you select. Windows NT comes with a wide selection of drivers. Printer manufacturers also distribute drivers and updates through their Web sites or through their other support venues. In most cases, printers come with a set of drivers on disk or CD-ROM.

6. Browse for your printer manufacturer by using the right pane of the dialog box shown in Figure 4.2. Find the specific printer you wish to install using the left pane. If your printer isn't part of this list or you wish to install updated drivers located in a different location, click the Have Disk button and then use the standard Windows NT dialog boxes to locate the driver files either locally or on a network.

The Driver Place

The Web is the best place to locate a driver for your printer if you can't locate your distribution disks or CD. Try the manufacturer first, but there are also many sites on the Web dedicated to stocking these drivers. If it is available, it's likely available on the Web.

This example sets up Kodak ColorEase printer by choosing the manufacturer (Kodak) in the left panel and the specific printer in the right, as you can see in Figure 4.3.

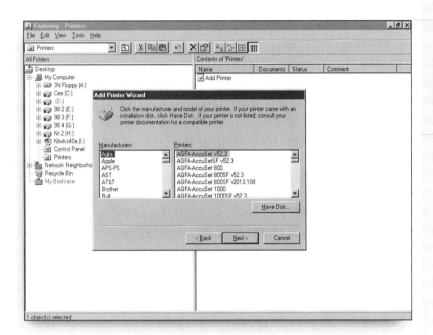

FIGURE 4.2.

You need files to "drive" your printer. Microsoft supplies many with the Windows NT distribution CD. Printer manufacturers also supply drivers for their products.

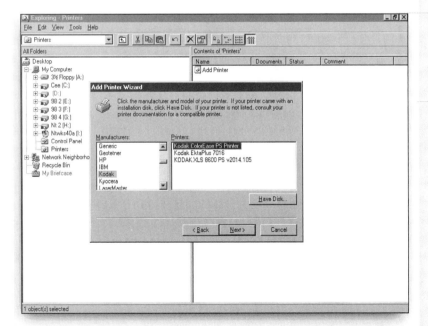

FIGURE 4.3.

This dialog box contains all the printers and printer manufacturers supplied with your Windows NT distribution CD.

7. At this point, you have specified three things to Windows NT: whether the printer is local or remote, the port where your computer can find the printer, and the specific type of printer you're installing. To move on, click Next.

8. You need to create a name for your printer. Choose a descriptive name if you don't wish to keep the default name. This isn't the same (necessarily) as the name the printer will be shared as over the network—if you choose to share it.

9. Click Next to move on after naming or accepting the printer name. Here is where you can choose to share your printer (allow access to) with others on your network. If you choose to share, you need to decide on a shared name. In this case the shared name is Tiri's Kodak. You also need to know if other operating systems, such as Windows 95, will be using this printer. If so, you will later be prompted for those specific drivers. Figure 4.4 shows how to share a printer by giving it a descriptive name. This printer won't be used by other operating systems.

FIGURE 4.4.

By naming this printer Tiri's Kodak, you tell others on your network that this printer is the Kodak attached to Tiri's machine. Some organizations dislike using personal names for resources. These organizations prefer the use of terminology such as HR's Kodak to free the names from individual identities. This enables them to downsize without creating ambiguity for network resource names.

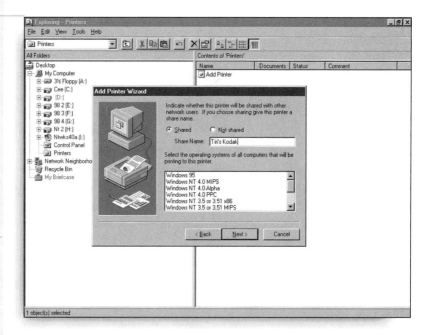

10. Click Next to move to the Test Page dialog box. It's a good idea to print a test page for every printer you set up to make sure its operating properly. If you choose to print the test page, Windows NT asks whether it went right. In either case, Windows NT installs the printer. If you tell the Test Page Success dialog box that the test page print didn't go right, it will bring up the Printer Troubleshooter section of Help. If you declined the test page or you signaled success at the test page, you're done. Figure 4.5 shows the Help section brought up if you tell the Test Page Success dialog box that the page didn't print correctly.

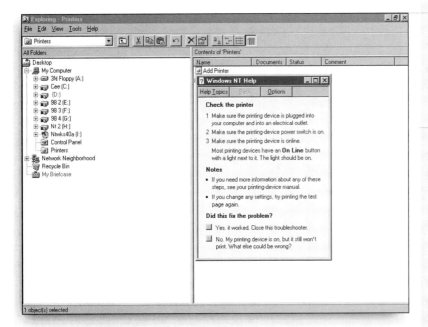

FIGURE 4.5.

Things will go wrong. The Printer Troubleshooter will give you step-by-step instructions to diagnose and fix most printer problems resulting from failed setups.

Network Printers

Installation of a printer on a network is almost identical to installing a local printer. The chief difference is that you need to start the wizard off knowing that the printer currently exists and is set up somewhere on your network. To do this, select the second option button in the first dialog box of the Add Printer Wizard. You then need to use a standard dialog box to browse

Printer Troubleshooter

You can also start the Printer (or Print) Troubleshooter manually by choosing the Start menu entry Help. Choose Troubleshooting from the Contents dialog box to open it, and then choose it if you have trouble printing from the detail entries.

for the printer you wish to set up. Figure 4.6 shows an example of such a dialog box.

SEE ALSO

➤ *See Chapter 8, "Networking Fundamentals," and Chapter 13, "Sharing Resources."*

FIGURE 4.6.

You need to browse to or name the network printer you wish to set up in the Add Printer Wizard.

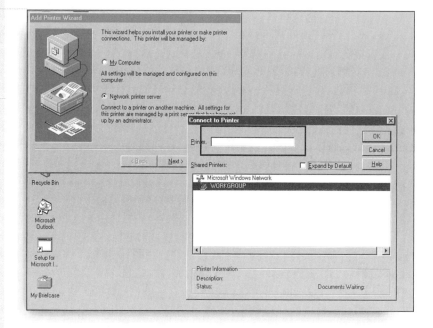

Once at Figure 4.6, locate the workstation or server that acts as the local computer for the printer you wish to set up, and then identify the printer itself. Some workstations or servers have more than one printer attached to them.

If you know the name of the printer and its server, you can avoid the browse step by directly entering their names in the Printer text box. That's the text box with a rectangle drawn around it in Figure 4.6. If the printer is named HP and it's attached to the computer Tirilee, for example, you enter

```
_\\Tirilee\HP
```

in the Printer text box to instantly jump to setting up that printer. You also need to specify the printer port as being part of the LAN rather than one of the local ports.

Depending on the files already installed on your computer, the Add Printer Wizard might or might not ask you for the location of the driver files at the end of its run.

Printer Properties

After setting up your printer, your Printers folder will contain a new entry showing that you have now set up a printer.

Viewing and optionally editing the properties of any printer on your system

1. Open the Printers folder by choosing the Printers entry in the right pane of Explorer or choose Start | Settings | Printers from the main Windows NT menu system. Figure 4.6 shows the Explorer method.

2. Right-click on the printer you wish to see or edit and choose Properties from the context menu. Figure 4.5 shows this operation.

Fast Printer Installs

If there is a printer already defined on your network, you can set it up locally by dragging it from its current location to your Printers group in Explorer.

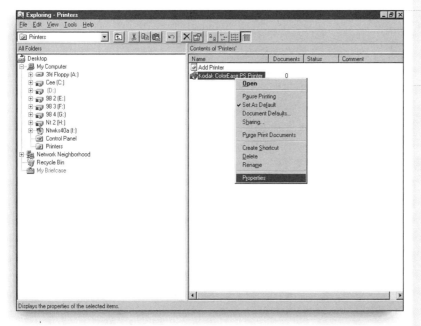

FIGURE 4.7.

You can modify or update a printer using its Properties dialog box.

3. You can do some modifications, such as Sharing, from the context menu or you can open the Properties tabbed dialog box to see them all. Figure 4.7 shows the Properties dialog box for this Kodak printer. As shown in Figure 4.8, the actual entries on the tab and the tabs themselves can vary depending on the specific printer you are working with.

FIGURE 4.8.

The properties for any printer vary depending on the features for the printer.

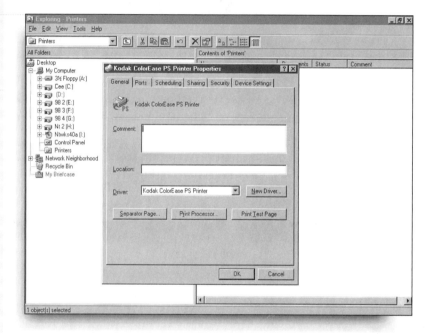

4. Make or examine any properties by choosing the appropriate tab and setting.

Here are the tabs for this Kodak printer along with their settings. This printer is well featured, but your specific printer settings will surely vary, and might vary widely, from this example:

- *General.* Set comments for the printer, choose the options for whether a separator page should exist between jobs, format for the spool file output (Print Processor), print a test page, and install a new driver for this printer.

- *Ports.* Add, delete, configure printer ports. Specify a new port for this printer. Enable bidirectional printing and print pooling.

- *Scheduling*. Set spooling options and priority for the printer. Set the time span the printer will be shared.

- *Sharing*. Enable, disable, or change the drivers for printer sharing.

- *Security*. Very similar to file and folder security. See information about doing this in Chapter 12, "Managing Users—NT Security."

- *Device Settings*. This is the tab that will vary most printer to printer. This is where settings specific to this printer exist. Figure 4.9 shows this tab for the Kodak printer. To change a setting, click on it and then change the setting displayed in the text box at the bottom of the tab.

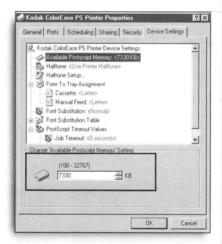

FIGURE 4.9.

The Device Settings tab entries will vary depending on the capabilities of the "device" or printer.

Troubleshooting Printing Problems

The Printer Troubleshooter part of the Help system has a good, if unimaginative, set of steps you might take if your printing isn't coming out or not coming out the way you hope. The following are some of the most prevalent causes and cures for printer woes:

- *Garbled or odd characters in the print job*. This is almost always caused by the wrong printer driver, so double check to make sure that you not only have installed the correct driver for the printer, but that you're using a proven driver version. If the printer was working before and stopped after a new driver install, try de-installing the new driver then re-installing the old. In some rare cases, a bad printer port, a bad cable, or a loose cable causes spurious characters. Cables seem to go bad for no reason whatsoever. If in doubt, replace the current cable with a known good one. Check the Font Substitution table (if it exists) to make sure it's the correct one. The Font Substitution table is on the Device Settings tab of the printer's Properties dialog box. Figure 4.10 shows a Font Substitution table for the Kodak printer installed on the Speedie workstation.

FIGURE 4.10.

Some printers, most notably PostScript types, have a Font Substitution table to fine-tune their page layouts.

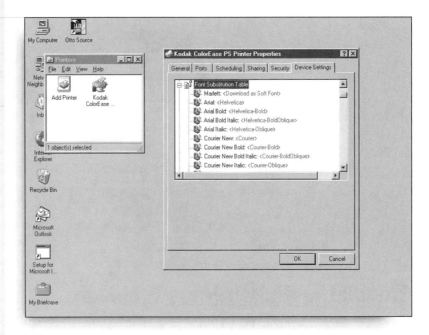

- *The network printer doesn't produce any output.* Make sure the printer works from its local server (computer). Try to access other resources on the server (such as a file) to make sure you're connected to the server. See the following item.

- *The local printer doesn't produce any output.* Make sure it's on. Make sure it's connected through the proper port. Make sure it's online. If the printer has a self-test, run that. Make sure the cable and port are functioning properly. Make sure there is paper in the printer. Run Windows NT Diagnostics and check the Devices display in the Resources tab to make sure the port exists. Check the IRQ and I/O buttons to make sure there is no conflict. If the printer connection goes through a switchbox or another device, try to connect directly to see whether the intermediary is the problem.

Printer Security

You can secure a printer by using the printer's security options within its context menu. The chief advantage to securing a printer is that unauthorized persons will not have access to print spooler files.

SEE ALSO

➤ *See Chapter 12, "Managing Users—NT Security," and Chapter 13, "Sharing Resources," for more on security.*

Setting security on your printer

1. Open the Printers folder either through the menu or through Windows Explorer.

2. Right-click on the printer you wish to secure.

3. Choose Properties from the context menu.

4. Click on the Security tab.

5. Set security as you would in any other aspect for Windows NT. For information on this see Chapter 12.

Fonts

Fonts are predefined character shapes. Although most modern printers can create a page from a bitmap, doing so takes a lot of processing power and time. Printers themselves come with certain predefined "hardware" fonts. Windows NT is bundled with

Custom Troubleshooting

Most manufacturers include a troubleshooting guide as part of their printer documentation. Unlike the troubleshooter in Windows NT, these 'shooters tend to be specific to the printer in question.

Many manufacturers have Web sites with FAQs (frequently asked questions) or other guides to solving printer problems.

several additional "soft" fonts the operating system can download to the printer for any given job using those fonts. Those fonts then act the same as if the printer came from the factory knowing the shape of those fonts. Additionally, many applications, notably those from the Corel Corporation, come bundled with fonts either as an added bonus or to facilitate the operation of the application itself.

If Windows NT doesn't have the font needed for a particular job, it substitutes the closest match available.

By far the vast majority of user-specified fonts within Windows NT are TrueType (TT) fonts. These fonts are stored as outlines within Windows NT and can be scaled, rotated, and otherwise manipulated for precise page layout. TrueType fonts act both as screen and printer fonts. They can also be called into service as system fonts, although this use isn't very common nor are the results usually worth the bother. This means that a document can be rendered in print identically as it appears on your screen. Although this might not seem that big a deal if you're new to computing, this had been a serious issue until the past few years. A person would lay out a document perfectly onscreen, only to find that minute differences in printer font rendering would—after a page or two—trash his design into something unrecognizable.

Those days are past if you use a modern operating system such as Windows NT and native applications. Today you can lay out a document onscreen and have full confidence that it will appear the same way when rendered by a modern printer.

Font Information

The number of fonts on your computer will vary from installation to installation. Many programs install, or offer to install, bundled fonts. In some cases programs require the installation of certain fonts to ensure proper outcome. The program Microsoft Picture Publisher 98, for example, demands certain fonts or its wizard-generated designs won't work. In theory these programs could use an identical font already on your system, but they won't because they can't recognize them as identical.

Screen Fonts

Windows NT uses both screen and printer fonts. Some fonts and font families are both for use by the display and any installed printers. Windows NT also has certain system fonts that can print, but are there primarily for items such as menus and dialog boxes within the operating system.

Windows NT has a facility to display its installed fonts and classify them according to how closely they resemble each other.

Viewing fonts installed on your computer by listing and similarity

1. Open the Control Panel and double-click on the Fonts icon. Alternatively, you can use the Explorer to locate the Fonts icon within the Control Panel.
2. Windows NT responds with a list of the fonts installed on your workstation. You can control the way the font names are displayed by choosing an option under the menu selection View or from the appropriate button on the toolbar. Figure 4.11 shows a typical font selection using the Details view.

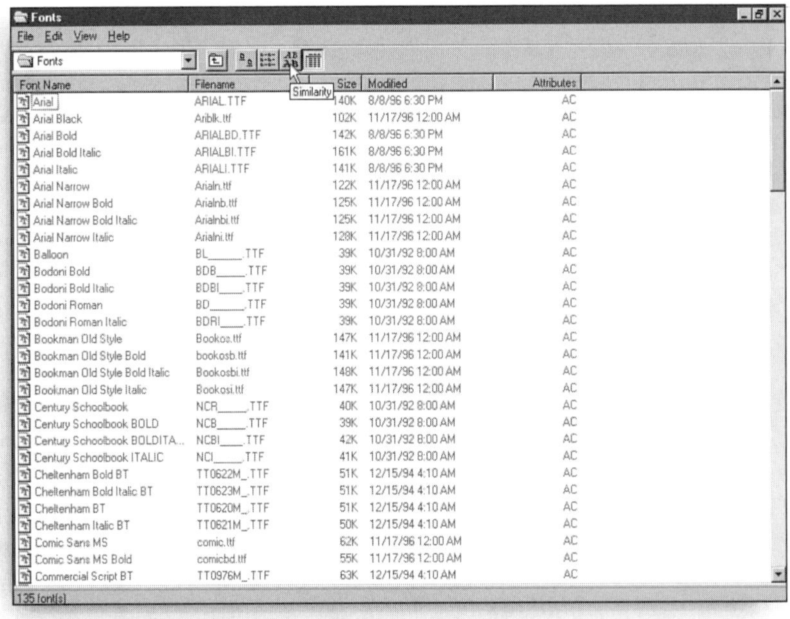

FIGURE 4.11.
The Fonts icon in Control Panel is a folder within the Windows NT directory structure. The display is slightly optimized for the display of font files.

3. By default, Windows NT displays the fonts using an alphabetic sort-by-file (font) name. To show fonts by similarity, choose the View | Toolbar option to display the toolbar if it's currently not displayed, and then click the Similarity button shown in Figure 4.11. You can also choose List Fonts By Similarity from the View menu.

Identical Fonts?

The name and hinting of a font can be copyrighted, but not the basic font shape itself. Therefore it is possible to have more than one identical font installed with each, using a different name. Pirating fonts is a big business. *Hinting* a font means a way the publisher alters the aspect of a font as it scales so that it always looks its best.

4. To see how fonts compare, pull down the combo box circled in Figure 4.12, choose a font, and Windows NT will re-sort the list with the most similar at the top. Figure 4.12 shows this re-sorted list.

FIGURE 4.12.

The Fonts display can sort by similarity as well as other Explorer views.

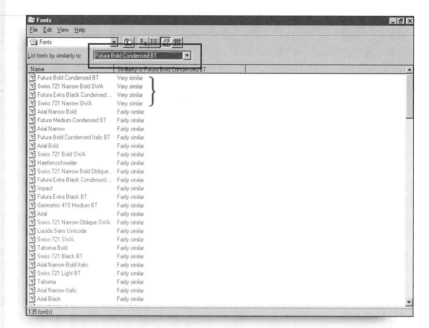

5. Note that in Figure 4.12 the two fonts, Swiss 721 and Futura, are listed as very similar. Windows NT learns about the font similarity from its Panose information. Both these fonts are derived from the same font, often called Helvetica.

You can also inspect fonts for their design. To do this, follow these steps:

Why Don't I Have These?

The fonts installed on your computer will vary from the ones shown in the book. Some, like Arial, are common to most Windows NTs. Others installed here aren't.

1. Open the Control Panel and double-click on the Fonts icon. Alternatively, you can use the Explorer to locate the Fonts icon within the Control Panel.

2. Windows NT responds with a list of the fonts installed on your workstation. You can control the way the font names are displayed by choosing an option under the menu selection View or from the appropriate button on the toolbar. Figure 4.11 shows a typical font selection using the Details view.

3. Double-click on any font name. Windows NT brings up a window with the font displayed. Figure 4.13 shows this window with the Futura font opened for inspection.

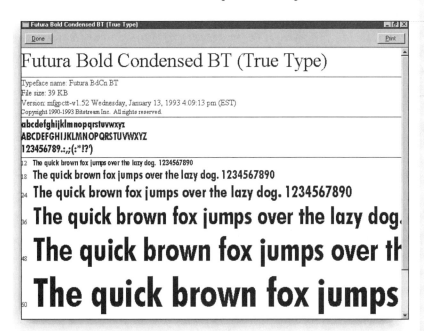

4. Figure 4.14 shows two windows containing the "very similar" fonts Swiss 721 and Futura. Figure 4.15 shows two windows, each with fonts that aren't similar at all.

You might believe that having many fonts that are very similar is a waste of disk space. In a way, you would be right. The problem with ridding yourself of the similar fonts is that you might delete a font required by an application program. If you do so, that program might refuse to run until you re-install the font or it might run poorly. Microsoft Office 97 requires the Tahoma font, for example, or it will complain bitterly upon startup. It will run, substituting another font for Tahoma, but it won't be happy about it.

FIGURE 4.14.

Although the font in the top window is heavier, the similarity between it and the font in the bottom window is obvious.

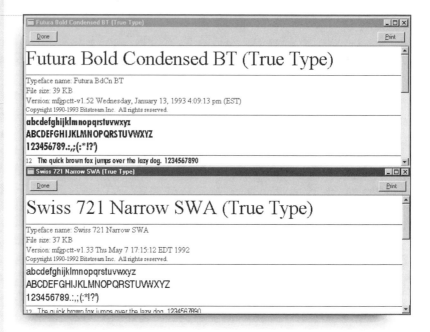

FIGURE 4.15.

No matter the weight, nobody would mistake the font in the lower window for the one in the top.

Adding and Deleting Fonts

Fonts are files with font descriptions located in the Fonts folder within the Windows NT directory structure.

Adding a font

1. Acquire the font file from a vendor or know its location on your network.

2. Open the Control Panel and double-click on the Fonts icon. Alternatively, you can use the Explorer to locate the Fonts icon within the Control Panel.

3. Windows NT responds with a list of the fonts installed on your workstation. You can control the way the font names are displayed by choosing an option under the menu selection View or from the appropriate button on the toolbar. Figure 4.11 shows a typical font selection using the Details view.

4. Choose File | Install New Font from the menu in Figure 4.11. Windows NT responds with a browse dialog box as shown in Figure 4.16.

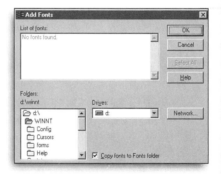

Comparing Fonts

The best way to compare fonts is to print them out by clicking the Print button shown in Figures 4.13 through 4.15. That enables you to move the fonts over one another for a close inspection.

FIGURE 4.16.

You can install a new font either from distribution media or your network.

5. Locate the font or fonts you wish to install. Highlight them by clicking on them in the List of Fonts list box using the Shift or Control (Ctrl) keys to select more than one font if you desire. Click OK.

6. You can use fonts physically located on your local machine or on your network (or any other available source).

If you wish to access the font(s) without installing them on your hard disk (to save space), uncheck the check box circled in Figure 4.16. Keep in mind that remote fonts won't be available if the resource having the physical font installed isn't available.

Deleting Fonts

Deleting fonts is an obvious and simple process. Here it is.

Deleting fonts

1. Open the Control Panel and double-click on the Fonts icon. Alternatively, you can use the Explorer to locate the Fonts icon within the Control Panel.

2. Windows NT responds with a list of the fonts installed on your workstation. You can control the way the font names are displayed by choosing an option under the menu selection View or from the appropriate button on the toolbar. Figure 4.11 shows a typical font selection using the Details view.

3. Highlight the font or fonts you wish to delete. You can use the Shift and Ctrl keys just as you can when selecting conventional files in Explorer. Figure 4.17 shows several fonts selected in this manner.

4. Press the Delete (Del) key or choose File | Delete from the Fonts menu. After confirmation, Windows NT deletes the font from your font selection. Fonts deleted from the Fonts window move into the Recycle Bin.

Font Properties

Fonts have properties just like any other files. These properties include security provisions identical to any other file, although few Windows NT users see the need to secure a particular font or font family.

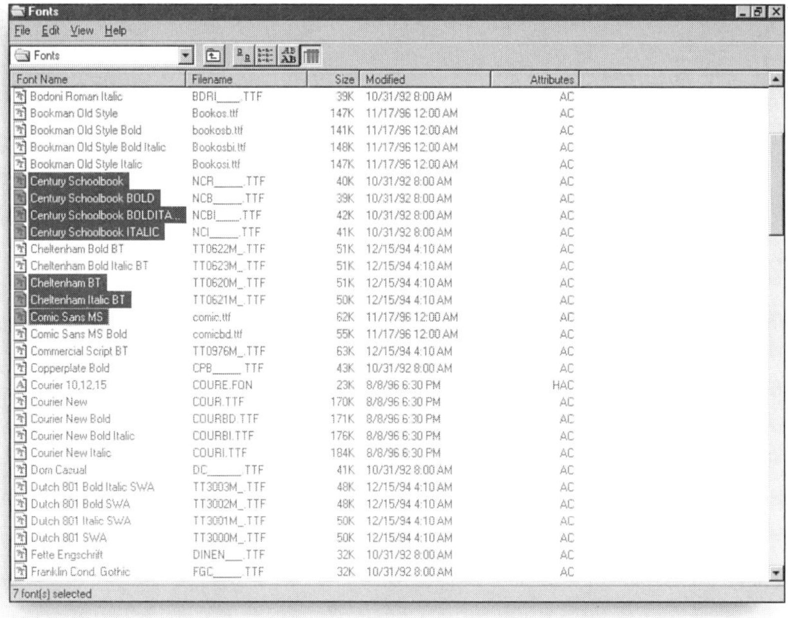

FIGURE 4.17.

Fonts are files. The Fonts window is the Explorer, so Shift and Ctrl work identically in the Fonts window as elsewhere in Explorer.

Inspecting a font's properties

1. Open the Control Panel and double-click on the Fonts icon. Alternatively, you can use the Explorer to locate the Fonts icon within the Control Panel.

2. Windows NT responds with a list of the fonts installed on your workstation. You can control the way the font names are displayed by choosing an option under the menu selection View or from the appropriate button on the toolbar. Figure 4.11 shows a typical font selection using the Details view.

3. Right-click on the font you wish to inspect. Choose Properties from the context menu. Alternatively, you can choose File|Properties from the menu. Figure 4.18 shows the resulting tabbed dialog box.

4. Note that the Fonts window displays both the font filename and the actual font name—the name that appears in your applications. However, the Properties dialog box shows only the font filename. Figure 4.18 displays the Balloon font (the font name), but the Properties dialog box uses the filename BL____.TTF.

FIGURE 4.18.

Fonts are files, and like files they have properties, including security.

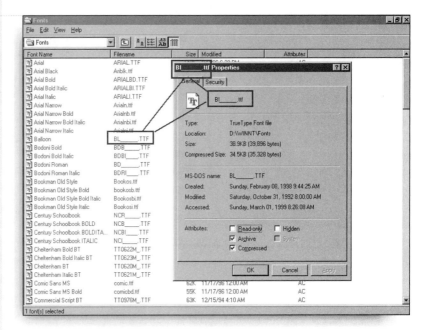

5. Click the Security tab and you will see three familiar buttons, as shown in Figure 4.19. To learn how to set security features, see Chapter 12.

FIGURE 4.19.

You can set all the Security features common to Windows NT for your fonts. You will have to be logged on with administrator rights to do so, however.

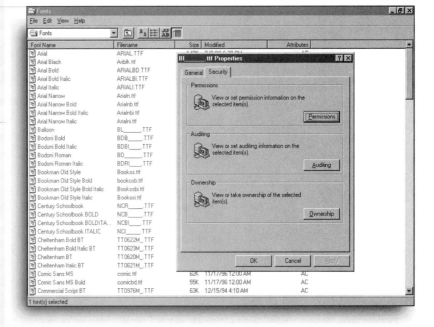

Common Windows NT Printer Terms

Some of the terms used by Windows NT for printing and printer services aren't obvious. Here are some of the most obscure or confusing:

- A *print device* is the actual printer hardware itself. This is different from the Windows NT definition of a printer.

- A *printer* is the driver or software interface between the computer and print device.

- A *print job* is the output from an application program sent to a printer, usually through a spool file.

- A *spool file* is the output from an application program written to file on your hard disk.

- *Network interface printers* are print devices that can connect to a network without the need for a computer to act as a printer server.

Fonts and Typefaces

Some people refer to fonts as typefaces. The use of the word *fonts* with its imputed meaning in this chapter is accepted by most of the computer industry.

CHAPTER

5

Installing and Uninstalling Applications

Installing Applications

Windows NT for Intel processors will run a variety of programs, including the following:

- Programs written specifically for Windows NT
- Programs written for another version of Windows (such as Windows 98) but that conform to the requirements of Windows NT
- Programs written for obsolete versions of Windows such as Windows 3.11
- Programs written for MS-DOS
- Programs written for OS/2 (Character mode only)
- POSIX programs

The overwhelming majority of people never need to run programs in the last two categories. Also Windows NT has somewhat varied success running programs written for MS-DOS or older versions of Windows, although you can do some tricks to increase your chances of success with those. Here are the techniques to install these options.

Conforming Programs—Those with an Install Routine

These programs just about install themselves. Part of Microsoft's requirements for a Windows program is a standard install or setup routine. These techniques work for any program, Windows or MS-DOS, that has an Install or Setup program meant to install it onto your machine.

Installing an application

1. Insert the distribution CD or disk, or know on the network where the distribution files exist.

2. Choose the menu options Start | Settings | Control Panel | Add/Remove Programs. Your screen should resemble Figure 5.1.

Does It Conform?

Some programs made for Windows 95/98 fully conform to Windows NT, but aren't certified as being so. The only way to be sure is to try them.

FIGURE 5.1.

The Add/Remove icon in Control Panel serves as the key to installing conforming programs.

3. Click the Install button. Click the Next button to start the Installation Wizard. The applet will search your drives for a file called SETUP or INSTALL. Upon finding such a file, the wizard will offer to run it. If you agree, you launch the installation routine for your application program. Follow the prompts onscreen. These prompts differ from program to program, depending on the needs and options of the application you're installing.

4. If the wizard doesn't find a file called INSTALL or SETUP on your removable drives, it will bring up a browse dialog box shown in Figure 5.2. You can enter the path to the install program or browse for it using the same techniques you do in Windows Explorer.

FIGURE 5.2.

If the Installation Wizard fails to find a program it recognizes as an installation routine, it offers you a chance to specify its location or browse for it.

You have an alternative way to install a program if you know the name and location of the setup program.

Installing applications (alternative method)

1. Choose the menu selections Start | Run.

2. Fill in the path to the installation routine or browse for it. Figure 5.3 shows this operation in progress.

FIGURE 5.3.

You can take a shortcut to an installation routine by bypassing the Add/Remove Programs applet.

Using Windows Explorer to install applications

1. Use the Windows Explorer to locate the installation program.

2. Double-click on it to launch or highlight it and choose File | Open from the Explorer menu. Figure 5.4 shows this in progress.

FIGURE 5.4.

You can shortcut all dialog boxes by using the Windows Explorer directly.

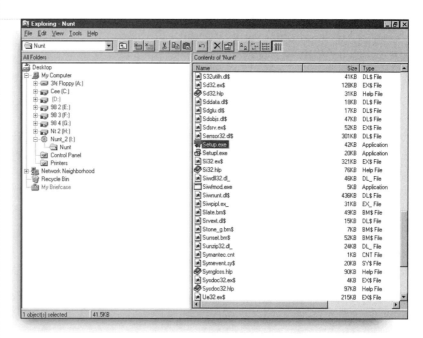

Some CDs have an Autorun routine that fires upon insertion of
the disk unless you have this facility disabled in your workstation. Figure 5.5 shows one such routine that launched itself
when the CD was inserted in the drive.

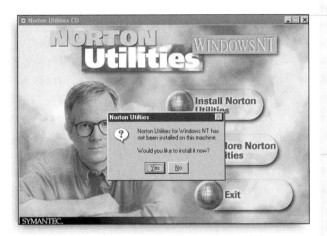

FIGURE 5.5.

Most program distribution CDs
will automatically launch into
their installation routines if you
let them. This installation routine not only launched itself,
but also sensed that the program wasn't currently installed
on the workstation.

Installing for All Users or One Profile

Installation routines need to decide whether, by default, to install
themselves for the logged on user or all users. Some routines,
such as the one shown in Figure 5.6, offer you a choice.

Most setup routines won't offer you such flexibility as the one
shown in Figure 5.6. If you have installed for one profile and
wish to make the program available to all users, you have the following option.

Making the program available to all users

1. Log on with the one profile or Administrator rights so that
   you can access the restricted program.

2. Launch the Windows Explorer. Locate the shortcuts for the
   installed program under the appropriate profile.

3. Move the program shortcuts from its restricted location to
   the Programs section (make a new folder if you wish) of All
   Users. Figure 5.7 shows this operation.

Disabling Autorun

To prevent an Autorun-enabled
CD from starting when inserted,
hold down the Shift key when
putting the CD in the drive.

FIGURE 5.6.

A sophisticated installation routine will offer you a choice about program access.

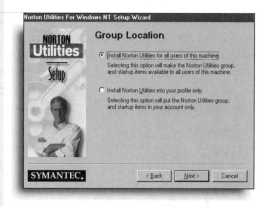

FIGURE 5.7.

Shortcuts can be moved to the Programs section of All Users.

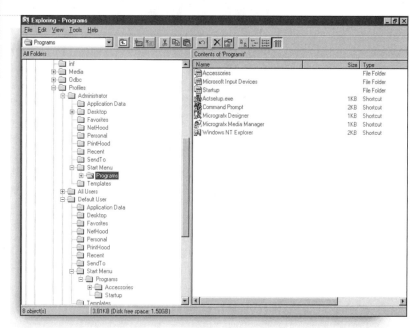

Moving shortcuts to All Users will allow greater access. Moving the shortcut to Micrografx Designer from the Administrator profile to the All Users profile, for example, will enable all users to access the program unless you secure it otherwise.

Moving a program from All Users or any user to another user

1. Log on with the appropriate rights. To be sure, log on with administrator rights.

2. Launch the Windows Explorer.

3. Locate and then move the shortcuts from one user's profile to another's. To make the programs available to more than one user, but not all users, copy the shortcuts into more than one user's profile.

4. Alternatively, you can manage program accessibility using security. To explore this, see Chapter 12, "Managing Users—NT Security."

Installing Programs Lacking Standard Setups

Installing programs, generally utilities and older programs, lacking a standard (conforming) setup routine depends on the program itself. Some small programs, such as the utilities found on the Internet, often don't need a true setup routine. You can just create a folder and put the program with any support files in there. You can then run the program using the Windows Explorer by double-clicking on it or using File | Open. Alternatively, you can create a shortcut to the program on the desktop or in any folder you have access to.

The .INF Installation

Many small utilities, such as the famous PowerToys (TweakUI) from Microsoft, use their .INF files for installation. To install these programs, right-click on the .INF file and choose Install from the context menu. Figure 5.8 shows this operation.

Simple MS-DOS or Windows Installs

In some cases, such as older or very simple MS-DOS programs, you need only to copy files to a folder and then manually create a shortcut to the program or launch directly from the Windows Explorer.

Some of these older programs present special difficulties when run under Windows NT. If you run into problems, see the "Troubleshooting" section later in this chapter.

FIGURE 5.8.

Some programs such as utilities and drivers can install from their .INF files.

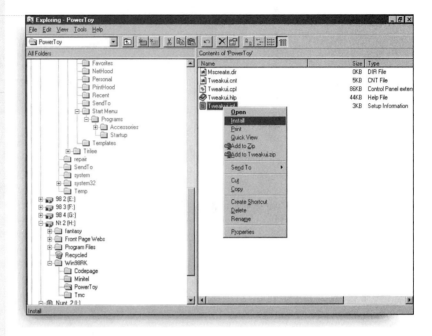

FIGURE 5.8.

Some programs such as utilities and drivers can install from their .INF files.

Web Installs

Many vendors, including Microsoft, have decided the Internet—especially the World Wide Web—is an ideal distribution medium for their installs or updates. The license issue prevents many vendors from doing true distribution from the Web because there is no reliable way to pay for a product while assuring customers they have a good distribution medium.

There are Web-based distributions where no license issue exists. The two general categories are free programs such as Internet Explorer and updates to either programs or drivers. There are two basic ways to install programs from the Web. Either you can download the program with its setup routine, or you can run the setup routine from the Web.

Technically, the first option isn't a Web install at all, just an alternative to a physical medium. The second option, setup directly from the Web, has gained some following notably with Microsoft's distribution of Internet Explorer.

There is no standard way to use a Web-based installation. If it is available, just visit the site and follow the instructions. In most cases, the routine downloads a small boot loader type program to your disk and that routine automatically launches and completes the setup using the Web site in place of a distribution medium. There also might be some security issues when trying a Web install; but the error messages, in these cases, will be self explanatory.

Uninstalling

The term "uninstall" means to remove an installed (or set up) program or part of Windows NT. In some cases it has been likewise applied to removal of hardware and drivers, but that's rare.

Uninstalls are usually the opposite analog of an install.

Uninstalling a conforming program

1. Choose the menu options Start | Settings | Control Panel | Add/Remove Programs. Your screen should resemble Figure 5.1.

2. Highlight the program you wish to uninstall in the list box.

3. Click the Add/Remove button shown in Figure 5.9.

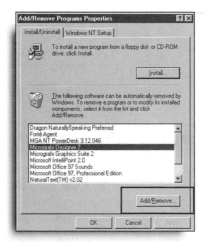

> **Danger on the Web**
>
> Watch out for virus and trojan horse programs when installing from the Web. Although this type problem isn't nearly as prevalent as sometimes portrayed, a prudent person will run a virus monitor when doing such installations.

FIGURE 5.9.

The Add/Remove button calls on the setup program for the highlighted program. How well the setup program uninstalls depends on the diligence of the programmers.

4. Follow the prompts.

Uninstalling simple Windows or MS-DOS programs often means nothing more than removing them from your computer. To do this, highlight the folder they are in, and then delete the entire folder structure. You might also need to search and delete any shortcuts that refer to this install.

The one problematic area for older Windows programs is the two .INI files, System and Win. Both exist in Windows NT for compatibility with 16-bit Windows (Win16) programs. These programs only understand looking for their initialization parameters in the two .INI files as the concept of the digital Registry was invented after their time.

Many, even some simple Win16 programs, modify one or both of these .INI files and often also install support files in the \system folder within the Windows NT folder structure. Few of these Win16 programs have setups that clean up after themselves, so you have to do it manually. There is no magic bullet here. You have to edit the .INI files, deleting the entries for the Win16 program you wish to uninstall, and also manually remove the referred to support files usually in \system—but they can also be anywhere.

Figure 5.10 shows the System.ini file from Windows NT with a Win16 program called Fast Eddie installed. This program initiated a new section of System.ini and also copied two files, flyout.drv and Tirilee.vxd, to the hard disk. To fully remove this program, you must remove the program files and then remove the entries in System.ini. The penalty for failure to remove the files themselves is slight—just a little lost disk space.

Troubleshooting

If you have problems running programs that conform to Microsoft's specification for Windows NT programs, you need to contact the vendor or your system administrator. These types of problems should be rare indeed. In fact, they shouldn't occur at all.

Partial Setups and Uninstalls

The Add/Remove button calls the general setup routine for the highlighted program. Often, as in the case of Office suites, this enables you to not only remove the entire suite, but also to change the installed components.

The Handy Semicolon

Adding a semicolon to the start of any line in Win.ini or System.ini will disable that line. This is a good way to test the effect of removing suspicious lines. If the semicolon addition has no effect, you're safe in fully removing the line and driver/program if it exists.

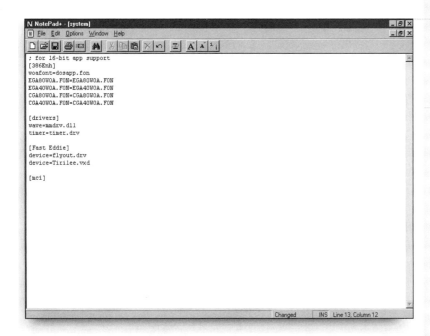

FIGURE 5.10.

Windows NT can use the System.ini and Win.ini files for Win16 programs that demand them.

The problems running programs under Windows NT come from running nonconforming, usually older, programs written for the Win16 (Windows 3.11, and so on) or for MS-DOS. These programs were written without Windows NT in mind and often disregard good programming practices. In some cases, this disregard stems from master programmers going around standard practice to improve performance to inept programmers making simple errors.

There are two aspects to tweaking older, nonconforming programs. The first to try to get them to run at all, if they don't. The second is to prevent them from ruining the performance of other nonconforming applications that might be running at the same time. This latter problem applies only to Win16 applications. MS-DOS programs run in their own memory space.

Allocating Discrete Memory for Win16

Each program (process) in Windows NT runs in an allotted memory space and is prevented from stepping on other running programs or NT itself. By default, all Win16 programs run in the same memory space. This allows them to mess up each other, but not Windows NT or conforming programs. The

The Pit of the Peach

The most common reason for older programs failing to run under Windows NT (or running poorly) is their use of undocumented calls to the operating system.

advantage of running this way is conservation of memory. Creating a space for each nonconforming program eats up a lot of memory, so it is efficient to stuff them all in the same place.

If you have a nonconforming program that crashes regularly—and especially if those crashes adversely affect other nonconforming programs—you can isolate that program from all others. This won't stop it from crashing (usually), but will prevent it from doing any damage when it does so.

There are several ways to run a process in its separate memory area. The first is using the Run dialog box.

Running a process in its separate memory area

1. Choose Start | Run from the Windows NT menu.

2. Enter the path and program name in the displayed text box.

3. Make sure you check the Run in Separate Memory Space check box in the Run dialog box. Click OK. Figure 5.11 shows this dialog box with the check box highlighted.

FIGURE 5.11.

The Start | Run dialog box is one way to run a program in its own memory space.

You can also create a shortcut to an application and tell the shortcut to order Windows NT to run it in its own memory space.

Windows NT and the TSR

TSR or MS-DOS "pop-up" programs often run well under Windows NT 4—an improvement over previous versions of Windows NT.

Running a program in its own memory space with a shortcut

1. Create a shortcut to a Win16 application.

2. Right-click on the shortcut, and then choose Properties from the context menu. You can also locate it in Windows Explorer, highlight it, and then choose File | Properties.

3. Click the Shortcut tab. Locate the Run in Separate Memory Space check box and select it. Figure 5.12 shows this tab and the check box.

4. Click OK to exit the Properties dialog box.

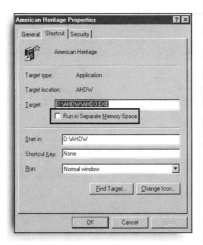

FIGURE 5.12.

You can set a shortcut to force a Win16 application into its own memory space.

Finally, you can use the CLI (command line interface) to run a Win16 application in its own memory space.

Running a Win16 application in its own memory space with the CLI

1. Start a CLI session. You can do this by choosing Start | Run and then entering CMD in the dialog box.

2. Enter the word Start in the command line, followed by a slash, the word Separate, followed by the path to the application. To run the application used as an example in this section, you enter,

   ```
   Start /Separate d:\ahdw\ahd3
   ```

3. Press Return (or Enter).

Figure 5.13 shows the Task Manager with two instances of the same program running, each in its own memory space. The NTVDM entry means NT Virtual Device Manager—the way Windows NT runs nonconforming programs. The WOW entries you will see in Task Manager mean Windows on Windows. Microsoft coined that term for the way Windows NT runs Win16 programs.

MS-DOS Programs

You can use a huge variety of settings and combinations to diddle problematic MS-DOS programs into running well under Windows NT. If your MS-DOS program isn't running correctly, you needn't throw in the towel.

FIGURE 5.13.

Each of the two instances of the same program can get their own memory space. This prevents one's malfunction from causing a problem with the other.

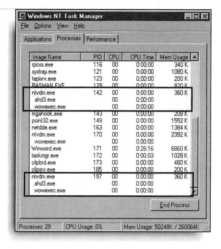

CMD and Command

Windows NT 4 has two command shells, CMD and Command. CMD is specific to Windows NT and contains NT-only commands. Command conforms to non-NT Windows and MS-DOS command line interfaces for the most part.

The problem with recommending a way to fix a malfunctioning MS-DOS program is that I can't know where to start making generic recommendations. The vast majority of problems in these programs stem from the programmers having used non-standard practices. Windows NT can allow for (trap really) most of these practices, but you need to have some idea what they are before you can begin doing any custom settings. I've had excellent luck getting MS-DOS programs to run under Windows NT Workstation; but in truth, I haven't tackled the most problematic class of programs—action games—very often. My business is focused on consulting with, well, businesses, and that's where I have kept my focus.

Here are my steps in determining a way to approach an MS-DOS program using Windows NT.

Adjusting an MS-DOS program for use under Windows NT

1. Is the vendor still in business? If so, does it have any ideas how to force its program to run under Windows NT?

2. Does the program issue any useful error messages when it fails? These can be invaluable when solving this class of problems.

3. Does the documentation offer any hints about running under any version of Windows? Those hints can often be applied to Windows NT too.

4. Does the failure imply the problem? A scrambled screen, for example, implies that you should look first at display settings.

5. If nothing else helps, follow your nose. After a while people develop an instinct for these things.

To adjust settings for an MS-DOS program, right-click on the program or its shortcut and choose Properties from the context menu. This brings up a dialog box with tabs relevant to these settings. Figure 5.14 shows one such dialog box.

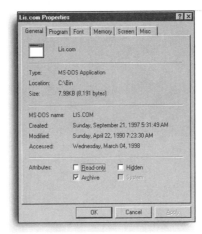

FIGURE 5.14.

The Properties dialog box of an MS-DOS program contains a blizzard of settings.

Each tab refers to a specific area of customization for a program. Windows NT is very good as sensing what a program demands, but its sensor isn't infallible. Figure 5.15, for example, shows the Screen tab. Here you can force Windows NT to treat a program's display services in a particular way.

One of the most useful areas of MS-DOS program customization is Windows NT's capability to use different MS-DOS initialization files for a program. As this capability is often overlooked, I decided to emphasize it here.

Changing the MS-DOS–type initialization files (in MS-DOS, AUTOEXEC.BAT and CONFIG.SYS)

1. Right-click on the MS-DOS program or its shortcut.

2. Choose the Program tab.

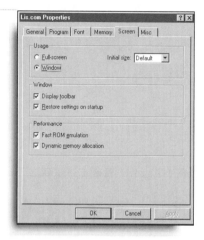

FIGURE 5.15.

The Screen and Memory tabs are the two most often used tabs to force MS-DOS programs to run under Windows NT.

Making an NT .PIF

When you exit the Properties dialog box for an MS-DOS program, Windows NT automatically creates a .PIF (program information file) for that application in the form of a shortcut. The shortcut contains your custom settings or, if you don't set anything special, it preserves the default settings for that program.

Zero-Based Budgeting

The easiest way to fix a poorly behaved ancient program is to replace it with a modern program that does the same thing. Sometimes people run these older programs out of habit or inertia, not because they really depend on them.

3. Click the Windows NT button.

4. Windows NT responds with a dialog box having two text boxes.

5. Change the entries to any custom text files you wish to use in place of AUTOEXEC.NT or CONFIG.NT.

Figure 5.16 shows this dialog box.

Windows NT permits custom initialization files for MS-DOS programs. Say, for example, that your program, "Jet Death to Infidels," requires the following line:

```
Device=zoomzoom.exe
```

As part of CONFIG.SYS when running under MS-DOS, you would provide this facility by specifying a special configuration file for use when that program launches. Windows NT can configure an environment that foxes the older programs into thinking that they have utter control over the computer and that their special environment rules.

Using custom configuration files for older programs

1. Locate the file zoomzoom.exe.

2. Create a text file containing the following line:

```
device=[path]zoomzoom.exe
```

3. Save the file using a unique name.

4. Right-click on the MS-DOS program or its shortcut.

5. Choose the Program tab.

6. Click the Windows NT button.

7. Windows NT responds with a dialog box having two text boxes. Enter the path to your text file in the text box labeled Config Filename.

After doing this, OK your way out of the dialog boxes. Now when you start your MS-DOS program, it will have the services of the device zoomzoom.exe.

Use an identical technique to create a custom file that can act as an AUTOEXEC.BAT file if you need that.

Figure 5.17 shows the Memory tab of the Properties dialog box. This tab is the third most used place to fix ill-running MS-DOS programs. Note the large number of settings possible. For the most part, Windows NT works fine when left to AUTO for these settings. In some cases, usually flagged by a memory error message, it won't. That's what this tab is for.

Protected from What?

The Protected check box in the Memory tab provides protection for system services. It does not change the allocated memory space for MS-DOS programs. In all instances, these processes run in their own space. This is fundamentally different from Win16 programs.

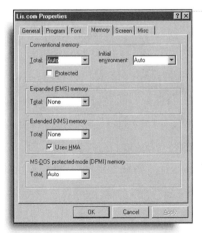

Communicating with Windows NT Workstation 4

Using Outlook Express

The Amazing Compatibility of Outlook Express

Outlook Express, or OE, is the email and news side of both Internet Explorer and the Windows Explorer. (IE and Windows Explorer can really be viewed as alter egos.)

There's a method behind this overlap. Microsoft has been on a campaign for a while now to make the function similar for all its application programs and operating systems. This follows the lead of Apple, which long ago stated that to be fully right for its Macintosh, programs must adhere to certain guidelines. This concept means computer users will have transferable skills among programs or, in this case, elements of the operating system itself.

There is only so far you can take this concept, however. Windows Explorer is primarily a files and folders management system. Internet Explorer is primarily a Web and FTP browser. Outlook Express is an email and news client. As each application has a different function, each also has some specialized extensions exclusive to it.

They also all have elements in common or at least very similar. OE's left pane, for example, is a tree view similar to Windows Explorer's left pane. Therefore users familiar with Windows Explorer will immediately understand and know how to use at least some parts of Outlook Express.

Active Desktop and Outlook Express

What's a Client?

A client application is the side of a program that runs on a local workstation (your computer). To operate, such a system also needs a server side—the other part of a client/server system. In email, for example, you operate your client (Outlook Express), which in turn establishes a connection with a server of some sort (Microsoft Exchange, an Internet account, or something similar).

SEE ALSO

➤ *For more information about the Active Desktop, see Chapter 3, "Customizing the Active Desktop."*

If you installed any version (other than Browser Only) of IE4 or higher to gain the Active Desktop discussed in Chapter 3, "Customizing the Active Desktop," you also installed Outlook Express. This is a messaging system for use in email and newsgroups on the Internet, a LAN, and Internet-like systems.

The advantage of using Outlook Express as an email and news client is its simplicity and similarity to other parts of Windows NT such as Explorer. Because OE and the browser part of Internet Explorer are both from Microsoft and designed with compatibility in mind, they work together in a very well-integrated fashion with other Microsoft products. That doesn't mean that non-Microsoft clients can't integrate well also, only that these do.

Generally speaking, people like to use suites. This means that people who use IE as their browser tend to be more comfortable using OE as their email and news client, but it's not mandatory. I have used IE as a browser with Agent (from Forte) as a news-reader and Eudora (from Qualcomm) as an email client, and have all working in perfect harmony. Similarly, I have used different Internet clients with various versions of Netscape's Navigator browser and had no problems whatsoever. By no means think that your browser—IE, Navigator or any others you might prefer—ties you to a set of clients.

Although most of these programs will work in harmony, this isn't even necessary for the most part. As nice as it is for you to click a link in an email and bring up your browser or click an email address on a page to invoke your email client, you can live easily with copy and paste. You also shouldn't feel bullied into using IE because you're using a Microsoft operating system, Windows NT. In fact, you could (if company policy allows) search around to find your own ideal Internet suite of an email client, a newsreader, and a browser. I, for example, have used several solutions that don't include any components from either Netscape or Microsoft. You can too.

> **Suite Harmony**
>
> When you install Internet Explorer 4, Setup will try to set it as your default browser and Outlook Express as your default email/newsgroup client.

For most people, however, the easy and obvious solution to an email client and newsreader is Outlook Express. Therefore this chapter addresses that program exclusively.

Standard Features

If you let the Active Desktop Setup run its course using its defaults, it installed three ways to launch Outlook Express. You will find an icon on the desktop, another icon in Quick Launch, and yet another shortcut in the Start menu under Programs|Internet Explorer. Using the method you prefer, launch OE.

Figure 6.1 shows Outlook Express opened. If you have added any services to your OE, your screen might also show those services. This system has already had a news service (Usenet) added. You can see that as the last entry in the left pane.

FIGURE 6.1.

Outlook Express has all the familiar Windows NT elements such as bars and windows.

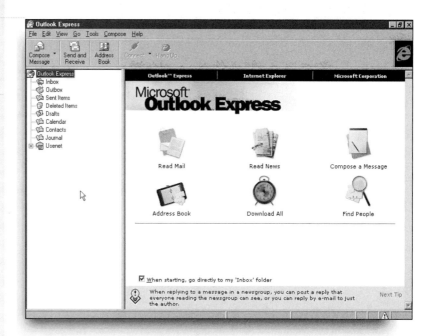

Outlook Express Versus Outlook Local?

Outlook Express is part of the entire Outlook application program. The Express part doesn't mean that it's faster than Outlook, but that it's only part of it (functionally speaking). The entire Outlook is part of the Office 97 suite. Later versions of Outlook are and will be part of subsequent Office suites. Microsoft also makes updates to the original Outlook (such as Outlook 98) available on its Web site.

When you first start OE, it is good for nothing until you establish what services and which accounts you wish to use it for. You will need certain information. Assuming you have established your Internet (or intranet or extranet) connection, you will also need interactive (logon) information.

Here's what you need to know before using OE.

For mail:

- Your logon name(s)
- Your password(s)

- Your POP (or other post-office–type service) server IP
- Your SMTP (or other send-mail–type service) server IP

For news:

- Your news server IP
- Your logon (for secure servers)
- Your password (for secure servers)

Before going on, let's take a closer look at all these IDs. An Internet IP is in the raw form of a series of numbers in this format: ###.###.###.###, where numbers from 0 to 255 are legitimate entries for each numeric series, such as:

- `198.112.100.1`
- `112.100.1.100`
- `155.155.155.2`

Most people have trouble remembering number series such as these, so the Internet has a translation service where an alphanumeric substitutes for IPs. If your server has a registered alphanumeric, you can use those in most places where you would normally use the IP. Examples of such addresses are as follows:

- `zhaggie2.unm.edu`
- `happy.irg.com`
- `election.phil98.org`

If you need to set up to use Outlook Express over your company's LAN, see your network administrator for some of these IPs. If you use an Internet service provider (ISP), that company should have a specification sheet with the required information. In the case of a private news service, you need to gain information from that service. So let's go.

Setting Up an Email Account

After you have your information, setting up an email account is easy.

Uniformity Reigns

Most companies standardize on a particular email client. Network administrators can get quite touchy if you replace that choice with one of your preference. Avoid conflict. Ask first!

Setting up an email account in Outlook Express

1. Launch Outlook Express.

2. Choose the menu selections Tools | Accounts. Click the Mail tab to see whether you have any accounts established. There is no benefit to creating duplicate identical email accounts. You will also need to decide, in the case of you having more than one account, which is to be your default one. Technically speaking, you can skip this step. Your screen should resemble Figure 6.2. Although if you have never used OE before, there will be no established accounts.

FIGURE 6.2.

You add accounts (services) to Outlook Express through a familiar tabbed dialog box.

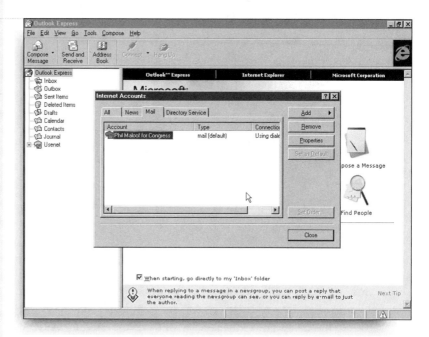

3. Click the Add button, and then click Mail from the fly-out menu. This invokes a wizard.

4. Fill in a display name of your own choosing. This will appear in the From field when others receive mail from you. Click Next.

5. Fill in your email address. This is usually in the form of a name followed by the *at* sign (@), followed by your domain. Tirilee@cassel.com, for example, is an email address. Figure

6.3 shows this section of the wizard filled in with my real email address. If in doubt, you can get your email address from your network administrator or ISP—that is, whoever administers your Internet access. Click Next.

FIGURE 6.3.
You need to know the name of your email account (where people send you mail) for this section of the wizard.

6. Select the type of inbound server type you have (IMAP or POP3) and fill in your incoming and outgoing server IPs or addresses. Figure 6.4 shows this for my service. Click Next.

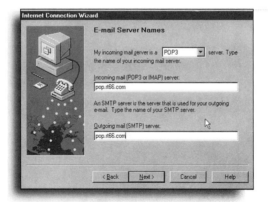

FIGURE 6.4.
This dialog box demands the technical information about your email service.

7. Enter your logon (often called your interactive logon) and the accompanying password. The password will appear onscreen as a series of asterisk (*) characters. Click the SPA option button if instructed to by your administrator. Click Next.

   8. Enter a name for this service to appear in Outlook Express. This example uses `Paul's Mail`, as you can see in Figure 6.5.

FIGURE 6.5.

Now done with the technicalities, you get to choose a display name for your new service.

   9. Click Next. Choose the way you will be connecting in this dialog box. Click Next to see the congratulations message. Click Finish to end the wizard.

   10. After you finish, OE will add the service under the name you chose in step 8. Figure 6.6 shows an example of such an addition.

FIGURE 6.6.

Unlike other email clients, Outlook Express enables you to add multiple email accounts. This OE now has two.

The default email account is the one OE will use to send email. You can direct it to use non-default accounts also.

Configuring Outlook Express for Newsgroups

Adding newsgroups to Outlook Express is very similar to adding email accounts, but in most cases you won't need either a logon or a password. These apply only to private newsgroups such as those established by companies for their internal use only. Most news servers such as the Usenet and MSNEWS are public. This permits all to participate without established accounts.

Adding a news account to Outlook Express

1. Launch Outlook Express.

2. Choose the menu selections Tools, Accounts. Click Add, and then click News from the fly-out menu to start a wizard. This example configures OE to receive news from Microsoft's server.

3. Enter a display name for the new account. This is the name that will appear in your news postings. Use your real name or a handle, depending on your preference. This example uses the real name `Paul Cassel`. Click Next.

4. Enter your email address so that people can email you from the public or semi-public news areas. Enter a fake address if you don't want people to be able to email you. Click Next.

5. Enter the news server's IP. In this example that is `msnews.microsoft.com`. If you wish to contact another news server, you need to consult your ISP or your administrator for its address. If your server requires you to log on, click in the check box. That will add a dialog box to the wizard giving you places to add your logon name and password.

6. Add a friendly name to use for this newsgroup to be displayed in the left pane of Outlook Express. This example used Microsoft News.

7. Click Next and tell the wizard how you will be connecting to the server. Click Next to see the Success screen. Click Finish.

8. Close the Accounts dialog box. OE will offer to download the newsgroups using the screen shown in Figure 6.7.

Verify and Check

Some outbound mail servers require verification. This will require even more settings. If this is so, click the established email account, choose the Properties button, choose the Servers tab, and check the My Server Requires Verification check box. Click the Settings button and enter the information given you.

FIGURE 6.7.
You can download the news-groups now or later.

After you have finished downloading, a dialog box with the downloaded newsgroups appears. If you choose not to download immediately, OE will offer to do this when you try to use this news service.

Directory Services

A Directory Service is a server or cluster of servers containing the network equivalent of a telephone white or yellow pages. Using these services, such as the well known Switchboard or Four11, you can look up people, businesses, and other entities both for their online and real-world information such as address, phone, or email.

Outlook Express comes configured with several Directory Services set up. Figure 6.8 shows the list at one stage of OE's cycle. Your OE might have different Directory Services installed at the factory.

FIGURE 6.8.
Outlook Express comes with several Directory Services installed at the Microsoft factory.

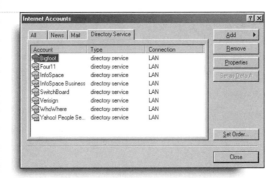

Adding a new service is quite simple. Here's how.

Adding a new Directory Service

1. Launch Outlook Express.

2. Choose the menu selections Tools, Accounts. Choose New, and then choose Directory Service from the fly-out menu. This launches a wizard.

3. Enter the address of the new service using Internet Protocol. (For example, the address of Switchboard is `ldap.switchboard.com`.)

4. Click Next and enter whether you wish the service to attempt to look up email addresses by clicking the appropriate option button.

5. Click Next and enter a friendly name for the new service. Click Next, and then click Finish to end the process.

Locating a person using a Directory Service

1. Launch Outlook Express.

2. Open the Address Book by choosing it from the toolbar or the Tools menu.

3. Click the Find button on the Address Book's toolbar. Pull down the combo box at the top of the Find dialog box and select a Directory Service. Figure 6.9 shows this operation.

Do I Need Directories?

Directories are analogous to telephone directory books. You don't need them if you know the contact information of your correspondents or just wish to participate in newsgroups.

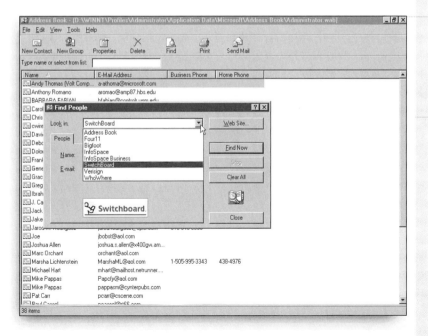

FIGURE 6.9.
The Find utility in Outlook Express's Address Book can search the Address Book itself or any registered Directory Service.

4. Enter whatever information you have on hand. This example uses "Paul Cassel" for lack of a better idea.

5. Click the Find Now button. This searches the service for the name (or email or both) that you have entered. Figure 6.10 shows the results of the "Paul Cassel" search.

FIGURE 6.10.

There are a lot of guys out there with the same name.

6. If at first you don't succeed, try again. Figure 6.11 shows the results of searching another service using the same string. Note the vast differences in returns for the two services.

FIGURE 6.11.

As the Four11 service shows, there are many guys who use odd variants of the real name.

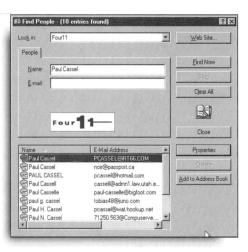

Using Outlook Express to see messages in a newsgroup

1. Launch Outlook Express.

2. Click the news server you wish to use. The servers you have available to you are located in the left pane of OE. This example uses the Microsoft news server configured in the earlier exercise.

3. If you haven't subscribed to any newsgroups, OE will invite you to do so. If you haven't downloaded the groups, OE will offer to do so. You must download the groups before using a news server. Figure 6.12 shows the dialog box asking you whether you wish to view a list of the newsgroups for this server. You can always see this list again by clicking the Newsgroups button in the toolbar when this server is selected.

FIGURE 6.12.

Until you subscribe to at least one newsgroup, Outlook Express will invite you to do so whenever you launch the server.

4. Figure 6.13 shows a list of the newsgroups for the Microsoft news server at the time the screen was shot. These groups change regularly, so your list might look different from the book's. To subscribe to a group name, click it and then click the Subscribe button (or double-click the group name). This example subscribed to two Access groups, "gettingstarted" and "queries." When subscribed, the groups appear in an Explorer-like display under the server in the left pane. Figure 6.14 shows this. Close the Newsgroups dialog box after you finish.

5. To see messages, click the group you wish to view. OE will download the current headers placing them in the upper-right pane of OE.

FIGURE 6.13.

Most news servers have a wide selection of groups, each of which address a particular interest.

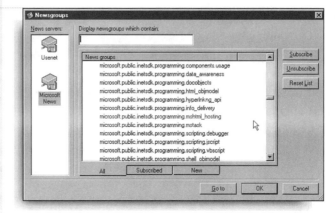

FIGURE 6.14.

Subscribed-to groups appear in an Explorer-like manner under the server.

6. To see the messages themselves, click any header (expand headers using the usual Explorer techniques). The message will appear in the lower pane, the Preview pane. Figure 6.15 shows message headers and one message.

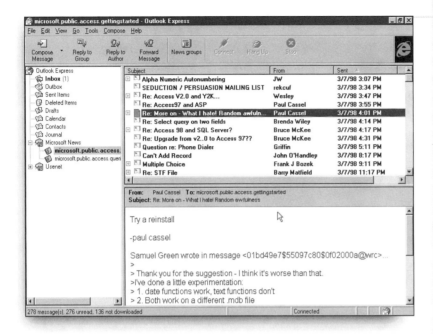

FIGURE 6.15.

The interface of Outlook Express is of the drill-down style. The left pane shows services and servers, the upper-right pane shows headers, and the lower-right pane shows the messages themselves.

Practical Uses for Outlook Express

The two purposes of Outlook Express are email and news-groups. Here's how to use it for both.

Using Outlook Express to respond to news messages

If necessary, review the preceding exercise called "Using Outlook Express to See Messages in a Newsgroup."

1. Use Outlook Express to see the message headers in the newsgroup you have selected to participate in.

2. Double-click a message to open it, or let your cursor linger on it long enough for Outlook Express to open it in the Preview pane (bottom-right pane). Figure 6.16 shows a message in the Preview pane and also opened in the bottom-right pane.

3. To post a reply to the newsgroup (for all to see), click the toolbar button Reply to Group. To reply privately (through email) to the poster, click Reply to Author. If the poster didn't use his or her real email address when posting, the email option will fail, but the Group Post option will work.

Salty Going

Unmoderated newsgroups (those where anybody is free to post anything) can get quite salty in the dialogs. Don't log on to these groups if you're feeling sensitive. Some groups have, by way of their content, quite a bit of acrimony. Some don't. You can usually get an idea of the tone you might anticipate by the title. For example, `alt.impeach.clinton` can get pretty wild; `alt.fan.osmond`, on the other hand, usually won't.

FIGURE 6.16.

It's quite easy to reply to a newsgroup post, which accounts for the many hasty and often rude exchanges in the Usenet.

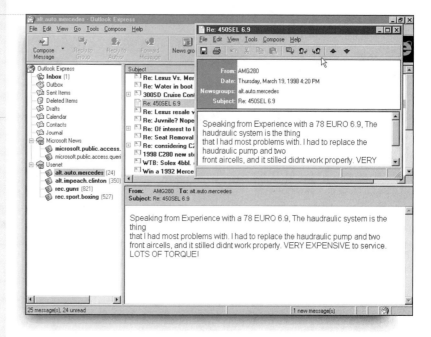

4. After composing your reply, click the Post or Send button in the toolbar to post the message to the group or to send it to the author privately. Figure 6.17 shows a reply being created for posting to the group.

Creating a new newsgroup message is similar to replying to an existing one. Here's how to do this.

Composing a new newsgroup message

1. On- or offline, click the newsgroup you wish to post into. The newsgroups appear in the left pane of Outlook Express.

2. Click the Compose Message button. This opens an Edit dialog box where you can create your message.

3. Enter a subject for your message. This will appear as the header in the newsgroup.

4. Optionally, click the icon to the left of the name of the newsgroup in the header part of the Message dialog box. This opens up a dialog box that enables you to post your message in more than one group from a list of your subscribed-to groups. Figure 6.18 shows this dialog box as well as a new message being composed.

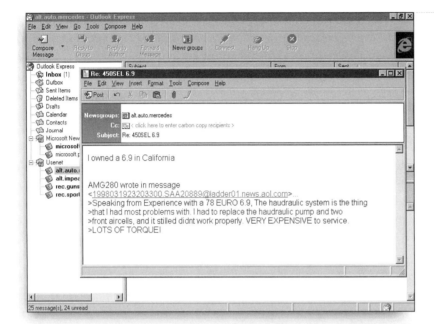

FIGURE 6.17.

You can post to the group for all to see and comment on or reply privately to the poster.

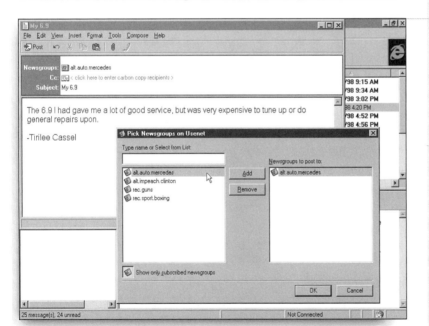

FIGURE 6.18.

There's no limit to the number of newsgroups that you can post to, but as you can see, some newsgroups would be more relevant to the topic of Mercedes purchasing than others.

They Will Get Back at You

If you use your real email address for a newsgroup server, be careful what you post; it might result in unpleasant returns to your email account. If you post derogatory messages about well-known Democrats in `alt.fan.democrats`, for example, expect to get some static back.

5. After you finish creating your message, entering a subject/header, and adding any additional newsgroups you wish to post to, click the Post button.

Creating a new email is almost identical to creating a new newsgroup post. The Address Book is a great help with email, so the next two exercises take a look first at the Address Book and then new email.

Using the Address Book

1. Open Outlook Express.

2. Open the Address Book by clicking the Address Book icon on the toolbar.

3. Add or edit any entries you wish. To edit, double-click the entry. To add, click the New Contact button. You can also use the Find button to find entries for editing. Figure 6.19 shows the Address Book open for editing.

FIGURE 6.19.

You can edit existing entries in the Address Book by double-clicking the entry in the Address Book list box.

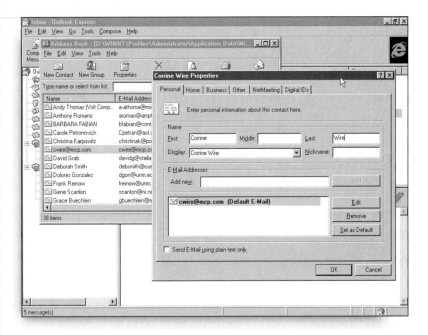

4. A handy and often overlooked feature of the Address Book is the creation of groups of addresses for mass email distribution. To create a group, click the New Group button when the Address Book is open. Create a name for your group and then add email addresses either from the existing list or by manually adding new email addresses. Figure 6.20 shows the creation of a group called "Union Members."

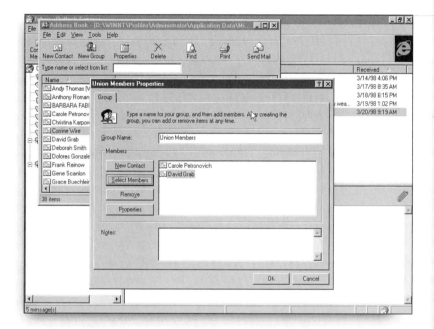

Creating a new email message

1. Open Outlook Express.

2. Click the Inbox or other email-related icon in the left pane to tell Outlook Express that you are intending an email transaction.

3. Click the Compose Message button on the toolbar. This will open an Edit dialog box where you can enter your message, a subject (header), and places to specify copies to be sent.

4. Enter an email address, a name from the Address Book, or double-click on the Rolodex-like icon to the left of the line in the To field to open the Address Book.

5. If in the Address Book, double-click on a recipient or recipients to add them to the To line.

Fast Address Book Entries

To add the email address of a correspondent to the Address Book, open a message from that person, right-click the return (from) address, and then choose Add to Address Book from the context menu.

6. Proceed identically to add other recipients in the Cc: or Bcc: lines. Cc: copies the message to another email address with the original addressee seeing the Cc:. The Bcc: is the "blind copy." This copies without the recipient seeing the fact that the message is copied. Cc: and Bcc: are optional entries. Figure 6.21 shows the use of Address Book to add an address to a new email.

FIGURE 6.21.

You can add as many recipients as you choose to an email message.

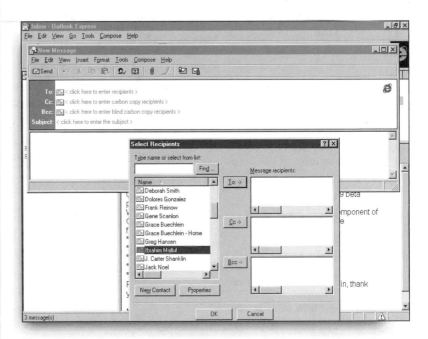

7. Add a Subject. This is optional.

8. Enter the message in the space provided. When you wish to send your message, click the Send button.

Keep in mind that you can create folders and subfolders within Outlook Express just like you can Explorer. You can freely move and copy files (messages) within these folders using the same techniques as you use in Windows Explorer. See Chapter 1, "Using and Understanding Windows NT 4," and Chapter 2, "The Windows NT Framework," for information on using Windows Explorer.

SEE ALSO

➤ *For more information on Windows Explorer, see Chapter 1, "Using and Understanding Windows NT," and Chapter 2, "The Windows NT Framework."*

Send Now or Later

If you don't wish to send a message now, you can click menu options File|Send Later. This will file the message in the Outbox for sending later. When you click the Send and Receive button, all messages in the Outbox will go out. You can also choose File|Save As or File|Save while composing a new message to file the message in the Drafts folder for later editing or sending.

Filtering Out Unwanted Messages

You can filter messages to prevent display in newsgroups of a person or person you find offensive. You can also filter your incoming email to eliminate email from sources you specify.

Both related features are available within the Inbox Assistant. Here's how to create some filters.

Adding a filter to your Outlook Express

1. Open Outlook Express.

2. Choose Tools | Inbox Assistant from the menu. Choose Add to create a new rule for filtering.

3. Add the criteria and an action to take. This example uses the word *sex* to filter the action to remove those messages from the server without downloading. Figure 6.22 shows this setup.

Receiving Email

When launched and at regular intervals (set in Tools|Options|General), Outlook Express will check for email. If you wish to check for email manually, click the Send and Receive button in the tool-bar or choose Tools|Send and Receive from the menu.

Auto Addresses

One of the settings in Tools|Options|General is to have those you reply to by email automatically entered into your Address Book.

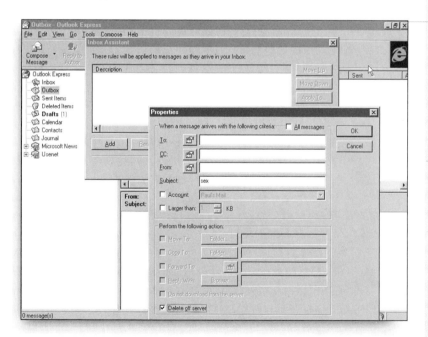

FIGURE 6.22.

Using the Inbox Assistant to filter unwanted mail or news messages can make your online experience much more enjoyable. This setup eliminates the download of any messages containing the word *sex* in the subject area.

4. Add as many criteria and actions as you choose, clicking OK after each one to add it to the Inbox Assistant dialog box. Table 6.1 shows some filtering ideas. Figure 6.23 shows several rules added to the Inbox Assistant dialog box. These rules will cut down on, but not eliminate, salacious messages. Click (OK) your way out of the Inbox Assistant after you finish.

FIGURE 6.23.

Nothing eliminates all unwanted messages, but you can cut down on the volume by using the Inbox Assistant.

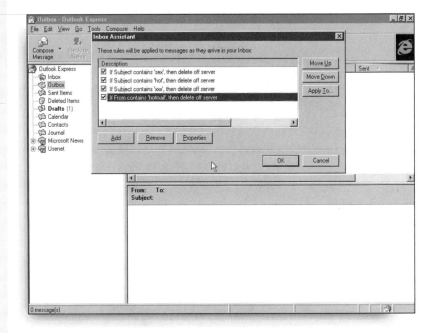

TABLE 6.1   **Filtering email**

To Filter Out	Enter
Anybody from the server "Hotmail"	Hotmail in the From text box
A specific email address	The email address in the From text box
All messages with the word *sex* in them	sex in the Subject text box
Copied to a particular person	The email address in the Cc: text box

Let's take a look at why you would want to do some of these things. Say you notice that you are getting a lot of unwanted email from a variety of senders having the same domain (the information after the @ sign in an email address). By entering that domain in the From text box, you will block all senders from that domain. Keep in mind that by using this technique you will also block senders from whom you might want to hear, too.

In some cases, you might see unwanted email coming to you bearing certain words or phrases. I, for example, never have gotten a wanted email with either the word *free* or *sex* in the subject line, but I get a lot of unwanted mail with those words; therefore I filter out (and delete from the server without downloading) all email bearing these words in the Subject line.

This does have a downside. I might someday get an email from a friend asking in the Subject line, "Are you free for lunch?" My rule will filter out this email too, an unwanted byproduct. I take the risk, however, to also filter out all the silliness. If the friend doesn't hear back from me, he or she can try again or just phone.

After you have been online, especially in a company email system, you will notice that many people copy all their email to everybody. You can block this by filtering out any email that's Cc:'d to another to whom you should have no relation. This too runs the risk of filtering out a legitimate email. I leave it to you to balance the risk and rewards of all these filters. I tend to filter like crazy because my time is more valuable than the risk of missing a legitimate email that by coincidence meets my filter rules.

Outlook Express Options

You can add fancy formatting to your newsgroup or email messages, but use this feature with care. Many email clients and newsreaders can't translate these formats and the use of fancy formatting increases the size of your messages often drastically.

Adding stationery (fancy formatting) to your messages

1. Open Outlook Express.
2. Choose Tools|Options|Send to see the options for sent messages.
3. Make sure you have HTML checked for each service you wish to apply your stationery to. Figure 6.24 shows this applied to mail, but not news.

Newsgroup Filters

You can also filter newsgroup messages by sender, domain, and subject. To do this, highlight a news server or group in the left pane of Outlook Express and then choose Tools|Newsgroup Filters from the menu. Because of the differences between email and news, there are fewer options than with the Inbox Assistant, but then again, there is less possible.

FIGURE 6.24.

You can get really fancy for either email or news or both by setting options for Outlook Express.

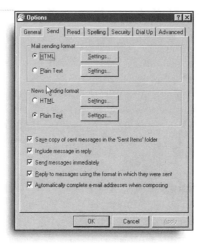

Fancy Bloat

Adding stationery or other fancy formatting to your messages enlarges them significantly. Most email messages total less than 1000 bytes (1KB); even simple fancy messages, however, take up to 10 times that amount of space. If you tend to send many copies, especially to internal company people, making the mail fancy will eat up quite a bit of internal resources. This will often annoy network administrators who don't see that your need for self-expression is as important as network storage space. You have been warned!

4. Click (OK) your way out of the Options dialog box.

5. Choose Tools|Stationery from the menu.

6. Choose the tab you wish to assign Stationery to. In this case, it's Mail.

7. Specify the font you wish to use by clicking the Font button. Click the This Stationery option button, and then click the Select button to open the Stationery browser.

8. Choose a stationery from those supplied. You can browse for any HTML file to use as a stationery or choose the Get More button to launch the IE browser and go to a Microsoft site. You can choose the Edit button to edit an existing HTML file. Figure 6.25 shows a stationery selection in progress.

9. Click (OK) your way out of the dialog boxes after you have made your choice. From now on, all your new messages will use this stationery. Figure 6.26 shows this in action.

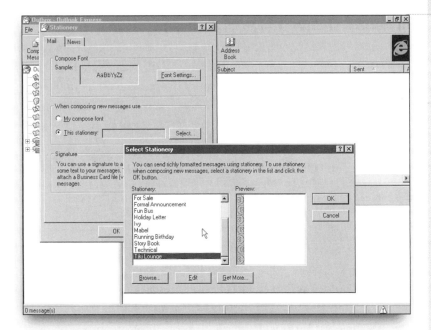

FIGURE 6.25.

You can choose a stationery from any HTML file. Microsoft supplies some sample stationery with Outlook Express.

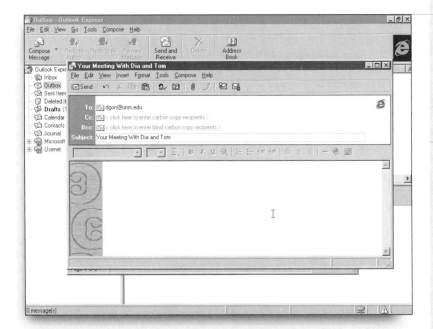

FIGURE 6.26.

Stationery makes for an interesting backdrop for your email or news posts, but make sure that the increased size and complexity of stationery is appreciated by your intended recipients.

Signatures

You can add a "signature," a phrase that gets tacked on the end of all your messages, by clicking the Signature button in Tools | Stationery.

Cleaning Up

To compact message space, remove message bodies or message bodies and headers from Outlook Express. Choose File | Clean Up Files when any news server folder is highlighted. Compaction isn't enabled when an email folder is selected.

Advanced Outlook Express Configuration

Open the Options dialog box of many tabs by choosing Tools | Options from the menu. Most of the entries are best left at default or are self explanatory. Here are some useful options and their tabs.

- **Tools | Options | General.** To set the interval where Outlook Express checks for new mail.

- **Tools | Options | General.** To set Outlook Express as your default MAPI client.

- **Tools | Options | Send.** To file send messages in Outbox instead of sending them right off.

- **Tools | Options | Send.** To send using plain text (filtering out HTML) only. Choose the Plain Text option buttons.

- **Tools | Options | Send.** To prevent Outlook Express from filing sent messages in the Sent Items folder.

- **Tools | Options | Read.** To turn off automatic preview.

- **Tools | Options | Read.** To specify the number of news messages headers to download at a time.

Using Internet Explorer 4

Browsing the Web

It is somewhat difficult to decide what Microsoft means when it says "Internet Explorer (IE)." Starting with version 3 and more so with version 4, IE grew into a suite of messaging tools for use over networks—especially TCP/IP networks such as the Internet.

For most people, IE means the browser part of the suite only. This chapter, and the rest of the book for that matter, discusses IE based on that popular meaning. Keep in mind that Microsoft will often, but inconsistently, refer to non-Web–related parts of Internet messaging as IE.

You can see a good example of this when you install IE4 or higher and take a look at the Internet Explorer entry in Start|Programs (see Figure 7.1). Note that only one of the entries in the list is the actual browser. The rest are auxiliary programs for the browser.

FIGURE 7.1.

Microsoft refers to both its browser and the entire suite as Internet Explorer.

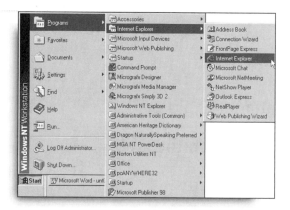

Using Internet Explorer for Various Sites

You need a connection to whatever you wish to browse before using IE. This can be your company's intranet, extranet, LAN, or most commonly, the Internet. As explained later in this chapter, you can also use IE to browse your local disk.

To use IE4 to reach a network site, follow these steps:

Using Internet Explorer to navigate to a known site

1. Launch the Internet Explorer either through the IE desktop icon, the Quick Launch icon, or from the Start|Programs|Internet Explorer menu.

2. Click Ctrl+O (Control plus the letter o). This is Internet Explorer talk for "open," as in "open a site." Figure 7.2 shows the dialog box where you enter an address. If the address is in IE's memory and you have Use Auto Complete checked in the Advanced tab of Internet Options (see Chapter 11, "Installing and Configuring Internet Explorer 4 or Netscape Communicator 4," for more information on this), IE will attempt to finish the address for you.

SEE ALSO
➤ *See Chapter 11 for more information on configuration issues.*

FIGURE 7.2.

If you know the address you wish to visit, you can enter the address in the Open dialog box.

3. Enter the address of the site you wish to visit. Press Enter or click OK to start IE on its quest.

Once installed, Internet Explorer is fully integrated with the desktop and what was formerly the Windows Explorer. This can be spooky at times if you're not prepared for it.

Seeing Internet Explorer's integration

1. Launch the Internet Explorer either through the IE desktop icon, the Quick Launch icon, or from the Start|Programs|Internet Explorer menu.

2. Press Ctrl+O. The Open dialog box appears.

3. Enter `file:c:\` in the space provided. Press Enter or click OK.

4. IE seems to open up a list of files and folders on the root folder of your C: drive. Figure 7.3 shows this view.

FIGURE 7.3.

You can use the Internet Explorer to view file lists on your computer and your LAN.

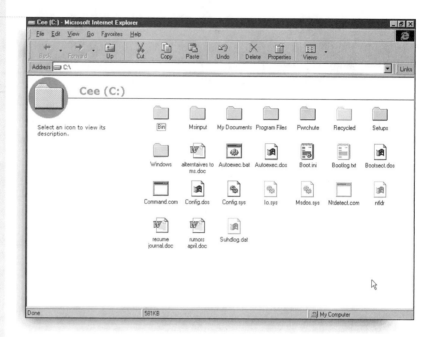

5. Keep in mind that the specifics of your screens will differ from the book's and any other computer containing different files. Pull down the Address combo box and choose Internet Explorer from the list that looks a lot like the left pane of Windows Explorer. (It is the same list.) Figure 7.4 shows this.

FIGURE 7.4.

The Address combo box holds your navigational history information or the same view as the left pane as Windows Explorer, depending on its mode.

6. Windows NT will launch a new instance of Explorer, this time with your default home page loaded. If you look at your taskbar, you will see that you have two instances of Explorer running—one at your local drive, and one at your home page.

Similarly, you can use the Windows Explorer mode to launch the Internet Explorer mode if you have a local file used by (associated with, really) Internet Explorer. By default, two such files are those with the .HTM, .HTML, and .GIF extensions. If you have any such files, you can try this.

Launching Internet Explorer mode through Windows Explorer

1. Start the Windows Explorer using any means you prefer.

2. Using any means you prefer (such as Find), locate a file bearing the extension .HTM, .HTML, or .GIF. Navigate to that file and double-click on it. Figure 7.5 shows such a file located in Windows Explorer.

3. Windows NT will launch Internet Explorer with the file loaded. Figure 7.6 shows that file launched and loaded.

The preceding launch example, even accompanied by the figures, might be difficult to follow just by reading about it. The best way to see what occurs is to try those steps yourself.

Fancy Formatting in Email

You can add HTML commands to email messages. This can create interesting effects if your recipient has an email client capable of deciphering such. Doing so does enlarge the size and bandwidth demands of your email, however.

FIGURE 7.5.

Before asking Windows Explorer to autolaunch Internet Explorer, you need to have a file to experiment on.

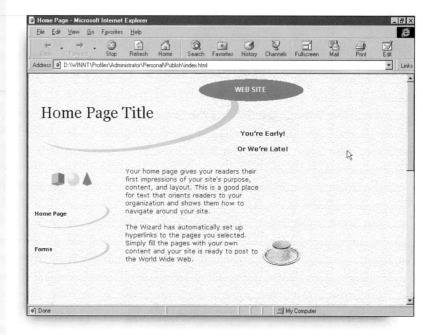

You can also use IE as an FTP site download utility. This isn't as handy or as full featured as a true FTP utility program, but if your need (as is most people's) is just to download files from an FTP site, IE will do the job. Here's how.

Using Internet Explorer to download files from an FTP site

1. Launch the Internet Explorer either through the IE desktop icon, the Quick Launch icon, or from the Start | Programs | Internet Explorer menu.

2. Press Ctrl+O. The Open dialog box appears.

3. Enter the FTP address such as `ftp://microsoft.com` or, as this example uses, `ftp://rt66.com/`. Press Enter or click OK to begin IE's search. Figure 7.7 shows an FTP site opened within IE.

Each underlined entry in Figure 7.7 is a folder (directory) or a file. Clicking on a folder will open it (drill down). After you are below the root directory, IE will also display an entry to move up a level. You can also jump back up to the root or wherever you started by using the Ctrl+O "open" method you might have used to get there to begin with.

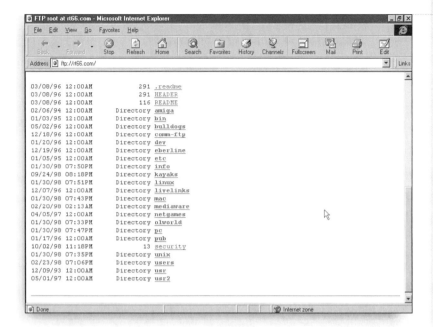

FIGURE 7.7.

Internet Explorer not only can open an FTP site, but it can display it reasonably well too.

If you find a file you wish to download, click on it. Internet Explorer will ask you where you wish to store it, or if you wish to open it in some cases. After telling IE your wishes, IE will, if you have given it the go ahead, download the file to the folder you specify.

Using Internet Explorer on the Web

By far the most common use for Internet Explorer is for browsing (surfing) the World Wide Web (Web) sites. The following sections use the Internet for examples, but could just as well use a private intranet or extranet too.

Using Internet Explorer to visit a public Web site

1. Launch the Internet Explorer either through the IE desktop icon, the Quick Launch icon, or from the Start|Programs|Internet Explorer menu.

2. Press Ctrl+O. The Open dialog box appears. Enter the address you wish to visit. This example uses www.rt66.com. Figure 7.8 shows this site. If you choose to visit this site,

Extra What?

An extranet functions like the Internet but uses a separate infrastructure.

note that it might have changed in between the time of the screen shot included here and your visit.

FIGURE 7.8.

Most Web surfs start with a home page. This is the home page of a Internet service provider, Route 66.

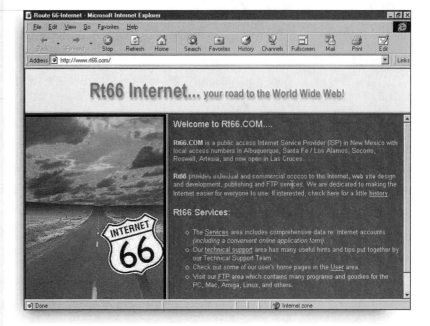

3. The underlined words or phrases are links to other places. A link will jump you to the Web site (or file or whatever) that this site is linked to. Other things besides underlines can be links too. Common links are buttons and hot spots on graphics. This example jumped first to a business directory. By using another link (Ciudad or Cd.), the business directory site transferred to a City of Juarez, Mexico site. Figure 7.9 shows the directory for this city.

4. At any time, you can use the Back arrow (left on the toolbar) to return to the preceding site. You can also use the Forward button to return to the site you just went Back from.

5. This example chose two links that brought Explorer to the leading *diario* (newspaper) of Morelia, Michoacán. Michoacán is one of the states of Mexico. Figure 7.10 shows the home page of this newspaper.

FIGURE 7.9.

Many international sites such as Ciudad Juarez have multi-language capacity. This site can display in Mexican Spanish, English, or French.

FIGURE 7.10.

Most sites, including foreign (for U.S. persons) newspapers, have English sections. This reflects English as the business language of the world as well as the U.S. dominance of the Internet.

The World Awaits

As you can see, a few clicks can take you anywhere in the world where the Web exists. There is an amazing amount of important news that never seems to make to it the U.S. airwaves or print media.

Surprisingly, many foreign newspapers are available in English. Even those non-English editions are fairly readable to English speakers with any familiarity with the local lingo.

Travelers will tell you that the easiest thing to read in any language is a newspaper. Not only do they teach language; they teach perspective. How many "Norteamericanos," for example, read the Mexican perspective on NAFTA?

After you have started on the Web, you can use some more of the services Internet Explorer provides.

Using the History facility of Internet Explorer

1. You will need to have used IE some to have any history to use. If you worked through the preceding step-by-step using the actual sites or any others, you have enough of a history to follow along.

2. Open Internet Explorer.

3. Click the History button on the toolbar.

4. IE opens a new pane to the left of the main pane. Click to open any day. This example uses Today. Figure 7.11 shows this pane from one IE user's computer.

5. To return to any place in History, click on the link. Figure 7.11 shows the pointer hovering over the link to the diario at Morelia, Michoacán in Mexico. To close the History pane, click on the History button again or click on the close icon in the History pane.

FIGURE 7.11.

Internet Explorer stores your travels within its History folder.

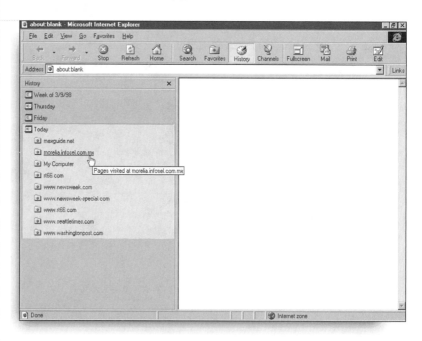

History is fine, but IE will only store those links for a short while. To make sure you can return, again and again, to any place you have been, store it in your Favorite Places folder. Here's how.

Using favorite places

1. Launch Internet Explorer.

2. Go to any site you wish, using any technique you prefer (such as Ctrl+O).

3. Click Favorites | Add to Favorites. This opens the dialog box shown in Figure 7.12.

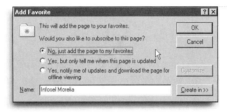

FIGURE 7.12.

Once added to your Favorites folder structure, sites remain quickly available for as long as you wish.

4. You can add the site to your Favorites list by clicking OK. You can add to a specific folder within the Favorites list by clicking on the Create in >> button. This example adds the displayed site to a folder called Publications.

5. Click on the Create in >> button to open a new dialog box. Create the Favorites folder you wish to store the site in or choose an existing folder. Figure 7.13 shows this operation.

FIGURE 7.13.

Just throwing sites onto the Favorites menu will soon clog it up. Use folders to organize your favorite sites.

6. After creating or opening the folder you wish to use for storage, click the OK button. This enters the site into the folder for later use.

7. To return to the site so stored, click on the Favorites menu, click on the folder where your site is stored, and then click on the site. Figure 7.14 shows this for the site stored earlier in this step-by-step.

FIGURE 7.14.
Once added to your Favorites
folder structure, sites remain
quickly available for as long as
you wish.

Where Are My Faves?

The Favorites folder structure is under
your profile in the Windows NT folder
structure. Favorites for the
Administrator profile, for example, is
located in \WINNT\Profiles\
Administrator\Favorites, assuming
that your Windows NT is located in
the root folder \WINNT.

Internet Explorer also has a built in capability to harness the
power of certain existing Web search engines. Here's how to
search the Web.

Using Internet Explorer to search the Web

1. Launch Internet Explorer.

2. Click the Search button on the toolbar. This opens a left
   pane.

3. Use the search engine that pops up, or click the Choose a
   Search Engine link at the top of the left pane. Figure 7.15
   shows the search engine that came up by default after clicking on the circled "choose link."

4. Enter any string (number, words, or phrase sequence) you
   wish to search on. This example uses the name "Cassel."
   Click the button or link your search engine uses to start the
   search and IE will fill the left pane with links to found sites.
   Note that search engines will vary widely in their returns.
   Click on a left pane link to launch the site in the right pane.
   Figure 7.16 shows the populated left pane along with one
   site (a genealogical one) and a view of ancestor Cassels.

Try Another

The indexing of search engines differs. If you aren't having any luck
with the first one you choose, try
another.

5. The left pane remains static, enabling you to browse its sites
   in the right pane. If your search yielded more sites than can
   fit in the left pane, the search engine will add navigation
   buttons that enable you to move forward and backward
   through the list of returns. Figure 7.17 shows another site
   from the left pane; this one is a hospital in the UK.

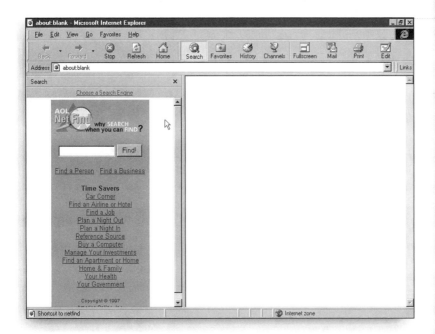

FIGURE 7.15.

You can use the search engine defaulted to by Internet Explorer or choose another.

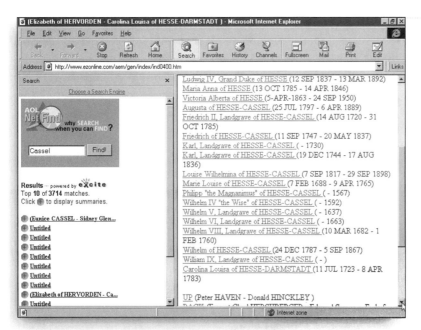

FIGURE 7.16.

Was Adam's last name Cassel? Only a genealogical search will tell for sure.

FIGURE 7.17.

Cassels have their own psychiatric hospital. This one stresses the psycho-social model for therapy. We need it.

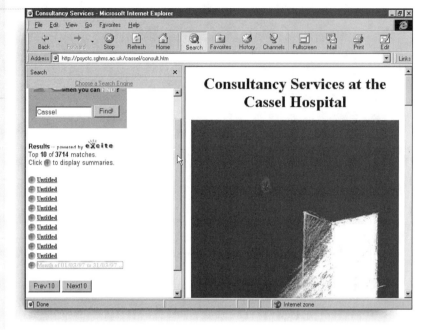

6. One of the delights of the Web is the ability to browse around. Clicking on a link or two in the left pane, for example, revealed that a Cassel was married to the daughter of George II of Great Britain. Yeah, the real George II. Figure 7.18 shows the proof. Close the Search pane by either clicking on the Search button again or clicking on the close (x) icon in the Search pane.

That should give you enough of a push in the right direction to get you surfing away over the Web. IE has other interesting features you should experiment with, especially its capability to call up other programs such as mail or news through the Go menu or by clicking on those specialized links.

Chapter 6, "Using Outlook Express," covers the mail and news features of Internet Explorer in depth. Internet Explorer will call Outlook Express automatically when demanded to do so.

SEE ALSO

➤ *See Chapter 6 for more information on the mail and news features of Internet Explorer.*

Web Source and IE

Although it is a minor feature, IE can display the HTML source for a Web page. To see this in action, load a page and choose the menu selections View|Source. Figure 7.19 shows this for the page displayed normally in Figure 7.6.

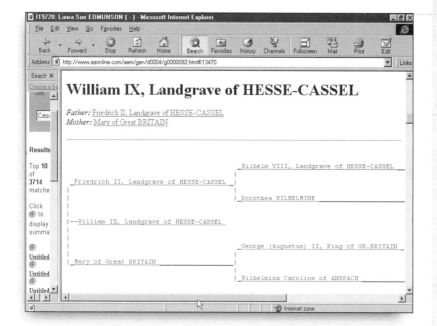

FIGURE 7.18.

Cassels have always had a nose for royals, even old-time ones like Mary, daughter of George II. The nose persists, but not the connections.

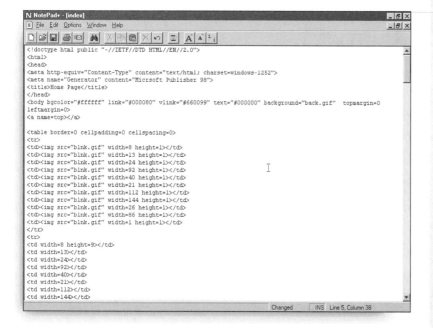

FIGURE 7.19.

Source is source. This is the inside view of a Web page loaded by ID into Notepad. You can only edit pages this way if you have sufficient access rights.

PART

III

Networking with Windows NT Workstation 4

Networking Fundamentals

Networking Overview

Computer networking is the linking of two or more computers in such a way that they can share resources. This very powerful and exciting technology enables persons across the office or across the globe to share files, printers, and other resources. You, too, can use computer networking to increase your productivity and make your computing experience more enjoyable.

Computer networks come in many sizes. A LAN, or local area network, connects a relatively small number of computers that are usually geographically close. You would typically find a LAN in a school, office, or home setting. On the other hand, a WAN, or wide area network, may connect many thousands of computers spanning multiple cities, time zones, or even continents. The Internet is the ultimate WAN, connecting millions of computers all over the world. Using the Internet, you can communicate instantly around the world using popular tools such as email (electronic mail) and the World Wide Web (WWW).

Before jumping into configuring your Windows NT Workstation to participate in a network, it is important to look briefly at some network background information.

Computer Networking Is Layered

Internet or internet?

The term *internet* is short for *internetwork*. An internetwork is just a network that connects other networks. The Internet is one such network, which connects many thousands of smaller LANs and WANs all over the world using the TCP/IP protocol. Custom demands using the word *Internet*, capitalized, when referring to that particular network. When referring to internetworks in general, custom dictates using the noncapitalized term *internet*.

Computer networking makes use of various protocols layered on top of each other to abstract aspects of the communication. This allows an Apple Macintosh in the United States to easily talk with an IBM mainframe in Zimbabwe over some connection such as a copper wire or a satellite link. A *protocol* is just a set of well-known and agreed-upon rules that govern such communications. The protocol for sending a postal letter most anywhere in the world is to place a postal address on the front-center of an envelope, a stamp in the front, upper-right corner, and to seal the communication inside. Furthermore, various protocols govern the layout of the postal address (PO Box, international, and so on). Computer networks use similar techniques to abstract the information being transmitted (the letter) from the information needed for delivery mechanics (the postal address).

In computer networking, the lowest layer is the Physical layer. This layer consists of your network adapter and the cables, hubs, gateways, and other network hardware between your computer and the one you are talking to. Physical-layer protocols directly govern the transmission of electrons through wire, light pulses through fiber-optic lines, and electromagnetic waves when wireless media is being used. The network card in your computer operates at the Physical layer. Windows NT refers to network cards and other Physical-layer interfaces as adapters.

One or more protocols sit on top of the Physical layer protocol. These allow computers to address other specific computers or groups of computers. The term *transport protocols* refers to this class of protocols. This layer doesn't know or care whether the communication will travel over a copper wire or a satellite link; it completely depends on the Physical layer to handle the gory details. This is not unlike the postal system. My letter may travel by truck, boat, or air, for example, and neither the stamp nor the envelope know or care about it. I don't need to worry about how exactly my letter will get to its destination when I write the postal address on it. This is the beauty of the layered approach— we have completely abstracted the physical medium out of our addressing scheme.

Popular protocols that operate at the Network Transport layer are TCP/IP, NWLink, and NetBEUI. All these are covered in detail later. Windows NT collectively refers to all transport protocols just as *protocols*. This is unfortunate, because in the strict sense of the word all layers of the network are made up of protocols. After we finish this discussion of layered protocols in the next paragraph, however, I will attempt to follow Microsoft's convention whenever possible to avoid confusion that might be caused by differences between this book and Microsoft's documentation.

The highest layer is called the Application layer. There, you will find the set of protocols that enables you to do something useful with the network. Application protocols include NetBIOS, NCP, HTTP, SMTP, and many others. These protocols enable us to share files and printers, browse the Web, and exchange email. Some of these protocols are individually discussed later.

Be Careful with the Term *Protocol*

Remember that the term *protocol* just means an agreed-upon method of communication. Many, many network protocols operate at many, many different levels. When Windows NT refers to a protocol, it is likely referring to a transport protocol such as TCP/IP.

Windows NT refers to some, but not all, protocols at this level as *services*. Specifically, the protocols that enable file and printer sharing using Microsoft or Novell protocols are installed as services. NetBIOS (Network Basic Input/Output System) and NCP (NetWare Core Protocols) are Microsoft and Novell's protocols, respectively. These enable us to share files and printers over the network. Windows NT implements NetBIOS functionality in the Server and Workstation services. NCP functionality is implemented in the Client Service for NetWare service.

The others previously mentioned—HTTP and SMTP—are not explicitly installed as services, but come free of charge when the TCP/IP transport is installed. This will become less confusing later, so don't worry if you are not with me 100% here.

Figure 8.1 shows an illustration of layered networking.

FIGURE 8.1.

The three layers of computer networking. Information flows vertically from user to transmission medium. Note that each layer needs to communicate only with the two adjacent layers. The parenthesized terms are what Windows NT calls each layer.

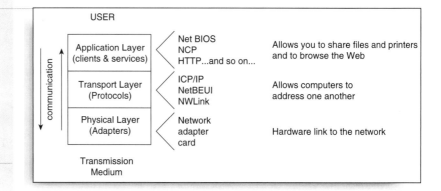

Windows NT requires that we separately install and configure the software for at least the Physical and Transport layers. Again, these three layers are referred to by Windows NT as the adapter (which is a device driver), protocols, and services. Most of the common protocols and services are installed by default, but you will still want to look over the next few pages to be sure that all the items you need are indeed installed and configured correctly.

Again, just installing TCP/IP enables many top-level application protocols, which then don't need any further effort on our behalf. Examples are HTTP (Web browsing) and FTP (File

Transfer Protocol). The following sections review the setup and configuration of all these layers in detail.

Now that you have a handle on the very basics of computer networking under Windows NT, let's get off of our hands and on to the Net!

Getting Ready

To place your computer on to a network, you need a few things. First, you need a network adapter card (sometimes called a network interface card, or just NIC). Windows NT favors the term network adapter, so I will do the same.

You also need a bit of wiring or other method of connections to join the network adapter in your computer to the network. Because discussing the physical setup of a network is beyond the scope of this book, I suggest picking up a good book dedicated to computer networking if you are setting up your first network from scratch: *Using Networks*, Que Publishing, ISBN 0-7897-1596-1 or *Networking with Microsoft TCP/IP, Second Edition*, New Riders Publishing, ISBN 1-56205-713-8. You will want to keep this book handy, however, because it will be a valuable resource when it comes time to place your Windows NT Workstations onto your new network.

The next sections discuss each of the three networking layers individually. You have some choices when it comes to which protocols you will install at each layer. Most likely, you will be connecting to an existing network and you will need to talk with your network administrator or Internet service provider to learn which protocols you need to install. If connecting to the Internet or other TCP/IP network, you need to get some configuration details from him or her as well.

Network Adapters

The network adapter is the physical device that connects your computer to a network. I will assume that the card is already properly installed into your computer chassis and is physically connected to an appropriate network.

Because this is a physical device, Windows NT requires that we install a device driver. A device driver is the (only) piece of software that talks directly to the device and is usually provided by the hardware manufacturer on a disk or CD. For convenience, many device drivers can also be found on the Windows NT Workstation CD. I suggest using the drivers shipped with the device whenever possible, however, because they are likely to be more current and are sure to be written explicitly for that device. Check with your hardware manufacturer for the most recent drivers and keep up with driver revisions whenever possible. Most hardware manufacturers make their drivers available on a Web site for easy download.

Installing a network adapter device driver

1. From the Start menu, choose Settings, Control Panel, and then choose the Network icon. This presents you with the Network Configuration dialog box shown in Figure 8.2. You will quickly get used to this dialog box; almost all network configuration activity in Windows NT starts here! Note that you can also get to this dialog box by right-clicking on the Network Neighborhood icon from the desktop and choosing Properties.

FIGURE 8.2.

The Network Configuration dialog. Most network-related configuration tasks in Windows NT start here.

2. Click the Adapters tab and choose Add.

3. If you have a disk or CD that shipped with the hardware, click Have Disk and you will be prompted for the location of the drivers. Otherwise, select your driver from the list. In Figure 8.3, I am adding an Intel EtherExpress PRO/10+.

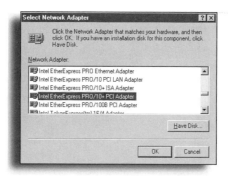

FIGURE 8.3.

Adding a network adapter is as easy as point and click!

4. At this point, Windows NT copies the necessary software to your hard disk. Depending on the driver, you may be asked for additional configuration information such as the I/O base address and interrupt (IRQ) level. See the documentation that shipped with your hardware for more information about these items. After driver installation is complete, Windows NT will ask for a reboot. After you have rebooted, your device is ready to use.

There are not really many configuration options to worry about with a network adapter; the defaults will suit most purposes just fine. However, we will take a brief look at common configuration settings here.

Your new adapter should now appear in the list of adapters under the Adapters tab. Click on the adapter, and then choose Properties. This bring ups the Configuration dialog box for the adapter. Note that this dialog box may differ considerably from adapter to adapter because this dialog box is specific to the driver, which is usually written by the hardware manufacturer, not by Microsoft. Figure 8.4 shows the configuration for the popular Intel PCI cards.

FIGURE 8.4.

If your adapter ever needs configuration attention, it is usually quick and easy. Here, the properties for Intel PCI adapters are shown. Note that this dialog box will differ considerably between hardware manufacturers.

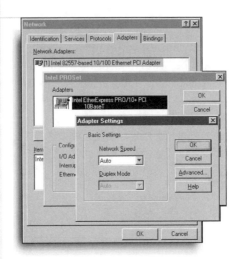

Aside from hardware settings such as I/O base address and IRQ, the following are some of the other common settings you might see:

- *Network speed*. Either standard Ethernet (10Mbps) or fast Ethernet (100Mbps).

- *Duplex mode*. Some cards support full- and half-duplex mode.

- *Media type*. Combo cards will have 10BASE-2 and 10BASE T connectors on the card. Most cards will successfully autodetect the connection type. Under some rare circumstances, however, you may need to set the type manually.

Fortunately, modern network cards almost never need configuration adjustments; they can autodetect all the previously discussed settings and act appropriately. If you are having problems with the default network adapter configuration, see your hardware documentation. Also, your network administrator can help with questions about your network speed, media, and so on.

Multiple Adapters

It is possible, and in some cases necessary, to have multiple network adapters in one computer. The most common occurrence of multiple adapters is in Dial-Up Networking, where a special "dial-up adapter" is installed and bound to your modem.

SEE ALSO

➤ *See the section titled "Dial-Up Networking" in Chapter 9, "Using Dial-Up Networking (DUN)/Remote Access Service (RAS)."*

In a few instances, you might want to have multiple network cards and cable connections linking one computer to multiple networks. A computer with multiple network interfaces is said to be multihomed. You can repeat the preceding process for all the network adapter cards installed into your computer. If you are multihoming your Windows NT Workstation, you will want to pick up a book dedicated to NT networking that will cover this topic in more detail. The vast majority of times, the topic of multihoming is one that only applies to Windows NT Server, not to Windows NT Workstation.

Installing Transport Protocols

If you are connecting to an existing network, you need to install the appropriate transport protocols to match. If you are implementing a new network, however, you have some choices when it comes to which transport protocol or protocols you want to use.

Choosing the Right Protocol for the Job

This section compares and contrasts three popular protocols—TCP/IP, NetBEUI, and NWLink—to help you determine which one you should use. If you know which protocol(s) you need to install, you can skip to the next section, which discusses installation and configuration of each in detail.

TCP/IP

TCP/IP is an acronym for Transmission Control Protocol/ Internet Protocol. TCP/IP is actually a suite of several protocols designed to allow many computers on large networks to communicate efficiently. The Internet, for example, is a completely TCP/IP network. Most large corporations and universities also run TCP/IP networks that are usually connected to the Internet. If you want to use email, the Web, FTP (File Transfer Protocol), and other popular Internet services from your Windows NT Workstation, you need to run the TCP/IP protocol. If you use an ISP (Internet service provider) to connect to the Internet, you need to install TCP/IP as well.

Given the current popularity of the Internet, I assume that you will be connecting to a TCP/IP network either directly or through a dial-up connection. TCP/IP requires slightly more configuration than the other protocols, so I have dedicated an entire section to it (following in just a few pages).

TCP/IP is, however, a bad choice for small networks where only a few computers will be connected. If you are in a small home or office setting and not connecting to the Internet, consider running NetBEUI.

NetBEUI

Microsoft introduced NetBEUI (NetBIOS Extended User Interface) as the Transport layer for its LanManager products many years ago. NetBEUI was designed to be a small, fast protocol suitable for small LANs. NetBEUI is not routable, which makes it completely unusable in large networks. NetBEUI also relies heavily on broadcast packets, a communication sent to every computer on the network, to locate other computers. This is the electronic equivalent of yelling, "Where is Joe?" in a crowded mall. You can imagine the problems that quickly arise if you have many computers on the network.

On the up side, NetBEUI is completely Plug and Play. That is, there is virtually no configuration that needs to be done. It is very fast and requires little memory on the client computers. NetBEUI is well suited for small LANs such as that in a small office or at home.

NWLink

NWLink is a Microsoft-developed transport protocol that is compatible with Novell's IPX/SPX protocols. In fact, Windows NT rarely makes mention of the term "NWLink," and instead refers to the protocol as "IPX/SPX-compatible protocol."

TCP/IP

TCP/IP stands for Transmission Control Protocol/Internet Protocol.

NetBEUI

NetBEUI stands for NetBIOS Extended User Interface.

NWLink, like NetBEUI, is virtually Plug and Play. Little to no configuration is required. The bonus with NWLink is that it is a routable protocol suitable for use on large networks. The downfall is that there is little support for NWLink outside of Novell and Microsoft. The only reason to use NWLink is if you need to connect with Novell NetWare servers. If you don't need to connect to Novell resources, I recommend sticking with NetBEUI for small networks and TCP/IP for large ones.

Choosing the Right Protocol Is Important

It is important to choose the right transport protocols to install. If you are connecting to the Internet, your network administrator or Internet service provider can provide additional assistance.

TABLE 8.1   Rough guidelines for choosing the right transport protocol

If You Are:	You Should Use:
Sharing files/printers in a small network	NetBEUI
Sharing files/printers in a large network	TCP/IP
Connecting to NetWare servers	NWLink
Connecting to the Internet	TCP/IP (in addition to any others chosen)

Now that you have chosen your transport protocols, you are ready to configure them. The following sections take a look at each protocol individually.

The TCP/IP Protocol

To configure TCP/IP correctly, we need to look at a bit of background information first.

TCP/IP Background and Theory

The postal address "123 Main Street, Cleveland, OH 44070 USA," like all postal addresses, is guaranteed to be unique. Otherwise, sending letters would be ambiguous. Computers also

TCP/IP Is Very Complex

If you will be administering a TCP/IP network, I suggest picking up a good book dedicated to discussion of the TCP/IP protocols. Some good examples include *Sams Teach Yourself TCP/IP in 14 Days, Second Edition*, Sams Publishing, ISBN 0-672-30885-1 and *Inside TCP/IP, Third Edition*, New Riders Publishing, ISBN 1-56205-714-6.

have unique addresses called IP addresses. Each computer on a TCP/IP network must have a unique IP address that no other computer will have at the same time. Let's take a look at IP addresses in more detail.

IP Addresses

An IP address is just a 32-bit value. We humans, however, tend not to remember 32-bit binary values too easily. Therefore IP addresses are almost always expressed in what is called dotted-decimal form. To express an IP address in dotted-decimal form, we just break the address up into four 8-bit values. These 8-bit chunks are called octets. We then convert the 8-bit binary numbers to base-10 decimal numbers and separate the octets with a period (.). That's how we get the familiar *nnn.nnn.nnn.nnn*-style address. Figure 8.5 shows this process.

FIGURE 8.5.

Converting a binary IP address to the popular and convenient dotted-decimal form.

32-bit IP Address:	10101010110010111011101000000101			
Split into 8-bit octets:	|10101010|	|11001011|	|10111010|	|00000101|
Base-10 equivalent of each octet:	170	203	186	5
Dotted-decimal form: 170.203.186.5				

Just How Many IP Addresses Are There?

An octet is 8 bits. Recall that if we have 8 bits, we can represent $(2^8)-1 = 255$ unique base-10 numbers: namely, 0–255. Valid octets fall in the range 0–255, which means complete valid IP addresses are in the range 0.0.0.0 through 255.255.255.255. Not all these addresses are usable, however, because some have special purposes (discussed later). After we remove those, there are roughly 2 billion unique IP addresses in existence.

Some IP addresses have special purposes and cannot be assigned to a particular computer:

- The use of 255 in an octet signifies broadcast traffic that will go to all computers with any value in that octet, with exceptions. Sending a message to 110.28.36.255 would send a message to every computer whose first three octets were 110.28.36 (whose complete IP address was of the form 110.28.36.*xxx*). Likewise, sending a message to 110.28.255.255 would target every computer having an IP address of the form 110.28.*xxx*.*xxx*.

- Any address where 127 is the first octet (127.*xxx*.*xxx*.*xxx*) is called a loopback address. Messages sent to these special IP addresses always go to the local machine only, and they are never actually output onto the wire.

- The first octet cannot be greater than 223. Those addresses are reserved for multicast and experimental purposes.

- The last octet cannot be zero (0).

Subnets

TCP/IP was designed to connect many smaller networks. An internetwork is a combination of smaller networks, called subnets. There are two types of subnets:

- *Physical subnets*. Computers connected to the same piece of physical wire, hub, or cascaded hubs. All computers on the same physical subnet see all of each other's traffic. Your network card watches the network for traffic addressed to your computer.

- *Logical subnets*. Computers that share one or more octets (contiguous from left to right) in their IP addresses. This type of subnet has nothing to do with the physical layout of the network; it is just a grouping of IP addresses. The logical subnet is very important to TCP/IP networking because each computer assumes that all other computers on the same logical subnet can be addressed directly, without the help of a gateway. To address any computers outside the logical subnet, they need to employ the help of a gateway. Note that we are not taking the physical network layout into consideration at all here. Computers on different logical subnets do not see each other's traffic.

An example of physical subnets would be the airline's handling of luggage when traveling by air. When picking up your luggage from the carousel, you see not only your luggage, but also that of everyone else on your flight. It's up to you to scan each item and determine whether it belongs to you, and to act accordingly. We can say that your luggage is on the same physical subnet as that belonging to the other passengers on your flight. However, there is luggage that has been routed such that it doesn't wind up on your carousel. That luggage is not on your physical subnet.

Broadcasting to the Entire Internet?

Would a message to 255.255.255.255 reach every computer on the Internet? No. There is little legitimate use for a message like that, and the potential problems are obvious. Therefore no gateway would pass such a request. In fact, few gateways pass broadcasts at all. So, a message sent to 255.255.255.255 would wind up going only to every computer on your physical subnet. (Subnets are discussed in the next section.)

Message Delivery

On simple networks, delivery of a message between computers is easy because all computers are on the same physical and logical subnet. Every device can directly address every other device; therefore, to send a message to any other computer, all we need to do is drop a note on the wire saying, "TO: Computer B; FROM Computer A; MESSAGE: Hi!" Figure 8.6 shows such a simple network. Every computer must look at each message that goes by and determine whether it needs to take action. This works great for small networks with few computers, but large networks need some kind of more intelligent handling of traffic.

FIGURE 8.6.

A simple single-subnet network. All computers may address each other directly.

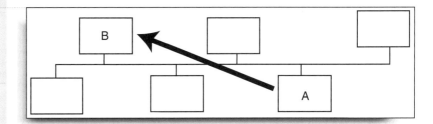

Enter TCP/IP. TCP/IP is a routable transport protocol. That means that the network can be broken up into smaller physical and logical subnets and connected by special computers called gateways. Gateways are just multihomed computers that forward traffic between their interfaces. There are many different terms for gateways: routers, bridges, and switches. Although there are subtle technical differences between some of these, they all basically do the same thing: intelligently forward traffic between different logical subnets. Windows NT favors the term *gateway*; therefore I will use that term as well. Figure 8.7 shows a complex network with multiple physical and logical subnets connected by gateways.

Figure 8.7 shows multiple physical subnets. The computers in these physical subnets are given IP addresses corresponding to matching logical subnets. That is, each physical subnet is also a logical subnet.

Gateways that intelligently pass network traffic between their interfaces (between subnets) allow computers on different physical and logical subnets to communicate with one another. To get a message from computer A to computer B, therefore, we need to send it to the gateway to handle delivery.

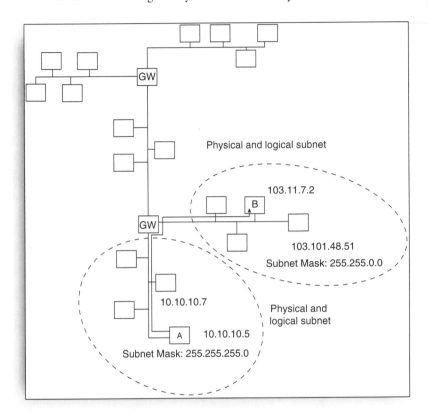

FIGURE **8.7.**

A complex multisubnet inter-network where gateways connect multiple physical subnets.

Your computer needs to know how to determine whether the remote computer is on its same logical subnet and can be addressed directly, or whether it needs the help of a gateway. The subnet mask tells the computer which octets define the logical subnet. Subnet masks "mask out" all the octets that don't help define the logical subnet. If an octet helps define the logical subnet, the respective position in the subnet mask will be 255. If an octet doesn't help define the logical subnet, its corresponding octet in the mask will be 0. All octets in a subnet mask are 255 or 0, and defining octets must be contiguous from left to right. Therefore 255.255.0.0 is a valid subnet mask, but 255.0.255.255 is not.

Mixed Logical and Physical Subnets

The original implementers of TCP/IP expected that, most of the time, each physical subnet would contain exactly one logical subnet. In other words, physical and logical subnets would correspond exactly as in Figure 8.7. Today as IP addresses become more and more scarce, however, physical subnets containing multiple logical subnets are becoming very common. In large TCP/IP networks, it is not unusual for one physical subnet to contain IP addresses from three or more different logical subnets. It is likely that in a corporate or campus environment, you, too, will encounter mixed logical and physical subnets.

When logical and physical subnets are mixed, some interesting problems are presented. Assume, for example, that two computers are sitting next to each other and attached to the same physical network cable; they are obviously on the same physical subnet. Let's also assume that they have IP addresses belonging to different logical subnets. These computers cannot communicate directly. They need the gateway to forward traffic between them, as in Figure 8.8.

FIGURE 8.8.

Multiple logical subnets on one physical subnet. Even though these two computers are directly connected, the gateway is needed to forward traffic between them because they are on different logical subnets. They won't see each other's broadcast messages either.

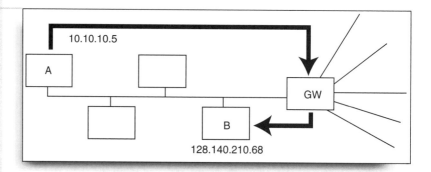

Most importantly, IP subnet broadcasts will only reach computers on the same logical subnet. Therefore those same two computers in Figure 8.9 won't see each others' broadcast messages because they are on different logical subnets. This has important implications (discussed when we look at NetBIOS over TCP/IP later).

Computer Names

Remember that we use dotted-decimal notation almost exclusively when noting IP addresses because humans don't remember 32-bit binary strings too well. Well, I have a fairly poor memory and don't remember strings of 4 octets with much more success! Apparently I'm not alone; a method was invented to give computers cute English names that map to IP addresses. In fact, an entire naming hierarchy exists to help humans better address remote computers. These English names correspond directly to one or more IP addresses and, in almost all places, can be used in place of clunky IP addresses. Think of it like the speed-dial on your phone: Pressing the button labeled "Jacalyn" is a convenient shortcut to dialing the phone number.

Users can't be allowed to assign completely arbitrary names to their computers. If we could, there would to a million computers named "HAL" and no way to figure out which "HAL" was which. There needs to be some kind or organization. Fortunately, a clever heretical naming scheme exists on the Internet. This naming scheme enables us some degree of freedom in naming our computers, while providing useful names to humans and a level of assurance that the computer names are unique.

An organization can group their IP addresses into one or more IP domains. An IP domain is just a group of one or more IP addresses issued to the same organization. Familiar examples of IP domain names are `ibm.com` and `microsoft.com`.

On a TCP/IP network, each computer is called (for historical reasons) a host. The name we assign to our host is, naturally, called a hostname. This is different from the NetBIOS name (or just computer name) that you assign to your computer during initial computer setup or in Microsoft Networking setup, as discussed later.

SEE ALSO

➤ *See the section titled "Computer Setup" in Chapter 19, "Setting Up Windows NT."*

To address a specific computer in any domain, just use the form `hostname.domain name`. `mybox.osu.edu` refers to the computer with the hostname `mybox` with an IP address belonging to the `osu.edu` domain. A `hostname.domain name` referring to a particular computer is called a fully qualified hostname or FQHN. When you

Broadcasts Aren't Always Broadcasts

If a single physical subnet contains multiple logical subnets, broadcast traffic won't reach all computers on the physical subnet. This is a source of confusion with Windows networking, which relies on broadcast traffic to announce computers and locate resources. Those issues are addressed in the discussion about NetBIOS networking later in this chapter.

view Microsoft's Web site (www.microsoft.com), you are just talking to the host named www belonging to the microsoft.com domain. www.microsoft.com is an FQHN.

DNS is an acronym for domain name service. DNS is the service that translates the English host and domain names into IP addresses. Host and domain names, although very descriptive and memorable for humans, are virtually useless to computers. Network routing mechanics rely on numeric IP addresses to get traffic to their destination. DNS servers are special computers that can look up host and domain names and return the IP addresses of the host they refer to. As Figure 8.9 shows, quite a few things happen when I point my Web browser at www.microsoft.com.

FIGURE 8.9.

A typical DNS resolution. My computer will first ask a DNS server to resolve the FQHN www.microsoft.com into an IP address. Then, my computer will use the IP address to communicate with the remote host.

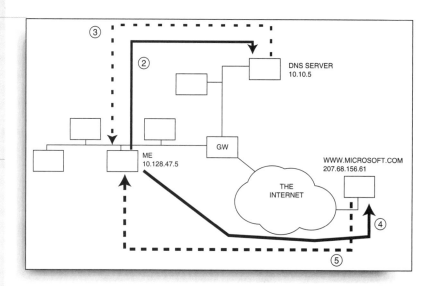

Adding exact IP addresses

1. I type http://www.microsoft.com into my Web browser.

2. My computer asks the DNS server what to do with www.microsoft.com.

3. The DNS server replies with the IP address associated with host www belonging to microsoft.com. Here, it is 207.68.156.61.

4. With this new information (the exact IP address), my computer can now communicate with that host, and thus, request the Web page.

5. The remote host returns the requested page.

DHCP–Domain Host Control Protocol

If you are lucky, your network administrator or Internet service provider will have a DHCP server to configure the TCP/IP settings on your workstation. If DHCP is in place, your computer at boot will acquire an IP address and all the appropriate settings from the DHCP server—without you needing to get involved at all!

Now that you know more about TCP/IP than you ever wanted to, let's configure your Windows NT Workstation to take part in a TCP/IP network.

Installing and Configuring TCP/IP

If you are connecting to an existing TCP/IP network, you need to obtain some information from your network administrator before beginning. You need to find out whether the network has a DHCP server or whether you need to configure your workstation manually. If DHCP is in place, you have an easy ride ahead. Windows NT Workstation, by default, expects DHCP configuration; therefore, you won't need to go through the following steps. For those without DHCP in place, you need to obtain the following from your network administrator:

- Your IP address.

- Your subnet mask.

- Your hostname and domain name.

- The gateway address(es).

- The DHCP server(s) address(es).

- The WINS server(s) address(es) (if necessary). A WINS server resolves names in a Windows-only network.

If you are connecting to the Internet through an ISP, it is unlikely that you will be provided with (or need) a WINS server. Therefore, don't worry if your ISP doesn't provide you with one.

SEE ALSO

➤ *See the WINS discussion in the "NetBIOS over TCP/IP" section of this chapter.*

The TCP/IP protocol may have already been installed during setup. Check to see whether it is listed as an installed protocol on the Protocol tab of the Network Configuration dialog box. If it's not, here's how to install it:

Adding TCP/IP

1. Right-click on Network Neighborhood and choose Properties. This bring ups the Network Configuration dialog box.

2. Click the Protocols tab and choose Add.

3. Select TCP/IP Protocol from the list as in Figure 8.10. Click OK.

FIGURE 8.10.

Adding the TCP/IP protocol.

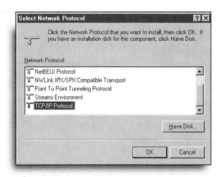

Now that TCP/IP is installed, let's configure it.

Configuring TCP/IP

1. Right-click on Network Neighborhood and choose Properties. This brings up the Network Configuration dialog box.

2. From the Network Configuration dialog box, click the Protocols tab. This shows the list of protocols installed on your workstation. If TCP/IP doesn't appear here, follow the preceding instructions for adding the TCP/IP protocol and reboot.

3. Click the Protocols tab, choose TCP/IP, and click Properties. This raises the TCP/IP Properties dialog box, as shown in Figure 8.11.

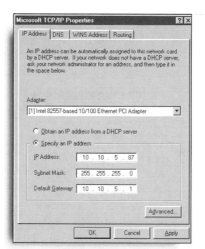

FIGURE 8.11.

The TCP/IP Properties dialog box. If you have a statically assigned IP address, you will enter it here.

4. The IP Address tab will be in front. If DHCP is in place on your network, be sure that Obtain an IP Address from a DHCP Server is selected. Otherwise, carefully type the IP address, subnet mask, and gateway address that your network administrator or ISP provided to you in the appropriate boxes. Take a look at my IP address configuration in Figure 8.11.

5. Bring the WINS Address tab forward by clicking on it. If you were provided with WINS address(es), enter them here. You don't need to enter an address for a secondary server if two addresses weren't provided to you. If DHCP is in place, you don't need to do anything here; your computer will obtain WINS server addresses from the DHCP server when auto-configuring. If your TCP/IP hostnames match your NetBIOS names, you can enable DNS for Windows Resolution. I talk about this trick when discussing NetBT ("NetBIOS over TCP/IP," later in this chapter). Figure 8.12 shows my WINS setup.

6. Click the DNS configuration tab. If DHCP is in place, you won't need to do anything here. Otherwise, fill in all the values provided by your network administrator or ISP. Again, you will likely only be provided with one address, but multiple addresses may be added to the list. I have several DNS servers noted in Figure 8.13. In most cases, you won't be

provided with additional domain suffixes; therefore you can leave the bottom portion of the dialog box empty, as in my setup.

FIGURE 8.12.

The WINS configuration dialog box. If you were provided WINS server addresses, you need to enter them here.

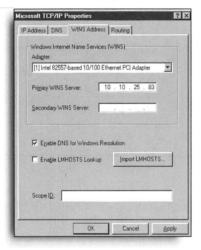

FIGURE 8.13.

You will enter your DNS configuration information here in the DNS properties tab. Note you may not be provided with multiple DNS server addresses or any additional domain suffixes.

7. Click OK to close the dialog box. Congratulations, you are done configuring TCP/IP! Your computer will now ask for a reboot.

If you don't have a DNS server available, you can still create static FQHN-to-IP address mappings for a corporate or campus TCP/IP network by making use of the HOSTS file. Note that if you are connected to the Internet, you have access to one or more DNS servers; therefore, this discussion would not apply. You only need to use the HOSTS file if you are participating in a private TCP/IP network that isn't connected to the Internet and want to use hostnames to address computers rather than IP addresses.

The HOSTS file sits in %systemroot%\system32\drivers\etc and contains static mappings between FQHNs and IP addresses. It performs the same lookup function that DNS servers provide. If a DNS server is not available or configured, Windows NT will check your HOSTS file to see whether the FQHN can be resolved to an IP address there. If there is no DNS available or configured, and the FQHN is not listed in HOSTS, the resolution will fail and your computer will be unable to communicate with the remote host.

Installing and Configuring Other Protocols

Although TCP/IP is required for communicating on the Internet and is the protocol of choice for large networks, there are reasons to use other protocols. Other protocols may be used either in conjunction with or rather than TCP/IP. There may be more than one transport protocol installed on a Windows NT Workstation. We will take a look at two popular protocols: NetBEUI and NWLink.

NetBEUI

As stated earlier, NetBEUI is an excellent choice for small networks. It is also a snap to configure. You will want to be sure that all the computers you want to communicate with are on the same physical subnet if you use NetBEUI. That is, your network should be small, simple, and look something like Figure 8.6, not like Figure 8.7.

You can use NetBEUI on a single physical subnet of a larger (probably TCP/IP) internetwork. There may be multiple transport protocols on one physical network and often are. Keep in mind, however, that no gateway will forward NetBEUI traffic;

IP Routing

It is possible to have your Windows NT workstation perform IP routing–that is, forward network traffic between multiple interfaces. IP forwarding is enabled in the Routing tab under TCP/IP configuration. If you will be configuring your workstation to perform routing, I suggest an advanced text on Windows NT networking–for example, *Networking with Microsoft TCP/IP, Second Edition*, New Riders Publishing, ISBN 1-56205-713-8.

When to Use the HOSTS File

If you have a relatively small TCP/IP network, using a HOSTS file is an easy way to implement DNS functionality without the cost or administrative time involved in maintaining a full-blown DNS server. The HOSTS file is simple in layout, and a sample file (HOSTS.SAM) is provided for you. Remember to rename the sample file to just HOSTS if you decide to use it!

therefore, you will only be able to communicate with other computers on the same physical subnet.

SEE ALSO

➤ *See the section titled "Protocol Security" in Chapter 13, "Sharing Resources."*

This behavior is sometimes desirable because it can isolate interoffice file/printer sharing traffic from Internet traffic. Chapter 13, "Sharing Resources," talks more about security. Let's look here at installing and configuring the NetBEUI transport.

Installing NetBEUI

NetBEUI does not install by default on Windows NT Workstation. Therefore, if you want to use NetBEUI, you need to install it first.

Adding NetBEUI

1. Right-click on Network Neighborhood and choose Properties. This brings up the Network Configuration dialog box.

2. Click the Protocols tab and choose Add.

3. Select NetBEUI Protocol from the list, as in Figure 8.14, and click OK.

FIGURE 8.14.

Adding the NetBEUI transport.

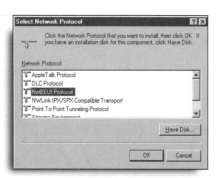

Configuring NetBEUI

Nothing to do here! Literally nothing; the Properties button is grayed. There aren't any options to set even if you wanted to. The beauty of NetBEUI is that it completely takes care of itself. If only everything were this easy!

NWLink

If you need connectivity with an existing IPX/SPX (or NWLink) network or internetwork, NWLink is for you. Installing and configuring NWLink is easy. The next sections look at those tasks.

Installing NWLink

NWLink does not install by default on Windows NT Workstation. Therefore, if you want to use NWLink, you need to install it first.

Adding NWLink

1. Right-click on Network Neighborhood and choose Properties. This brings up the Network Configuration dialog box.

2. Click the Protocols tab and choose Add.

3. Select NWLink IPX/SPX Compatible Transport from the list, as in Figure 8.15, and click OK.

FIGURE 8.15.
Adding the NWLink transport.

Configuring NWLink

Like NetBEUI, there is little to do here. Looking at the NWLink Properties dialog box, shown in Figure 8.16, the only option we have is to adjust the frame type. The default value of Auto Frame Detection is almost always the best option. However, your network administrator can help if the autodetect doesn't seem to do the trick.

FIGURE **8.16.**

Configuring NWLink. Under most circumstances, you will want to stick with Auto Frame Detection.

Windows NT and NetWare Integration

If you are integrating your Windows NT workstation into a Novell environment, I highly suggest a book dedicated to the subject; it is quite involved and beyond the scope of this text.

Application-Layer Clients and Services

At the top layer, we find the protocols that we interact with most. These are the protocols that enable us to connect with other computers to accomplish something useful.

We will look at the NetBIOS client (Microsoft Networking) as well as NCP (the Novell Client).

Client for Microsoft Networks—NetBIOS

NetBIOS is the Network Basic Input/Output System. It is a set of Application-layer protocols that enable users to share files and printers among Microsoft clients. It is likely that the majority of your file and printer sharing will be accomplished using NetBIOS, so we will spend considerable time discussing its intricacies.

The NetBIOS client installs in the following two pieces:

- *Server service.* Makes local resources available to the network.

- *Workstation service.* Enables you to connect to and use resources on other computers.

These two services are installed by default. If they were removed for some reason, however, here's how you can reinstall them:

Adding the Server service

1. Right-click on Network Neighborhood and choose Properties. This brings up the Network Configuration dialog box.

2. Click the Services tab and choose Add.

3. Select Server from the list, as in Figure 8.17, and click OK.

FIGURE 8.17.

Adding the Server service. The Server service makes resources available to the network via the NetBIOS.

Adding the Workstation service

1. Right-click on Network Neighborhood and choose Properties. This brings up the Network Configuration dialog box.

2. Click the Services tab and choose Add.

3. Select Workstation from the list, as in Figure 8.18, and click OK.

FIGURE 8.18.

Adding the Workstation service. The Workstation enables you to connect to resources on the network using NetBIOS.

Before we look at configuring our NetBIOS interface, let's get a better feel for how NetBIOS works.

Workgroups, Windows NT Server Domains, and Computer Names

The Identification tab in the Network Configuration dialog box enables you to set your computer's NetBIOS name and workgroup/domain membership. Figure 8.2 shows this dialog box.

Each computer taking part in NetBIOS networking must have a unique name. For further human convenience, NetBIOS enables you to group your computers into workgroups. Membership in a workgroup doesn't do anything other than affect browsing, which is discussed in a bit.

An NT domain is an administrative unit defined by one or more Windows NT Servers. If your workstation will participate in an NT Server domain, your network administrator will need to configure your computer. Usually domain membership is configured at the time of computer setup, but, we will take a look at it here.

SEE ALSO
➤ *See the section titled "Windows NT Domains" in Chapter 13, "Sharing Resources."*

Adding a Windows NT workstation to a domain

1. Right-click on Network Neighborhood and choose Properties. This brings up the Network Configuration dialog box.

2. The Identification tab is already in front. Click the Change button.

3. Select Domain and type the name of the domain in which you want to enroll.

4. In most cases, you will want to check Create Computer Account in Domain and fill in the next two input fields.

5. You need to provide an administrator username and password. This password must be of an administrator of the Windows NT server that controls the domain, not just your local workstation. See Figure 8.19 where I'm joining the Accounting domain.

IMPORTANT: Joining an NT Domain

Because joining a Windows NT Server domain has significant security consequences, an administrator password will be required. Your network administrator will have this password and will likely do this procedure for you.

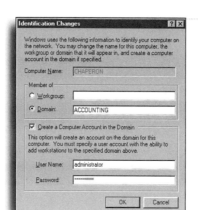

FIGURE 8.19.

Your administrator will usually add your workstation to a Windows NT server domain if necessary.

6. If your workstation was successfully added, you will see a note to that effect and a request for a reboot.

When establishing NetBIOS connections with other computers to share files and printers, you use the NetBIOS name exclusively. This name is completely unrelated to the TCP/IP hostname discussed earlier. It is good practice, however, to use matching hostnames and NetBIOS names. Imagine if the same computer on your network answered to both "Bob" and "Joe."

Browsing

There are a number of places where your computer will try to display a list of all the other computers and resources that are available to you. Double-click on the Network Neighborhood icon from the desktop and your computer will display all the other computers in your workgroup or domain. You can view other workgroups and domains by clicking on Entire Network and navigating from there.

NetBIOS relies heavily on broadcast messages. When you first turn your computer on and then periodically thereafter, it sends messages to every other computer on the physical subnet saying essentially, "I'm here, this is my name, and these are the resources I am sharing." Similarly, if you want to connect to a computer named "Joe," your computer will broadcast a message saying, "Hey, Joe, are you out there? I want to connect to a resource you own."

Hostnames Versus NetBIOS Names

If you have installed TCP/IP and NetBIOS, your computer will have a hostname and a NetBIOS name. These names are technically unrelated and may be different, but it is a good idea to keep them the same for human sanity sake! It also enables you to use little tricks such as Enable DNS for Windows Resolution, which you will see in the "NetBIOS over TCP/IP" section coming up.

If your transport protocol is NetBEUI, browsing will usually work fairly well. If your transport is TCP/IP, browsing is slightly less consistent, especially if you are connected to a large inter-network. NetBIOS is discussed in more detail in the following section.

NetBIOS over TCP/IP (NetBT)

NetBIOS was originally designed to operate over the top of the NetBEUI transport. With the popularity of TCP/IP, however, modifications were made and NetBIOS over TCP/IP (also called NetBT) is a quite common and effective method of sharing information. NetBT combines the capability of TCP/IP to handle large networks with the ease-of-use inherent to NetBIOS.

If you will be using NetBT, however, you should be aware of the following issues:

- *NetBIOS-name-to-IP-address resolution.* If you are on a TCP/IP network, your computer will need the IP address of the remote computer to communicate. The NetBIOS name is useless, and broadcasts won't get out of the local physical subnet. NetBIOS-name-to-IP-address resolution is accomplished through the use of WINS (Windows Internet Naming System) servers or through the %systemroot%\system32\LMHOSTS file. A WINS server and LMHOSTS file work identically to the DNS/HOSTS file scheme discussed earlier. WINS servers are configured in the TCP/IP Setup dialog box. Note that if your NetBIOS names exactly match your hostnames, you can enable DNS for Windows Resolution, as I did in Figure 8.13. This tells your computer that your NetBIOS names match your hostnames and it can resolve NetBIOS names by asking a DNS server.

SEE ALSO
➤ *See the section titled "Computer Names" earlier in this chapter for a discussion of DNS and the HOSTS file.*

- *Browsing.* Again, the broadcast nature of NetBIOS doesn't fit nicely into the very point-to-point–oriented TCP/IP. The "Hey everybody, I'm here" style of NetBIOS will work over TCP/IP only when all computers are on the same physical and logical subnet *or* a WINS server is in place.

One or more WINS servers is nearly essential in a large TCP/IP network where NetBIOS sharing (NetBT) will occur. WINS servers reduce broadcast network traffic and make location of resources across complex internetworks possible.

Client for NetWare Networks—NCP

The client for NetWare Networks is not installed by default. To install the NetWare client, just follow these easy steps:

Adding the client for NetWare networks

1. Right-click on Network Neighborhood and choose Properties. This brings up the Network configuration dialog box.

2. Click the Services tab and choose Add.

3. Choose Client Service for NetWare, as in Figure 8.20, and click OK.

After the client is installed, you can connect with NetWare resources including file and print shares.

Configuring Novell Client Services

After the Novell NetWare Client Services are installed, you need to do some basic configuration. Because NetWare Client

---

Name Resolution

Remember:

- DNS servers resolve host-names (or FQHN) into IP addresses.

- WINS servers resolves NetBIOS names into IP addresses.

- The HOSTS file resolves hostnames (or FQHN) into IP addresses.

- The LMHOSTS file resolves NetBIOS names into IP addresses.

What Is an LM host?

The *LM* in LMHOSTS is short for LanManager. Microsoft's original workgroup LAN product was called LanManager and introduced the NetBIOS protocol and NetBIOS name.

FIGURE 8.20.

Adding the Client Services for NetWare. This allows your Windows NT workstation to connect to NetWare resources using NCP.

Services will only bind to (talk to) NWLink, configuration is simple because TCP/IP issues don't get involved. And, NWLink is a snap to configure.

You can also bring up the Client Services for NetWare configuration dialog box by double-clicking on the CSNW icon in the Control Panel. Talk with your NetWare administrator and fill in the necessary configuration options. Figure 8.21 shows my NetWare configuration.

FIGURE 8.21.

Configuration of the NetWare client is simple. You will likely need to obtain some of these values from your NetWare administrator, however.

Because a full discussion of Windows NT and NetWare integration is beyond the scope of this book, we will end our discussion of the NetWare client here.

Testing and Troubleshooting Your Network Connection

Now that your network is all set up, let's perform some simple tests and look for common configuration errors. The following sections are broken down by application and transport protocol. Take a look at the sections that correspond to protocols.

NetBIOS over NetBEUI

NetBIOS over NetBEUI is about as simple as it gets when it comes to troubleshooting.

If you are on a network with other computers, you can verify proper operation by double-clicking on the Network Neighborhood icon on the desktop. There, you should see the other workgroups and computers on your LAN, as in Figure 8.22. If you don't see other machines, try explicitly connecting to another computer using one of the techniques in Chapter 13.

FIGURE 8.22.

If your NetBIOS connection is working, you can browse the network by double-clicking on the Network Neighborhood icon on the desktop. Here, I have drilled down a few levels into the workgroup called "Extension."

If the explicit connection fails, the problem is likely one of the following:

- You may not be properly logged on or may not have sufficient permissions to browse the network.

SEE ALSO

➤ *See the section titled "User Permissions and Accounts" in Chapter 12, "Managing Users—NT Security."*

- Your network adapter card has failed or is not configured correctly. This could be a problem with the base I/O address or interrupt (IRQ) setting. Check your hardware documentation for more information.

- If you have a combo card, the card may not be correctly set to the correct media type (either 10BASE-2, which is coaxial cable, or 10BASE T, which is twisted pair). Follow the instructions that shipped with your hardware to verify this setting. There are rare instances where an adapter will not correctly autotype the media type. If so, try setting it manually.

- Check the physical network for broken cables, an unterminated end (10BASE-2), or a hub that may have failed or be misconfigured.

NetBIOS over TCP/IP (NetBT)

To verify that your NetBT connection is functioning, follow the preceding procedures. If both the browse and explicit connection fail, follow these steps to attempt to isolate the problem:

Troubleshooting TCP/IP

1. Start a command prompt session: Start, Programs, Command Prompt.

2. Double-check your TCP/IP settings. A quick way to do this is to run the ipconfig program. From the command prompt, type ipconfig /all. You should see something similar to Figure 8.23 if you *are not* using DHCP. Verify that all the addresses are correct. If DHCP is in use, verify that you have an IP address and that the lease has not expired. Figure 8.24 shows ipconfig output if DHCP is in use. Correct any misconfigurations using the Network Configuration procedures discussed earlier in this chapter. If DHCP configuration failed, check with your network administrator.

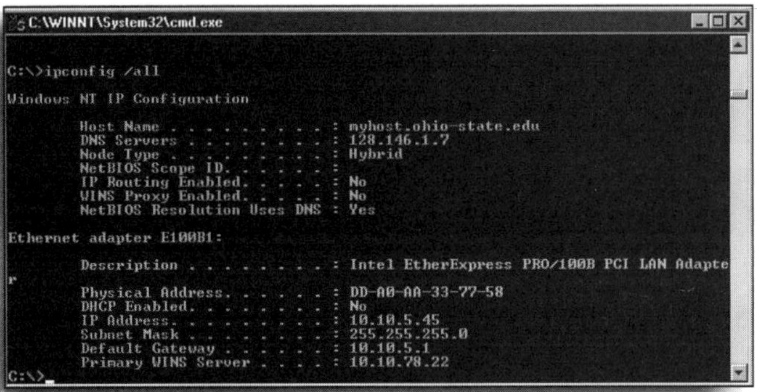

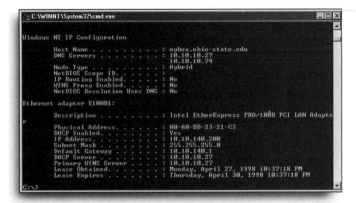

FIGURE 8.23.

Reasonable ipconfig output when DHCP configuration is not in use.

FIGURE 8.23.

Reasonable ipconfig output when DHCP configuration is not in use.

FIGURE 8.24.

Reasonable ipconfig output when DHCP configuration is in use. Note that a reasonable IP address has been assigned and that the lease expiration date is in the future.

3. Attempt to Ping your loopback address. A Ping does nothing more than say "hi" to the remote host and wait for a "hi" back. Ping is a very useful tool in TCP/IP diagnostics. Pinging your loopback address will verify that your TCP/IP stack is installed and running. To do this, at the command prompt type `ping 127.0.0.1` followed by Enter. A successful Ping where all the requests were answered looks like Figure 8.25. A failed Ping would not indicate any replies and would report errors similar to either of the two Ping sessions in Figure 8.26. The first Ping session shows the most common Request Timed Out error. If Pinging your loopback address failed, check that TCP/IP is properly installed on your workstation.

FIGURE 8.25.

Ping is a valuable diagnostic tool in TCP/IP. This is a successful Ping. Note that all four of the requests were returned in a reasonable amount of time.

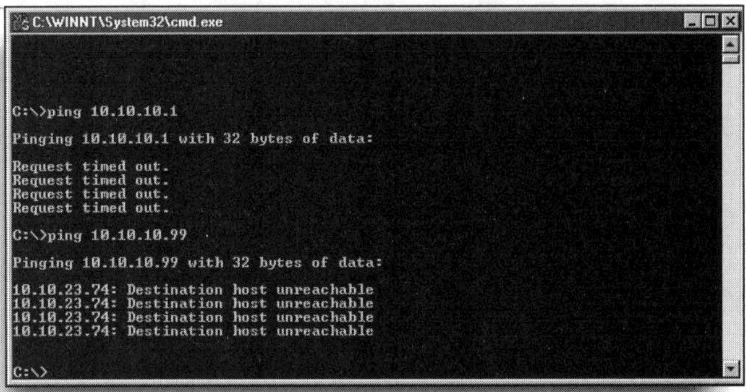

FIGURE 8.26.

Failed Pings will report errors of some kind. This figure contains two failed Ping sessions: the first where the request timed out; the second where the host was reported as unreachable by a gateway somewhere along the way. The gateway that reported that the host was unreachable is identified: here, it is 10.10.23.74 that reported the unreachable host.

4. Attempt to Ping your gateway IP address. If you don't have a gateway, Ping an IP address of a known-good host on your local physical and logical subnet. If the Ping fails, check the following:

   * Your IP address

   * Your network card (see the suggestions in the section titled "NetBIOS over NetBEUI")

   * The physical network, including the cable connection to your network adapter

5. Attempt to Ping an IP address outside of your local logical subnet. If connected to the Internet, Ping a known-good IP address out there. (204.146.18.33 is a good one to use; it's www.ibm.com.) If the Ping fails, check your IP address, subnet mask, and gateway address.

6. If connected to the Internet, attempt to Ping a host using an FQHN rather than an IP address. This will check the DNS lookup procedure. I usually use ping www.ibm.com. If this Ping fails, but the one in step 5 succeeded, there is a problem with your DNS server. Double-check the DNS address(es). Try Pinging your DNS server IP address. If DHCP is being used, see your network administrator.

7. If you have gotten to this point, you have successfully Pinged a host outside of your logical subnet by FQHN. Congratulations, your TCP/IP transport is working correctly!

If your TCP/IP transport is working, but you still can't connect to NetBIOS resources (file and print shares), double-check your WINS server configuration and/or LMHOSTS file. If you are still unsure, contact your network administrator for further assistance.

Using Dial-Up Networking (DUN)/Remote Access Service (RAS)

About Dial-Up Networking/Remote Access Service

Windows NT Workstation includes software called Dial-Up Networking (DUN) that enables you to establish a network connection to the Internet or a corporate network over phone lines. Remote Access Service (RAS) is the technical name for Dial-Up Networking under Windows NT; the terms are interchangeable. This connection is the type of connection you would have on a local area network, but slower.

If you sometimes work at home or travel, Dial-Up Networking enables you to remotely access your corporate network, the Internet, or another PC to check email, retrieve files, or use a Web browser.

Windows NT Workstation has the capability to access remote networks and the Internet using modems, ISDN terminal adapters, or X.25 communications adapters. Because modems are the most popular piece of equipment to use with Dial-Up Networking, this discussion primarily focuses on using Dial-Up Networking with a modem.

Installing Dial-Up Networking

Dial-Up Networking is provided with the Windows NT Workstation CD-ROM. You can install Dial-Up Networking during the initial installation of Windows NT, or after Windows NT is installed and working properly.

To use Dial-Up Networking, you need to have a modem, ISDN terminal adapter, or an X.25 communications adapter installed. You should follow the installation instructions supplied with the equipment. Most people will use Dial-Up Networking with a modem. You also need the Windows NT Workstation CD-ROM, and the newest Windows NT Service Pack (at the time of publishing this is Service Pack 3 [SP3]).

Adding a Modem to Windows NT

If you are using a modem with Dial-Up Networking, the first thing you must do is install a modem within Windows NT so that the operating system knows you have a modem. Except in extraordinary circumstances, you will be using a modem to use DUN. Therefore if you don't have a modem installed both physically and within Windows NT, you must do this first.

After physically installing a modem—either through a port such as a serial, parallel (rare), or USB, or internally—you need to set up that modem for use within Windows NT. To do this, follow these steps:

1. Open the Control Panel by selecting it under Start | Settings | Control Panel.

2. Double-click on the Modems icon. If you already have a modem installed, the Modem Properties dialog box will appear. If your modem is in the dialog box, you can proceed to installing the Dial-Up Networking software. If you do not have a modem already installed, the Install New Modem Wizard will appear. Figure 9.1 shows the start of the modem installation wizard.

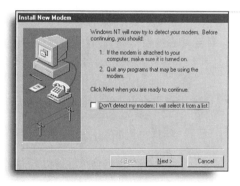

FIGURE 9.1.

The Install New Modem Wizard walks you through the process of installing a modem.

3. Most modems can be autodetected by the wizard, so select the Next button. The wizard will attempt to find and identify your modem.

4. If the wizard cannot detect your modem, you will be asked to select a modem from a list. Manufacturers will be listed in

a list box on the left, and the right-hand side will display modem models for a particular manufacturer. Find your modem's manufacturer on the left, and then select the modem model on the right.

5. If you do not see either the correct manufacturer or model for your modem, your modem probably came with a disk or CD-ROM containing a configuration file that Windows NT and Dial-Up Networking can use. If you do have such a disk or CD-ROM, insert it into your computer and select the Have Disk button. If the wizard can find the file immediately, you will be shown one or more modems to select. If the wizard does not find the information, you will have to select the Browse button to find the modem configuration file (which will be called either modem.inf or another filename with an .inf extension.) The .inf extension is Microsoft-talk for "information."

6. After you have your modem selected, you can click the Next button in the wizard. You will be asked, On which ports do you want to install it? Select the correct communications port where your modem is installed, and select Next. The wizard will install the modem. Figure 9.2 shows the dialog box that enables you to specify your port.

FIGURE 9.2.

The wizard asks what communications port your modem is attached to.

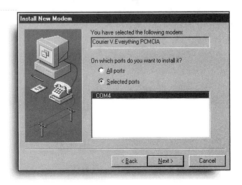

7. After the wizard has installed the modem, the Modem Properties dialog box will appear. The next step is to ensure the dialing properties are properly set.

Setting Dialing Properties

Dial-Up Networking and other communications-related
Windows NT components can share common dialing settings.
These dialing settings could include any digits or codes you
would need to be dialed before a phone number (for example, 9,
to access an outside telephone line in your office). You can create
separate dialing properties for different locations, such as your
home or office. If you have not previously defined any dialing
properties, Windows NT creates dialing properties for a location called Default Location. Figure 9.3 shows the dialog box
with these options.

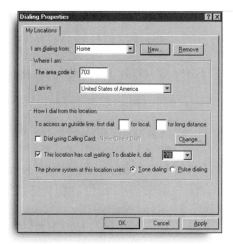

FIGURE 9.3.

Setting your modem's dialing
properties enables you to dial
any special numbers to access
an outside line or disable call
waiting.

1. In the Dialing Properties dialog box, select the Dialing
   Properties button. A dialog box appears that enables you to
   set dialing properties. If you like, you can change the
   Default Location name to something more relevant to you,
   such as My Office, in the text box next to the I am dialing
   from label.

2. Fill out the text boxes with the required information, such as
   area code and country. If you need to dial a number to
   access an outside line for local or long-distance calls, enter it
   in the appropriate text boxes. Usually you will want to add a
   comma to the number to tell the modem to wait a moment
   before dialing the remaining digits of the phone number.

3. If your location has call waiting, you will want the modem to disable it before dialing so that the call waiting tone does not interfere with your call. To do this, select the drop-down list next to the This location has call-waiting. To disable it, dial:__ label. Select the appropriate prefix (in most locations it is *70). This setting can usually be found in the front of your phone book.

4. If you need to use a calling card to make your call, check the appropriate box and select the Change button to specify your calling card type and number. If you use pulse (or rotary) dialing, select it in the dialog box.

5. After you have set your dialing properties, you can click the OK button. If you want to add additional locations, you can select the New button in the Dialing Properties dialog box.

Installing the Dial-Up Networking Software

After the modem or communications adapter is installed, you are ready to install Dial-Up Networking (DUN).

Installing DUN or RAS networking

1. Open the Control Panel and select Network. The Services page will list the network services currently installed.

2. Select the Add button, and choose Remote Access Service from the list that appears. (As mentioned earlier, Remote Access Service is the technical name for Dial-Up Networking under Windows NT; the terms are interchangeable.) Figure 9.4 is the dialog box enabling you to choose among various network services including RAS.

FIGURE 9.4.

You install the Dial-Up Networking software by adding the Remote Access Service to the computer's network services in the Network Control Panel.

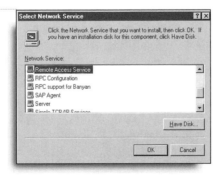

3. After you have selected Remote Access Service, you will be prompted for files from the Windows NT CD-ROM. You can specify a location for these files, always specifying the i386 subdirectory for Intel or Intel compatible-based PCs (for example, e:\i386).

4. A dialog box labeled Add RAS Device will appear. By default, the list box labeled RAS Capable Devices will have your modem selected. If you want to use another modem or device, you can select it from the drop-down list box. Then select OK to proceed.

5. The Remote Access Setup window appears. The devices configured for use with RAS, such as your modem, appear in the list box. You will have a choice of RAS devices to choose from, as shown in Figure 9.5.

FIGURE 9.5.

Remote Access Setup asks what device you would like to use. Your modem should be selected.

6. You are now ready to configure how you intend to use the Remote Access Service. Figure 9.6 shows this dialog box. Select your modem in the list box, and click the Configure button. In the dialog box that appears, you can select how you would like to use Remote Access: to dial out to other networks (Dial Out Only), to act as a Remote Access server to allow calls into your network or PC (Receive Calls Only), or to do both (Dial Out and Receive Calls).

FIGURE 9.6.

Click the Configure button after selecting a modem.

7. In the main Remote Access Setup window, you can configure the modems, devices, and networks that the Remote
Access Service and Dial-Up Networking will use.

8. Using RAS as a server to enable people call into your network or PC is discussed later in this chapter. Select Dial Out
Only to allow you to dial in to the Internet or in to a corporate network. Figure 9.7 shows this dialog box. Click OK to
return to the Remote Access Setup window. The next step is
to configure what network protocols you would like to use
with RAS.

FIGURE 9.7.

Configuring the Remote Access
Service to dial out, receive
calls, or do both.

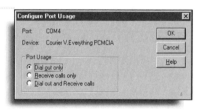

9. In the Remote Access Setup window, Figure 9.6, click on
the Network button. A dialog box will appear, as shown in
Figure 9.8, listing your protocol options. You should choose
all the protocol(s) that you will be using with Dial-Up
Networking. Networks that you call into with Dial-Up
Networking can use multiple protocols, and there is no
harm in selecting extra protocols at this point if you are not
sure.

FIGURE 9.8.

Choosing which protocols to
allow the Remote Access
Service to use.

10. For calling the Internet, you will use TCP/IP. Check the
box labeled TCP/IP.

11. If you are calling in to a Novell NetWare-based corporate
network, the most probable choice is IPX. NetWare

networks that use NetWare/IP can use TCP/IP as well, but the largest majority of Novell networks will use IPX.

12. If you are calling in to a Windows NT-based network, you can use any or all of the three protocols (NetBEUI, TCP/IP or IPX). It is best to ask the network administrator of the network you are dialing in to.

13. When you have selected all the protocols you intend to use with Dial-Up Networking, select the OK button. You have fully configured the Remote Access Service, and you can select the OK button in the Remote Access Setup window. You will be prompted to restart your machine; you must reboot Windows NT before Remote Access and Dial-Up Networking will function properly.

If you can, eliminate all but needed protocols. Extra protocols won't necessarily cause any trouble, but they will delay connection speed, because Windows NT will have to decide by a time out that they are invalid for this connection. When in doubt, leave it out.

Applying a Windows NT Service Pack

After the PC has rebooted, it makes sense to apply (or reapply) the Windows NT Service Pack (SP3). You should do this because original system files were copied from the Windows NT CD-ROM during the RAS installation, and Service Packs often replace some of the system files that RAS uses from the original Windows NT CD-ROM. Instructions on applying a Service Pack are covered in Chapter 3, "Customizing the Active Desktop."

Adding a Dial-Up Networking Entry

After you have installed the Remote Access Service, applied any Service Packs, and rebooted your system, you are ready to create Dial-Up Networking entries that contain the settings you need to dial in to a network. We will cover two scenarios: connecting to the Internet, and connecting to a corporate network, such as a Windows NT or NetWare network.

Novell IntranetWare Client for Windows NT and Service Packs

If you have the Novell IntranetWare Client for Windows NT installed on your machine to access your Novell NetWare network, you should be very cautious in applying Windows NT Service Packs. The Novell software replaces some Microsoft-supplied system files. The Windows NT Service Packs can unknowingly overwrite the Novell-supplied files, potentially leaving your system in an unbootable state. To be safe, you should uninstall the Novell IntranetWare Client for Windows NT before applying a Service Pack and then re-install the Novell software.

Connecting to the Internet

Before you connect to the Internet, you should know certain configuration information. You'll use the information as you create a Dial-Up Networking Entry. These items are discussed in detail below.

Information You Need to Know

Dial-Up Networking can connect to the Internet using a variety of remote access protocols and settings. Before proceeding, you should gather some detailed configuration information from your Internet service provider (ISP) to improve the chances of successfully establishing an Internet connection. The most basic information you should have includes the following:

- Access phone number(s)
- Protocol (PPP or SLIP)
- Whether you need to manually type in some text before connecting
- Whether it is necessary to manually specify DNS or workstation IP addresses

Creating a Dial-Up Networking Entry for the Internet

The first time you launch Dial-Up Networking, you will be notified that the phonebook is empty. The phonebook contains Dial-Up Networking entries for each network you want to connect to. If the phonebook is empty, the New Phonebook Entry Wizard appears. If the phonebook already has entries in it, the Dial-Up Networking window will appear. Clicking the New button in the Dial-Up Networking Window will launch the New Phonebook Entry Wizard.

Using the wizard to add an entry for DUN/RAS

1. After you have started it, the wizard will prompt you for a name for the entry. This can be anything you would like it to be; in our example it will be called Internet. The default name is MyDialUpServer. After you have given your entry a name, click the Next button. Figure 9.9 shows the start of the Add Wizard.

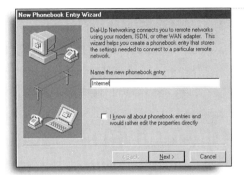

2. The wizard will now want to know what type of server you will be calling. Because we are creating an entry for the Internet, check the box next to I am calling the Internet. Figure 9.10 shows an illustration of this section of the wizard.

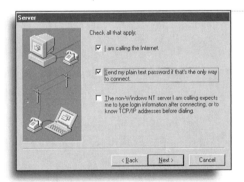

3. The next check box is asking whether your ISP will accept encrypted passwords. Dial-Up Networking supports various password encryption methods (PAP, CHAP, MS-CHAP, and so on) to prevent your password from being compromised, although your ISP may only accept clear text (that is, unencrypted) passwords. Checking this box almost always guarantees success, although your password may be at risk. It is good to leave this box unchecked, and change the security settings if you have connection problems. Changing the password security settings is explained later.

4. Sometimes you will have to manually type in some special commands, such as a separate logon name or password, before establishing a connection. Or your ISP could assign a permanent IP address to you that you need to tell Dial-Up Networking to use. Checking the third check box tells Dial-Up Networking to present a terminal window where you can type in these special commands or IP address information before establishing a connection. If your ISP uses SLIP as a dial-in protocol, you should check this box (see sidenote "SLIP Versus PPP").

5. After you have filled out the Server page of the Add Phonebook Entry Wizard, click the Next button.

   The wizard will request a phone number and related information for your Internet connection. You should enter the phone number and area code of your ISP. Figure 9.11 shows the dialog box in which you fill in this information. You can select the Alternates button to type in additional phone numbers for Dial-Up Networking to use. This is useful if you have multiple phone numbers to choose from; if the first number is busy, Dial-Up Networking will try each number in the Alternates list. If you set dialing properties when you installed the modem, check the Use Telephony Dialing Properties box. This enables you to use different dialing settings for different locations, such as your home or office.

FIGURE 9.11.

You need to tell Dial-Up Networking what phone number you should call to establish a connection.

6. Click the Next button on the wizard.

If you checked the third box on the Server page of the wizard, labeled The non-Windows NT server I am calling expects me to type login information, you will be prompted with several additional pages.

7. If you need to type logon information after the modem if connected to the ISP, you can either type that information in manually or you can automate this logon with a script that supplies the relevant information for you. Dial-Up Networking includes predefined logon scripts, which you can select using the drop-down list box as shown in Figure 9.12. Some scripts are generic or are templates for you to customize; if you use CompuServe, you should use the script named CIS.SCP. If you want to type this information in manually, select the option Use a Terminal Window. If you do not need to enter any information, select None. When you are done, click the Next button.

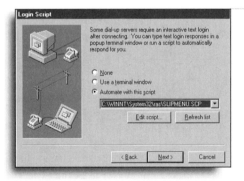

FIGURE 9.12.

You can specify a logon script to use to automate some commands that need to be typed into a terminal window, or you can have a terminal window appear for you to type commands into.

8. The next step in the wizard, seen in Figure 9.13, asks whether you will be using PPP or SLIP as your dial-up protocol. SLIP is now a rare protocol. If you do not know which protocol to use, try PPP first, because this is a newer and more reliable protocol (see the following Note).

9. Click the Next button after choosing the right protocol.

The next page, seen in Figure 9.14, asks about how your IP address will be set. If your ISP has assigned you an IP address to use each time you call in, specify it here. If you are using SLIP or PPP, the server will assign the address each time you connect. Leave the address at 0.0.0.0, and click the Next button.

FIGURE 9.13.

Choose whether your connection will use PPP or SLIP.

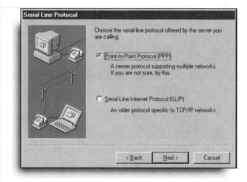

FIGURE 9.14.

If you will always use the same IP address for this Dial-Up Networking connection, enter that address on this page.

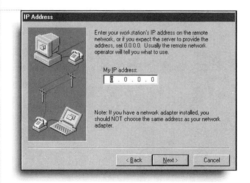

10. The Internet uses servers running a service called DNS (Domain Name Service) for matching IP addresses to hostnames (for example, the hostname www.microsoft.com to IP address 207.46.130.139). The Name Server Addresses page, shown in Figure 9.15, asks you for a DNS server's IP address. If this is automatically supplied by the ISP's server, leave the address at 0.0.0.0. Otherwise fill it in with the IP address the ISP has given you. The box labeled WINS Server is used for Windows NT-based networks and is discussed in the section titled "Connecting to a Corporate Network."

11. Click the Next button to finish.

FIGURE 9.15.

If the server you are calling does not automatically communicate DNS server addresses, you must enter your Internet service provider's DNS server IP address.

The New Phonebook Entry Wizard should now be complete, and you can click the Finish button. You are then presented with the main Dial-Up Networking window. You can now proceed to the section titled "Establishing a Connection."

Connecting to a Corporate Network

Windows NT's Dial-Up Networking can connect to a variety of corporate networks. These networks can be running Windows NT Server, Novell NetWare, UNIX, OS/2 LAN Server, any other network operating system, or a combination of all these systems. The instructions here apply to connecting to a Windows NT- or NetWare-based network using the two most common methods: the industry-standard PPP protocol and/or Microsoft's Remote Access Service.

Information You Need

These instructions assume you are familiar with the basic Add New Phonebook Wizard and the main Dial-Up Networking window as described in the section in this chapter titled "Connecting to the Internet."

Creating the Phonebook Entry

The first step is to create the phonebook entry using the Add New Phonebook Entry Wizard. The wizard will start automatically if you do not have any existing phonebook entries, or you

SLIP Versus PPP

If you are connecting to the Internet, the most common communications protocol you will be using is PPP (Point-to-Point Protocol). SLIP (Serial Line Interface Protocol) is an older alternative to PPP, and is still used in some environments, particularly universities and organizations with long-standing Internet capabilities. If your ISP or organization supports both protocols, you should use PPP because it is faster, supports multiple protocols (TCP/IP and IPX), is more secure, and automatically sets your PC's IP address and network configuration. If you must use SLIP, you enter this configuration information into the terminal window that you use to type the commands you use to establish a SLIP session (specified by your ISP).

Remote Access Server (RAS) and remote access servers

The term *remote access server* can be confusing. A remote access server is a network device or computer connected to a network that enables users with modems to dial in to the local network. Remote users have the same type of network connection as users connected directly to the local network, with the exception that the connection speed is significantly slower. Microsoft offers remote access capabilities in its Remote Access Service, which comes with Windows NT; a Windows NT machine that runs the Remote Access Service to allow incoming calls is often called a Remote Access Server, or RAS server. Usually the term *remote access server* refers to a general-purpose remote dial-up server, and the term *Remote Access Server* applies to a remote access server specifically running Microsoft's Remote Access Service.

can start it from the main Dial-Up Networking window by clicking the New button.

Using DUN/RAS for a corporate connection

1. Start the Add New Phonebook Entry Wizard from the DUN window by choosing the New button.

2. Give your phonebook entry a name on the first section of the wizard. This example named it Corporate. You can use any name you like; the default is MyDialUpServer. Select the Next button.

3. The next section sets the Server type. Because you are connecting to a corporate network and not the Internet, do not check the first box labeled I am calling the Internet. There is no harm in checking this box; if you do, the wizard then assumes that TCP/IP is the only protocol you will be using.

4. If your remote access server does not use encrypted passwords, you should tell Dial-Up Networking to send clear-text passwords by checking the box labeled Send by plain-text if that's the only way to connect. Click the Next button to proceed to the next page.

5. The next section asks you for the phone number(s) of the remote access server you will be dialing in to. You can enter multiple phone numbers by clicking the Alternates button. If you entered telephony dialing information when you installed the modem (for example, specified a number to dial to access an outside line or to disable call-waiting), check the Use Telephony Dialing Properties box. When you have entered the phone number, click the Next button.

6. That is all you need to enter into the wizard. Now you can click the Finish button. You will then be returned to the main Dial-Up Networking window.

Your phonebook entry may enable you to connect to your network without any further modifications to the entry. However, there is some fine-tuning you can perform to ensure your entry will work. The best thing to do is to try to establish a connection now. If you have problems, you will need to manually edit the phonebook entry details.

Manually Changing Phonebook Entries

If the connection doesn't go smoothly, you might have to manually tune the entry. Here's how to do this.

Editing a DUN/RAS entry

1. Open the entry in the combo box, and then click the More button. Figure 9.16 shows this drop-down list. A drop-down menu will appear. Select Edit Entry and Modem Properties.

FIGURE 9.16.

In the main Dial-Up Networking window, you can manually edit phonebook details by clicking the More button.

2. The Edit Phonebook Entry dialog box appears. It has several pages: Basic, Server, Script, Security, and X.25.

3. The Basic tab, shown in Figure 9.17, covers such information as the entry name, comments, and the phone number. If you have multiple modems installed in your computer, you can choose to use either a single modem or multiple lines in the Dial Using list box. If you select multiple lines, you can use Dial-Up Networking's multilink PPP features to aggregate multiple connections. To use whichever modem is not busy, check the Use Another Port if Busy box. If you want to change the default modem settings, such as the speed, speaker, or compression settings, you can select the Configure button.

FIGURE 9.17.

The Basic tab enables you to modify the name, phone number, and modem selection for the phonebook entry.

4. The Server tab, Figure 9.18, enables you to specify what type of server you are dialing in to, as well as the network protocols to use for the connection. In the Dial-Up Server list box, you choose what type of server you are dialing in to. The default is PPP: Windows NT, Windows 95 Plus, Internet. This is the most common server type. Other options are SLIP (for older TCP/IP-only networks) and Windows NT 3.1 and Windows for Workgroups 3.11 (which use an older proprietary protocol).

FIGURE 9.18.

The Server tab contains settings related to the remote server and the protocols you will be using.

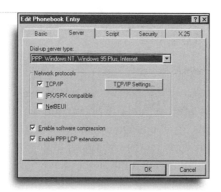

5. You should select which protocols the remote access server supports. You can select all three if you like, and Dial-Up Networking will attempt to use all three the first time you connect, but that will slow things down quite a bit. You can then specify that future connections will only request the protocols that were successfully used.

TABLE 9.1 **Common network types and typical protocol settings**

Network Type	Common Protocol Settings
Windows NT	NetBEUI, TCP/IP, or IPX
Windows 95	NetBEUI, TCP/IP, or IPX
UNIX	TCP/IP
Internet	TCP/IP
Novell NetWare	IPX/SPX, TCP/IP
OS/2 LAN Server	NetBEUI

6. If you enabled TCP/IP as a protocol, you should verify some detailed settings. Select the TCP/IP Settings box. A new dialog box appears. If the remote access server specifies your workstation and name server IP addresses automatically (most do), you do not need to change the default settings. Otherwise enter the IP addresses you have been assigned and/or the IP addresses of primary and secondary DNS and WINS servers.

The last check boxes, Enable Software Compression and Use LCP PPP Extensions, should be checked by default. If you have problems establishing a connection, you can experiment with disabling these settings.

7. The Script tab, shown in Figure 9.19, enables you to specify either a script to be run or the pop up of a terminal window to be run after the modem has established its initial handshaking. If you want a script or window to execute before the modem begins to dial, you can specify this by selecting the Before Dialing button.

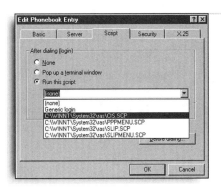

FIGURE 9.19.

You can specify a logon script to run after your modem has first connected to the remote server. Our example shows the selection of the script for CompuServe.

Dial-Up Networking Scripting

You have several scripting options with Dial-Up Networking. The most common reason you would use scripting is to automate repetitive, simple commands you need to enter before you can establish a PPP or SLIP connection. The simplest way learn how to use scripts is to look at the sample scripts that come with Dial-Up Networking, which are stored with other Dial-Up Networking files in the <winnt>/system32/ras directory. In this directory, there is a detailed scripting manual called script.doc. Script files are also stored there as text files with the extension .SCP. There is also a script file called switch.inf that can contain scripts as well. This file is heavily commented and contains a generic logon script as well as an example of logging on to a remote access server using SLIP.

8. The Security tab, shown in Figure 9.20, in the Edit Phonebook Properties dialog box is for security settings related to how the remote access server handles password encryption and authentication. You can specify to allow the use of clear-text passwords, to only allow the use of encryption, or to only allow the use of Microsoft-specific encryption. Most remote access servers will work with the middle option, the use of encryption. If you are calling into a Microsoft Remote Access Server, you can select the third choice (Microsoft-only encryption). This enables you to specify the requirement for data encryption on your dial-up session. You can also specify to automatically use your existing Windows NT credentials (your username and password) for the RAS session. Your network administrator may require Microsoft encryption and data encryption for security reasons. If you previously chose to have your username and password saved for this phonebook entry, selecting the Unsave Password button will clear the saved user credentials.

FIGURE 9.20.

You can choose how Dial-Up Networking will handle authentication security and the use of a clear-text password for authentication.

9. The X.25 tab, shown in Figure 9.21, is for X.25 communications adapters, and should be left blank unless you use X.25. If you don't know whether you use X.25, you probably don't use it. You can enter the X.25 service provider, the network address of the X.25 server you want to connect to, and other configuration information.

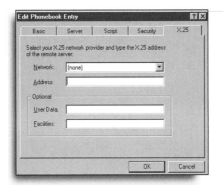

FIGURE 9.21.

Dial-Up Networking supports the use of X.25. This tab is where you select the network and enter X.25-specific configuration information.

10. After you have entered all the phonebook details, you can click the OK button for your changes to be applied. You can now establish a connection to you corporate network.

Establishing a Connection

After you have created the phonebook entry for your Internet or corporate network connection, you can initiate the connection by launching the main Dial-Up Networking window by either double-clicking on the Dial-Up Networking icon in My Computer or by the Start Menu shortcut under Start | Programs | Accessories | Dial-Up Networking.

Using a dial-up connection

1. Start DUN/RAS by choosing Start | Programs | Accessories | Dial-Up Networking.

2. In the main Dial-Up Networking window, select the phonebook entry for the connection. If this is the only phonebook entry, it will already be selected. Note that the phone number will contain any special dialing strings specified in the Telephony settings for your location. If you have defined multiple dialing locations, you can select the appropriate one under the Dialing From list box.

3. When the information in the window is correct, click the Dial button. You will then be presented with a dialog box, shown in Figure 9.22, for you to type in your username and password. There is also a box labeled Domain; this is the

Windows NT domain name and can usually be left blank for connections to the Internet or Novell networks. Enter your username and password in the text boxes, and select Save Password box if you want to skip this step each time you connect.

FIGURE 9.22.

After you click the Dial button, you can enter your username, password, and the domain name (domain name is for Windows NT networks only).

4. You now begin the process of connecting to the remote network. A status window appears; you first see a message indicating the PC is dialing. After the initial modem handshaking has been established, you should see status messages first saying Verifying Username and Password and then Registering you on the Network. If the connection is dropped after verifying username and password, check that the username and password you supplied is correct (it may be case sensitive), and if that doesn't work check the password encryption settings (try clear text).

If your connection is established successfully, a dialog box appears notifying you that you connected correctly. If you don't want this window to come up each time, just check the box and proceed. The Dial-Up Networking connection status can be observed in the lower right-hand corner of the taskbar, where a telephone icon sits before two bars. This is the Dial-Up Monitor.

The Dial-Up Monitor

The Dial-Up Monitor, shown in Figure 9.23, enables you to observe the status of a Dial-Up Networking connection while you are online. After the Dial-Up Monitor is running on the taskbar, you can also use it to establish and hang-up Dial-Up Networking connections.

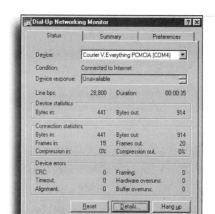

FIGURE 9.23.

The Dial-Up Networking
Monitor enables you to view
the status of an active connection.

The Dial-Up Monitor in its default configuration has two gray
bars above one another. The top bar turns blue for sending data,
the bottom bar for receiving. If you double-click the Dial-Up
Monitor, the Dial-Up Networking Monitor main dialog box will
appear. Here you can view usage statistics, such as bytes sent and
received, your connection speed, and how long you have been
online. If you click the Details button, you can view your IP
address. This is useful if you need to provide your IP address to
play online games, use video conferencing software, or run other
programs where you need to know your address.

You can also dial or hang up a connection with the Dial-Up
Monitor by right-clicking the Dial-Up Networking Monitor
icon on the taskbar. Select either Dial or Hang Up, along with
the phonebook entry.

Disconnecting

To hang up your Dial-Up Networking connection, you can
either launch the Dial-Up Networking main window and select
the Hang Up button, or right-click the Dial-Up Networking
Monitor icon as discussed in the preceding paragraph.

Making a Dropped Connection Redial

You will probably want a Dial-Up Networking connection to be automatically re-established if you are disconnected prematurely.

Using redial in DUN/RAS

1. Open the main Dial-Up Networking window, select the More button and choose the User Preferences window shown in Figure 9.24. In the window's Dialing page, you can enable an automatic redial by checking the Redial on Link Failure check box.

2. This tab also enables you to enable or disable automatic establishment of Dial-Up Networking sessions when you are attempting to use a resource usually accessed over a dial-up session.

FIGURE 9.24.

In the User Preferences window, you can specify to redial a dropped connection or to drop an idle connection.

Automatically Dropping an Idle Connection

You can have Dial-Up Networking hang up an established Dial-Up Networking session if the session remains idle for a predetermined number of minutes. This is useful if you start large Web or FTP downloads from the Internet and you want the phone line freed up after the download is done. To automatically drop idle connections, open the Modems icon in Control Panel. In the Modems Properties window, select your modem and choose the Properties button. In the Properties window for your modem, choose the Connection page. Check the Disconnect if Idle box and enter the desired number of minutes to wait before disconnecting. Click OK on each window until you have returned to the Control Panel.

Troubleshooting

Dial-Up Networking is very reliable after you have all the correct settings figured out. The best way to troubleshoot connection problems is to experiment with various settings. Nonetheless you may have problems that will confuse and confound you; here are some common problems and their remedies.

Connection Is Established but then Immediately Dropped

The most common cause of this problem is either an incorrect set of user credentials (username, password, and Windows NT domain name if applicable), authentication security settings, or subtle PPP version incompatibilities.

Troubleshooting immediate disconnections

1. Verify your user credentials. Is your username spelled correctly? Is your password case sensitive?

2. Verify your authentication encryption settings. Do you need to send clear-text passwords? Does the network require Microsoft encryption? Data encryption?

3. Experiment with PPP settings. Try disabling software compression or the PPP LCP extensions.

4. Enable PPP or modem logging to troubleshoot the connection. You can do this by editing certain Registry entries. For more information on logging, search for logging in the Dial-Up Networking help file. To access the help file, select Help under the More button in the main Dial-Up Networking window.

Sometimes you will find that your connection works, but connect speed is slow or connection is sporadically dropped.

Modem connection speeds depend on a wide variety of factors. One is modem speed, because modems can only connect at the lowest common denominator. This can especially be true for yet-to-be-standardized modem speeds. Another factor is phone-line quality. You may want to try connecting at lower speeds, or examine your phone wiring for corroded or aging contacts. Unfortunately there is often nothing you can do to improve phone-line quality.

Connections into a Windows NT Remote Access Server Work Fine with NetBEUI or IPX, but Do Not Work with TCP/IP

Troubleshooting TCP/IP connections

Phone-Line Quality and PBXs

If you are having sporadic connection problems in an office setting, one item to check out is the phone line and your office's PBX. A PBX (Private Branch eXchange) is a local phone switch that enables you to use fewer phone lines from the local phone company than phones in your office. A PBX also enables you make interoffice calls by just dialing an extension number. In most corporate environments, you access an outside line from the PBX by dialing 9 first. Most of the time this works fine for data and fax calls. However, some PBXs cannot handle the high speeds that today's modems use; some have problems sending data above 9600 bps. To tell whether this may be a problem for you, see the PBX documentation. If this is an issue, you can often program a line to bypass the PBX. Another solution would be to acquire a direct outside line that does not touch the PBX.

1. Ensure both machines have TCP/IP installed, and that the RAS server has a valid IP address.

2. Verify the TCP/IP protocol settings for the network in the Remote Access Setup window (in the Network Control Panel). Verify that your network either uses DHCP, or that there are at least two IP addresses in the specified range.

3. Make sure the Dial-Up phonebook entry contains the correct WINS address for your network in the TCP/IP settings on the Server page. If your network does not use WINS, get a copy of the correct LMHOSTS file for PC from the network administrator.

Using the Remote Access Service as a Server

The Remote Access Service or Dial-Up Networking that comes with Windows NT Workstation can serve as a server for incoming modem or ISDN connections. This allows computers to connect to a workstation running the Remote Access Service on a network and have the same type of network connectivity that a local network user has. You can also access a Windows NT Workstation that is not connected to a network, creating a network connection that you can use to access files or resources on the workstation itself. This is useful if you want to occasionally access files on your office PC from home.

You may be asking what the difference is between the Remote Access Service on Windows NT Servers and the same service on Windows NT Workstation. The difference is the number of connections supported. Windows NT Server supports up to 256 modems or adapters; Windows NT Workstation is limited to a single device for incoming calls.

Setting Up RAS for Incoming Calls

You should have the Remote Access Service already installed as described in the preceding section. These steps walk you through enabling inbound calls.

Using your computer as a DUN/RAS server

1. Open the Network Control Panel. Double-click on the Network icon, and go to the Services page.

2. Double-click on the entry labeled Remote Access Service.

3. In the Remote Access Setup window, select your RAS device (your modem or ISDN terminal adapter). Click the Configure button. This brings up the dialog box shown in Figure 9.25. In the Configure dialog box, select whether you want the device to support both incoming and outgoing calls (dial out and receive) or just incoming calls (receive only). Click the OK button when you are done.

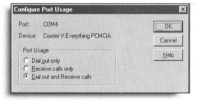

FIGURE 9.25.

Configuring the Remote Access Service to allow incoming calls.

4. In the Remote Access Setup window, click the Network button to bring up the dialog box shown in Figure 9.26. Select the protocols you want to support for dial-in sessions. For each protocol, you can choose the extent to which dial-in users can access the network. By selecting the Settings button next to each protocol, you can specify whether you want clients to access the entire network or limit access to the machine running the Remote Access Service. If you just click OK in the Network window, you will be walked through each protocol's Settings dialog box.

5. The IPX protocol's settings enable you to specify how IPX network addresses and numbers are assigned. You should not have to change any of these settings. For security reasons, you should avoid checking the box enabling users to request their IPX node number.

FIGURE 9.26.

The Remote Access Service can support a variety of protocols for both dialing out and accepting inbound calls.

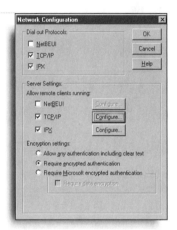

6. The settings for the TCP/IP protocol, shown in Figure 9.27, determine how IP addresses will be handled. If your network uses DHCP (Dynamic Host Configuration Protocol), the default settings will have the Remote Access Server request addresses on the local network from a DHCP server. If you allocate IP addresses manually, you must specify an inclusive range of IP addresses for the RAS server to allocate to clients. The IP addresses must be valid for the network where the RAS server resides, and you must allocate at least two addresses (one for the RAS server's modem and one for the client). If you need to exclude certain addresses in the range (that is, not allocate the addresses to clients), you can do so by adding the applicable range to the excluded ranges section of the dialog box. For security reasons, you should prevent users from being able to request a particular IP address.

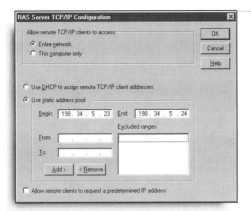

FIGURE 9.27.

TCP/IP addresses can be allocated to dial-in clients by a DHCP server on the local network or by specifying a particular address range to use. At least two addresses are needed for either end of the dial-up connection.

7. You can also set your authentication encryption settings. If all your dial-in clients run Microsoft Windows NT or Windows 95 and will use Dial-Up Networking as the client software, you can opt to require the use of Microsoft authentication encryption and to mandate data encryption. The default setting will still use encryption and will support non-Windows clients.

8. After your network settings are as you would like them, you can click the Continue button in the Remote Access Setup window. You will be prompted to supply the Windows NT distribution media. After the usual and mandatory reboot, you are ready to handle incoming calls.

Administering the RAS Server

You can set who can dial in to the server, monitor who is connected to the server, send users messages, and disconnect users by using the Remote Access Admin application in the Administrative Tools program group.

Specifying Who Can Access the RAS Server

To specify users who have the necessary permissions to access the RAS server, from the Users menu choose Permissions. The Permissions dialog box, shown in Figure 9.28, appears showing a list of users. Page through the list, and check the box labeled

Grant Dialin Permission to User for each user account you want to give dial-in permissions to.

FIGURE 9.28.

You specify each user who can use the Remote Access Server by selecting the user and checking the Grant Dialin Permission to User box.

It is a good idea to limit who can use the Remote Access Server. Each RAS-enabled account presents another window for hackers and security breaches. It is also a good idea to have every user use separate dial-in accounts. If multiple people use the same account, security administration becomes difficult should an employee leave the company while knowing the remote access password.

In the Permissions dialog box, you can also set each user's callback settings.

Using a RAS Server to Provide Internet Access

If your network is connected to the Internet, you can use the Remote Access Service to provide Internet access. To do this, you must enable some network settings.

Enabling RAS Internet access

1. Make sure the Windows NT Workstation and the client computer both have the TCP/IP protocol installed. You can check this in the Network applet within the Control Panel.

2. On the Windows NT Workstation that runs the Remote Access Server, verify Internet connectivity by successfully launching Internet Explorer or another Internet tool.

3. In the Network Control Panel on the RAS server, ensure that TCP/IP routing is enabled. To do this, select TCP/IP

on the Protocols page. Click the Properties button. In the Microsoft TCP/IP Properties window, select the Routing page and ensure that the check box is checked.

4. Configure the TCP/IP settings in the Remote Access Setup network window to allow access to the entire network, and ensure that IP addresses will be assigned correctly (for example, via DHCP or in the ranges).

5. If you have a firewall, check your security settings to ensure that information from the remote user's IP address will be able to be sent through the firewall.

Callback Security

One of Microsoft Remote Access Server's security features is client callback. Callback works like this: A user calls the remote access server. The user's credentials are verified. If the user is configured for callback, the server disconnects the client and then calls the client back. The client answers the phone, and the remote access session is fully established. The client can either enter a phone number in after the user authentication process, or the number can be predetermined by the system administrator. The ability to predetermine the call back phone number provides a certain level of security, because the user must be at the predetermined phone number. Another benefit is that any long-distance phone charges are born by the remote access server, eliminating the need for reimbursing employees for long-distance calls. A drawback is that callback does not work well for travelers, because hotel rooms do not provide the capability for direct inbound calls.

Personal Web Server

Personal Web Server (PWS) is a fantastic tool for quickly making Web pages available to a relatively small number of users. It is a scaled-down version of the very popular Microsoft Internet Information Server (IIS) that runs on Windows NT Server. PWS is designed to run on your Windows NT Workstation 4.0, and has a lot of wizards and other user-interface niceties to make Web publishing easy for anyone.

Because PWS was not designed to support high-volume Web sites, and because of license limitations on Windows NT Workstation, it does not include all the features found in the full-blown IIS.

Here's what isn't included:

- Microsoft Site Server Express
- Index Server
- Certificate Server
- HTTPS (secure Web) Server

But, you get everything else, including the following:

- *Active Server Pages*. Enables you to use server-side scripting to generate dynamic HTML pages on-the-fly. Combine with Microsoft's Active Data Objets (ADO), and you can write Web pages to interact with ODBC data sources.
- *Script debugging*.
- *Internet Service Manager*. A plug-in for the comprehensive, all-in-one administrator's tool called the Microsoft Management Console, or MMC.
- *Microsoft Transaction Server*. Facilitates the use of transactions in distributed applications.

So far, PWS has been used primarily by Web site developers and administrators for testing Web content before publishing it to a production server. It was developed as a adjunct to FrontPage, Microsoft's Web site creation program—FrontPage requires a Web of some sort to operate at all. It can just as well be used, however, to publish "real" content right from your desktop.

Because I could write an 800-page book on just Web publishing, I will limit my discussion of PWS to setup and basic maintenance of the Web server. I won't talk at all about Web design and authoring, nor will I talk about authoring tools such as the previously mentioned Microsoft FrontPage. If you are serious about publishing Web content, you will want to pick up some books on HTML, Web publishing, and the authoring tool(s) of your choice. If you are thinking about running a serious Web server that will likely see more than a couple dozen *hits* (or accesses) a day, you will want to consider a Windows NT Server running IIS.

This discussion very quickly reviews the basics, and then jumps right into PWS.

Web Basics

In 1989, a researcher at the European Particle Research Center (CERN) in Switzerland proposed a common method of formatting hypertext documents such that they would have a consistent appearance on any kind of networked computer. The researcher was Tim Berners-Lee, and his invention is what we know today as the World Wide Web.

HTML and HTTP

The proposal consisted of two separate but closely related parts:

- *Hypertext Markup Language* (HTML) for layout and formatting of documents.
- *Hypertext Transfer Protocol* (HTTP) for transmitting the documents between computers.

SEE ALSO

➤ *See the section titled "Protocols" in Chapter 8, "Networking Fundamentals."*

One of the most powerful features of HTML was that the documents could contain *hypertext links* (or just *links*) to other documents on the same computer, or on another computer on the Internet. This enabled people to browse information in a more human fashion—jumping among related documents in a nonlinear manner. This simple concept is likely one of the major reasons for the Web's amazing success.

Another Protocol

HTTP is the protocol that enables us to view Web pages. It operates at the Application layer on top of TCP/IP. We don't need to explicitly install HTTP into Windows NT; it comes free of charge when TCP/IP is installed. No further installation or configuration is needed.

Browsers

Your browser is the client software that runs on your local workstation. It requests HTML pages from remote servers using HTTP. It then parses the *HTML formatting tags* and displays the beautifully formatted Web pages you have undoubtedly come to know and love. Popular Web browsers include Netscape's Navigator and Communicator products and Microsoft's Internet Explorer.

Client/Server Computing and URLs

The computer that asks for data is known as the *client*. The computer that receives the request and sends the necessary data back to the client is called the *server*. That right there is the basis of the client/server model for distributed computing. Pretty simple, eh?

A *uniform resource locator* (URL) enables clients to locate and address servers. It is nothing more than a computer name preceded by a resource type identifier, and perhaps a file pathname at the end. The computer name may be a *fully qualified hostname* (FQHN), an IP address, or even a NetBIOS computer name if accessing a local intranet server. Keep in mind that usually one site can be accessed by using slightly different URLs. Remember, an FQHN is just a substitute for an IP address, and computers with Microsoft Networking installed will answer to a NetBIOS name as well as a hostname.

SEE ALSO

➤ *Part 3 of this book covers various aspects of networking. See Chapter 8, "Networking Fundamentals," for details about protocols.*

The following are all URLs:

- `http://home.netscape.com`
- `http://www.microsoft.com/windows/default.asp`

- `http://10.10.10.132/index.html`

- `http://mycomputer`

- `http://IntranetServer/Web/home`

- `ftp://ftp.ibm.com`

- `gopher://gopher.mit.edu`

- `telnet://10.10.10.132`

There are many resource type identifiers, but HTTP is by far the most common.

People will use an URL to access your Web site. In Figure 10.1, I am using Microsoft Internet Explorer (IE) to view my PWS-hosted Web site on my local workstation. The URL is `http://chaperon`. That's because my NetBIOS name is `chaperon`, and I'm using the local intranet to connect. There are also other ways I can connect to my computer and view the same page:

- `http://chaperon.mydomain.com` is the FQHN for my desktop computer. This URL will display the same page as shown in Figure 10.1. If I were making this page available to the Internet at large, this is the URL I would advertise. An URL composed of an FQHN is by far the most popular and useful.

- `http://10.10.10.77` is the IP address of my desktop computer. Remember, `chaperon.mydomain.com` is just an alias for `10.10.10.77`. Using the IP URL just saves the browser the task of doing the DNS lookup. This URL also will display the same page as shown in Figure 10.1.

SEE ALSO

➤ *See the section titled "Computer Naming" in Chapter 8, "Networking Fundamentals," for more on DNS, FQHN, and IP addressing.*

FIGURE 10.1.

Using Microsoft Internet
Explorer to access my PWS
hosted Web site. The URL is
http://chaperon.
chaperon is the hostname
and NetBIOS name of my
desktop workstation.

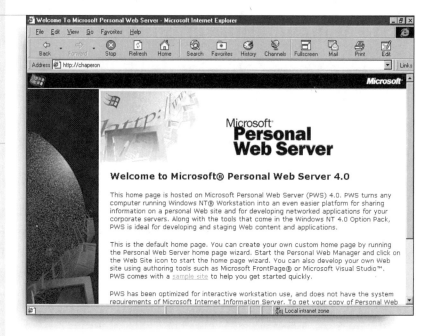

Obtaining and Installing PWS

Personal Web Server is included in the Windows NT 4.0
Option Pack that is, at the time of this writing, being distributed
online by Microsoft free of charge. If you own or buy
FrontPage, you will likewise get PWS. Check out Microsoft's
Web site if you need to download a copy. The URL is
http://backoffice.microsoft.com/downtrial/optionpack.asp.

The Option Pack includes some additional software including
Microsoft Transaction Server, Microsoft Message Queue Client,
Windows Scripting Host, FTP Server, and others. This chapter,
however, focuses on the Personal Web Server.

Before installing the Option Pack, you need to make sure that
your system meets a few requirements:

- Windows NT Workstation 4 with Service Pack 3 or higher.
  For Service Pack information, see
  http://www.microsoft.com/windows.

- TCP/IP transport protocol installed and properly configured.

SEE ALSO

➤ *See Chapter 8, "Networking Fundamentals" for more information on TCP/IP.*

For most purposes, I recommend the Standard installation. If you know that there are pieces that you definitely will or won't need, run the Custom configuration. If hard disk space is tight, and you plan on serving simple Web pages only, the Minimum configuration is for you. Figure 10.2 shows the Select Components dialog box for a Custom installation.

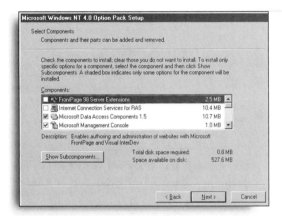

FIGURE 10.2.

Here's where you choose which components of the Option Pack you want to install. I suggest sticking with the standard configuration.

Looking at the subcomponents of Personal Web Server, you will see some additional documentation and samples that you might want to install if you are new to Web publishing. Also, if you want to install the FTP Server, you will have to enable it here; it is not installed by default (see Figure 10.3).

After Setup finishes, you will have just a bit of very basic configuration to do. You will be asked for the folders that will contain the files you want to publish, and the location of the program files that make up the servers. The defaults are fine under most circumstances.

When it's all done, you need to reboot.

FIGURE 10.3.

Subcomponents for Personal Web Server. The documentation and samples will be useful if you're new to this whole Web thing.

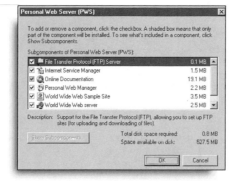

Personal Web Manager

When your computer comes back up, you will notice a new icon in your system tray—by the clock in the left corner of your taskbar. That icon brings up the Personal Web Manager.

Setup also installed a shortcut in Start, Programs, Windows NT 4 Option Pack, Personal Web Server. The shortcuts in the Option Pack folder vary, depending on which options you selected to install.

You can administer your PWS site in several ways. You can use the Personal Web Manager, which is a collection of wizards packaged in a very easy-to-use format. You can also use the Internet Service Manager, which is a plug-in for the new Microsoft Management Console (MMC). Both tools install by default with the Option Pack.

The Personal Web Manager interface is very easy to use and can take you through the basics of publishing and maintaining a very simple Web site—all without writing a bit of HTML code. A bit later in this chapter, you will use the Home Page Wizard to create a functional and appealing home page without writing any code.

The serious configuration you will want the Internet Service Manager for is beyond the scope of this text. We will look at the Personal Web Manager in detail, but for use of the Internet Service Manager MMC plug-in, you need to refer to a book on IIS 4.

Take the Tour!

I highly recommend taking the tour provided with PWS. From the Personal Web Manager, just click on the Tour icon, which is located near the bottom of the left column. It contains very useful information about your Personal Web Server, and the Web and Internet in general. Check it out!

A Book Is a Book

Personal Web Server is so similar to IIS 4.0 that a book on IIS 4.0 would be a great reference. (For example, see *Using Microsoft Internet Information Server 4, Special Edition*, Que Publishing, ISBN 0-7897-1263-6.) Just keep in mind the few differences previously mentioned and you will be fine.

If I've given you enough of a taste that you're considering running a serious Web site, you'll definitely want to grab a book or two dedicated to the discussion of Web publishing, and IIS in particular.

Go ahead and fire up the Personal Web Manager either by double-clicking on the Tray icon, or from the Start menu. Figure 10.4 shows the Personal Web Manager.

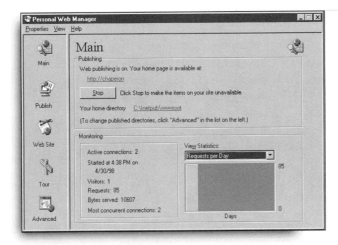

FIGURE 10.4.

The Personal Web Manager is a very user-friendly program comprised of several wizards that guide you through common administrative tasks.

Here you can see all the pertinent information about your Web server—the URL used to access your Web server, the root folder of your Web, and some cool statistics.

The root folder is the folder on your local hard drive that the Web server defaults to when no additional path information is specified in the URL. During the installation procedure, you were asked for this root folder. If you accepted the default, as I did, your root is also c:\Inetpub\wwwroot. What this means is that when I use the URL `http://chaperon`, the Web server changes to c:\Inetpub\wwwroot and looks for a default document.

Of course, a Web site can't be confined to publishing documents in a single folder alone. Later, this chapter discusses some ways to map other folders on your hard drive to URLs so that they may be accessed over the Web.

Administrators Take Note

MMC can host any number of plug-in modules to administer anything from a Web server to a coffee pot. Look for familiar favorites such as Event Viewer and User Manager to become MMC plug-ins in the future, because MMC will become the primary administration and configuration tool with the release of Windows NT 5.0. Even the Control Panel will likely get an overhaul. Therefore you might want to poke around in MMC a bit and get a feel for how it works; you will likely be spending a lot of time there in the future.

Publishing Content to the Web

Before you can use the Publishing Wizard, you need to run the Home Page Wizard first.

Making a home page

1. Open the Personal Web Manager and click Publish. You will be told that you need to run the Home Page Wizard first. Go ahead and click the Home Page Wizard button to run the wizard.

2. The Home Page Wizard starts, as shown in Figure 10.5. Click the >> button to proceed.

FIGURE 10.5.

The Home Page Wizard takes you through the process of creating your home page step-by-step.

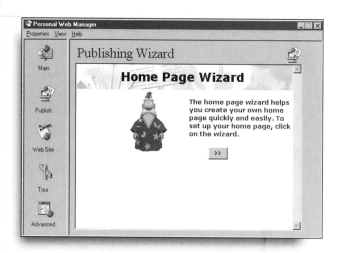

3. Now you need to choose the general template or style for your home page. In Figure 10.6, I have chosen the Gunmetal template. Click the >> button.

4. Next, you need to decide whether you want to include a guest book or not. A guest book enables people to leave their name, location, and other basic information. If you will be publishing your content on an office intranet only, it doesn't make much sense to have a guest book. If you're publishing to the whole Internet, however, it's always cool to

see who has accessed your site! In Figure 10.7, I have chosen to enable the guest book. Note the Theme link. As we progress through the wizard, you can jump back to any step just by clicking the link. Click >> to continue.

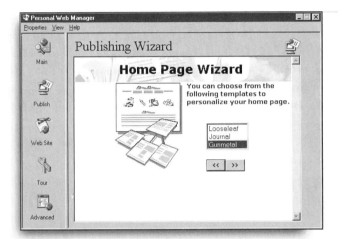

FIGURE 10.6.

A template determines the general look and feel of your home page. You can come back here and change the template later if you don't like it.

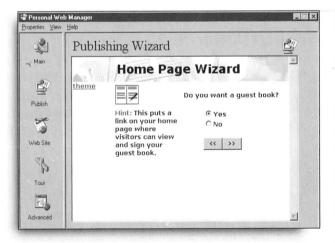

FIGURE 10.7.

Enabling this option enables your users to view and sign an electronic guest book.

5. You are asked whether you want a drop box. A drop box is a place where your users can leave you messages. Again, not very useful in an office setting, but you will probably want to enable this if you're publishing to the Internet; your visitors might want to drop you a line for many reasons. Click >>.

6. Great! You will get a confirmation like that shown in Figure 10.8. You are almost finished. Now it's time to enter some information about yourself!

FIGURE 10.8.

The wizard offers some encouragement along the way!

7. Now, the wizard fires up Internet Explorer. It's time to put some content on the Web! You will see a Web page like that shown in Figure 10.9.

FIGURE 10.9.

Adding content to your home page is done through a Web form itself!

8. Go through the form and enter the information that you want to publish. Notice that each field prompt is a link: Clicking it will produce a description of what is expected in the field. I have filled out the form in Figure 10.10. Note that I left out phone numbers and other information that I don't want on the Web.

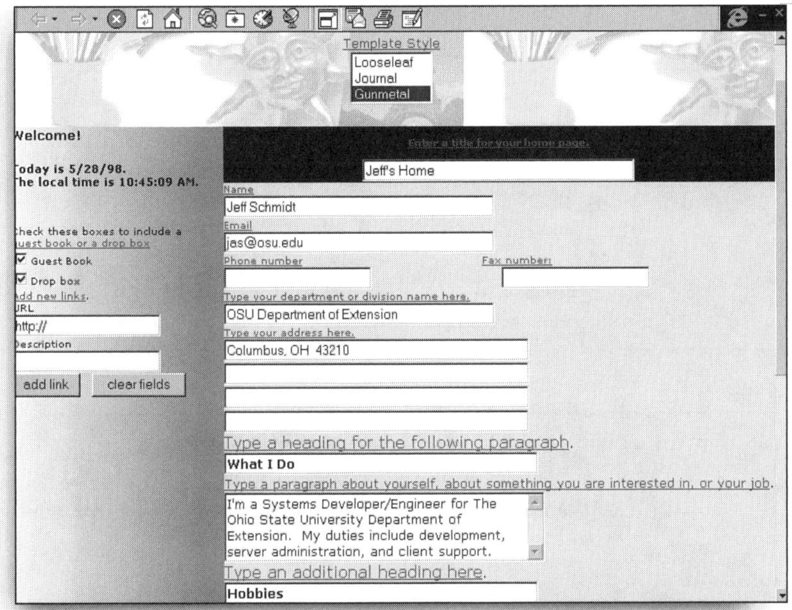

FIGURE 10.10.

The Home Page Wizard puts all this information into a visually appealing home page that will be available on the Web!

9. On the left, you can add some links to other pages. You might want to include links to your employer's main home page, your departmental page, friends, family, and so on. Just enter the URL, a short description, and click Add Link. Your list of links will then appear as in Figure 10.11.

10. When you are satisfied with the content, click the Enter New Changes button at the bottom of the form. You will then be sent to your brand-new home page! Figure 10.12 shows the one I designed here.

Oops

Check your typing carefully for spelling errors and typos; nothing is more embarrassing than publishing content to millions of users with a goof! Trust me, I've done it! As a tip: To make it easier to check large blocks of text, cut and paste them into Word and run the spell check before you publish.

FrontPage and other Web site makers such as PageMill have built-in spell checkers.

FIGURE 10.11.

You can add several links to your home page. Here, I have a link to a company's main home page and to a department within that home page.

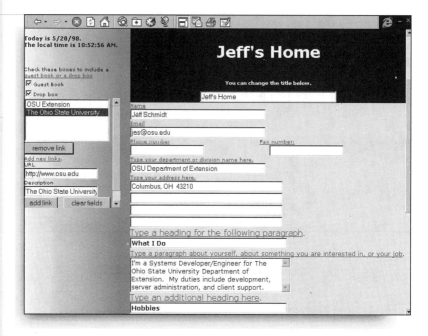

FIGURE 10.12.

My brand new home page! Wasn't that easy?

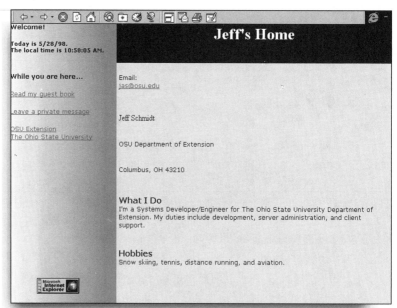

Adjusting and Maintaining Your Home Page

So, you want to make a change to the home page you just slaved over, eh? Don't worry, it is easy with the Personal Web Server wizards! Remember the form where you provided all of your personal information and additional links (Figures 10.10 and 10.11)? Well, you can get back to that form any time you want to make changes.

From the Personal Web Manager, click the Web Site icon in the left column. A screen similar to that shown in Figure 10.13 appears.

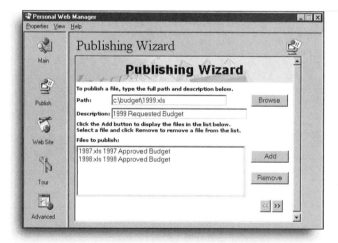

Here, you can query your guest book, view the messages left in your drop box, and, of course, make content changes to your home page. Clicking the Edit Home Page button takes you back to the form you filled out in Figures 10.10 and 10.11.

Publishing Additional Content

So, let's get some "real" content out on the Web. With the Publishing Wizard, this is easy to do.

Publishing documents to the Web

1. Open the Personal Web Manager and click the Publish icon. Note that a default installation of the Windows NT 4.0

Option Pack placed a shortcut on the desktop that will take you to this wizard as well.

2. Here, all you need to do is enter pathnames and descriptions of the files that you want to publish. Click the Browse button to look around your file trees for the content you want to publish. In Figure 10.14, I'm using the file/directory browser control to add another file. This browser operates just like the one you would expcct to find when opening a file in Word or Excel.

FIGURE 10.14.

If you are like most people and can't remember long pathnames, don't fret. You can browse as usual. Note that this browser is actually a control on the Web page, but it acts the same as any other file/directory browser.

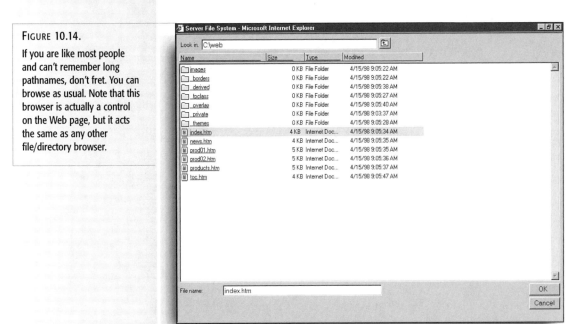

3. After you have added all the files and descriptions, click >>. A confirmation appears, like that shown in Figure 10.15. If you get an error here, click the << button and make the necessary changes. Usually the error will be a result of the requested file not existing.

4. Click >> to complete the task. A new dialog box appears, like the one shown in Figure 10.16.

FIGURE **10.15.**

The wizard will let you know that your pages have been published successfully.

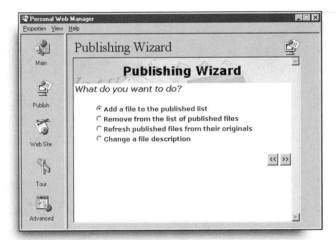

FIGURE **10.16.**

The Publishing Wizard starting point. From here you can add, remove, and modify your published documents.

Now if you point your Web browser at your local computer, you will see your home page with a new link called "view my published documents" in the left column, as shown in Figure 10.17.

If you click that link, you see a page similar to Figure 10.18. Here are the three Excel budgets that I just published.

FIGURE 10.17.

My home page now contains a link to my published documents.

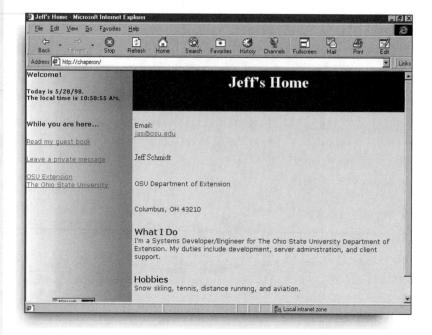

FIGURE 10.18.

The pages I have published.

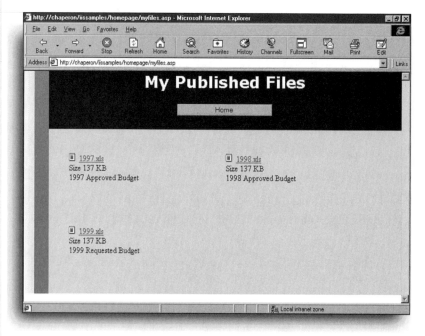

Removing Content

Now you have decided that you don't want the whole world to see your 1999 proposed budget. Removing a page is just as easy.

Removing a previously published page

1. Fire up Personal Web Manager and click Publish. This brings up the Publishing Wizard. After a click of the >> button, you will see the familiar dialog box shown in Figure 10.16.

2. Select Remove from the List of Published Files, and click >>.

3. A dialog box similar to Figure 10.19 appears, containing all the files you have published. These are the three budget files we added earlier.

4. Just highlight the page or pages you wish to remove. In Figure 10.20, I am removing the 1999 budget requests workbook. When you finish, click >>.

5. If the page was removed successfully, the usual congratulations and confirmation appear, like the one shown in Figure 10.21.

Yeah, Now What?

If the guest viewing this page has Excel installed on his or her computer and is browsing using Microsoft Internet Explorer (IE), clicking any of these *.xls files will automatically fire up a session of Excel within IE. If the guest doesn't have Excel and IE (or a program registered to read .xls files), the guest will see a dialog box asking what to do with the file. The guest will have the option to save it or specify a program to use to open it.

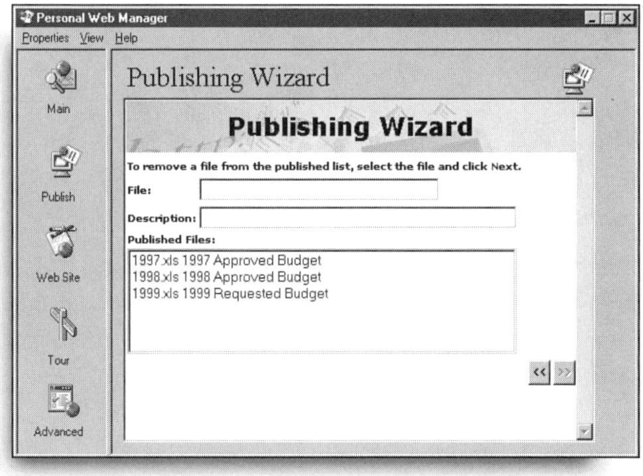

FIGURE 10.19.

Removing documents from publication is even easier than publishing them!

FIGURE 10.20.

I'm removing my 1999 budget requests from the Web. After careful thought, I have decided that the world doesn't need to know how much I spend.

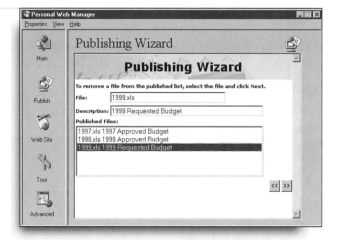

FIGURE 10.20.

I'm removing my 1999 budget requests from the Web. After careful thought, I have decided that the world doesn't need to know how much I spend.

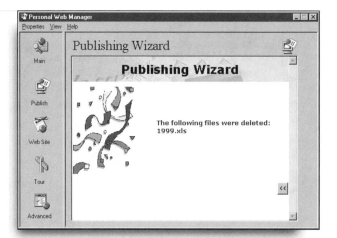

FIGURE 10.21.

The wizard again congratulates you on a job well done!

The Main Icon and Usage Statistics

Now that you have some content out there, let's again take a look at the "main" area of the Personal Web Manager shown in Figure 10.4.

The top half gives you some information about your URL and root directory. These are actually links that will bring up your Web browser and Windows Explorer, respectively. You also have a button that gives you the opportunity to start and stop the server, depending on its current state.

The bottom half gives you some access statistics for your Web server as a whole. If you pull down the View Statistics menu, you will see the several different bar charts that are available. The chart you select appears immediately beneath the pull-down menu.

To the left of the bar chart, you will also see some usage numbers.

These numbers represent global statistics tallied since the last time the server was started. The statistics are as follows:

- *Active Connections*. The number of connections currently in use and transferring data.
- *Started at*. The date and time the server was last started.
- *Visitors*. The number of unique addresses that have connected to the server since the server was last started.
- *Requests*. The total number of requests (hits) that have been received since the server was last started.
- *Bytes Served*. The total amount of data that has been sent by the server to all clients since the server was last started.
- *Most Concurrent Connections*. The maximum number of connections opened to the server simultaneously—again , since the last server restart.

The Advanced Icon

In the Advanced Options dialog box, you can manage virtual directories, default documents, security permissions, and logging.

Virtual Directories

To publish from any directory not contained within your root directory, you need to create a *virtual directory*. A virtual directory is a directory not physically contained in the root directory, but one that appears to client browsers as though it were.

A virtual directory has an *alias*, a name that your guests will use to access that folder. Because an alias is usually shorter than the pathname of the directory, it is more convenient for users to

More About Visitors

If the same person visits the site more than once, subsequent visits are not counted. Only 50 addresses are stored for comparison. Repeat visitors might be counted again if more than 50 unique addresses have been added to the list since their last visits. This shouldn't be an issue with the type of low-traffic Web site you should be hosting with Personal Web Server.

What's a "Request"?

Each time a guest's browser asks for a file, that is called a *request*. This is synonymous with the term *hit*, which is also used frequently. Keep in mind that a page with three graphics on it will count as four requests or hits: one for the HTML page, and three for the graphics.

type. An alias is also more secure. Users do not know where your files are physically located on your hard drive and cannot use that information to potentially mount an attack. Aliases also make it easier for you to move folders in your site. Instead of changing the URL for the page, you change the mapping between the alias and the physical location of the page. You can move files and folders around on your local hard drive all you want; as long as you keep the aliases pointing to the right places, your visitors will never know the difference.

In other words, all we are doing is taking an URL such as `http://myworkstation/alias` and mapping it to a location on your hard drive outside of the root folder.

Here, we create a virtual directory that will map the URL `http://chaperon/Salary` to c:\SalaryProject.

Creating a virtual directory

1. Start the Personal Web Manager and click the Advanced icon. The Advanced Options screen appears, as in Figure 10.22. You may already have a good number of virtual directories, as I do here, depending on the components you selected to install. These directories contain documentation and samples.

FIGURE 10.22.

In the Advanced Options screen, you can do some additional configuration that isn't possible through the wizards.

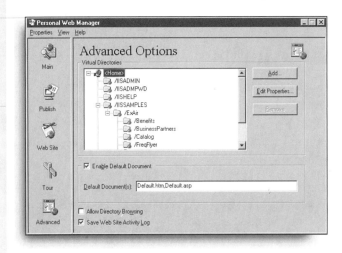

2. Because this will be an alias from the root, highlight the top level of the tree (<home>) and click Add. The dialog box shown in Figure 10.23 appears.

FIGURE 10.23.

You need to know the name of your email account (where people send you mail) for this section of the wizard.

3. Enter the local directory and alias as I have done. You can also assign permissions defining what kind of access you will allow through this share and operate independently of NTFS permissions. See the section titled "Security" later in this chapter. Click OK.

4. You will now see that your new virtual directory is listed in the tree, as in Figure 10.24.

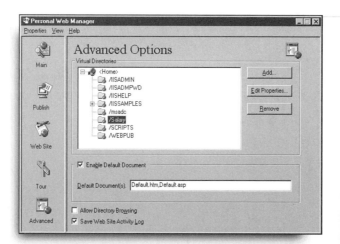

FIGURE 10.24.

The new virtual directory Salary is in place. A client can use the URL http://chaperon/salary to access this directory.

The properties for any of the virtual directories just consist of the local pathname, alias, and permissions, just as you saw in Figure 10.23. You can display a virtual directory's properties by double-clicking the directory or by highlighting the directory and clicking Edit Properties.

Removing a virtual directory is also very straightforward. Just highlight the directory and click Remove. You will be asked to confirm.

You're Not Actually Deleting Anything

Don't forget these are just aliases that map URLs to locations on your hard drive—not unlike shortcuts that map a representative icon to the actual file somewhere else. When you delete an alias, you don't delete any content files; just like when you delete a shortcut (*.lnk file), you don't delete the file it points to.

Publishing Content Using Windows NT Explorer

Now that you know all about virtual directories, we can talk about yet another method of making pages available to users on the Web. The Windows NT Explorer provides an interface for you to quickly and easily create virtual directories, without ever having to bring up the Personal Web Manager.

Using Windows NT Explorer to create virtual directories

1. Open Explorer and navigate to the folder you wish to publish. In Figure 10.25, I'm using the same c:\SalaryProject folder I used in the preceding example.

FIGURE 10.25.

Select the local folder that you want to make available to the Web.

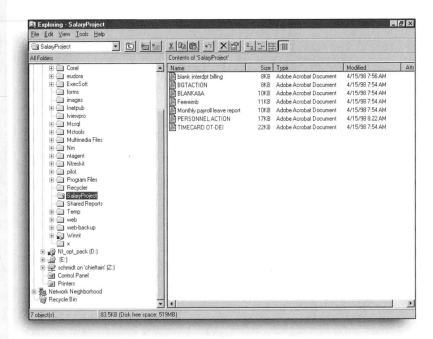

2. Highlight the folder by clicking it. Right-click and select Properties from the context menu. Click the Web Sharing tab, as shown in Figure 10.26.

3. Selecting Share This Folder automatically brings up the familiar dialog box you saw in Figure 10.23. I will shorten the alias to "salary," as I did in the preceding example. I will leave the permissions alone for now. Click OK and you will

see Figure 10.27, confirming that we added the virtual directory.

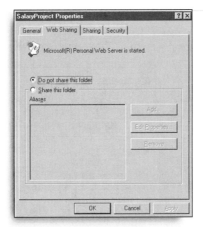

FIGURE 10.26.

Explorer provides a vehicle to create virtual directories.

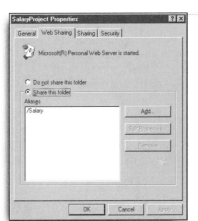

FIGURE 10.27.

The virtual directory has been added. Just as with the preceding technique, a client can use the URL `http://chaperon/salary` to access this directory.

4. Click OK to return to Explorer.

That was easy, wasn't it? Editing the properties of an existing virtual directory and deleting a virtual directory are just as straightforward.

Security

Remember from the discussions in Chapter 12, "Managing Users—NT Security," and Chapter 13, "Sharing Resources," that no one gains access to a Windows NT computer unless he or she is logged on to an account. Well, users browsing our Web pages are, of course, no exception. They must be logged on under some account.

Go ahead and fire up User Manager. If you have installed the Option Pack, you will notice two new accounts:

- *IUSR_machinename*. This is the account that anonymous Web users are mapped to. When a guest connects to your Web server, Windows NT logs him on under this account. This is a very important account, because the permissions that it has are given out for free to any anonymous user who comes along and browses your Web pages.

- *IWAM_machinename*. A special account used by the Web Application Manager.

When a user requests a Web page from your Web server, here's what happens:

1. The desired access is checked against any restrictions placed on the virtual directory in which the requested file sits. If the virtual directory doesn't allow the requested access type, the client is not served the page. I will talk about these permissions next.

2. The server *impersonates* the IUSR_machinename account. That is, the Web server takes on the account properties of the IUSR account, including the most important characteristic: security access permissions.

3. The server, operating under this new security context, tries to access the page as requested. If the NTFS file and folder permissions allow the request, it succeeds and the Web server serves the file. If the IUSR account doesn't have permission to access the file, the server prompts the user for a username and password and attempts to log the user on

using a local account. If a satisfactory account is found, the request suicides. If no satisfactory account exists, the request will fail.

The IUSR account, by default, has only guest access to your Windows NT system. You want to be sure that it stays that way.

Remember to give the IUSR account access to all your content folders. Perhaps the most common problem when setting up a Web server is forgetting that your common, anonymous users will be assigned the IUSR account during the time they are on your system. Therefore anything you want them to be able to do, you need to allow IUSR permission to.

Restrictions on Virtual Directories

In addition to NTFS permissions, you can also enforce restrictions based on the virtual directory that the resource is being accessed through. Like file shares, the actual working set of permissions will be the union (most restrictive) of the two sets.

Technically the home (root) directory is a virtual directory that maps to the null alias. In Personal Web Manager, under Advanced, look at the properties for the <home> entry. You can assign permissions just as you would for any other virtual directory. Therefore every page you serve is being accessed through a virtual directory, and is thus securable.

Take a look at the permissions and what they mean:

- *Read.* The read permission enables Web clients to read or download files stored in the virtual directory. If a client sends a request for a file that is in a directory without read permission, the Web server returns an error message. Generally, you should give directories containing information to publish (HTML files, for example) read permission. You should disable read permission for directories containing common gateway interface (CGI) programs and other executable code to prevent clients from downloading the files.

NTFS = Two-Step Process

Hopefully you are working on an NTFS volume where security is possible. Security is good, but you need to remember there is slightly more administration required. When you create each and every new virtual directory, for example, you will likely need to add permission to the IUSR account to read the folder on the NTFS volume. Without read (or better) permission, your users won't have access to the content.

- *Execute*. The execute permission enables any application to run in this directory, including script engines and Windows NT binaries (.dll and .exe files). For security reasons, do not give standard-content (HTML) folders execute permission.

- *Scripts*. The scripts permission enables a script engine to run in this directory without having the more dangerous execute permission set. Use script permission for directories that contain ASP scripts, Internet Database Connector (IDC) scripts, or other scripts. Scripts permission is safer than the execute permission and should be used whenever possible.

Installing and Configuring Internet Explorer 4 or Netscape Communicator 4

Service Problems

Choosing a Communications System

Dual Communication System Installations

Profiles and You

Installing Communicator

Installing Internet Explorer

Using Communicator

A Guide to Newsgroups

282

PART III

CHAPTER 11

Networking with Windows NT Workstation 4

**Installing and Configuring Internet Explorer 4 or
Netscape Communicator 4**

As odd as it sounds now, when Windows NT Workstation 4 was introduced it came with Internet Explorer version 2. This browser seems antediluvian by today's standards. Anybody but the most casual user of the Internet will want to upgrade to a modern set of Internet and intranet communication tools. This is especially true today, because the modern communication suites such as Internet Explorer 4 (and up) as well as Netscape's Communicator 4 are free, aside from connect time or media cost. This chapter covers the installation and configuration of these two dominant communication suites.

Choosing a Communications Suite

Computer-oriented magazines have knocked themselves out (and will continue to do so) trying to pick a winner between these two suites. They laboriously review features lists and compatibility between arbitrarily shifting standards in their quest for the superior suite. You may wish to choose a product based on these evaluations.

The truth of the matter is that these are equivalent products. If you remember the *Mad* magazine competition of "Spy vs. Spy," you have a good idea of what Netscape and Microsoft are locked into. As soon as one implements a good idea, the other incorporates it into its product. There are slight differences in bias and operational intent, however. People tend to like one over the other not because of some feature list, but because they enjoy the way a much used operation works. Additionally, Internet Explorer, unsurprisingly, integrates itself into (actually replaces) the Windows NT shell or user interface. You might regard that as a feature or a bug, depending on your point of view.

Pick Your Favorite

Netscape fans accuse Microsoft of being a copycat. Microsoft fans accuse Netscape of being an intruder. Choose your side and join in the fun where passions run higher than for a World Cup or a Super Bowl.

You should look at your situation before deciding. If you use the office suite Corel WordPerfect, Communicator integrates right into it through CorelCENTRAL. That's a plus. Some people also hold political views that make them happy using non-Microsoft products under a Microsoft operating system. Again, Communicator, from Microsoft's archrival (one of them, anyway), rises to the fore.

Some people are crazy over the integration of Internet Explorer and its Active Desktop into the Windows NT shell. Some others reason that because both Windows NT and Internet Explorer (IE) come from Microsoft, IE will be more reliable than other browsers. Although not proven, this does stand to reason. In actual field use with hundreds of clients and anecdotal evidence from thousands more, I have not seen a difference in reliability.

If you have the time and an engineer-type mind, why not try them both? Don't do this at the same time unless you are an adventurous engineer. I have actually wrestled them both on to the same machine, but consider myself somewhat lucky to have succeeded at this. Anyway, having the two fighting on the same Windows NT workstation isn't a fair test. If one fails in reliability, is it due to the other's existence or is it a real-world failure?

Give each a week. That's long enough, assuming you log on at least once a day, to see which one works the way you wish to work and to uncover any showstopper reliability issues on your specific machine.

The balance of this chapter goes over the initial installation and setup of Communicator from a CD-ROM and Internet Explorer from a downloaded file. Because this is a book about Windows NT Workstation, the chapter hits only the highlights of installation and configuration of these programs. It does not attempt to be comprehensive. To do so would take up the entire book.

Install Both?

A true "engineer mind" will surely be fatally attracted to installing both to see what blows up first. Why do you think I did it? Great fun, but make sure you have that backup and ERD before playing this game. (For more information on backup and ERDs, see Chapter 16, "Disaster Prevention," and Chapter 17, "When Problems Strike.")

Installing Communicator from a CD

Before installing any major program, be sure to back up your system. At the very least, make a new ERD. You can find instructions for doing this in Chapter 16, "Disaster Prevention," in the section titled "Making and Maintaining ERDs." Never rely on any program's uninstall routine to restore your system to its pre-setup state.

SEE ALSO

➤ *For more information on ERDs, see the section titled "Making and Maintaining ERDs," in Chapter 16, "Disaster Prevention."*

**Installing and Configuring Internet Explorer 4 or
Netscape Communicator 4**

Netscape and its strategic partners distribute Communicator in many different media. This example uses the setup of Corel's WordPerfect Office Suite Professional, version 8. Communicator is part of the setup for CorelCENTRAL in this suite.

Figure 11.1 shows the screen from a Custom option setup. If you run a Typical or Standard setup, you will end up with Communicator installed. As the Custom setup is more complex and more flexible, I will use it here to show you how to pick and choose among the suite's components.

FIGURE 11.1.

In the Custom Installation dialog box, you can choose which components, and which elements of each component, you wish to install.

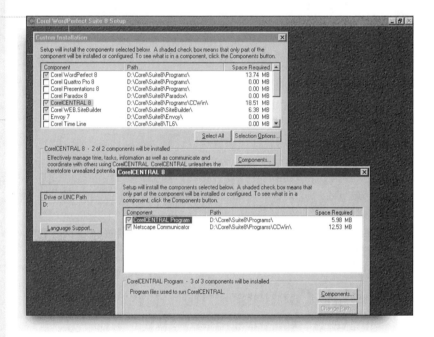

To get to this screen, run WordPerfect Office Suite Professional's Setup program, choosing the Custom option. Enter the information about username and serial number when requested. The meat of this Setup program is the Component Options dialog box shown in Figure 11.1. To see the screen like Figure 11.1, highlight (click) the CorelCENTRAL choice in the main dialog box and then click on the Components button (just peeking out at the top of the CorelCENTRAL 8 dialog box). This example accepts Corel's defaults for Communicator's setup. This installs all of Communicator, but not Netscape

Conferencing. If you wish to install that element, click the Components button in the CorelCENTRAL 8 dialog box and check its check box.

After choosing which elements of WordPerfect Office Suite you wish to install, click the Next button to start the copying and registration processes. Confirm that you really want to go ahead in the next dialog box and then sit back and wait. If nothing goes awry, you will be rewarded with the success dialog box shown in Figure 11.2. Exit the setup routine. You are now ready to configure Communicator.

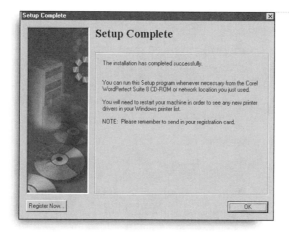

FIGURE 11.2.
The success dialog box positively tells you that the programs are installed and ready for use.

Starting Up

Setup will install all of Corel's suite in the main folder of Start-All Users rather than under Programs as is conventional. To start Communicator from this Setup routine, choose Start|Corel WordPerfect Suite 8|Netscape Communicator, as shown in Figure 11.3.

The initial startup of Communicator demands that you create at least one profile. A profile for Communicator works similarly to a profile for Windows NT itself. For more information about how NT does this, see Chapter 12, "Managing Users—NT Security."

SEE ALSO

➤ For more information about creating profiles, see Chapter 12, "Managing Users—NT Security."

FIGURE 11.3.

Corel's Setup deposits the shortcuts to its Office Suite in Start|All Users. If you installed Communicator using a different setup routine, your results might vary from the example.

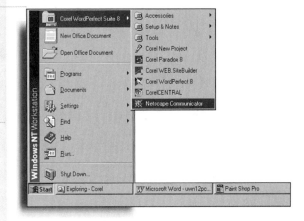

You will also need some way to connect to the Internet or an intranet (or extranet or some sort of net). For most users off a company LAN, this means a dial-up connection. For more information on this, see Chapter 9, "Using Dial-Up Networking (DUN)/Remote Access Service (RAS)."

SEE ALSO

➤ *For more information on dial-up connections, see Chapter 9, "Using Dial-Up Networking (DUN)/Remote Access Service (RAS)"*

With those asides put aside, it is time to return to Communicator. Figure 11.4 shows the initial startup screen for a Communicator installation with no profiles.

FIGURE 11.4.

You need to create at least one profile before using Communicator. This expert-style dialog box starts the process.

Click Next to start the configuration process. Here is the information you need to enter using the next series of dialog boxes.

- Your username (handle or real name).
- Your email address (yourname@yourserver.com).
- Your server's address for sending email. You will sometimes see this as your server's SMTP (Simple Mail Transport Protocol) identity.
- Your server's address for receiving email and the protocol it uses.
- Your news server's address.

Now to start the actual process. Enter your real name (if you wish to reveal it to the denizens of the Internet) and your email address in the spaces given.

Click Next to get to a screen where you name this profile and its folder. After entering this information, as shown by example in Figure 11.5, click Next.

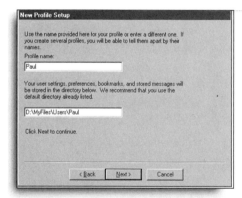

FIGURE 11.5.

Communicator needs a name and a folder location for each profile. Here's where you enter your choices for these options.

The next dialog box is a bit tricky; you need the first bit of technical information: your server's identity for sending email. If you're in doubt about this, consult with your Internet service provider (ISP) or your network administrator. You can skip this step and enter the information later, but you will need it sometime to send mail. This can be in the form of an address, such as

Pop.myisp.com

Privacy and Public Profiles

Some people like to use handles (a made up identity) to make a style statement or to protect their security while online. Others view such handles as the mark of a sniping coward afraid to face the consequences of his or her statements. Communicator, with its profiles, enables you to play it both ways. You can have a privacy profile and a public one.

or an IP (Internet Protocol) address such as

111.111.111.111

After entering this information, click Next to move onward.

You are again faced with needing technical information, this time your server's identity for you to receive mail. Like the preceding dialog box, you need to enter the information in an IP or an address. You also need to know what type of system your server uses when you pick up mail: POP or IMAP. Figure 11.6 shows this dialog box.

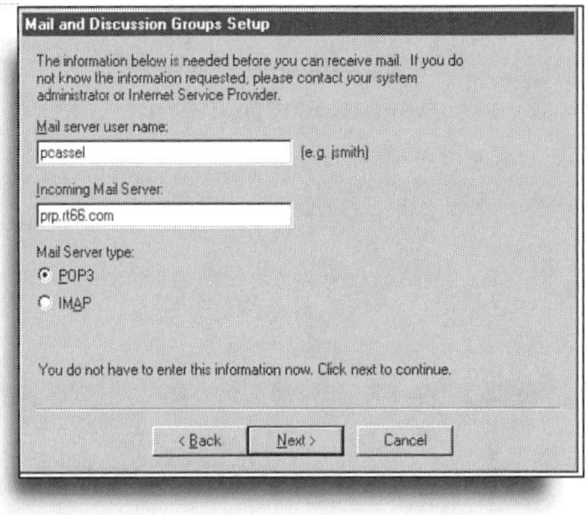

FIGURE 11.6.

You'll need to tell Communicator your server's identity to receive mail and also what kind of protocol it uses.

The final step is to tell Communicator your news server's address. Like in the other steps, if you're in doubt, seek the information from your ISP or network administrator.

You also need to change the port for your news server if it is not the default 119. This is very rare, and if so, your network administrator will let you know. (He had better if he wants a decent employee review!) If you use a secure news server, as in the case of some private company-only setups, check the Secure box. Again, your administrator will be his usual font of information regarding this topic.

Click Finish. Communicator's Navigator section checks to see whether it is the default browser. If not, it offers to make itself so. You can disable this check in the future. Unless you have reason not to, make Navigator your default browser. Figure 11.7 shows this check dialog box.

Give It Time

Items such as SMTP, POP3 and NNTP–along with their strange addresses–are not only baffling if you have never encountered them before, but they can be upsetting because of their newness. Just play along with the nonsense for awhile. As time goes by, you will watch the nonsensical items grow logical as your dweeb factor increases in step with your time on the Internet.

FIGURE 11.7.

Browsers are jealous over which one is the default. Here Navigator finds itself left out in the cold and asks to be let back in.

Finally, after all that, Communicator itself will start! It will try to log on to the Corel site on the World Wide Web (WWW). If you're not online, it will fail of course (and whine about it too). If you are online, and so is Corel, you will jump right to that site. If you have received Communicator from another source than Corel, you will either jump to a different site (such as Netscape) or to a blank page. Figure 11.8 shows Communicator offline after a failed attempt to reach the Corel site.

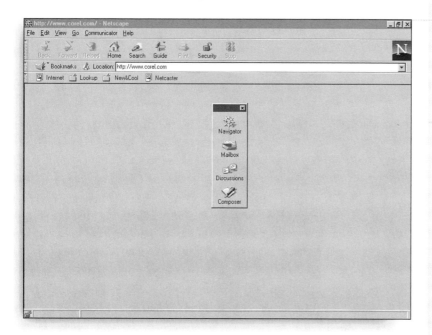

FIGURE 11.8.

The Navigator part of Communicator starts up trying to reach a predetermined Web site. In this case, the site is Corel Corporation.

The bar with the rectangle drawn around it in Figure 11.8 is the Component bar. This allows quick links to the various parts of Communicator. By default it floats over all applications (staying on top). This can be a distraction or actually impede the flow of your work. If you find that to be the case, right-click on its title bar and deselect Always on Top. You can get the Component bar back by choosing it from the Communicator menu.

Configuring

Communicator has an excellent centrally located configuration place. To see this, choose the menu selections Edit | Preferences from the main menu shown in Figure 11.8. Figure 11.9 shows the resulting dialog box.

FIGURE 11.9.

Communicator uses a hierarchical approach to user options rather than the more commonly found tabbed approach.

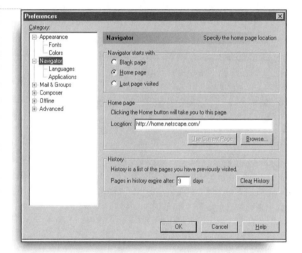

In the initial dialog box, you can change the initial startup site for the browser. This includes the option to start with a blank page—very useful if you use a modem and aren't always online, because it prevents the type of error message navigation you had to go through the first time you started Communicator.

In the dialog box shown in Figure 11.9, you can also enter the setup information you might have lacked when going through the initial expert-style setup discussed earlier in this chapter. You can also use these options to change settings if your server changes or changes its configuration. Here is a list of the hierarchy of the dialog box in Figure 11.9 and the major settings for each.

- *Appearance.* How Communicator formats its toolbar and what it launches on startup by default.

- *Appearance | Fonts.* The font set used by Communicator.

- *Appearance | Colors.* Colors for text, background (defaults), and links.

- *Navigator.* The startup page and settings for the history folder.

- *Navigator | Languages.* Add or remove language capacity from Communicator.

- *Navigator | Applications.* Add, edit, or remove helper applications necessary to display or manipulate certain Internet content such as multimedia or animation.

- *Mail&Groups.* Global settings for the display and handling of mail and newsgroup messages, including how to reply, whether to include the initial message in replies, and if to include a "reply" character.

- *Mail&Groups | Identity.* Your identity or alias online.

- *Mail&Groups | Messages.* Settings for outgoing messages.

- *Mail&Groups | Mail Server.* Settings for your outgoing and incoming mail server(s).

- *Mail&Groups | Groups Server.* Settings for your news server.

- *Mail&Groups | Directory.* A path-like search pattern for folders and sites making up a directory of addresses (similar to a sequential phonebook).

- *Composer.* Global settings for Composer, Netscape's Web publishing tool.

- *Composer | Publishing.* Specific information about your Web site such as its FTP and URL addresses.

- *Offline.* Options to work on- or offline.

- *Offline | Download.* Specific settings for downloading messages using your defined criteria.

- *Advanced.* Global settings for all of Communicator such as Java usage and cookie acceptance. A *cookie* is a file written by a server to your local computer so that the server can mark a place or identify your computer. Cookies worry some users, because they prefer the Web to remain passive. The technology behind a cookie can theoretically winkle out some information from your computer.

- *Advanced|Cache*. The space for the cache and the cache flush interval.

- *Advanced|Proxies*. Information about your proxy server if such exists. Your network administrator is the person to check with when it comes to proxy servers. If you dial up to an ISP, you don't need to fiddle with this dialog box.

- *Advanced|Disk Space*. How much total disk room you allow Communicator for messages.

That's a lot, but fortunately you don't need to visit any of these dialog boxes in most cases. The only adjustment most users like to make is the startup page from the Navigator dialog box shown in Figure 11.9.

Using Communicator

To follow along with the following sections on Communicator, make sure that you are online. Communicator is a full-fledged suite in itself. A comprehensive discussion of its features is clearly beyond the scope of this book. That's the bad news. The good news is that for most people, using Communicator is fairly obvious by inspection. The following sections deal with how to use the mail, newsgroup, and Web browser parts of Communicator. These are the parts used by 99% of users 98% of the time (percentages estimated, obviously).

Navigator or the Web Browser

Get online if necessary and launch the Communicator suite. If you have installed it identically to the book's example, it is in Start|Corel WordPerfect Suite 8|Netscape Communicator. The browser will launch giving you a screen similar to Figure 11.10. Note that the browser used in this example has been configured to open with a blank page loaded rather than a live Web site.

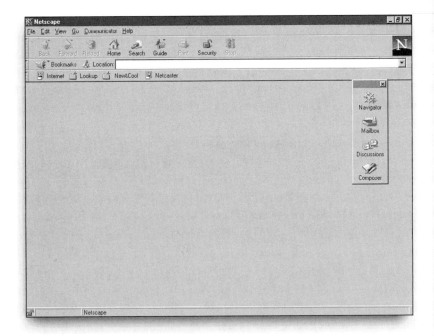

FIGURE 11.10.

After launch, Communicator is ready to do your bidding.

Several of the buttons in Communicator's toolbar take you to predetermined sites that change content on a regular basis. Choosing New&Cool and then What's Cool from the fly-out menu, for example, brings up a site with links and information the Netscape folks view as cool. They are, too. Figure 11.11 shows this site for one particular day. A visit on other days will bring up a similar, but different (content-wise) site. The URL (uniform resource locator) address for this site is

```
http://netscape.yahoo.com/guide/whats_cool.html
```

You can see this address shown in Figure 11.11.

If you wish to search the Web, click the Search button in the main toolbar right below and to the right of the Help entry on the main menu of the browser. Click any of the links to start the search engine of your choice.

If you know the URL of a site you wish to visit, you can enter it directly by choosing Ctrl+O (Control plus the letter *O*) and entering the URL directly. To jump to the MrShowBiz site, for example, press Ctrl+O and enter

```
www.mrshowbiz.com
```

A Short Guide for Nerds

I have seen dozens of beginner or intermediate users operate Communicator with nothing to guide them beyond following their noses and making logical guesses as to how something is done. Some book authors, present company excepted, worry about this. However, there is really no need for them to worry so. There are always the advanced users who need some guidance. It is for these advanced, nerd-like users that I have written this short guide to Communicator.

Explore Communicator

Communicator sports a fully modern user interface (UI). Explore it by right-clicking at any likely spot. The chances are if you suspect something works a particular way, it really does work that way.

294
PART **III**

CHAPTER **11**

Networking with Windows NT Workstation 4

**Installing and Configuring Internet Explorer 4 or
Netscape Communicator 4**

in the dialog box. The browser assumes the `http://` part of the address. Figure 11.12 shows the direct entering of an URL.

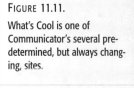

FIGURE 11.11.

What's Cool is one of Communicator's several pre-determined, but always changing, sites.

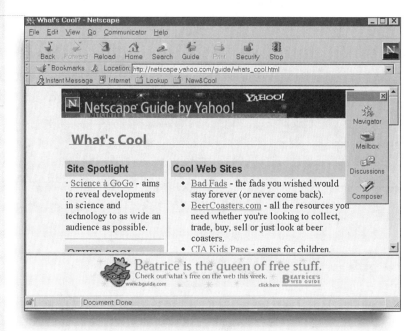

FIGURE 11.12.

If you know it, you can directly enter an URL for a page or file.

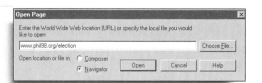

If you find a site along the Web you wish to visit again and again, you can "bookmark" it. To do this, visit the site, and then choose Bookmarks from the middle of the toolbar (middle by default). Communicator brings up a set of folders with predetermined bookmarks and enables you to add this site by choosing Add Bookmark from the fly-out menu.

After choosing Bookmarks, you can choose Add Bookmark to drop the URL on to the main Bookmarks menu, or you can File Bookmark to a folder. The Bookmarks menu fills up fast if you don't file your bookmarks in folders, so it's a good idea to do so.

Using Communicator

To visit a site (URL) already in the Bookmarks menu, choose Bookmarks and the folder (or URL) where it lives.

The two green arrow buttons on the far left of the main toolbar enable you to page forward and backward among pages visited this online session.

Communicator keeps a comprehensive history file of all sites visited. To see this list and to return to any site, open the history file by choosing the menu choice Communicator | History or by pressing Ctrl+H. Figure 11.13 shows such a history file.

Bookmarks May Vary

Your selection of predefined bookmarks can vary depending on your source for Communicator.

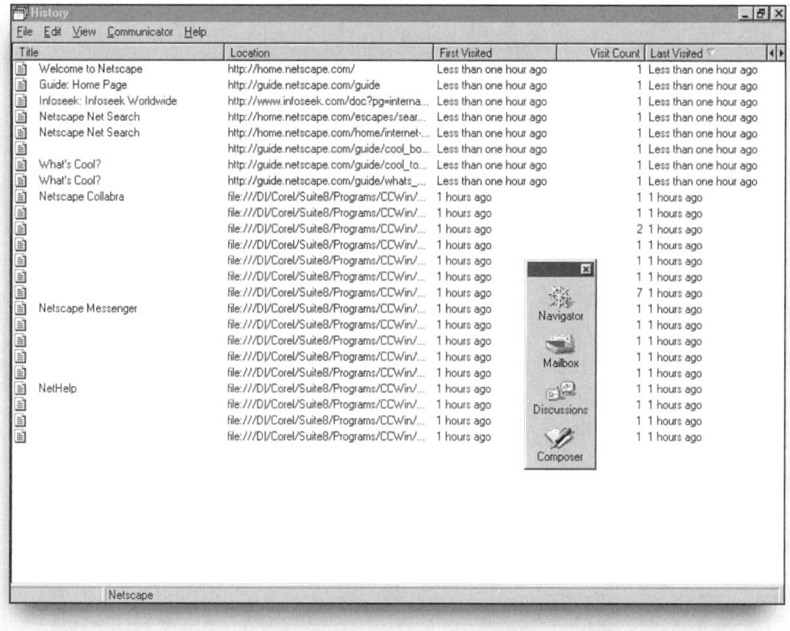

FIGURE 11.13.

Communicator watches what you do and records all of it.

You can return to any site by double-clicking on it in the History window. You can also rearrange the layout of the columns in the History window to suit your tastes.

No, that is not all there is to Navigator, but it's a start. Most people don't need more than direct URL entry, Bookmarks, and History to enjoy the Web in all its glory and variety. If you're ever curious to know how a site is put together, you can see the source code (the language) by right-clicking on the page and choosing View Source from the context menu. Try right-clicking elsewhere in Navigator to explore its capacities further.

The History Window

Your History window will vary from the example shown here, based on its layout and the places you have visited.

296

PART **III**

CHAPTER **11**

Networking with Windows NT Workstation 4

**Installing and Configuring Internet Explorer 4 or
Netscape Communicator 4**

This chapter promised only a taste, and a taste is what you have had; now it's time to move on to using newsgroups for a different taste.

Using Newsgroups

A newsgroup is a site for discussions. Such discussions are classified by newsgroup and by a thread (topical conversation) within a newsgroup. The newsgroup dedicated to Mercedes Benz automobiles, for example, is

`alt.auto.mercedes`

This example uses the Usenet, the most visited of the public newsgroups. Companies often maintain private (logon only) news servers for their employees and customers. In addition, some companies maintain private public-access news servers for their products. Microsoft, for example, maintains the `msnews.microsoft.com` server offering user-to-user information exchange (hopefully) about Microsoft-related topics.

To start Communicator's newsgroup utility, launch Communicator if necessary, and choose Discussions from the Component bar. Assuming you specified at least one news server during the initial configuration of Communicator, you will see that server (or servers) in the resulting dialog box. Figure 11.14 shows the Message Center brought up by clicking Discussions. Presently this computer has only one news server configured, `news.rt66.com`.

Before viewing any newsgroups, you need to download the list of all newsgroups from your server. Right-click on the news server you wish to access (in this example, `news.rt66.com`), and choose Subscribe to Discussion Groups from the context menu. The Message Center opens a new dialog box and downloads a list of all newsgroups. Figure 11.15 shows this dialog box after the download is complete.

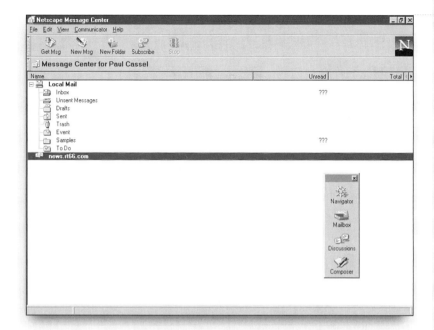

FIGURE 11.14.

Discussions is the Component bar entry you need to bring up the Message Center.

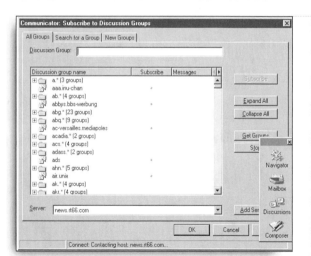

FIGURE 11.15.

You need to find out which newsgroups exist on a server before you can use any of them.

After you have downloaded the newsgroups, you can browse them using the dialog box shown in Figure 11.15. They are classified in a fairly straightforward hierarchical manner. If you wish to locate a newsgroup based on a keyword, you can by clicking on the Search for a Group tab and entering that keyword, and

Adding Additional News Servers

You can also add additional news servers from the dialog box shown in Figure 11.15. Note the Add Server button in the lower right.

then clicking the Search Now button. Figure 11.16 shows the results of searching on the keyword "Mercedes."

FIGURE 11.16.

The Usenet contains over 20,000 newsgroups. Browsing for any specific one can be tedious, so Communicator has keyword search capacity.

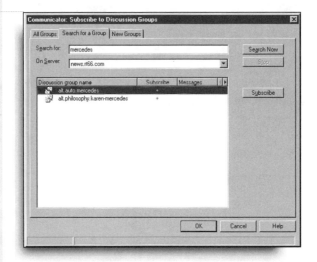

To subscribe to the newsgroup (add it to your list), highlight it and click the Subscribe button. This works the same in any of the three tabs of the dialog box shown in Figures 11.15 and 11.16. Figure 11.17 shows the highlighted group from Figure 11.16 after it's been subscribed to.

The numbers to the right of the newsgroup show the number of total messages that are posted and current on the newsgroup and how many you haven't read yet. To see these messages, right-click on the group you wish to see the messages in and choose Open Group from the context menu. This brings up a three-pane screen called, in this case, CorelCENTRAL. The top-left pane shows newsgroups and other Message Center folders. The upper-right pane shows the message headers (titles). The bottom pane shows the messages themselves.

If necessary, scroll down to the newsgroup you wish to view and click it to make it current. That brings up any message headers in the upper-right pane. Highlight a message header in the upper-right pane and the message body itself will appear in the bottom section. Figure 11.18 shows one message header highlighted in the upper-right pane with the actual message shown in the bottom pane.

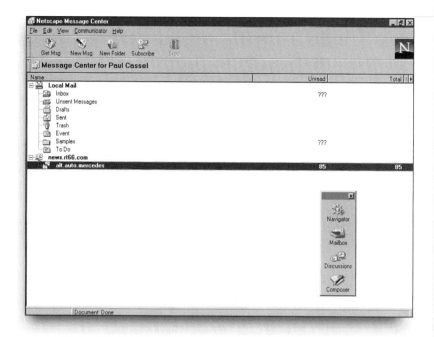

FIGURE 11.17.

Subscribed-to newsgroups appear under their news servers in the Message Center.

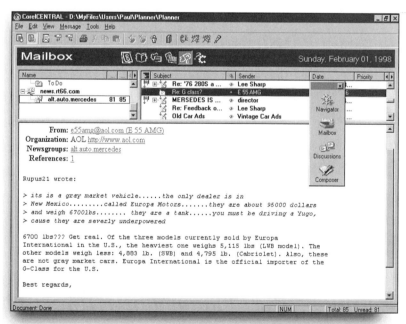

FIGURE 11.18.

The three-pane approach to newsgroup and email messages is fairly standard practice. CorelCENTRAL is no exception.

To reply (answer or comment on) to a message, highlight its header in the upper-right pane and choose the Reply button located in the toolbar. You have several options to reply privately (to sender), publicly (to group), or some combination thereof. You can also forward a message to a mail recipient by choosing that button.

If you wish to create a new message, click the New Msg button in the toolbar. That creates a new message; when you send it, it will be placed in the highlighted newsgroup.

That's a very fast and "lite" tour of newsgroups. Most of the rest is apparent by inspection. Other than a touch of security, email is almost identical in use to newsgroups, so let's move on to that.

Email

Email consists of private electronic communication. Most newsgroups are public, requiring no login. This isn't true of email, where the messages are directed specifically to you.

If necessary, get online and launch Communicator. Click the Mailbox choice in the Component bar. Communicator will prompt you for your password. Some ISPs call this your "interactive" password. Figure 11.19 shows this dialog box.

FIGURE 11.19.

Email is private and is therefore password protected.

Enter your password. Communicator will "echo" your password, using asterisks to prevent someone from snooping over your shoulder and learning your password. After a successful password entry, Communicator downloads your email. Figure 11.20 shows the Progress dialog box for email downloading.

Communicator will place any received mail in your Inbox, ready for your review and disposal. Figure 11.21 shows the Inbox with message headers in the upper-right pane and the message body in the lower pane.

FIGURE 11.20.

After you enter your password, Communicator will go out and fetch your mail.

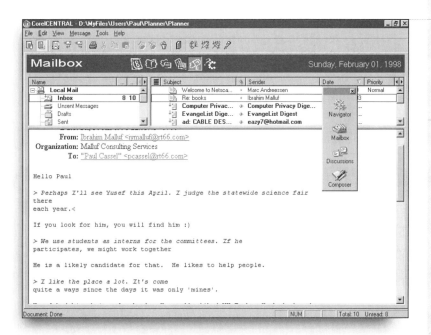

FIGURE 11.21.

You can read your mail by clicking its header or subject line. The message itself appears in the bottom pane of the screen.

You can treat email messages similarly to newsgroups in that you can reply or forward them as you see fit by clicking the appropriate button on the toolbar. You can also drag either class of message from the upper-right pane into the folders in the upper-left pane for later reference. Using the upper-left pane of CorelCENTRAL is similar to using the Windows Explorer. You can create or delete folders as you see fit.

You can also delete messages by clicking the Delete button on the toolbar or by pressing Del while the message header is highlighted.

To send a new message, follow these steps:

  1. Open the mailbox if necessary.

2. Click the New Message button in the toolbar or press Ctrl+M.

3. Enter the recipient's address in the space provided along with any cc: addresses. Figure 11.22 shows the pull-down To button, which allows these various entries.

4. Enter a subject in the space provided.

5. Enter the message in the space provided.

6. Click the Send button in the toolbar or press Ctrl+Enter. You can also file the message for later revising or send it later by choosing the appropriate entries from the File menu.

Figure 11.22 shows the Message Composition dialog box.

FIGURE 11.22.

Pull down the To button and you have the opportunity to enter the main recipient's and others' addresses for your new email.

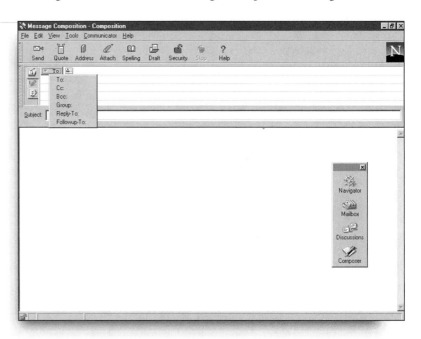

Conclusion for Communicator

This has been about the fastest tour of Communicator imaginable. As you might guess, many things have been left unsaid; but this should get you started using the program. People usually have no trouble using it. Here are the known troublespots for this program:

- Not knowing your server information or entering it incorrectly during the initial expert/wizard set of dialog boxes.

- Mixing up the server information—entering the DNS, for example, when you mean to enter the SMTP. I made that last sentence intentionally dense to demonstrate that it's awfully easy to get lost in the sea of acronyms. Proceed slowly and carefully until you're familiar with Internet and Internet-like jargon.

- Forgetting or incorrectly entering passwords.

- Trying to find a newsgroup by keyword in the All Groups tab rather than the Search for a Group tab.

- Clicking rather than double-clicking. If Communicator isn't responding, try giving it a double dose of clicks.

Jump In

Using the mail and discussion (newsgroup) sections of Communicator makes for a difficult read, but an easy set of operations. Remember, Netscape designed this application for beginners to start using without any instructions. The fact that it met its design goal is largely proven by the legions of users who are, well, communicating away with Communicator. Just jump in. If you get in any trouble or stuck anywhere, there is an excellent help system ready to bail you out. You probably won't need it.

Internet Explorer

If you think the section on Netscape Communicator was slam bang, wait until you see this one! This section covers only the installation and initial settings for Internet Explorer. There's a reason. Chapter 7, "Using Internet Explorer 4," goes over using the parts of Internet Explorer in reasonable depth,; therefore there's no sense in repeating that information here.

SEE ALSO

➤ *For more information on the parts of Internet Explorer and how to use them, see Chapter 7, "Using Internet Explorer 4."*

Microsoft has decided it should try and establish some sort of consistency between browsing the Internet and navigating on your desktop. You use a single mouse click to navigate between sites on the World Wide Web, for example, yet you have to double-click on your desktop folders. To address this whole "look-and-feel" issue, Microsoft developed a new way to interact with your Windows environment, called the Active Desktop.

The delivery vehicle for all these browsing and desktop enhancements is Microsoft Internet Explorer 4.0. This is Microsoft's latest and most feature-packed browser to date. The rest of this chapter outlines how you can take advantage of some of these features.

304

PART **III**

CHAPTER **11**

Networking with Windows NT Workstation 4

**Installing and Configuring Internet Explorer 4 or
Netscape Communicator 4**

Revealing the Internet Explorer Easter Egg

1. Start Internet Explorer.

2. Click Help | About Internet Explorer.

3. Hold down the Ctrl key and use your mouse to drag the Internet Explorer "e" icon from the top-right corner of the About Internet Explorer screen until it rests over the globe on the left-hand side.

4. Continue to hold down the Ctrl key and, using your mouse, drag the "e" icon to the text that says "Microsoft Internet Explorer 4.0," in the middle of the screen. You should see an Unlock button appear.

5. Click on the Unlock button. The globe should start to shake.

6. Hold down the Ctrl key and drag the "e" icon back over the globe.

What you see from the preceding exercise is called an *Easter Egg*. Easter Eggs are hidden programs or screens within major applications. Easter Eggs send messages or list credits for program development. The Internet Explorer 4 Easter Egg is of a credit screen type.

What's an Easter Egg?

Easter Eggs are hidden programs or screens within major applications.

Basic Configuration

You can access the browser-related configuration options for Internet Explorer 4.0 in two main ways:

1. If you already have Internet Explorer running, click View | Internet Options.

2. If Internet Explorer is not running, right-click the Internet Explorer icon on your desktop and select Properties.

Either of these methods brings up the Internet Options window shown in Figure 11.23.

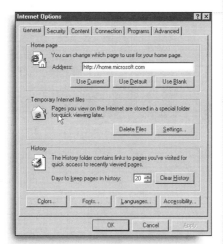

FIGURE 11.23.

The General tab of the Internet Options dialog box has the most often set properties for Internet Explorer.

Configuring Your Home Page, Temporary Files, and History Settings

In the screen associated with the General tab of Internet Options shown in Figure 11.23, you can modify some (appropriately enough) general aspects of Internet Explorer 4.0.

Your Home Page

To change the World Wide Web site that your browser connects to each time it starts up, you can modify the Home Page settings. You have a couple of options here:

- If you know the address of the site you want, just type it in the Address line. For example: `http://www.myFavouriteHomePageSite.com`. Note that you don't actually have to type the "`http://`" part, because Internet Explorer assumes this is what you mean by default. If you wish to use a file or any other non-HTTP item, you must specify the initial part.

- If you want to use the Web page currently open in your browser as your home page, click the Use Current button.

- If you want to use the Web page that was set by default when Internet Explorer was first installed, click the Use Default button. This is usually, but not always, `http://home.microsoft.com`.

306

PART **III**

CHAPTER **11**

Networking with Windows NT Workstation 4

Installing and Configuring Internet Explorer 4 or
Netscape Communicator 4

- If you prefer not to have your browser connect to a specific Web site when it starts up, click the Use Blank button.

Temporary Internet Files

To speed up your browsing experience, Internet Explorer saves a copy of Web pages you visit in a folder on your local hard disk. When you subsequently visit the same page, Internet Explorer can be configured to check whether it still has a local copy of the page. If so, it asks the Web site whether the page has been updated. If the page hasn't changed since you last visited, Internet Explorer displays the local copy; this is faster than retrieving it from the Web site. If the page has changed, Internet Explorer downloads the newer copy.

One thing to be wary of is that these locally stored files can use up a lot of space on your local hard drive. You can control the amount of space utilized as follows:

- To delete the locally stored copy of these Web pages (which is no big deal because the pages are available on the Web anyway), click the Delete Files button on the General Internet Options screen, shown in Figure 11.23.
- To modify settings for the temporary Internet files, click the Settings button. The screen shown in Figure 11.24 appears.

FIGURE 11.24.
This dialog box allows you to modify settings for temporary Internet files.

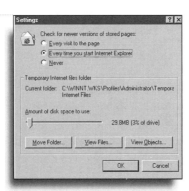

This is the place within the dialog box where you set options for temporary files. Note the slider control where you can set the amount of total space used by these files. This setting is often set too large by the Setup process.

Modifying temporary Internet file settings

1. To have Internet Explorer check for new versions of pages each time you visit a page—which means it effectively ignores the locally stored copy—click Every Visit to the Page. This option may slow down your navigation, but it should save you from having to hit the Refresh button in your browser to make sure the information displayed is current.

2. Click Every Time You Start Internet Explorer if you want Internet Explorer to check for a newer version of pages you previously visited. Contrary to what you might think, it doesn't check for newer versions of all the locally stored pages each time you start Internet Explorer. (This would take too long.) Instead, it checks for newer versions once during each session, wherein a session means the time from which you start Internet Explorer to the time you exit. If you visit the same Web page twice during a single session, you need to use the Refresh button to see whether the page has actually been changed.

3. Click Never if you always want Internet Explorer to use the locally stored copy of previously visited Web pages. Each time you revisit a Web site, you will have to use the Refresh button to make sure the information is current.

4. To change the amount of disk space used for temporary Internet files, use your mouse to drag the slider.

5. Click the Move Folder button and enter your preferred folder if you want to move your temporary Internet files to another location. You may want to do this if you're running out of space on your default drive and have a larger hard disk available.

6. To view the contents of the Temporary Internet Files folder, click View Files to see locally stored Web pages and graphic files, or click View Objects to see Java applets and ActiveX controls.

What About Changing My Default Search Page?

The Search button on the Internet Explorer toolbar enables you to create a list of your preferred search engines. You can also use the menu option Go|Search the Web to access a single predefined search engine. To change the default behavior of either of these options, you must resort to making changes to the Windows NT Registry as outlined on the Web at `http://support.microsoft.com/support/kb/articles/q171/8/53.asp`.

Configuring History Options

Internet Explorer maintains and organizes a list of every Web page you visit to provide you with quick access to previously viewed sites. Use the History button on the Internet Explorer toolbar to access this feature.

For your convenience, history information is sorted chronologically by day and further subdivided by Web sites visited and pages viewed on each site. Note that the history data stored on your hard disk only contains links to Web pages you visited, not the actual content. Regardless, this information can use up a considerable amount of disk space, so you may want to put some limits in place.

By default, 20 days of history is stored. To modify this, click View|Internet Options from the Internet Explorer menu. On the General tab, as shown in Figure 11.23, type a value in the Days to Keep in History box (or you can use your mouse on the spin buttons beside the number to increase or decrease the value). If you want to clear out your current history information to free up some disk space, click the Clear History button.

Configuring Your Connection to the Internet

There are two main ways to tell Internet Explorer how you connect to the Internet; both are available from the Internet Options|Connection screen, shown in Figure 11.25.

- The Internet Connection Wizard steps you through the various configuration options. Clicking the Connect button accesses this option.
- Change the options directly.

Modifying Your Proxy Server Configuration

A proxy server basically acts as an intermediary on your behalf when you access the Internet. Companies generally set up proxy servers for security reasons and to speed up access to the Internet. In circumstances where a proxy server is not used (for example, when you dial up to an Internet service provider), your browser connects directly to Web sites and retrieves the Web pages. In the case with a proxy server, your browser requests Web pages from the proxy server; the proxy server then retrieves the pages from the Internet on your behalf and returns the result back to your browser.

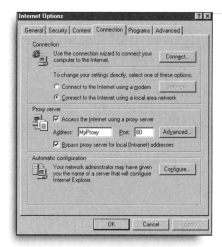

FIGURE 11.25.

Depending on your situation, you may need or want to alter these connection options. If you use a laptop, for example, you may connect to the Internet differently, depending on whether you're in the office or on the road.

Configuring proxy server settings

1. Click Access the Internet Using a Proxy Server, as shown in Figure 11.25.

2. Type the address of your proxy server in the Address field (for example, `myProxyServer.company.com`).

3. Type the port number in the Port field (this is typically 80).

4. If you are using Internet Explorer to access Web sites within your company's internal network (intranet), you may need to click on Bypass Proxy Server for Local (intranet) Addresses. Selecting this option will make your browser ignore the proxy server when accessing intranet sites.

5. Click the Advanced button to access other proxy configuration options (for example, setting up different proxy servers for different Internet services).

6. Click the Configure button if you know that your network administrator has already provided a configuration file for all

your Internet Explorer settings (which basically saves you the work of doing it yourself). If you don't know the location of an Automatic Configuration file for your network, leave this entry blank. If you do know the location of such a file (for example, `http://server.myCompany.com/ AutoConfigFile.ins`), enter it in the address line.

Using Auto-Dial Capabilities

If you're using a modem to connect to the Internet, Internet Explorer for Windows NT uses the built-in auto-dial capabilities of Windows NT to automatically dial up and connect to the Internet whenever you request a Web page or some other Internet resource. The point is to cut down on the number of steps required in accessing the Internet. Instead of the typical two-step procedure whereby you first dial in to the Internet using Dial-Up Networking and then fire up your browser to start navigating, the process is reduced to one simple step: start browsing. The Auto-Dial dialog box that comes up when you request a site needing a dial-up connection includes your username and password, so be sure to have these handy when connecting for the first time. After then, you will have the option to save these settings for your personal logon.

Configuring Helper Programs

Internet Explorer 4.0 includes several additional components beyond just the Web browser that you optionally can use and configure. These helper programs are selected from the Internet Properties|Programs screen, as shown in Figure 11.26.

Selecting helper programs

1. Select your default Internet email program by choosing one of the programs listed in the drop-down list box beside the word Mail. The program you pick will be automatically launched whenever you click a link in a Web page that points to an email address. (More technically, this is known as a Mailto link.) The default email program included with Internet Explorer 4.0 is Outlook Express, although other programs can be used.

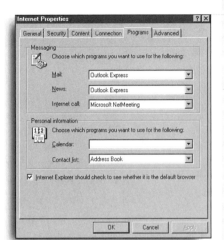

FIGURE 11.26.

Internet Explorer comes bundled with several useful corollary programs.

2. Select your default Internet news program by choosing one of the programs listed in the drop-down list box beside the News indicator. The program you pick will be automatically launched whenever you click a link in a Web page that points to an NNTP newsgroup. The default news program included with Internet Explorer 4.0 is Outlook Express.

3. Select your default Internet call program by choosing one of the programs listed in the drop-down list box beside the Internet Call indicator. The default Internet call program included with Internet Explorer is Microsoft NetMeeting, which permits you to chat, make video calls, share applications, and send files to other NetMeeting users.

4. Select your default Calendar and Contact List programs by choosing one of the programs listed in the drop-down list boxes beside the Calendar and Contact List indicators, respectively. Internet Explorer includes a default address book for storing contact list information. It does not include a default calendar, however. You must use other programs such as Microsoft Outlook to provide this functionality.

Using Languages Other than English

Some Web sites offer content in several different languages. To view these sites using your preferred language, you have to add support for those languages to Internet Explorer.

Adding support for other languages to Internet Explorer

1. Click the Languages button on the Internet Options|General screen shown in Figure 11.23.

2. Click Add.

3. Select the language you want to add and click OK.

4. You can arrange the languages in order of preference by clicking a particular language and then clicking Move Up (for higher precedence) or Move Down (for lower precedence). If a particular Web page is offered in multiple languages, Internet Explorer will show content from the language with the highest priority.

Note that adding a language does not necessarily mean that you have the proper fonts installed on your system to properly display a page written in that language. You may still need to install the Microsoft Multilanguage Support Packs if you are dealing with languages such as Japanese, Korean, Chinese, and Pan-European (Russian, Greek, and Turkish). To install these Support Packs (or to see whether they are already installed), click the menu option Help|Product Updates from the Internet Explorer main screen.

Although the Multilanguage Support Packs enable you to display Japanese and Korean Web pages, you still won't be able to write in these languages on a particular Web page that has forms or from the Outlook Express email program. If you would like to have this capability, you need to get the Internet Explorer Input Method Editor (or IME) 4.0 from Microsoft's site at http://www.microsoft.com/ie/ie40/ime.htm. This add-on enables you to communicate in Japanese or Korean without requiring Japanese or Korean versions of Windows NT 4.0.

Configuring the Active Desktop

The most dramatic new feature of Internet Explorer 4.0 is the Active Desktop, shown in Figure 11.27. If you select this option during installation, you will notice that your desktop now behaves more like a Web page with features such as single-click activation of programs and navigation. What might not be immediately obvious is that the desktop background is actually a customizable Web page, as are the views that you have for all your folders such as My Computer. Another interesting feature on the Active Desktop is the channel bar (the vertical bar to the right of the dialog box in Figure 11.27). You can subscribe to these and other channels (which are basically snapshots of selected sections of Web sites) such that you can view the contents of these Web sites even when you're not connected to the Internet. If you find the channel bar distracting, you can disable it as follows:

1. Click Start | Settings | Active Desktop | Customize My Desktop. You can also right-click on a blank area of your desktop and select Active Desktop | Customize My Desktop.

2. Click the Internet Explorer Channel Bar check box to disable (unchecked) or enable (checked) the channel bar.

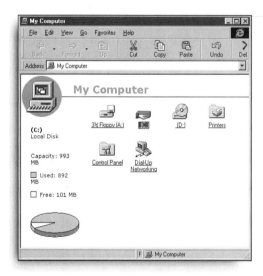

FIGURE 11.27.

This is what a local folder looks like when formatted to appear like a Web site via Active Desktop.

Each folder can be viewed in either Standard View or Web View. Your best bet is to experiment with both and see which one you prefer. Web View generally gives you more information on a particular folder and its contents; however, it is sometimes a bit slower than Standard View. By default, the view settings are applied on a per-folder basis, meaning that the Active Desktop will remember the view settings you apply to each folder.

A number of customization options are available for any given folder.

Configuring folder options

1. Click the folder you want to customize.

2. Click View|As Web Page to flip between Web View and Standard View for any given folder.

3. Click View|Customize This Folder to further modify options for a particular folder. This brings up a wizard that leads you through customizing the folder with options such as using a particular image as a background.

4. Click View|Folder Options to set the general behavior of all folders. This brings you to the Folder Options screen, from which you switch between Web Style View and the Classic View you are accustomed to with Windows NT. This option is also available from the Start menu by choosing Start|Settings|Folder Options.

5. Click the View tab in the Folder Options screen, shown in Figure 11.28, to further customize general folder options.

FIGURE 11.28.

The View tab of the Folder Options screen has a plethora of options available to you.

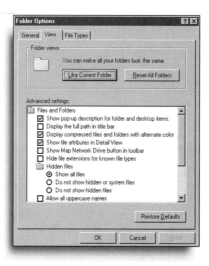

Using the Microsoft Wallet, Certificates, and Ratings

Many people have serious concerns about their safety on the Internet. Not their physical safety, but financial—that is, whether a site will misuse financial information such as credit card numbers. Microsoft Wallet is a way to create secure accounts with trusted vendors. Similarly, digital certificates guarantee the identity of a person or company when you're communicating with them.

Rating a Web site is an attempt to filter objectionable material. Philosophically, ratings work similarly to movie ratings. A site is rated according to content such as sex and violence. While no two people agree what exactly is objectionable, this system seems to strike a reasonable medium.

Using the Microsoft Wallet

If you have ever purchased goods over the Internet, you are familiar with the standard routine of visiting an online store, selecting the goods you want to purchase, and then entering a full screen of information on payment details such as your name, address, and credit card type and number. To simplify the final part of this procedure, Internet Explorer includes an electronic wallet that stores your address and payment information so that you don't have to type this each time you make a purchase.

Note that you will need to connect to Web sites that are capable of understanding the Microsoft Wallet in order to make use of its capabilities. You can check out a directory of some such sites at http://www.microsoft.com/commerce/wallet/directory.htm.

Before you can use the Microsoft Wallet, you must enter your address and credit card information from the Content tab of Internet Properties options, shown in Figure 11.29.

Entering your address information

1. Click View|Options within Internet Explorer.
2. Click the Content tab.
3. Click the Addresses button.

FIGURE 11.29.

The Content tab is where you supply the information Wallet needs for your secure transactions.

How Secure Is My Wallet?

The information you enter for each credit card in the Microsoft Wallet is protected by a password you select and a special encryption technique (specifically, the SHA-1 hashing algorithm). The Wallet also supports Secure Electronic Transactions (SET), a security standard for online payments co-developed by VISA and MasterCard. Add to this Secure Sockets Layer (SSL), which encrypts information travelling across the Internet, and you end up with a highly secure way of purchasing goods on the Internet.

4. Click Add.

5. Enter all the address information requested. If you have already used the Windows Address Book to store similar information, you can save yourself some typing by clicking the Address Book button.

6. Click the Home or Business icon to indicate what type of address you entered.

7. Click OK.

8. Click Add to add more addresses, Edit to change an existing address, or Delete to remove an address.

Entering your credit card information

1. Click View | Options within Internet Explorer.

2. Click the Content tab.

3. Click the Payments button.

4. Click Add and select the card type you want to add.

5. If this is the first card you enter, you will be prompted to accept a license agreement. Read it and click Accept.

6. Click Next and fill in your credit card information. When you are finished, click Next.

7. Click the drop-down arrow and select the address information you previously entered, or click New Address to enter another billing address.

8. Type a password. Type the password again for confirmation. Click Finish.

9. Click Close.

Using Certificates

Digital certificates are used to prevent someone from impersonating someone else (or you). Consider these the equivalent of electronic credentials. The contents of digital certificates are used to sign and encrypt digital information, such as sending encrypted email across the Internet. (This technology, supported in Outlook Express, is known as S/MIME [pronounced "ess-mime"].)

To take advantage of digital certificates, you have to obtain your own certificate from a trusted source known as a Certificate Authority, or CA. There are a growing number of CAs to choose from. Just point your browser to one of these authorities (the most popular of which is probably VeriSign at http://www.verisign.com) and follow the procedure for obtaining your own client-side certificate. This usually involves filling out some personal information such your name and address, as well as providing the CA with some form of payment for the certificate. After you complete the registration, the Certificate Authority will tell you the process for installing the digital certificate within Internet Explorer.

The configuration for certificates is controlled from the Content tab of the Internet Properties window of Internet Explorer, as shown in Figure 11.29.

Configuring digital certificates

1. Click View | Internet Options within Internet Explorer.

2. Click the Content tab.

3. Click Personal to view information about the personal certificates you obtained from a Certificate Authority. From this window, you can click Import to add certificates you previously exported, Export to save the certificate to disk for later importing, and View Certificate to check the contents of a given certificate. Click Close when you are finished.

4. Click Certificate Authorities to tell Internet Explorer about the CAs that you trust. You're supposed to click (or check) the authorities listed that you trust. The basic rule here is that if you don't know the identity of a given CA or the types of certificates the authority issues, you probably shouldn't check the box. This is somewhat of a catch-22, because most people don't know anything about most CAs. Your best bet here is to leave the default options selected and modify them afterward if something changes your mind. (For example, you may come across news that a given Certificate Authority is no longer reputable, in which case you probably don't want to trust certificates issued from that source.) Click Close when you are finished.

5. Click Publishers to see the names of software publishers you deem trustworthy. Whenever you download special programs over the Internet known as ActiveX controls or certain Java applets, you may be prompted (depending on your security settings) with a window informing you of who wrote the software and asking whether you want to trust this software publisher or the issuing CA. If you say "yes" to trust the publisher or CA, you won't be prompted in the future when you download digitally signed software from the same source. If you decide at a later time that you no longer trust a given source, highlight the questionable entry and click Delete. Click OK when you are finished.

Using Ratings

You can use the Internet Explorer Content Ratings feature to block out sites you deem inappropriate, such as sites that contain certain levels of nudity, sex, obscene language, or violence. Scenarios where this feature might be used include parents who don't want their children to access inappropriate sites and employers who want to restrict their employees from accessing certain sites. This is not a foolproof solution, in that it requires the authors of Web sites to rate their own content and include this information on their sites, but it is a step in the right direction.

The configuration for Content Ratings is controlled from the Content tab of the Internet Properties window of Internet Explorer, shown in Figure 11.29.

Configuring Content Ratings

1. Click View | Internet Options within Internet Explorer.

2. Click the Content tab.

3. Click Enable.

4. Enter a supervisor password, and confirm the password by entering it again. You can use this password to override the Content Ratings security you put in place. If you visit a site that contains inappropriate content but you'd like to view the page anyway, for example, you can enter the supervisor password and see the page. You will also need this password to subsequently change the settings for Content Ratings. Click OK to continue.

5. Select a ratings category (such as Language) by clicking it. Use the slider bar beside the word Ratings to set the level of potentially objectionable content that you will let someone view. You won't be able to view Web pages that are rated higher than the level you specify. Repeat this process for each ratings category. Click OK to finish.

6. Click OK to close the Internet Options window.

Configuring Security Zones

Internet Explorer security zones permit you to establish rules that limit how much access you give a specific group of Web sites (called zones) to your computer. This is particularly important when it comes to downloading potentially harmful software from the Internet such as ActiveX controls and Java applets. You may also want to customize how your browser behaves when you're prompted for passwords or need to run scripts. All these settings and more are controlled from the View | Internet Properties Security tab, as shown in Figure 11.30.

I Forgot My Content Ratings Supervisor Password!

What happens if you forget the supervisor password you entered for Content Ratings? You can recover from this dilemma by making modifications to the Registry. Specifically, you need to delete the value named "Key" from the following Registry location: HKEY_LOCAL_MACHINE\ Software\Microsoft\Windows\ CurrentVersion\Policies\Ratings. Restart your computer after making this change and the next time you need to use the supervisor password you will be prompted to enter a new one.

FIGURE 11.30.

The Security tab has settings to protect your computer from aggression. The Content tab protects you from objectionable content.

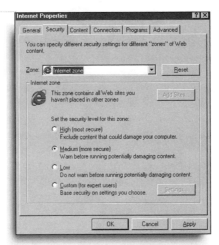

Four security zones are included with Internet Explorer 4.0:

1. *Local intranet.* By default, this group includes Web sites that aren't accessed through a proxy server, and internal network sites that use Windows networking computer names (also known as UNC names, short for *universal naming convention*).

2. *Trusted sites.* You have to specifically add the names of Web sites you trust to this zone.

3. *Restricted sites.* You have to specifically add the names of Web sites you *do not* trust to this zone.

4. *Internet.* These are Web sites not included in any other zone.

Each zone contains a set of default security settings that you are permitted to change. By default, the Restricted sites zone has the highest level of security, meaning that any content from the Internet that is potentially damaging is not permitted to run on your computer. The Trusted sites zone is the least secure in that it assumes you trust the Web sites contained therein and therefore permit programs from those sites to run on your computer without warning you.

You can set the default security behavior for each of these zones to High (the most restrictive), Medium (you're warned before any potentially damaging content is run and asked if it's okay), Low (no warnings are made), and Custom.

You may want to view what Custom settings are available by clicking the Custom radio button on the Security tab, and then clicking Settings. You will see a wide variety of options as shown in Figure 11.31 that are, for the most part, self explanatory.

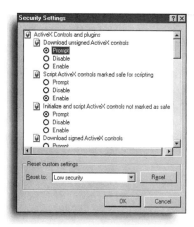

FIGURE 11.31.

The Security tab looks similar to Windows Explorer's View|Folder Options|View tab, but the options differ.

Advanced Configuration Options

One area that you will want to explore is the Advanced tab under the Internet Properties window, shown in Figure 11.32. From here you can control the behavior of Internet Explorer as it relates to accessibility for the handicapped, browsing, security, multimedia, and more.

To access these properties, select View | Internet Options from the Internet Explorer main window, and then click the Advanced tab. To enable or disable a specific behavior, just check or uncheck the item by clicking it. To restore the default settings, click the Restore Defaults button.

If you don't understand the behavior a particular Advanced option is influencing, you can get context-sensitive help by right-clicking the option and selecting What's This?

Although the default settings are fine for most people, you may want to change a few options (or at least take a few moments to understand them). Table 11.1 outlines these options.

Customizing the Security of Java Applets

One custom setting that even advanced users sometimes miss out on relates to the precision of security control available for Java applets. From the custom security settings shown in Figure 11.31, scroll down to Java|Java Permissions. When you select the radio button named Custom, a Java Custom Settings button "magically" appears on the lower left-hand side of the window. Click this button and you will see more ways to customize the security of Java applets than you probably thought existed.

FIGURE 11.32.

Don't be intimidated by the Advanced tab. Despite its name, the options here are for everybody, not just advanced users.

TABLE 11.1   **The Advanced tab explained**

Option	Default Setting	Description
Browsing I Use AutoComplete	Enabled	Specifies whether Internet Explorer automatically completes Internet addresses as you type by suggesting a match it derives from sites you have visited before.
AutoComplete		Most people like this feature because it saves on typing, but some find it disconcerting.
Security I Warn if Forms Submit Is Being Redirected	Enabled	Specifies whether to warn you if information you typed on a Web page is being sent to a different Web location. In the past, some Web sites took advantage of this redirection capability to send personal information you may have entered to undesirable recipients. However, many Web sites currently use this feature extensively to link related pages, so you may find having to click through the myriad warning messages counter-productive.

Option	Default Setting	Description
Security | Cookies	Always Accept Cookies	Web sites use what are known as "cookies" to store information on your hard disk so that when you visit a site again it can "remember" any preferences you set or other information you submitted. Although cookies are generally not harmful, some people don't like the idea of Web sites tracking their usage, nor do they like their hard disk to be populated with cookies without knowing about it. You may want disable cookie usage or be prompted before accepting a cookie.
Search | Autoscan Common Root Domains	Enabled	Internet Explorer has the capability to automatically complete Web short names or addresses if you enter them using incorrect root-level domains (where the term *root-level domains* denotes the last extension in a Web address, such as .com, .org, .edu, .gov, and others). If you type the word microsoft in the Address line, for example, Internet Explorer searches for logical extensions such as www.microsoft.com, www.microsoft.org, and more until it finds a match. Also, if you mistype an address (such as www.microsoft.org), Internet Explorer will search the other root domains to see whether it can find a logical match (such as www.microsoft.com).
Toolbar | Small Icons	Disabled	Using smaller icons on your toolbar gives you a bit more screen real estate for browsing, so you probably want to enable this option.

IV

Managing Windows NT Workstation 4

Managing Users—NT Security

Managing Users

Because the vast majority of users log on as the administrator (the default Windows NT logon) or with Administrator rights, they often wonder what value (if any) using NT's built-in security has for them. The answer is that it might have little value, but there are aspects of it that most users can avail themselves of. In the case of a workstation with several users—each of whom, or any of whom, desires privacy—the security capabilities of Windows NT makes it a vastly superior system to its siblings Windows 95 and Windows 98.

As mentioned in Chapter 1, "Using and Understanding Windows NT Workstation 4," you can create a logon for multiple users that will keep them away from the files of each other. This makes Windows NT a surprising first choice for many users who have a computer at home for their work use, but also need to allow their family access. There are many sad tales of files inadvertently lost due to the lack of true security in lesser operating systems. Combine the security of Windows NT with its flexibility in running legacy programs—found in the Chapter 5 ("Installing and Uninstalling Applications") discussion of older applications—and you will see that Windows NT has more possibilities as a general purpose operating system than most people give it credit for.

Two broad aspects comprise Windows NT security. The first is User Groups. These are classifications of users you can define as to their permissions. When you create a new user, you can assign him to a group that will confer the specific rights of that group to that user.

Unlike other Windows

Windows NT has been designed from the get go to be a secure operating system. Other versions of Windows have whatever security they possess tacked on.

False Security

Many people rely on encryption to keep their files secure from tampering, either intentional or not. This is effective against people reading or editing your files, but utterly useless against deletion by intent or oversight.

What's Permission?

The term "permissions" in computer security refers to what a user is allowed to do. Permissions stretch from logging on (the simplest permission) to doing security maintenance (the highest permission). In between there are tasks such as what folders a person might visit to run backups.

Getting Started in Windows NT Security

Configuring Windows NT Workstation's security is fairly simple and straightforward. Even novice users can use it without fear, assuming they keep their logon names and passwords straight. For that matter, even veteran users can get themselves into trouble losing either or both of those.

Some people shy away from using Windows NT security because they have heard how complex it can be. This is true for managing a network using Workstation's sister operating system, Windows NT Server. It is doubly true for other operating systems such as VMS or UNIX, but don't let those stories discourage you. Keep in mind these two points:

- Define User Groups and their permissions or use (modified, if appropriate) one of the User Groups predefined by Microsoft for Windows NT.

- Secure your logon name and password to use Administrator rights in a way available to you, but not others. Using the Administrator rights, you can undo any errors you might make in security.

User Groups

Microsoft has designed Windows NT security so that it's easier to first define a group, and then create a user identity, and finally assign that identity to a group. That way the user inherits the group's permission settings.

To get you going, Microsoft supplies Windows NT with several predefined groups bearing descriptive names. I have found that people get started fastest by first examining those predefined User Groups to get a feel for what permissions are out there and how they're reflected in a group definition.

To use the User Manager (not my idea of a good name), you need to be logged on with Administrator rights. Start the User Manager by choosing the Start menu choices Programs|Administrative Tools (Common)|User Manager. When started on a new system, the User Manager will look like Figure 12.1.

The top part of the User Manager shows the users already defined; the bottom part shows the User Groups. Because this part of the chapter is dedicated to User Groups, this discussion focuses on the bottom part of the User Manager for now.

The first item is to see who (if anyone) is assigned to a group. This is simple. Double-click on the User Group to bring up the Local Group Properties. Oddly enough, the logical right-click

FAT Security Is Thin

Applying Windows NT security to a FAT volume is much less effective than an NTFS volume. A FAT volume is vulnerable to being booted (mounted) by an MS-DOS or Windows 95/98 disk boot.

All NTFS the Same?

NTFS has remained the same from the first version of Windows NT to version 4. Starting with version 5, Microsoft will introduce a new NTFS. A service pack will patch Windows NT 4 (but not previous versions) to use the new NTFS.

and then choosing Properties from a context menu is missing here. This is very likely an oversight. For some aspects of security, however, the user interface is inconsistent.

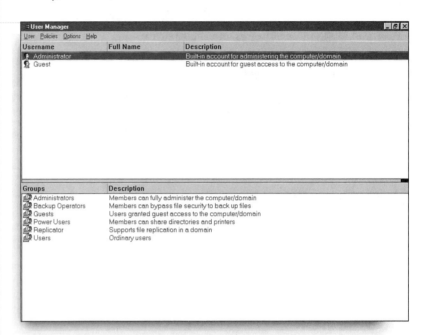

The Local Group Properties box gives a description of what these users are about and who (logon names) is a part of the group. Double-click on Users in the User Manager shown in Figure 12.1. This results in a screen similar to Figure 12.2.

The area of Windows NT where you set or see permissions is the Policy or Policies area.

To see the Policy for the group shown in Figure 12.2, close the dialog box in Figure 12.2 (if it's open), and then choose the menu selections Policies | User Rights. This opens the dialog box shown in Figure 12.3.

The screen in Figure 12.3 is the heart of assigning rights to users, so slow down a minute and examine this dialog box carefully.

Remember Context Help

Pressing F1 within the User Manager will almost always bring up help within the context of the current dialog box. This is an enormous help for occasional users.

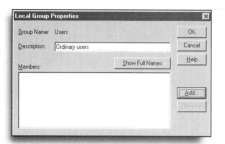

FIGURE 12.2.

The group Users doesn't have any members initially.

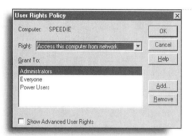

FIGURE 12.3.

Users are assigned to groups, and then groups are assigned policies. Here is where you can examine those policies.

Right under the title bar, you will see the name Speedie. This is the name of the computer where the User Manager is running. If, for example, you were to try to locate this computer on a LAN, you would search on the name Speedie.

Below the computer name is a combo box (pull-down box) with the label Right. These are the rights or permissions available on the local workstation. The right (permission) showing is the right to log on remotely, from the network.

The list box next down shows three User Groups. Those are the groups that currently have the right (or permission) shown in the combo box. So here's how to determine which groups have what rights:

Determining which groups have what rights

1. Log on with Administrator rights. Nothing less will do.

2. Start the User Manager by choosing the menu selections Start|Programs|Administrative Tools (Common)|User Manager.

3. From the User Manager, choose the menu selections Policies|User Rights.

4. Pull down the Right combo box and examine the User Groups displayed in the list box immediately below.

As you can see in Figure 12.3, for example, the User Group called Users can't log on remotely. Pull down the combo box labeled Right and scroll to Log on Locally as shown in Figure 12.4. As you can see, this is a right granted to the group called Users (and everybody else too). You might need to do some scrolling to find the group called Users if you try this.

FIGURE 12.4.

The group called Users can log on locally, but not remotely. Compare this screen with Figure 12.3 to see how the members differ.

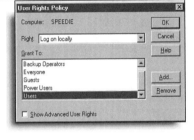

Creating a New User Group

This one's a piece of cake. Most of the work in creating a new group or a new member of a group is planning what permissions you wish to grant. Here you will create a new User Group called Kids and grant that group limited rights.

Creating a new user group and granting limited rights

1. Log on with Administrator rights. Nothing less will do.

2. Start the User Manager by choosing the menu selections Start | Programs | Administrative Tools (Common) | User Manager.

3. Choose the menu selections User | New Local Group. Fill in the name of the new group and a description. Figure 12.5 shows the filled-in dialog box.

4. Click OK to close the dialog box. When finished, Windows NT displays your new group in the User Group section of User Manager. Figure 12.6 shows this having occurred.

FIGURE 12.5.

You only need name a new User Group to create one. It's a good idea to fill in a description, especially if more than one user has Administrator rights on the machine.

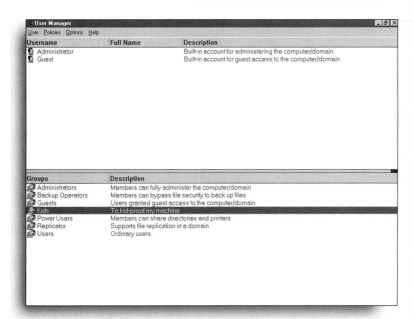

FIGURE 12.6.

You have now created a new group, but setting its rights or permissions still lies ahead.

Setting Policies for a User Group

A User Group needs to have its rights defined. You probably already have a good idea of how to do that from the earlier sections, but here's the step by step from the beginning. If your screen looks like Figure 12.6, you should ignore the first two steps.

Refining rights for a user group

1. Log on with Administrator rights. Nothing less will do.

2. Start the User Manager by choosing the menu selections Start | Programs | Administrative Tools (Common) | User Manager.

3. Choose the menu selections Policies | User Rights.

4. Pull down the combo box labeled Right to choose the right you wish to assign to a group. For this example, choose Log on Locally to assign to the new group Kids. The same procedure works for any right, however.

5. Click on the Add button. Locate the group Kids (or the group you wish to assign a right to) and click the Add button in the Add Users and Groups dialog box. Figure 12.7 shows this operation.

FIGURE 12.7.

Assign a right to a User Group through the Add Users and Groups dialog box. Here the Kids group is being permitted to log on locally.

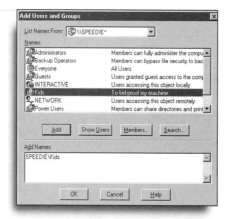

6. Click OK in the Add Users and Groups dialog box. That's the one on the right in Figure 12.7. Take a look at the User Rights Policy dialog box now. As you can see from Figure 12.8, the member of the new group Kids can now log on locally. If you have followed along, scroll through the Right combo box to confirm that that's all these members can do.

FIGURE 12.8.

New groups will have only those permissions or rights that you expressly assign.

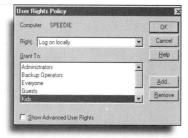

7. Click OK to close the User Rights Policy dialog box after you are satisfied that Kids (or your group) has, in fact, the new right or permission you assigned.

Removal of Rights and User Groups

Removing a right or permission from a User Group

1. Choose Policies|User Rights from the User Manager menu.
2. Locate the right you wish to remove.
3. Locate and highlight the group you wish to remove it from, and then click the Remove button.

Removing an entire User Group

1. Start the User Manager.
2. Locate the group you wish to delete. Press Del or choose User|Delete from the menu.
3. Windows NT will issue a stern warning. If you persist, you can delete the group by confirming clicks to the OK buttons.

That's all it takes to create or edit a User Group. The following section shows how to create the users themselves and assign them to a group so that they inherit a group's rights.

Creating New Users and Assigning Rights

Users, not User Groups, log on to Windows NT. The previous material in this chapter dealt mostly with User Groups as they come logically first when discussing Windows NT security. The reason for their coming first is that for the most part, people like to create a user identity and then assign that person to a User Group. Obviously for this scheme to work, the group must pre-exist the definition of the user.

Well, with that piece of confusing introduction complete, it's time to move on to the creation of a user identity. You will find some of the options or parameters for new users tend toward the

Relax

If you are familiar with insecure operating systems such as Windows or the MacOS, much of this is new to you. Take it easy and in small bites.

Right-Click and the User Manager

Right-clicking (clicking the non-default button) within User Manager is a hit-and-miss proposition. Some fields and dialog boxes are so enabled, but others aren't. You might think that right-clicking on a user would bring up a context menu allowing actions on that user, for example, but it doesn't.

needs of a professional network administrator. That's because with Windows NT, you have moved into the area of serious workstation-grade operating systems. The product would not have succeeded with security at the almost nonexistent level of other products such as Windows 98 or 95. Although the options exist, they aren't formidable. Remember that if you have no security issues, you can always just have all users sign on with Administrator rights by sharing that password with them.

You create users by using the User Manager. Don't blame me for this alliteration. I don't make the names up here.

Making a new user identity

1. Log on with Administrator rights. Nothing less will do.

2. Start the User Manager by choosing the menu selections Start | Programs | Administrative Tools (Common) | User Manager.

3. Choose the menu options User | New User from the User Manager. You will get a dialog box shown in Figure 12.9.

FIGURE 12.9.

The New User dialog box was created with the needs of the professional administrator in mind. Still, the options are decipherable by mortal users.

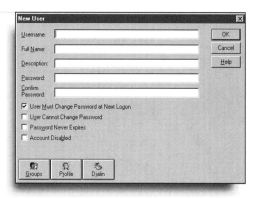

4. Fill in the New User dialog box. The Username is the logon name. It can be up to 20 alphanumerics, excluding certain MS-DOS type reserved characters such as [ ] / \ > < , = + * ?. It can contain periods and spaces, but can't be made up only of those characters. That is, a logon name of only a space or a period is illegal. Therefore, the following names

- Tirilee5

- Tiri_lee_5

- Tiri.lee.5()

- Tirilee 5

are legal, but

- Tirilee[5

- Tiri/lee

- Tiri>Lee

- Tirilee?

aren't legal.

For most standalone uses, you can leave the password alone and set it never to expire. For serious security work, you need to force the user to change the password at the next logon so that the password is one of his own, not yours, and set it to expire according to the settings in Maximum Password Age. You set the latter in Password Policies. To see the policies for an account, choose the menu choices Policies|Account from the User Manager menu system.

5. At this point, you can click OK to finish the definition of your new user or move on to the next section to learn how to associate the user with a group. You will need to set this user's permissions or rights somewhere; otherwise, the new user identity isn't, well, usable.

Users and User Groups

Users need rights or permissions to do anything. After you have created a new user, you can individually set his permissions or associate the user with a User Group. Earlier in the chapter, you saw how to create a new User Group. The example created this group and called it Kids. In the preceding section, you saw how to create a new user. The example created a new user (a kid) called Tirilee (my daughter, age 5). These steps show how to associate a user with a User Group. If you have completed the steps in the preceding section and haven't closed the New User dialog box, you can skip the following first three steps.

Hard Cases

Passwords in Windows NT are case sensitive! The password Tiri isn't the same as TIRI. Make sure your users know this or their logon attempts might be all in vain.

Associating a user with a user group

1. Log on with administrator rights. Nothing less will do.

2. Start the User Manager by choosing the menu selections Start | Programs | Administrative Tools (Common) | User Manager.

3. Double-click on the user you wish to associate with a User Group. This will bring up the User Properties dialog box shown in Figure 12.10. You can highlight the user and choose User | Properties instead if you prefer menus to mice.

FIGURE 12.10.

The User Properties dialog box is the place to edit the properties of previously defined Users.

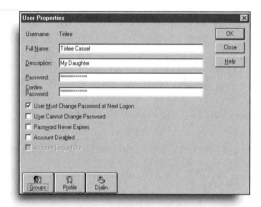

4. Click the Group button. Select the Group or Groups you wish to enroll the user in and click the Add button. To remove a user from a group, highlight the group and click Remove. Click OK when you're done adjusting the users' groups. Figure 12.11 shows this operation.

FIGURE 12.11.

A user can be part of several groups, or only one. Remember that the user's rights are restricted to those rights specifically enumerated in the definition of a User Group.

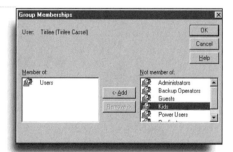

5. Finish making any edits you wish to such as changing the user's password or setting it to expire or not. Then click OK to close the User Properties dialog box.

Other Properties for the User

You saw in Chapter 1 that you can create profiles to make a logged on user see a familiar environment. The Profile button in the New User and User Properties dialog boxes are the place to associate a user logon with a particular logon. Figure 12.12 shows the dialog box for setting a profile for a user.

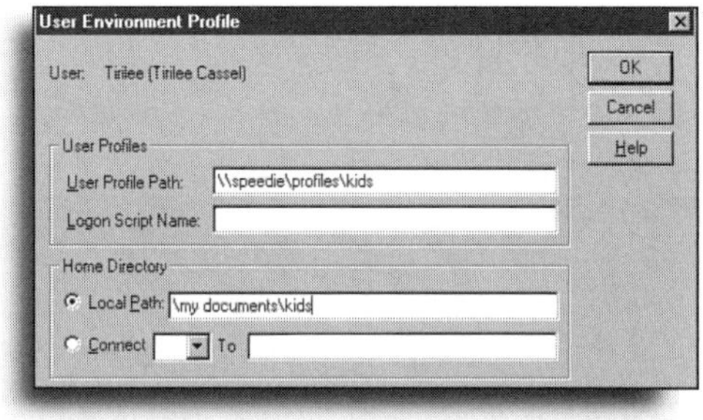

FIGURE 12.12.
You can set a profile for your users and also their home directories or folders. The latter is where, by default, applications look to open and close documents.

The other button is the Dialin button. This is a very important aspect of Windows NT security often overlooked by people. Assume that you wish to dial in to your computer, but you don't wish to expose your machine to the type of security risk this might pose. You can create a user identity for yourself having a fairly low set of rights or permissions. You can set those rights by creating a Dialin User Group or by setting them specifically for that user ID. This allows you to dial in, but once in, you— and anybody else who might dial in illegally by, let's say, stealing your laptop—have very restricted rights.

Be sure to set the Dialin rights for that user to permit a dial up connection. By default, no user has Dialin rights. Figure 12.13 shows the Dialin Information dialog box. The Call Back options on this dialog box set up a security feature that forces the host computer to call back either to a user specified phone or a preset one. This logs the phones used by callers or prevents a connection from an unauthorized remote location, respectively.

Can't Dial In

Remember, as it comes from the box (setup), Windows NT lacks dial-in rights to all users, including one with Administrator rights.

You must log on locally (at the console) with Administrator rights to start the process of granting dial-in rights.

FIGURE 12.13.

You need to set dialin rights explicitly. By default, users don't have dialin rights.

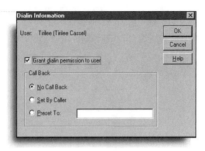

Account Policies

You can set the overall policies for an account using the User Manager. To see the dialog box where you do so, open the User Manager and choose Policies|Account from the menu. This brings up a dialog box shown in Figure 12.14.

FIGURE 12.14.

Windows NT comes with an account policy that's a good compromise for most uses. You can modify these policies to suit your own needs or desires.

If you are not at all concerned about security matters, you can change the policy to allow blank passwords. Although users do find remembering passwords a real chore, a blank password means that a pirate needs only to know the username logon to gain access to your workstation. The reason for expiring passwords is to force users to change them regularly. This is good security policy, but can lead to a revolt in the user ranks. Another good security policy is to lock out a user after a few (usually three) failed password attempts. This goes far in keeping password-guessing pirates away from a system.

The truth is that most users use familiar passwords such as their birthdays or their children's names. If you lock out after a few tries, unauthorized users who know personal details will have a lesser chance of hitting it right by trying all of them because they will have to get it in the first few tries.

Security in Action

The best way to see the effect of security is to create a User Group with restricted rights (or use one of the predefined groups), and then create a new user associated with that restricted group and logon as that user.

If you have created a custom desktop for yourself, the first thing you will notice is that your new logged on personality doesn't share that customization unless you have set them both up to the same profiles. You should also notice that the Start|Programs menu has changed. The bottom part, the All Users section, is the same; but the middle part is now bare of any programs that are the exclusive rights of the administrator. This user identity can install programs for his or her specific use too, and they will be unavailable to other restricted (non-Administrator) rights users. You will even find that programs, such as those in Microsoft Office 97, that conform to the logged on user will revert back to their default behaviors.

Finally, give Windows NT a few tests. Try to access the Administrator folder using the Explorer. If you can get in, either you have conferred more rights than you intended to the new user or you have broken Windows NT's security and made computer history. Figure 12.15 shows the results of trying to access the Administrator folder structure with less than Administrator rights.

You will also note a new folder structure with your new logged on identity. You can see a thin rectangle drawn around this folder in Figure 12.15. The restricted user here has the logon name Tirilee. She is a member of the Kids User Group defined earlier in this chapter.

The Internet Is Looking

If you don't use a firewall (blocker program) to access the Internet, something out there can "come back up the wire" and access your machine. This is rare and difficult to achieve, but possible. If you have sensitive material on your machine, you should only go online behind a firewall.

Security for the Administrator

A logon consists of a logon name and a password. If you use the logon name Administrator (Windows NT default) for Administrator rights logon, you're giving half the secret away. A better way is to create a new username with the same rights as Administrator, and use that logon name instead.

Security and Applications

You can create profiles for different conforming application programs by customizing those programs differently under various log on identities.

Finally, try running a Windows NT routine that should require higher rights than this user has. For example, try examining or changing a User through the User Manager. Trying to do so yields the message you can see in Figure 12.16.

You will find restricted rights throughout Windows NT. While logged on with restricted rights, try making system changes in Control Panel. You will find that, for the most part, you can't. You will have no problems making superficial changes such as environmental ones like the appearance of your screen. These changes will attach themselves to the user logon and not affect others, including yourself if you log on with your usual high rights under a different username.

For Your Own Security

Some owners enjoy defining a user logon name for themselves with less than full rights (Administrator-level rights) because this keeps them from inadvertently making changes that might adversely affect their computers. This is also a handy way to have several different environments (such as screen resolution) for different type tasks.

Final Check

Just to make sure all is how you suppose it should be, run the User Manager again if you have closed it. Assuming you followed along with this chapter's examples, either literally or using you own parameters for a User Group and/or a new user, you should see your results there.

Locate the new User Group you made, and then either double-click on it or highlight it. Choose User|Properties from the menu. Figure 12.17 shows the results for doing the procedures in this chapter so far.

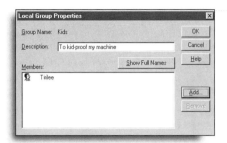

FIGURE 12.17.
Here is the new User Group and its only member so far, Tirilee, a kid herself.

Setting Rights Without a User Group

You can set up a new user account and set its rights without adding it to a User Group, although the work isn't really any less doing so. Here are the steps.

Setting up a new user account without adding it to a User Group

1. Log on with administrator rights. Nothing less will do.

2. Start the User Manager by choosing the menu selections Start|Programs|Administrative Tools (Common)|User Manager.

3. Create a new user, following the steps you learned earlier in the section titled "Creating New Users and Assigning Rights," but stop after you have created the new user definition. At this point, the new user has, assuming you've left Windows NT's policies at default, the rights of the User Group. This amounts to being able to log on locally. Figure 12.18 shows your screen at this point, using the username Jrobert.

4. Now choose Policies|User Rights. Locate the right or permission you wish to grant. Click the Add button. Your screen should resemble Figure 12.19.

5. Click the Show Users button shown in Figure 12.19. This reveals the names of users as well as User Groups, as you can see in Figure 12.20. Click the Add button in the Add Users and Groups dialog box. This gives the highlighted user or User Group the permission showing in the Right combo box. In the example, Jrobert is gaining the right to log on remotely. As Figure 12.20 shows, this particular user is granted this right after you click on OK.

Administrator

Create a new or keep the Administrator logon as a never-used "back door" logon. Use this account in case you forget your usual logon or passwords. If you create a new one, make sure this safety account has full Administrator rights.

FIGURE 12.18.

This is a new user defined for the purposes of this example. He's about to get Power User rights.

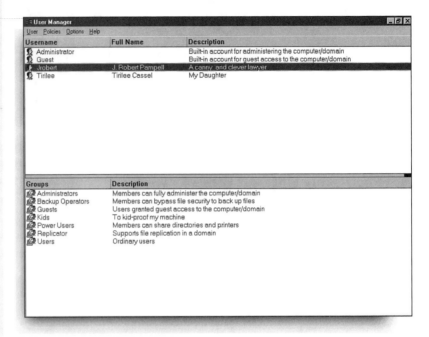

FIGURE 12.19.

By default, the Add button shows only User Groups. You can change that, however.

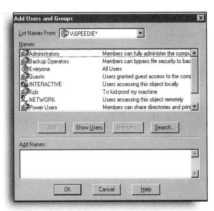

6. Using the same technique, you can create a unique set of user rights without creating a User Group.

File and Disk Security

You can set up Windows NT to allow or disallow access by file and folder (directory) if you choose. The example so far in this chapter created a User Group called Kids with very limited rights. A user who is part of this User Group can't, for example,

access the folder structure in the Windows NT Profiles\
Administrator structure. The person so logged on can access just
about everything else.

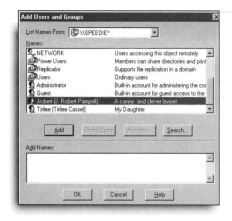

FIGURE 12.20.

The new user now has the right
to log on remotely (through a
network). This was granted him
without associating him with a
User Group already having that
right.

Restricting such access by file or folder

1. Log on with Administrator rights. Start the Windows
   Explorer.

2. Locate the file or folder to which you wish to restrict rights.
   Right-click on it. Choose Properties from the context menu.
   Alternatively, you can choose the menu selections
   File|Properties from Explorer's menu. Click on the Security
   tab. Your screen should resemble Figure 12.21.

3. Click the Permissions button. Note that this dialog box has
   two important check boxes: to apply the changes you're
   about to make to existing files, and whether to apply them
   to the entire folder structure. When making permissions
   changes, keep these check boxes in mind. Click Add.

4. This brings up a dialog box familiar to those having seen the
   User Manager. Figure 12.22 shows this dialog box.

5. Remember to click the Show Users button if you wish to
   assign a permission to a specific user rather than a User
   Group. Highlight the user or User Group you wish to
   assign the permission to and click Add. Pull down the

combo box at the bottom of the screen and choose the type of access you wish to confer. Figure 12.23 shows this operation in progress.

FIGURE 12.21.

The Security tab has three buttons, all of which relate to file or folder security in some manner or another.

FIGURE 12.22.

Once familiar with granting rights to users and User Groups, doing the same for permissions on files and folders is fairly similar.

6. You can also deny access for a user or User Group by specifying the type of permission as No Access. Click OK to return to the Directory Permissions dialog box. As you can see in Figure 12.24, the User Group Administrators has now been added to the Directory Permissions with Full Control.

7. At this point you can remove Everyone from the permissions to restrict access to those with Administrator rights.

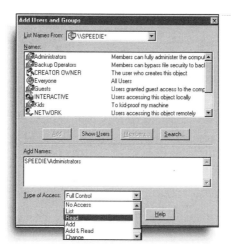

FIGURE 12.23.

You not only need to assign a user or User Group file and folder permission, but you need to set the type of permission.

Autediting

You can track or audit quite a number of events relating to files and folders in Windows NT. The Audit feature creates an entry in the Event log for every time your selected event occurs.

The facility to do this is in the Auditing button in the dialog box shown in Figure 12.21. Before applying any Audit features, you must activate the capability to audit through the User Manager.

Turning on auditing for an account—which in this case is Microsoft-speak for the local computer

1. Log on with Administrator rights. Nothing less will do.

2. Start the User Manager by choosing the menu selections Start | Programs | Administrative Tools (Common) | User Manager.

3. Choose the menu selections Policies | Audit. Your screen should resemble Figure 12.24.

4. Click on the Audit These Events option button, and then place a check mark in the Event check boxes where you wish to allow auditing. If you wish to track how often a user tries (and fails) to access restricted places on the computer, for example, place a check mark in the File and Object Access Failure column.

Beware Everyone, the Group

If you remove access for Everyone from the boot drive (usually C:), you can conceivably set security so tight that nobody, even Administrators, can access the machine. Don't do it.

FIGURE 12.24.

Before applying any audits to specific files or folder structures, you need to use the User Manager to set the policy allowing audits.

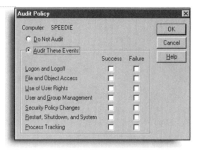

The Common Trap

The single most prevalent problem with auditing is failure to initialize (start) Auditing itself. Most people reasonably assume that it's on by default.

5. Close the Audit Policy dialog box and close the User Manager. You have now made auditing possible.

To apply auditing for a user or User Group, you need to return to the Explorer. Auditing means an entry is made in the Event log for every occurrence of your selected event or events.

Applying auditing for a user or User Group

1. Log on with Administrator rights. Start the Windows Explorer.

2. Locate the file or folder to which you wish to restrict rights. Right-click on it. Choose Properties from the context menu. Alternatively, you can choose the menu selections File | Properties from Explorer's menu. Click on the Security tab. Your screen should resemble Figure 12.21.

3. Click on the Auditing button. This brings up an Auditing dialog box consisting of a series of check boxes and a list box. Figure 12.25 shows this dialog box.

4. Click the Add button to bring up the dialog box from the User Manager where you locate users and User Groups. Be sure to click on Show Users if you wish to apply the audit to a user. If you wish to apply it to a User Group, they're there for you now. Highlight the User Group or user and click Add. This example adds the User Group Kids to the audit and applies the Audit Event Read to see how often the Kids try to read forbidden areas of the computer. Figure 12.26 shows the screen after having set this up.

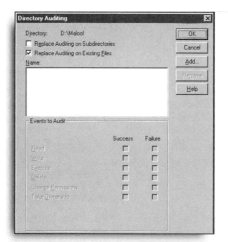

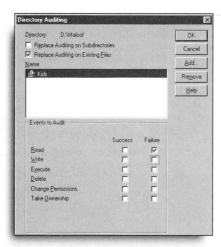

5. Click OK to exit the Directory Auditing dialog box and then close the Properties dialog box in Explorer if you're done. Now whenever the event you have set up to log occurs, you will see an event generated in the Event log.

After you have started auditing some events, you will need to open the Event Viewer to see whether any have occurred (which brings this discussion to the Event Viewer).

Auditing and File Systems

You can only audit file and folder accesses on NTFS volumes. FAT is out.

Event Viewer

The primary purpose of the Event Viewer is to monitor errors or warnings generated by your system. If a service scheduled to launch up on boot fails to start, for example, the failure will be recorded in an Event log. You can use the Event Viewer to see those and similar entries.

For the purposes of this book, I have set Auditing to catch certain events such as unauthorized file access of the Kids User Group created step by step earlier in this chapter. I then logged on as a member of Kids and tried some forbidden tasks. I also set Auditing on the Administrators User Group to generate some permitted event entries and also on the specific user Tirilee who is a member of the Kids User Group. This emulates a father wanting to track to see whether his kids are trying to gain access to his files.

Daddy Is Superman

The Event Viewer and Auditing is a great way to monitor what your kids are up to on your computer. Later telling them that you know without saying how you know can increase their awe of you considerably.

Unfortunately for me, my daughter has the Event Viewer figured out.

A run through of the Event Viewer and log

1. To review the Event log, open the Event Viewer by choosing the menu options Start | Programs | Administrative Tools (Common) | Event Viewer. You must be logged on with Administrator-level rights to view the Security log. Your screen should resemble Figure 12.27.

2. The screen shown in Figure 12.27 is the System log. Most of the entries in the Event log aren't of much use or are almost undecipherable to most users. They can be of interest in some cases, however, and can also aid support personnel in diagnosing System (or other) problems.

3. To see different logs, choose the Log menu, and then choose from the three choices: System, Security, or Application.

4. To see details on any event, double-click on that event. Figure 12.28 shows the details of the first event in Figure 12.27 as an example of a useful detail set; Figure 12.29 shows the details for the third event. Most people won't have any idea what sort of message the third event is trying to convey. (It's got to do with the IntelliPoint software.)

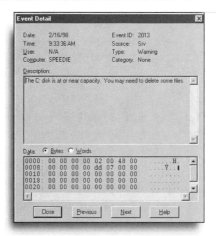

The Security log can be much more useful and informative if you have set audits for certain events. Figure 12.30 shows this log with the details of an event opened. As you can see, Tirilee tried to access the file maloof.txt, a file restricted to her. Windows NT not only prevented her from opening the file, but it also recorded the crime.

The Keys to the Kingdom

Administrator rights are the keys to the NT kingdom. Anyone having these rights can restrict access. This isn't like MS-DOS or Windows 98 where anybody with a boot disk can get at a FAT volume. NTFS is meant to be secure, and it is.

FIGURE 12.29.

Few (if any) people outside the most technically inclined geeks will know or care what this message means. It's only an advisory anyway of something that might be wrong.

FIGURE 12.30.

The Security log is where you find events triggered by the Audit feature.

The columns in the Event log are somewhat self-explanatory. Many System events occur despite a specific user being logged on. The screen in Figure 12.28 is a good example of that. In other cases, such as the Security log, the identity of the user is vital to know. The only column that might make for some mystery is the Event column. This should really be called the Event ID column. It records an event's ID—a Windows NT internal identifier as to event type. Each event ID is linked to a triggering application or other software, as shown in the Source column.

It is important that you understand the severity of any event. The key to that is the symbol in the extreme left column of the Event Viewer. Here are the symbols, their meanings, and their translations.

Symbol	Meaning	Interpretation
Key	Failure audit	Failed access attempt.
Padlock	Success audit	Access attempt succeeded.
The letter *i* in a small blue circle	Information	Rare, but significant successful operations.
The exclamation point (!) in a yellow circle	Warning	System is unsure whether the event is significant, so it records the event for the System Administrator to decide.
Stop sign	Error	Possible severe problem including data loss or system failure.

The Event log can get jammed with too many events for you to make out what's important and what's not. You can clear the log by using the menu options Log|Clear All Events or you can choose the View menu entry Filter Events to get them down to those of interest to you. Using the Log|Log Settings entry, you can set global options for the Event log such as how long to keep events. As even a modest system can generate many events, the default is to toss the entries after a week.

If you are on a network and have the rights, you can view the events of a different system by choosing Log|Select Computer. This brings up the other computers on your LAN. The remote computer must be on and Windows NT booted. You can't view the Event log of a remote dual-boot computer if it's running another system such as Windows 98 or 95—even though you can see that computer in your Network Neighborhood.

Finally, you can save Event logs and open them for later viewing by choosing the menu choices Log|Save As and Log|Open respectively. The Save As option gives you the option of saving as a native log format (.EVT) a text file or a comma-delimited file for use in database systems such as Microsoft Access. The latter option when used in conjunction with a database system is quite useful for organizing and referring back to your logs, because a decent system such as Access is much better at organizing and viewing logs than the Event Viewer itself. Figure 12.31 shows a log saved as a comma-delimited file and then read into Microsoft Access.

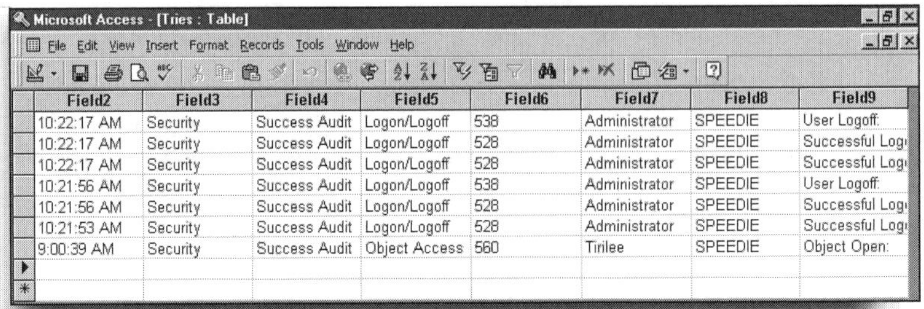

Field2	Field3	Field4	Field5	Field6	Field7	Field8	Field9
10:22:17 AM	Security	Success Audit	Logon/Logoff	538	Administrator	SPEEDIE	User Logoff:
10:22:17 AM	Security	Success Audit	Logon/Logoff	528	Administrator	SPEEDIE	Successful Log
10:22:17 AM	Security	Success Audit	Logon/Logoff	528	Administrator	SPEEDIE	Successful Log
10:21:56 AM	Security	Success Audit	Logon/Logoff	538	Administrator	SPEEDIE	User Logoff:
10:21:56 AM	Security	Success Audit	Logon/Logoff	528	Administrator	SPEEDIE	Successful Log
10:21:53 AM	Security	Success Audit	Logon/Logoff	528	Administrator	SPEEDIE	Successful Log
9:00:39 AM	Security	Success Audit	Object Access	560	Tirilee	SPEEDIE	Object Open:

FIGURE 12.31.
The Save As a comma-delimited file function brings the possibility of using a database management system to organize your Event logs.

Gads—An Event!

The Event Viewer contains many events you can safely ignore. For example, the Intellimouse software when installed with the MS IntelliMouse InPort (wheel mouse) will often generate several warning messages on startup. The start of the Event Viewer itself will generate an event entry.

Special Groups

As already discussed, in Windows NT you can create groups and organize your user accounts in a multitude of ways. I am sure that by now you have noticed several built-in groups. Let's take a look at those groups:

- *Administrators*. A local group, the most powerful group on the computer. Administrators can do just about anything, and they can take ownership of any object (even the ones they don't have access to).
- *Domain Administrators*. Global group with users who have rights to administer multiple servers in the domain.
- *Everyone*. Literally everyone. All user accounts including guest.
- *Domain Users*. A global group. Usually holds all accounts in the workstation's home domain.
- *Users*. A local group. Usually holds all the local accounts and Domain Users. So, all users with domain or local accounts.

- *Guests*. Miscellaneous nonprivileged users.

- *Interactive*. Only the user physically sitting at the console.

- *Network*. Users accessing the workstation from the network session.

- *System*. The Windows NT operating system itself, including drivers and services configured to run in User mode. It is usually fine to give System Full Control.

- *Power Users*. Have some administrative access over the workstation. Power Users can change the system time by default, for example; normal users cannot.

- *Creator Owner*. A special ID that refers only to the user account that created the file.

- *Operators*. Come in several different flavors. Printer Operators have administrative control over the printers, Server Operators can manage and reboot servers, Backup Operators can run backups.

These groups are shown in the standard NTFS file permission dialog box shown in Figure 12.32.

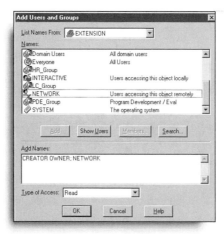

FIGURE 12.32.

The built-in groups provide a foundation to build your security on.

Copying and Moving Protected Files

So, you have got the permissions set just right on all your files. Now, you want to move some files around; will your permissions stay as you set them, or will the files inherit the defaults of the directory they are copied/moved into?

When you copy a file or directory, you are creating a new file and filling it with the contents of an existing file that will still reside somewhere else. Therefore your new files and directories will inherit the default file and directory permissions and owner of the new parent directory.

When you move a file or directory to a new location *on the same partition*, the permissions will stay intact. The difference between copying and moving is that Windows NT doesn't actually move the file data when you move a file, it just rearranges some pointers and housekeeping lists. Therefore the permissions are still valid and never touched.

Moving a file or directory *off of the partition* is a different story, however. It is not a move like the preceding example. Windows NT will actually make a copy to the new location, and then delete the old file. Because this is a copy, the permissions of the destination's parent directory will be inherited.

File Ownership

For each file on an NTFS volume, Windows NT has assigned a user as its owner. File ownership is very important because the file owner always has at least enough permission to change the security on the file—even if he or she can't access it directly. Let's say that I own a file, but for some reason the security on the file is set such that I have no access. As the file owner, I can always edit the security on the file and give myself back the necessary permissions.

Similarly, if the administrator is locked out of an account, he or she can take ownership and then grant whatever permissions are necessary. In Figure 12.33, I am logged on as administrator, but am locked out of the directory c:\web.

What to do now? Here's how to take ownership of the c:\web subtree first.

Confused Yet?

- If you copy, assume that the copy inherited the default permissions at the destination.

- If you move to the same partition, assume that your permissions are intact.

- If you move to a different partition, assume that the permissions of the destination will be inherited.

But, don't take my word for it. It's easy to double-check!

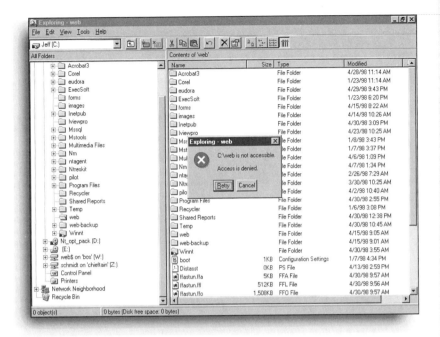

FIGURE 12.33.

Even the administrator can get an occasional access denied error. Here, I have removed my own access to c:\web.

Taking ownership of a file or folder

1. You will need to be logged on as an administrator.

2. Launch Windows NT Explorer and navigate to the file or folder that you wish to take ownership of.

3. Right-click on the file or folder and select Properties, Security Tab, Ownership. Figure 12.34 shows the Owner dialog box.

FIGURE 12.34.

The owner of the directory happens to already be the Administrators group, but it could have been anyone. An administrator can "take owner-ship" from any other user.

4. Even though the Administrators group already owns this directory, I still can't access it because I don't have read, list, or execute permissions. Windows NT will alert me to this and ask whether I want to give myself Full Control while we're taking ownership, as in Figure 12.35. I will say yes to this and all the contained subdirectories.

FIGURE 12.35.

Windows NT volunteers to give me Full Control, which of course I will accept.

5. When it's done stepping through the directory tree, I will have full control over the entire subtree.

Ownership can be taken, but not assigned. After you have taken ownership of something, it remains yours until another user or administrator takes it from you. Not even the mighty Administrator account can assign ownership. This is done for security reasons, so that the administrator doesn't quite have free reign over the system.

Conflicting File Permissions

With a large network with many users, groups, files, and shares, permission conflicts are bound to occur. When a user is a member of many groups, some of these groups may specifically allow access to a resource; some groups may deny that same access. Also, permissions might accumulate. A user might obtain read access to a directory because he's a member of Domain Users, for example, but also have Change Access because he's a member of the Accounting group. Windows NT determines the working set of access privileges in the following manner:

1. Administrators will always have Full Access, one way or another. Access will be denied to an administrator if privileges aren't expressly given to administrators—that is, until an administrator takes ownership.

2. NTFS permissions are combined to allow the most permissive access based on permissions assigned to that user as well as permissions assigned to groups to which that user belongs.

3. An explicit No Access always overrides any granting of access.

4. When resolving conflicts between NTFS and share-point permissions, Windows NT always chooses the most restrictive permissions—that is, the logical intersection of all NTFS permissions and all share-point permissions.

Overview of Security

Although you can create new users and set their rights or permissions individually, most people prefer to create a User Group (or use one of the predefined groups) and make new users part of that group. By setting up user identities, you can make sure that people don't get where they don't belong or mess things up either intentionally or unintentionally.

Many people prefer a working user identity with limited rights even on a machine where they have Administrator rights. This prevents even them from making unintentional mistakes. It's also a way to create different profiles for when they need to use the computer to do different tasks. For most people, the use of Windows NT security is optional; but it's nice to know it's there just in case.

You can monitor the use of a workstation by setting Audit Policies. First activate Audit through the User Manager and then you can set your audits for files and folders using Explorer on NTFS volumes.

You can view the Events logged by the system, its applications, and your security settings by using the Event Viewer. You will need to be logged on with Administrator rights to view the Security part of the Event log.

All or Nothing

When a user or program requests use of a file, he must specify whether he wants read, write, or read/write access. All of these permissions must be allowed or no permissions will be granted. If a user requested read/write access to a file that he was only allowed to read, for example, no access would be granted.

Sharing Resources

Security Concepts

Security is a very important part of networked computing, because potentially millions of people all around the world may be able to access your Windows NT Workstation if it is connected to the Internet. In this section, you learn how Windows NT enables you to assign just the permissions you want to just the people that you want to have them. This chapter is an extension of the concepts and methods from Chapter 12, "Managing Users—NT Security." There is some overlap between the two chapters because Chapter 12 and this one approach resources from slightly different angles.

Before proceeding, I need to expand on some of the security concepts discussed in Chapter 12.

Windows NT Domains

It's a Dangerous World

If you plan to use your Windows NT workstation to serve resources across the Internet, I suggest picking up a book dedicated to the discussion of Windows NT network security. If your Windows NT workstation is connected to a corporate or campus network, check with your network administrator to see what security precautions you need to take.

All Domains Aren't the Same

Don't confuse a Windows NT domain with the IP domains that were discussed in Chapter 8, "Networking Fundamentals." A Windows NT domain is some logical grouping of users. In a large corporation, the Accounting Department may have their own domain called "Accounting," the Purchasing department may have their own domain called "Purchasing," and so on. These domains have nothing to do with the TCP/IP protocols.

The basic administrative unit of a Windows NT network is the *domain*.

SEE ALSO

➤ *See TCP/IP domains in the section titled "Computer Names" in Chapter 8, "Networking Fundamentals."*

Windows NT domains almost always correspond to some high-level human organizational scheme, such as departments in a corporation. Each domain will have one or more Windows NT Servers that act as *domain controllers*. User accounts exist within these domains. If the Marketing Department has its own domain, all the employees of the Marketing Department would be members of the Marketing domain and have accounts that reside on the Marketing domain controllers.

Domain controllers are the central repositories for account information for all the member users. In other words, all the account information for all employees in the Purchasing Department will reside on the domain controllers that manage the Purchasing domain. You can see that this scheme is much better than the other option, which is having account information distributed over possibly hundreds or thousands of individual workstations all over the place. In this way, network administrators can do account maintenance easily from the domain controllers without the need to maintain local accounts on many workstations.

When I say *account information*, I am referring to username, password, permissions, and all the other information visible in User Manager. User *credentials* refer just to the username/password pair.

Authentication is the process of determining that a user is indeed who he or she claims to be. In the computer world, authentication is usually accomplished by comparing credentials presented by the user to an account database. If I say my name is Jeff and I present Jeff's password, the computer will assume that I am indeed Jeff and not Tirilee.

Authentication in the physical world is usually accomplished with a driver's license or some other government issued ID card. This offers a perfect parallel to what we computer scientists call a *trusted third party*. Assume that a man walks up to me and claims his name is Joe. He proceeds to show me a reasonable Ohio driver's license reinforcing his story.

If the license does indeed corroborate all the information he has given me, including a matching photo and the name Joe, there is a good chance that I will believe he is indeed Joe. We can say that I trust Ohio to have properly authenticated Joe using alternative means such as birth certificates, government records, and so forth.

After this *initial authentication* by the state, I don't need to DNA-type Joe myself to establish his identity to my satisfaction. Here, the State of Ohio is a trusted third party. The same can be said if I was introduced to Joe by a good friend of mine. I trust my friend, therefore I trust he provided me with accurate information and that this guy is actually named Joe. Here, my friend is the trusted third party.

Domain controllers perform the initial authentication usually by requesting username/password credentials at Windows logon. If you are using a domain account, when you press Ctrl+Alt+Del and log on to your computer first thing in the morning, you are authenticating with the domain controller. If your credentials

Domain Controllers

For each domain, there must be at least one Windows NT Server designated as a primary domain controller (PDC). There may be zero or more backup domain controllers (BDCs) that exist to distribute load and provide fault tolerance in the event of a PDC failure. For our purposes, all domain controllers perform identical tasks and thus I refer to any and all PDCs and BDCs collectively as *domain controllers*.

Better Authentication Methods

Using a password for authentication isn't particularly effective because passwords are usually written down, shared, or easily guessed. Therefore other methods of computer authentication are becoming more popular, including digital ID cards (smart cards).

match a valid account, the domain controller is satisfied that you are who you say you are.

The domain controller will then serve as a trusted third party and authenticate you to other servers and workstations that are configured to trust the domain controller. All workstations and servers that are members of the domain "trust" the domain controllers—that's what it means to be a member of a domain. Those servers and workstations (and others, if configured) may ask the domain controllers to authenticate users for them. This eliminates the need for multiple accounts, as you will see here. Let's look at three scenarios to illustrate these security concepts.

The goal: You work for the Payroll Department, which has a Windows NT domain called Payroll. Using your Windows NT Workstation, you want to make some sensitive data files available to only three people, also in the Payroll Department. The files are stored locally on your workstation's hard disk.

Method 1: You create a single local account, PayrollUsers, assign a password to it, and give the account the necessary permissions to access the files. You will need to distribute the (common) password to the users in some secure manner (see Figure 13.1).

FIGURE 13.1.

A single local account shared by all users needing to access the shared resource.

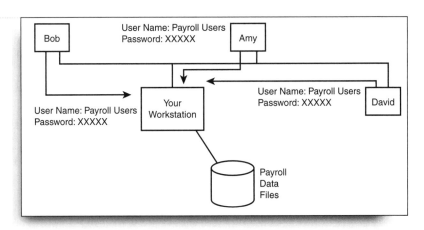

Advantages:

1. Easy initial setup.

2. Only one account to maintain.

Disadvantages:

1. No user granularity. You can't determine which user does what. Auditing is basically useless.

2. The common password will quickly become known to everyone, except (possibly) the Pope. This is a result of human nature to share and write down passwords.

3. All users will have the exact same permissions. If you want different permissions given to different users, you will have to make separate accounts.

4. You are now a network administrator with accounts to maintain. If you share many resources with many people, this could become quite time consuming. Users will forget their usernames, passwords, and so on. You will need to create new accounts for new employees and delete accounts when employees leave or no longer need access to the resource.

5. The users will have to log on to the resources individually using a different username and password pair than their Windows logon credentials. This can be confusing, especially if they connect to many resources that have many usernames and passwords.

Method 2: You create three local accounts on your workstation for the three employees. You will need to select passwords for the users and communicate the passwords to them in some secure manner (see Figure 13.2).

Advantages:

1. User granularity. Through audit, you can now track which user has done what.

2. Passwords will be more secure.

3. You can assign different permissions to each individual user.

A Bad Security Practice

It is very poor security practice to share a single account among multiple users, as I have illustrated in method 1. When more than one user share common username/password credentials, there is no accountability. You cannot use Windows NT's excellent auditing facilities to track usage because you are not certain which actual user is using the account. This is an example of resource-based security, which, luckily, went out with Windows 3.11.

FIGURE 13.2.

Individual local accounts for each user needing access to the resource.

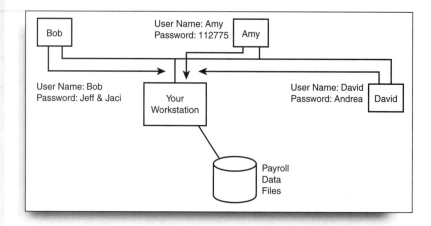

Disadvantages:

1. See #3 and #4 in the preceding Advantages list.

Method 3: Because all your Windows NT workstations are participating in the domain Payroll, you can use the domain controller as a trusted third party to authenticate the users (see Figure 13.3).

FIGURE 13.3.

Using a Windows NT Server domain controller to act as a trusted third party. Users are authenticated using their Windows logon credentials.

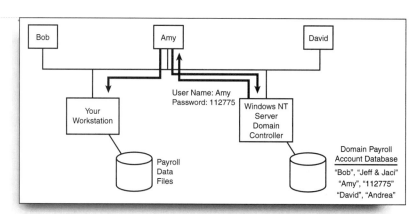

Advantages:

1. #1 and #2 from the preceding Advantages list.

2. You aren't a network administrator, because you aren't creating and maintaining accounts locally. You're using the authentication vehicle already in place, the Windows logon.

You don't have to deal with lost passwords, new accounts, and so forth. Let the real network administrators deal with that; after all, it's their job!

3. Easy for the users. Connecting will be transparent; they won't even be asked for a username/password pair because they have already authenticated with the domain controller.

Disadvantages:

1. Not possible unless there is a Windows NT domain in place that authenticates all the users to whom you need to grant access.

2. You can only authenticate users who have domain accounts in this way. If a user you need to assign permissions to doesn't have a domain account, you will need to use method 2.

In method three, your workstation uses the domain controllers as a trusted third party to authenticate the users. NT people use the term "trusted third party" because both computers trust the domain controller to provide accurate information, even though it isn't directly involved in the transaction—just as the State of Ohio isn't directly involved in every authentication using a driver's license.

Method three is called *domain authentication*. Account credentials are passed to the domain controller for analysis. The domain controller, armed with the account database, validates the credentials and returns the user's permissions and related account information to the requesting source.

Domain authentication is often used in multiserver, multiworkstation environments, as shown in Figure 13.4. If domain authentication weren't used, each server and each workstation would need to maintain accounts for each user. In a situation where there are many servers and many users, disaster would quickly ensue.

Accounts and Logging On

You learned in the preceding chapter that every Windows NT user has an account and that the permissions assigned to that account define what the user is and is not allowed to do.

Domain Authentication Fits NT Architecture

The preferred architecture of a Windows NT Server network is to have multiple servers each performing specific tasks, as in Figure 13.4. This differs from the traditional UNIX network architecture where there was typically one "super-server" doing everything. Hardware prices are the primary reason for this difference: UNIX runs on large, expensive computers; Windows NT, on the other hand, can run on comparatively small, inexpensive computers. Note that this trend is changing as UNIX becomes more popular on Intel platforms and RISC architecture computers drop in price.

Networked computing is no exception. Every user who connects to your workstation over the network will be authenticated and will be assigned permissions from an account.

The Guest Account

By default, Windows NT Workstation's guest account is enabled. Because you will likely be sharing files with a group of known persons, you will probably want to disable the guest account. This prevents your computer from allowing connections by persons who do not have accounts. When persons without explicit accounts access your computer and are logged on using the guest account, it is called *anonymous access.*

Disabling the guest account

1. Open User Manager.

2. Double-click the account named "guest."

3. Check Account Disabled in the User Properties dialog box, as in Figure 13.4.

FIGURE 13.4.

Disabling the guest account prevents users without accounts from accessing your workstation.

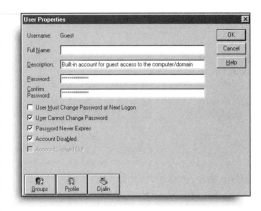

4. Click OK.

SEE ALSO

➤ *See the sections titled "User Manager Accounts," in Chapter 12, "Managing Users—NT Security."*

Different Types of Logons

A user may log on to your Windows NT workstation in two ways:

- *By using an account on the local workstation.* This includes the local guest account, if enabled. Windows NT Workstation will request logon credentials and compare them to those stored in the local account database.

- *By using a domain account on either the domain your workstation is a member of, or, a domain that is trusted by your home domain.* Windows NT Workstation will request logon credentials and forward them to the appropriate domain controller for authentication. We will talk about trust relationships next.

These two types of authentication were shown in Figures 13.1 and 13.3. No matter which form of authentication is used, every user accessing your computer will have a Windows NT account associated with him and her.

Fully qualified account names have two parts: a domain (or machine) name followed by a username. The two parts are separated by a backslash (\), as follows:

- Accounting\JBarnett (Domain: Accounting; User: JBarnett)
- HR\Carlson (Domain: HR; User: Carlson)
- BigServer\Administrator (Domain: BigServer; User: Administrator)

This lets Windows NT know which domain controller can authenticate your account. Fully qualified account names are used heavily when we start authenticating between domains.

Trust Relationships

Building on the preceding example, let's say that, in addition to the Payroll domain, there is also an Accounting domain and a Human Resources (HR) domain. These domains each have their own Windows NT Server domain controllers that maintain the list of accounts in each domain.

Disabling the Guest Account Is a Good Idea

When the guest account is enabled, any user can connect to or directly access your workstation. Users who don't have accounts will inherit the permissions of the guest account. Under most circumstances, this behavior is undesirable and you will want to disable the guest account. Windows NT Server installs by default with the guest account disabled, but on NT Workstation you will need to disable the guest account in User Manager.

Why All This Security?

Windows NT is a secure operating system. It differs in this from other Microsoft operating systems such as Windows 98. Using NT, unlike Windows 98, you can make sure that nobody but authorized people accesses your workstation at all. Similarly, you can secure various resources such as folder structures or whole volumes from unauthorized use.

I, for example, use NT security to make sure my five year old daughter doesn't inadvertently erase or otherwise meddle in my business files. There is really no way to ensure this using a non-NT Microsoft operating system.

It isn't unreasonable to assume that there might be times that someone from the HR domain might want to run a report on personnel salaries. For this, he needs to access resources in the Payroll domain and/or the Accounting domain. Users in the Payroll Department might also need access to HR and accounting records. Now we have the same problem we looked at a few pages ago: Must we create duplicate accounts, one in each domain, for the users that need access resources in several domains?

Luckily, the answer is no. Microsoft included a vehicle in Windows NT Server that allows domains to use domain controllers from foreign domains as trusted third parties to perform user authentication. Therefore a user in HR can access a resource in Payroll without a separate logon, assuming of course that he or she has the appropriate permissions. The Payroll domain would trust that the HR domain properly authenticated the user and would grant the assigned permissions. Figure 13.5 shows the trust relationships between the domains.

FIGURE 13.5.

Domain trust relationships allow computers in different domains to authenticate with one and other. In this figure, user Jaci, a member of the Accounting domain, is logging on to computer B, which is a member of the HR domain.

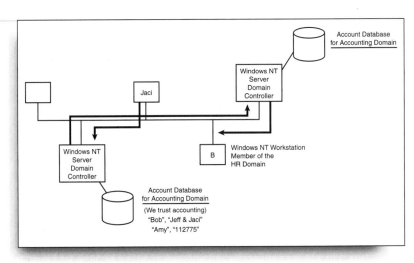

So, why does this matter to you? If the domain your Windows NT workstation belongs to is involved in trust relationships, you are free to grant access and assign permissions to any user of any trusted domain, not just your local domain. Say, for example, that my computer is a member of the Accounting domain, and

Accounting has trust relationships with HR and Purchasing. I can grant access and assign permissions to users in the HR and Purchasing domains just as easily as if they too were members of Accounting. No additional accounts are required and no additional logons will be asked of the users. Windows NT takes care of all the authentication detains behind the scenes. This is a big plus and will make your life much easier. We will take a look at permissions again when we actually secure and share some resources in just a bit.

Assigning Permissions

Now, let's put the previous two sections together and look at actually assigning permissions. I know we haven't looked at sharing anything yet, we will get to that in the next section. The procedure for assigning permissions is basically the same for all resources.

Let's look at some common folder, file, share point, and printer permissions and what they mean in English.

Folder Permissions

- *List*. The user can list the contents of the folder. No files can be read, executed, or altered, nor can any new files or folders be added. Permissions on the folder and contained files may not be altered.
- *Add*. The user can add files and folders to an exiting folder and list the contents of the folder. The user may not read, execute, or alter existing files. Permissions on the folder and contained files may not be altered.
- *Read*. The user can read and execute existing files in the folder as well as list the contents of the folder. New files or folders cannot be added nor can any existing files be altered. Permissions on the folder and contained files may not be altered.
- *Add & Read*. Add combined with read. The user may add new files and folders as well as read and execute existing files. Existing files may not be altered. Permissions on the folder and contained files may not be altered.

- *Change*. The user may read, write, and execute any file in the folder. Contents of the folder may be listed. Permissions on the folder and contained files may not be altered.

- *Full Control*. Same as change, but permissions may be altered.

File and Share Point Permissions

- *Read*. Contents of the file may be read and the file may be executed. The file contents and permissions cannot be altered.

- *Change*. Contents of the file may be read or changed, but the permissions cannot be adjusted.

- *Full Control*. Same as change, but permissions may be altered.

Printer Permissions

- *Print*. The user can print to the printer and pause, resume, or delete his or her own jobs.

- *Manage Documents*. The user can change the status of print jobs belonging to anyone, but may not change printer configuration settings.

- *Full Control*. The user is allowed complete access to adjust user print jobs and printer configuration settings.

The No Access Permission

You can assign the No Access permission to any resource. Assigning this permission expressly denies access to a particular user or group. However, this is rarely necessary because not granting access is the same as denying access. The only time you will want to use the No Access permission is if you want to refine a group permission to exclude several users or groups. Assume Jaci is a member of the Accounting group, which has Change permissions on a resource. For whatever reason, you want to remove only Jaci's access to the resource, but maintain access for the rest of the users in Accounting.

You have two choices: either remove the Accounting group completely and add each individual user (except Jaci) or keep the Accounting group and add a No Access permission for Jaci. A No Access permission is absolute and has precedence over any and all other permissions. Except for refinement as in this example, No Access should not be used. Don't think you're improving security by using No Access all over the place, because you're not. You will just be creating an administrative nightmare.

Figure 13.6 shows the folder permissions. This particular dialog box is discussed in more detail in just a bit.

FIGURE **13.6.**

Folder permissions are given easy-to-understand names in Windows NT.

In Figure 13.7, I have a standard Directory Permissions dialog box.

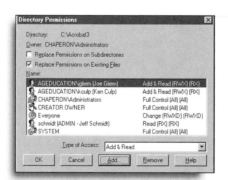

FIGURE **13.7.**

The standard Directory Permissions dialog box.

No Access Is No Good

Avoid use of the No Access permission unless it's used to refine a permission, as in the example in the text.

Note that in Figure 13.7 most of the account names are actually fully qualified account names of the form Domain\Username. The non-fully qualified names are built-in local groups. The permission assigned to the user or group is shown on the right.

The account names are either fully qualified account names or names of built-in local groups. In Figure 13.7, I have permissions assigned to several groups and users from several domains and local accounts have permissions.

When I click Add, I see the Add Users and Groups dialog box, as in Figure 13.8. We add permissions one at a time, perhaps to multiple users. Let's walk through adding a permission.

FIGURE 13.8.

In the Add Users and Groups dialog box, you can choose accounts to assign a permission to from other domains as well as local accounts and accounts on your home domain.

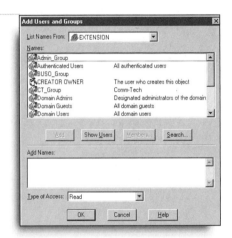

In Figure 13.9, Chaperon is my computer name, Extension is my home domain, and AgEducation is a domain that has a trust relationship with Extension. Note the fully qualified names appear in the bottom window when I add an account.

1. In the List Names From pull-down, I select the domain where the user accounts I want to assign the permission to reside. After I select which domain I want to browse, I select the users and groups I want to add the permission for. In Figure 13.9, I'm browsing the Extension domain. Note that I have clicked the Show Users button so that the individual users are listed. Note that Windows NT will also search for

a particular user for us. Click the Search button to execute a
search.

FIGURE 13.9.

This is the listing of the groups
in the Extension domain. I have
clicked the Show Users button,
so individual user accounts are
listed as well as the groups.

2. Add group and usernames to the Add Names area either by
highlighting the user/group name and clicking the Add button or by double-clicking on the user/group name. The
names that appear in the Add Names area represent the list
of users and/or groups that will receive the permission.

3. I have repeated steps 1 and 2 to select multiple users and
groups from multiple domains.

4. After all the necessary users and groups are selected, choose
the permission you want to assign to them. This is done
with the Type of Access pull-down at the bottom of the dialog box. All the users and groups you have listed will be
assigned that permission. In Figure 13.10, I am assigning
various users and groups the Change permission.

5. Clicking on OK returns me to the Permissions dialog box,
with my additions noted as in Figure 13.11.

Removing a permission is as easy as highlighting the permission
and clicking Remove.

Adding and removing permissions for all securable resources
basically follows the preceding example. Now that you know
how to assign permissions, let's share something!

Where Are My Users?

Because you will usually assign
permissions to groups not to
individual users, and because a
domain might have a considerable number of users, Windows
NT does not by default list the
individual domain users'
accounts in the Permissions dialog boxes. To see all the users
so that you may assign permissions individually, just click the
Show Users button and the
users for the selected domain
will appear at the bottom of the
group listing, as in Figure 13.9.

FIGURE 13.10.

Assigning the Change permission to a couple of users and groups from different domains.

FIGURE 13.11.

My new permissions have been added.

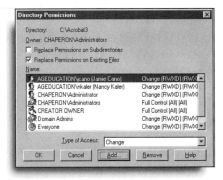

Sharing Files

Windows NT allows you to *share* files, folders or entire volumes on your hard drive. Sharing is hierarchical. It makes the folder, and the files and folders in it, available to other users on the network.

More Security

No FAT here...

For security reasons, I highly suggest using an NTFS partition when you are sharing folders, as it won't be possible to assign detailed file-based permissions otherwise.

First, let's look at the security involved with sharing folders. Windows NT enables you to specify security at two places: the *share point* and the file system (if NTFS). If you're not using the NTFS file system, you can only assign permissions at the share point.

Windows NT will enforce the union of these two sets of permissions—that is, the elements they have in common. All else will be denied, consistent with the "all that is not expressly allowed will be denied" security paradigm. Assume this scenario, for example:

Share point permissions:

- Accounting\RobS: Full Control
- Purchasing\LindaJ: Read Only
- Administrators: Full Control

NTFS permissions:

- Accounting\RobS: Read Only
- Accounting\GareW: Read Only
- Administrators: Full Control

The union is as follows:

- Administrators: Full Control
- Accounting\RobS: Read Only

These are the permissions that Windows NT would enforce given the preceding situation. No other users would be allowed access. Although LindaJ and GareW are given access to the share point and the NTFS volume, respectively, remember we look at the union of the two permission sets. LindaJ isn't mentioned in the NTFS permissions and GareW isn't mentioned in the share point permissions. Because we don't grant access unless specifically enabled, no access is granted to these two users.

The flowchart in Figure 13.12 illustrates how Windows NT determines whether a user will be allowed access to a file.

UNC—Universal Naming Code

UNC is an acronym for *universal naming code*. UNC is a naming convention for files, which provides a machine-independent means of locating the file. A UNC name will usually include a reference to a shared folder and filename accessible over a network instead of specifying a drive letter and path.

FIGURE 13.12.

The process used by Windows NT to determine whether a user will have access to a shared folder.

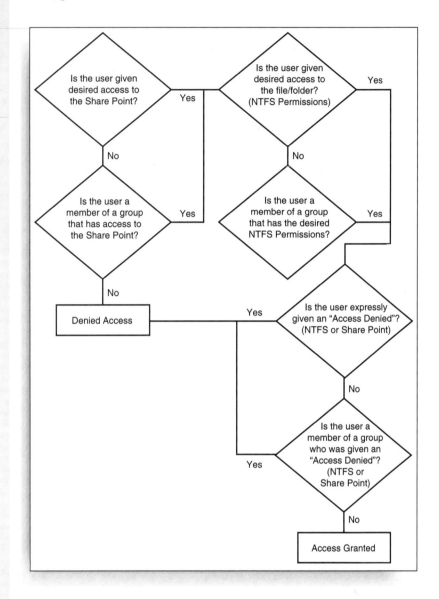

To access a workbook named budget.xls on a shared folder named Excel on the computer called MyWorkstation, for example, you could use the UNC name \\MyWorkstation\Excel\budget.xls. The share point is just \\MyWorkstation\Excel.

Making a Folder Available to the Network

Sharing a folder and setting the permissions

1. From Start, Programs, choose the Windows NT Explorer.

2. Select the folder you wish to share.

3. Right-click and choose Properties from the context menu. Figure 13.13 shows the property sheet for the folder called Shared Reports.

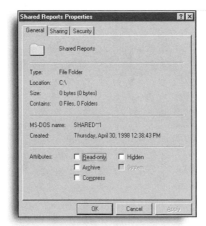

FIGURE 13.13.

Properties for the Shared Reports folder.

4. Click the Sharing tab, select Shared As, and type a meaningful name. This is the name that your folder will go by on the network. You may add a comment as well. In Figure 13.14, I have named the share point "Reports."

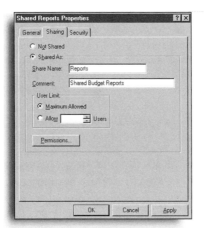

FIGURE 13.14.

Assigning a share name to our folder.

Hidden Shares

When people browse your computer, they can see a list of all the share points you are making available to the network. If you don't want a particular share to be displayed, just append the share name with a dollar sign ($). The share "secret$" won't be visible when browsing, but users who know that it is there can connect to it explicitly.

5. You may limit the maximum number of simultaneous connections to the resource. There is little reason to change this from the default of Maximum Allowed.

6. Click the Permissions button to set share point permissions. Figure 13.15 shows the dialog box. The procedure for assigning permissions, and what each share point permission means, were previously discussed.

FIGURE 13.15.

Setting permissions on the share point. Don't forget that the union of these permissions and the NTFS permissions (if an NTFS volume) determines the access to the resource.

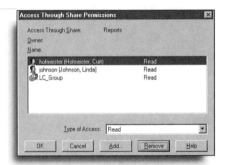

7. If the folder exists on an NTFS volume, click the Security tab and the Permissions button. Set the NTFS permissions accordingly, using the preceding procedure. Figure 13.16 shows my NTFS permissions.

FIGURE 13.16.

NTFS permissions for a shared folder are the same as those for any other folder.

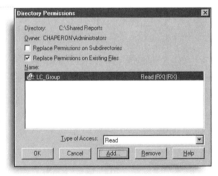

8. If you want to audit use of your files, click Auditing and enable the desired events. In Figure 13.17, I am auditing some common events.

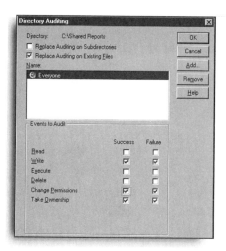

Enable Auditing First

Remember that to audit file accesses, you need to fire up User Manager and enable File and Object Access auditing.

SEE ALSO

➤ *See the sections titled "Auditing" and "Event Viewer" in Chapter 12, "Managing Users—NT Security."*

9. Double-click OK to get out of the share setup, and you're done! Other users can now connect to your share.

Sharing Printers

Windows NT makes it possible for you to allow other people to print to your locally attached printers. Now that you know all about security, we can jump right into making a printer available on the network.

Sharing a printer

1. From the Start menu, choose Settings, Printers. This brings up the Printer Control Panel.

2. Double-click the printer you want to share. This raises the printer configuration dialog box shown in Figure 13.18. Note that it must be a locally attached printer, usually connected to your computer's parallel port.

3. Select Printer, Sharing. A dialog box similar to Figure 13.19 will appear. Select Shared and choose a name for your printer.

FIGURE 13.18.

Printer configuration.

FIGURE 13.19.

Under the Sharing tab, you name your printer and specify any additional drivers you want to install to make life easier for those who connect to your printer.

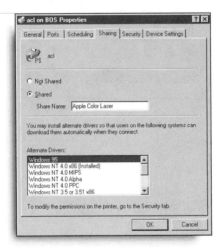

4. You can keep additional drivers for your printer on hand so that the people who connect to your printer won't need to go looking for installation CDs when they connect for the first time. Instead, their computer will just grab the necessary driver from yours. In Figure 13.19, I have asked that the Windows 95 driver be loaded. Note that I will be asked for the Windows 95 CD!

5. Click the Security tab, and then click Permissions. Assign permissions as necessary using the techniques previously discussed. Click OK. Figure 13.20 shows my permissions.

6. If you want to audit use of your printer, click Auditing and enable the desired events. Figure 13.21 shows the events I usually audit.

Have Some Installation CDs Handy

The Windows NT Workstation CD doesn't have the Windows 95/98 or the Windows NT 3.x drivers on it. You will be asked to supply an appropriate installation disk if you select non-NT 4 drivers.

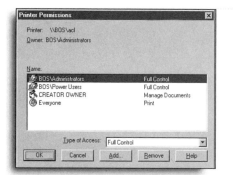

FIGURE 13.20.

Printer permissions are just as intuitive as file permissions.

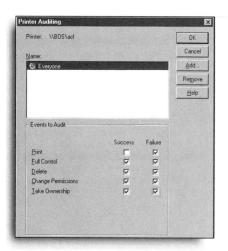

FIGURE 13.21.

Printer auditing is a nice way to keep tabs on use of your printer.

7. Click OK. Your printer is now available to the network!

Connecting to Shared Folders

Connecting to a remote share point is easy. Even if you don't know exactly where you're going, you can still browse the network and hopefully locate the resource you are in need of.

Your C: drive is a logical drive that maps (relates) to a certain partition on your local hard disk. When you connect to a share point, you map the space on the remote drive to a logical drive letter on your own machine. You will map network drives such that you will access storage on remote disks using a local logical drive letter.

Connecting to a share point

1. From the Start menu, choose Programs, Windows NT Explorer.

2. In Explorer, choose Tools, Map Network Drive. A dialog box similar to Figure 13.22 appears. You can also click the button on the Explorer toolbar corresponding to the connect function.

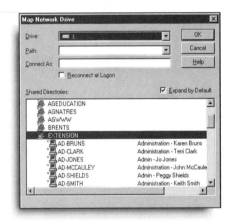

3. Windows NT automatically selects the next available logical drive letter to be mapped. You can change this to a different letter if you have a preference. Note that the UNC name of previously mapped drives appear in the drop-down list, as in Figure 13.23.

4. You have a choice here. If you know the UNC name of the share point you want to connect to, you can type it in the Path input box. Otherwise, you can browse the network below. Double-clicking on a computer exposes a list of shares it is offering. Double-clicking on a domain or workgroup enumerates all the computers in the domain or workgroup. I have located my resource through browsing in Figure 13.24. When I double-click on the share point, Windows NT enters the UNC name into the Path text area.

Nothin' but 'Net!

Fire up a good old-fashioned command prompt and check out the net command. There are a whole slew of net commands that can do just about everything network related—all quickly from a command line session. This functionality is great for use in batch files and Windows Scripting Host scripts. For example: net use R: \\MyServer\Reports will map the local logical R: drive to the share point \\MyServer\Reports. Do a net help and prepare to be impressed!

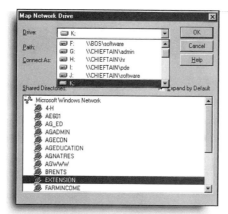

FIGURE 13.23.

Windows NT reminds you of previous drive mappings by placing the UNC name with the local logical drive letters in the Drive pull-down list.

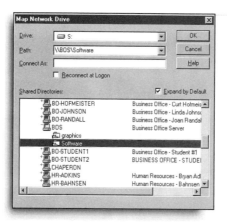

FIGURE 13.24.

Here I'm connecting, or mapping, the local logical S: drive to the share point \\bos\software. I used the browser, but I could have typed the UNC name just as easily.

5. It is possible to connect to a resource using a username/password pair that is different from that of your current logon session. If you want to connect using a different account, type the fully qualified account name in the Connect As text box.

6. Click OK. Your network drive will appear on the drive tree on the left. You may now use the mapped drive as if it were local (see Figure 13.25).

Windows NT will remember which network connections you had at logoff and attempt to restore them when you next logon. You can connect and disconnect to network drives at will. The following example shows you how to disconnect from a network drive.

Browsing Isn't a Walk in the Park

The list of resources you will get performing the operation illustrated in Figure 13.22 is not an exhaustive list, because browsing is far from perfect (especially in large networks). You are also asked which logical drive letter to map and the UNC name of the share point if known.

The sure way to find a resource isn't to browse, but to know its UNC and enter it directly. This isn't too much of a problem on small- or medium-sized networks. Let experience with your particular network be your guide.

FIGURE 13.25.

Network drives, once mapped, behave identically to local drives. The S: drive tree shown here is the network drive we just mapped.

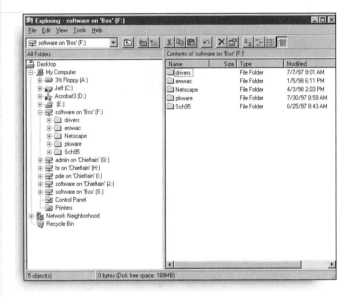

Disconnecting from a network drive

1. From the Start menu, choose Programs, Windows NT Explorer.

2. Choose Tools, Disconnect from Network Drive. You will be presented with a list of all network drives, as in Figure 13.26.

FIGURE 13.26.

Choosing which network drive to disconnect from.

3. Choose the drive you want to disconnect, and then click OK.

Adding/Configuring Hardware

Compatibility Versus Robustness in Windows NT

The Hardware Compatibility List (HCL)

Generic Add Hardware Method for PnP and non-PnP

Determining Windows NT Resources

Installing PnP and non-PnP Hardware

Installing the PnP Service for Windows NT

Hardware and Windows NT

Windows NT is less tolerant of hardware, the nuts and bolts of your computer, than the other Microsoft family of Windows operating systems. This is by design. Microsoft faced a tradeoff between making Windows NT solid and compatible. Because one of the prime goals of Windows NT was robustness, solid won out over compatible.

The tradeoff is most apparent with legacy hardware. Legacy hardware is any hardware existing prior to the introduction of an operating system or version of that operating system. Luckily for the users of Windows NT, the very success of Microsoft's premier operating system makes for a wide selection of hardware designed with Windows NT in mind—most late hardware is.

In some cases, either Microsoft or the manufacturer of legacy hardware will adapt drivers (if possible) to later versions of Windows NT. In some cases the manufacturer of a product believes that his target market isn't using Windows NT, so he doesn't provide drivers for this operating system. Those products are becoming rarer as Windows NT continues its explosive growth. As it is for so many things, the Web is a great place to find updated drivers and other related information about your hardware.

Microsoft maintains a Hardware Compatibility List (HCL) at its Web and FTP sites. This lists all hardware currently certified by Microsoft as working under Windows NT. All items on this list will work; some not on the list will work also, but haven't for one reason or another been certified by Microsoft. The conservative way, however, to hardware installs or purchases if you are running Windows NT is to consult the HCL first, and buy second.

Success Breeds Success

The very success of Windows NT is enticing more hardware vendors to tailor their wares for the operating system. Once Windows NT-specific hardware was rare. Now it's rare for a newly introduced piece of hardware to fail to have NT support.

The Installation Method

The generic method for installing hardware under Windows NT is similar to other Microsoft operating systems. Here it is for non-Plug and Play hardware.

The generics of installation

1. Determine resource requirements for the new hardware.

2. Determine which resources are available in your installation of Windows NT.

3. Configure the hardware for available resource. If necessary, you might have to shuffle resources around for existing hardware to accommodate the new hardware.

4. Install the hardware into or onto the machine.

5. Install drivers or other needed software.

In some cases, steps 3 and 4 are reversed. Most hardware is configured outside of the machine. Some is configured after physical installation by using an installation program of some sort.

If you have Plug and Play (PnP, or autoconfigure) hardware, the steps are a bit different. The steps are as follows:

1. Install (if necessary) or activate (if necessary) the Plug and Play service.

2. Install the hardware physically into or onto your computer.

3. Install necessary drivers by following the onscreen prompts.

Determining Resources

No general rule determines the resource requirements of your new hardware. You must consult the manufacturer, vendor, or documentation. Windows NT does have a complete diagnostic program to determine which resources are available on your machine. The resources that might be in conflict are IRQs, I/O addresses, and DMA channels. New hardware developments such as USB (Universal Serial Bus) will make these problems go away or reduce them considerably, but these are still some time off. For now, users struggle to allocate limited resources to resource-hungry hardware. Here is how to determine which resources are currently available on your computer.

Using Diagnostics to determine hardware resources

1. Choose the Start menu selections Programs|Administrative
Tools (Common)|Windows NT Diagnostics. As with all
Administrative Tools applets, you should be logged on with
Administrator level rights. Your screen should resemble
Figure 14.1.

FIGURE **14.1.**

One of the most used administrative tools is Windows NT
Diagnostics.

2. Each tab of the Windows NT Diagnostic dialog box has a
different set of information. The Version tab, the one shown
in Figure 14.1, has complete version information including
which, if any, Service Packs are installed. The processor
information is valuable in those rare instances where support
personnel believe a problem stems from a processor fault.

3. Click on the Resources tab. Your screen should resemble
Figure 14.2. Each button along the bottom will reveal a different set of resources. This makes for a simpler display than
if all the information was stuffed into one list box.

4. If you want to see a complete display of resources, check the
Include HAL Resources check box. This will reveal all
resources, including those you can't alter. HAL stands for
Hardware Abstraction Layer—the layer of Windows NT
that lies in between the hardware and the rest of the system.

Resources and Your Computer

Generally speaking, two hardware
devices can share the same
resources, but can't share them at
the same time. Resource 1 and
Resource 2 can share the same IRQ,
for example, as long as Resource 1
and Resource 2 never run simultaneously.

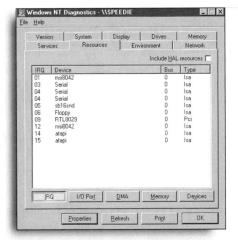

FIGURE 14.2.

The first three buttons on the Resources tab represent the resources where most conflicts arise.

5. Click the button for the resource or resources you wish to determine. You can use the menu to save or print a resource report by using the File I Save Report or File I Print Report entries, respectively. You can also click the Print button to output any display you wish to preserve.

6. To see some details about any resource, highlight that resource and then click on Properties. To see details about the serial ports, for example, click the Devices button, and then highlight the Serial entry, and finally, click on Properties. Figure 14.3 shows the results of doing this on one computer.

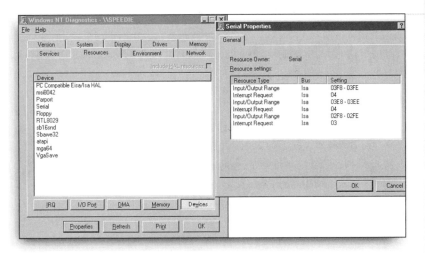

FIGURE 14.3.

The display of Diagnostics isn't particularly user friendly. With a little concentration, however, most people can winkle out the meaning of the display. Here a system has three serial ports with some IRQ conflict.

Modern Times

Most current production hardware has a great deal of flexibility as to computer resources. Older hardware and some specialty modern hardware might require specific hardware addresses or IRQs. In some cases, software will demand particular hardware configuration. For example, I recently had to struggle with a custom software communications program that could only recognize (address) COM2:.

7. Note that although each of the three serial ports has its own address space (I/O), two share IRQ 4. Compare Figure 14.3 with Figure 14.2 and you will see pretty much the same information there, too. Windows NT Diagnostics displays IRQ as IRQ in the dialog box in Figure 14.2, but calls it Interrupt Request in the dialog box in Figure 14.3.

Using Diagnostics

1. You want to install a device that can use IRQ 11 and an I/O address space of 0E24-0E40. Will that work in the computer shown in Figures 14.1–3?

2. From the screen shown in Figure 14.1, click on the Resources tab. Examine the display to see whether any device is using IRQ 11. Figure 14.2 shows this display. As you can see, no device is apparently using this resource. Now click on the I/O Port button. Figure 14.4 shows the resulting screen.

FIGURE 14.4.

Clicking on the I/O Port button on the Resources tab produces a listing of devices.

3. The I/O display is a bit troublesome to understand until you realize it is in hexadecimal, or BASE 16 format.

4. As you can see, the requested I/O starts above the Sbawe32 (SoundBlaster) device's ending address and ends below the RTL8029 (network adapter) card's starting address.

This makes letting the new device use IRQ 11 and the I/O address OE24-OE40 a safe thing to try.

Not all devices and resource eaters appear as they should in Windows NT Diagnostics. Also, some devices don't configure as their manufacturers and documentation says they do. Although you have found what you think are safe places to address your new hardware, be alert to system malfunctions after installation.

If you choose to allow a conflict that you believe is safe, be especially observant when using the devices in conflict. The machine used for illustration here, for example, has a tablet (Wacom Artpad II) sharing an IRQ with the modem. This works fine as long as the modem and the Artpad aren't used at the same time—something that never seems to occur. Previously the modem was set up to share an IRQ with the UPS (uninterruptible power supply). This caused the UPS to think something at the computer malfunctioned whenever the modem got used, an unsatisfactory arrangement.

Installing Drivers

As with determining new hardware requirements, no generic rule(s) applies to installing drivers for your new hardware. You must consult your hardware documentation, the vendor you got the stuff from, or go right to the manufacturer.

Because driver installation is supposed to be a user operation, manufacturers tend to make it as user friendly as they can. After all, if you have a nightmare installation with a Wowie-Zowie video card, you are unlikely to buy another. Manufacturers know you have a wide selection and respect that you do.

In the case of downloaded drivers, usually from the Internet, you might find valuable documentation embedded in the download. If the download requires an extraction (such as unzipping a ZIP file or running a self-extracting program), examine the files for anything that looks like a document. Such files usually have extensions of .WRI, .DOC, or .TXT. Be sure to review these files before attempting the driver setup. Some driver installs, such as those for some Creative Labs' SoundBlaster line, require

What Would Happen?

Running two devices sharing the same resources at the same time isn't fatal by any means. The only problem that can occur is the failure of one or both to function.

In some cases, the failed resource needs a full power off reset. Don't be shy about testing two hardware devices sharing the same computer resources. You can't hurt the hardware, the computer, or your Windows NT setup by doing so.

multiple setups in the proper order. Failure to adhere to the setup requirements will result in a malfunctioning piece of hardware, as well as a great deal of frustration for you.

If things go utterly awry, you can remove the device from your system either through the Control Panel or by actually pulling the new device and then removing its driver. To remove a multimedia device such as a sound card, for example, open Start|Settings|Control Panel|Multimedia|Devices. Figure 14.5 shows this display.

FIGURE 14.5.

The Devices tab of the Multimedia applet enables you to remove or examine related devices.

Web Information

If the hardware you are about to install is new or complex, try visiting the vendor's Web site before you try. You might find information that will save you a lot of frustration. It's not at all rare for vendors to put poorly tested hardware in the field in hopes that users will find out what can go wrong. As the vendor learns where the problems are, he usually posts them for subsequent users' elucidation.

Locate and highlight the device you wish to remove, click the Remove button, and it's "Hasta la vista, baby" to the offending piece of hardware.

Adding Plug and Play to Windows NT

Microsoft defended the lack of Plug and Play (PnP) in Windows NT 4 by saying it will be there in Windows NT 5. Curiously enough, the company has been very quiet about the perfectly functional, but somewhat limited, PnP in Windows NT 4. This service isn't installed by default.

Some hardware for Windows NT requires the PnP service for configuration. If you decide to install some such hardware, you must first locate and install the PnP service into your version of Windows NT. There is little, if any, advantage to installing this service without compliant hardware.

To install PnP, first locate the driver on the distribution CD or wherever you have your distribution file. The standard CD has the Intel driver located at [Drive:]\DRVLIB\PNPISA\X86. Figure 14.6 shows this directory (folder).

FIGURE 14.6.

Plug and Play lives in Windows NT 4! You just need to know where to find it.

To install PnP, right-click on the INF file and choose Install from the context menu, as shown in Figure 14.6. This action starts the install process. From that session on, you will have a new service started at each session. Figure 14.7 shows the new service up and running in Windows NT.

To see the display shown in Figure 14.7, choose Start I Settings I Control Panel I Services.

Figure 14.8 shows a post-PnP boot screen when Windows NT detects new hardware without a driver. (I forced this screen by leaving the PnP joystick port enabled, but with a disabled (removed) driver. Windows NT detected the port and realized that it didn't have a driver, so it commented on the fact.)

Just for the Heck of It

There is no upside and some risk to installing the PnP Service unless you need it. Even if it causes no trouble, it will eat resources and do no good. In other words, don't bother unless you have to.

FIGURE 14.7.

After installation, Plug and Play
will be started automatically.

FIGURE 14.7.

After installation, Plug and Play
will be started automatically.

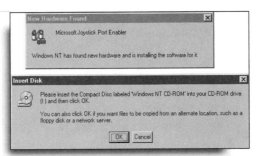

FIGURE 14.8.

The dreaded and welcomed
dialog boxes showing PnP
active. They are dreaded when
the hardware is detected
incorrectly. They are welcomed when PnP works properly, as it is doing here.

Is PnP Installed?

Plug and Play (PnP) is a service
under Windows NT. When installed,
it appears in the Services list
(Control Panel|Services).

PnP works fine until it doesn't. In some cases, PnP will detect
phantom hardware and demand drivers for these nonexistent
devices. You can either try to diagnose and fix these errors
through applets such as Windows NT Diagnostics or Control
Panel, or you can just ignore these messages by clicking on
Cancel to remove the dialog boxes. PnP wakes up only upon a
boot up, therefore error detection messages won't appear on
workstations left on permanently.

Optimizing

Overview of Optimizing

By just installing Windows NT on a recommended hardware platform (as opposed to the minimum Microsoft asserts that Windows NT will run under), you will get yourself a finely running machine. You can, however, make certain tweaks or adjustments to have your computer running even better for the tasks you actually perform.

Windows NT, unlike many other small computer operating systems, comes with a full set of diagnostic tools that you can use to determine areas where you can improve performance for your particular installation. In some cases the only way to significantly improve performance is to change hardware. In these cases, you will have to make a cost-benefit analysis of your own. At the very least, you will know what you can do and how much benefit it will likely yield.

You need to keep two things in mind. First, what is the aim of optimization? Are you trying to decrease response delays, for example, or trying to increase the rate of processing for such tasks as 3D rendering?

Second, you must recognize that some metrics aren't tunable from within Windows NT. If you have a slow video card, for example, no tuning will make it a fast card. The best you can hope for using the techniques in this chapter is to get the most from what you have. To get more than that, you need to change what you have.

Determining Performance

The goal of optimizing is to relieve bottlenecks. A *bottleneck* in computer talk is a place, or a hardware subsystem that's significantly slower than the rest of the computer. A Windows NT computer running a 400+ MHz processor with an ultra SCSI disk, but with 24MB of RAM will be bottlenecked by the amount of RAM, for example. That's an easy thing to see, quite obviously. In actual use, most bottlenecks are much tougher to determine. So, how you can find these things out? Read on.

The single most effective tool for determining the performance of your system's individual subsystems (to isolate bottlenecks) is the Performance Monitor. Here's an overview of the Performance Monitor.

Using the Performance Monitor

1. Select the Start menu choices Programs|Administrative Tools(Common)|Performance Monitor. Your screen should resemble Figure 15.1.

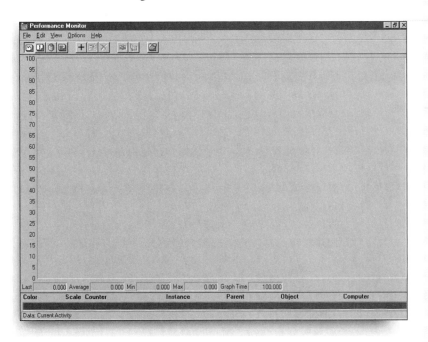

FIGURE 15.1.

The Performance Monitor starts with nothing monitored. The tool is a blank slate awaiting your input.

2. To start monitoring an aspect of a computer, choose the menu selections Edit|Add to Chart, or click on the plus icon in the toolbar. Performance Monitor will open a dialog box.

3. Choose a computer to monitor (the local workstation will be the default), an object to monitor (class of monitoring), and a specific counter for an activity of that object. To monitor the amount of time the CPU works, for example, choose Processor as an object, and %Processor Time as a counter. Click on the Explain button for a short explanation of any

Obviously Elementary

Don't forget the obvious when examining performance. Windows NT needs to have its files defragmented just like earlier Windows versions. Unlike Windows 98, Windows NT doesn't come with a defragger. You need to buy one such as Diskeeper or Norton Utilities for Windows NT.

counter. Figure 15.2 shows these choices for the local work-station, Speedie.

FIGURE 15.2.

These choices will monitor the amount of time the CPU is busy processing tasks, and by the inverse, its idle time.

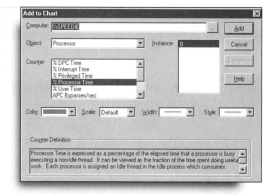

4. You can change the way the display looks by altering the selections along the bottom row of combo boxes shown in Figure 15.2. Click on Add, and Performance Monitor will add the CPU usage counter to the Performance Monitor main screen. Figure 15.3 shows this. Click on the Close button to clear the dialog box.

FIGURE 15.3.

You're now monitoring CPU usage for the selected workstation.

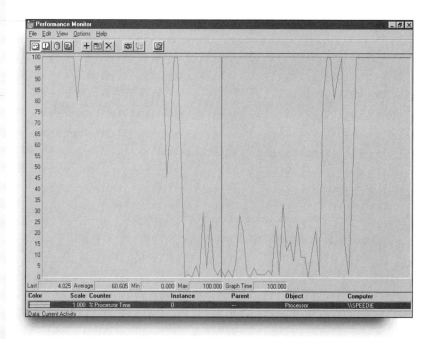

5. The display in Figure 15.3 shows that this CPU varies its usage from almost idle to 100%. (I manipulated this monitor by starting and stopping processes to give a good display for this screen.)

6. You can change the look of the chart by using the Options|Chart (or Ctrl+O) menu selections. That will enable you to vary the sample time and to change the display from a line chart to a bar (histogram). Figure 15.4 shows this dialog box.

FIGURE **15.4.**

You can vary the Performance Monitor Chart Options by using this dialog box. The more frequently you set the Interval, the more the Performance Monitor affects the performance that it is supposed to be monitoring; so take it easy.

7. Figure 15.5 shows the histogram display for a single counter—the same one used for the rest of this example. This isn't a very useful display. Look at the bottom of the figure, however, or launch the Performance Monitor on your computer and look at the bottom two display rows. The second to the bottom row contains summary information, and the absolute bottom row is a legend. The legend isn't important with one or two counters. When you have several running, however, it is vital!

Now you have had a quick look at the Performance Monitor. Here's some other things you can do with it.

Reporting

You can change the view of the Performance Monitor to a Report (View|Report, or click on Report in the toolbar) that will, in effect, give screen space to the display in the second to last row in the Chart display—the one shown in the Figures 15.1–15.5. Figure 15.6 shows a Report format for several counters of two objects, Processor and Thread.

Removing Counters

To remove any counter in any module of Performance Monitor, highlight the targeted counter, and then click the Delete Selected Counter button (the one with the *x*) on the toolbar.

FIGURE 15.5.

The Performance Monitor can be changed into report format.

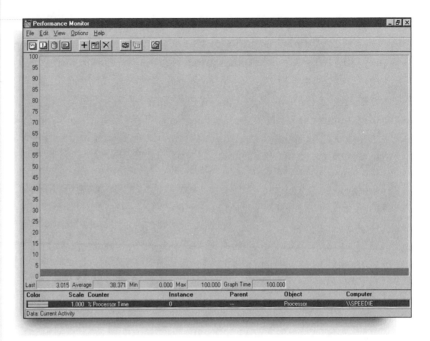

FIGURE 15.6.

The Report format shows an easy-to-read display of all the counter summaries.

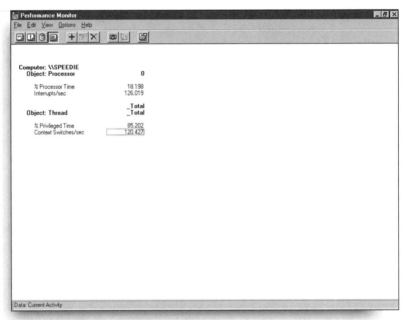

The Processor in the display for Figure 15.6 is labeled 0, as it is the first (and only) processor in this workstation. Windows NT workstations can have multiple processors, each of which you can monitor separately using Performance Monitor.

The bottom section shows the *thread(s)*. Think of threads as individual tasks within an application or system service. An application running under Windows NT can spawn many threads. A word processor, for example, might launch a thread to do a search and replace while still allowing editing. A single-threaded application can't allow two (or more) "thoughts" to happen simultaneously. In reality, the threads only "appear" to happen at the same time. In fact, Windows NT is switching between them like crazy.

How often Windows NT switches its attention from thread to thread is shown in the last report in Figure 15.6. As you can see, this computer was switching its attention from thread to thread at a rate of 120 per second when this Performance Monitor session was occurring.

You can export a report using the File | Export Report into a format used by Performance Monitor or to a comma-delimited text file that you can, in turn, import into most applications.

Logging

Logging means to collect and write to disk Performance Monitor data gathered at a user-specified interval. Here's how to use Performance Monitor to create a log.

Using the Performance Monitor log

1. Start the Performance Monitor.

2. Choose View | Log from the menu or make the appropriate toolbar choice.

3. Choose Options | Log from the menu. Your screen should resemble Figure 15.7.

Swept Away

Don't get carried away tweaking performance to the last ounce. A few percentage points in performance won't be noticeable, but your lost time fiddling will be.

How Fast Is Fast?

A 400MHz processor executes at 400 million cycles per second. A modern computer has no trouble executing quite a few processes within a single second, or even a small fraction of a second.

What Are These Things?

Even expert computer people have some trouble remembering what each counter in Performance Monitor does and what its significance is. Keep in mind the Details button, which offers some explanation for all of them. In many cases, this explanation is a bit thin, but at least something's there.

FIGURE 15.7.

You need to supply a unique name and path for your log file.

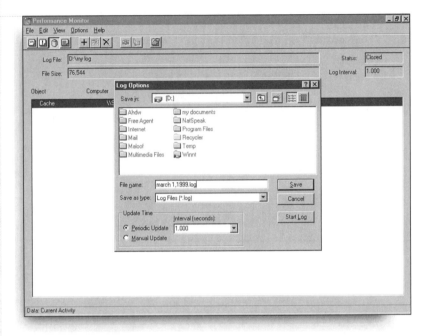

FIGURE 15.7.

You need to supply a unique name and path for your log file.

4. Enter a name for your log file. Change the update time from default if you wish. You might, for example, wish to increase the sample interval.

5. Click on the Start Log button.

6. The Log window will now start to display the size of the log file in the File Size text box near the top of the screen.

7. When you have logged enough information, choose the menu selections Options|Log and click on the Stop Log button. Windows NT will write the log to the file specified in step 4.

Setting Alerts

You can have the Performance Monitor watch your computer for instances where a metric (a measurement) will fall outside of a parameter you set. You can set an alert to record the instance and optionally run a program, for example. Here's how.

Using Performance Monitor alerts

1. Open Performance Monitor.

2. Choose View|Alert or Ctrl+A or the appropriate button on the toolbar. Click on the Add button on the toolbar, or choose Edit|Add to Alert from the menu. Your screen should resemble Figure 15.8.

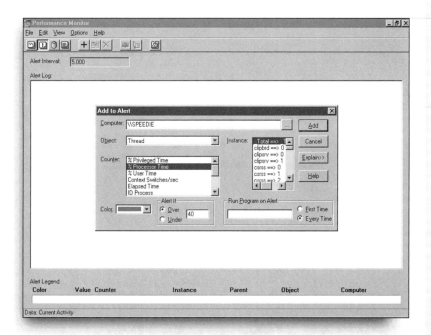

FIGURE 15.8.

Here's where you can add a variety of objects, counters, and parameters to set for an alert.

3. Add the object and counter you wish to set an alert for. Set the values you wish to monitor for (over or under). This example uses a Thread setting that will generate many alerts. This isn't a practical setting, but one chosen for demonstration. Enter a program you wish to run when an alert occurs. This is optional.

4. Click on Add, and then click on Done when you have finished adding counters and objects. Whenever the computer enters the condition you set, such as the settings in Figure 15.8, Performance Monitor will generate an entry. You can see a series of such entries in Figure 15.9.

FIGURE 15.9.

Each time a computer enters the targeted zone, Performance Monitor will generate an entry in the Alerts module.

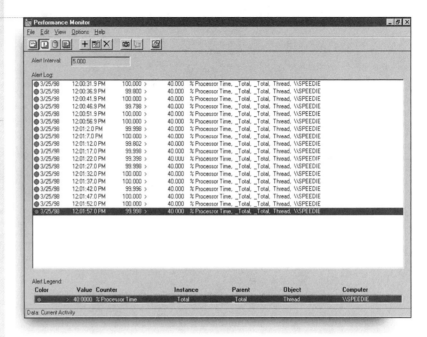

5. To remove any counter, select the counter and click on the Delete Selected Counter button on the toolbar.

Using alerts to monitor your computer's performance areas makes much more sense than sitting there watching the metrics.

Using the Performance Monitor

Now that you know how to use the various features of the Performance Monitor, you need to understand what to use it for. Certain metrics work in concert, so they need to be measured together. Windows NT uses a disk cache (RAM) to speed up disk performance, for example. If you have too little RAM, your disk will run slowly—but not because of inherently slow characteristics. Adding a faster hard disk without adding more RAM won't help much, if at all. Adding more RAM to the computer while keeping the existing disk, however, might be all it takes to get a significant speed increase.

By monitoring various aspects of your computer, you will learn what your often used tasks require in the way of computer resources. This way you can plan your upgrades and future purchases.

Before monitoring any disk-related performance, you need to enable it for the computer you wish to monitor. Here's how.

Using disk monitoring within Performance Monitor

1. Open a command-line window by choosing the menu selections Start | Run and entering `cmd` in the dialog box. Press Enter.

2. Enter the command `diskperf -y \\computer`, substituting the name of the computer you wish to monitor. If left off, the last parameter will indicate to Windows NT that you wish to start monitoring on the local workstation.

3. Close the command-line window by entering `exit` at the command prompt and pressing Enter. Reboot to start disk monitoring.

Note that the Uncertainty Principle from good old physics applies to any monitoring situation. The very act of monitoring elements of your computer changes the actual performance of that computer.

Take a look at Figure 15.10. This Performance Monitor is set to measure disk reads/writes, cache misses, processor times, and interrupts per second. You might be able to see these counters at the bottom of the figure, but as the legend is in color and the book's figures aren't, I will narrate what the figures mean.

The machine in Figure 15.10 is running all the usual (common) services along with five applications. These are a bitmap editor, a large word processor program, Microsoft Access, the Clipboard Viewer, and the Performance Monitor itself. Generally, the activity of the computer is low with spikes for disk reads/writes and processor usage. The spikes are generally where Windows NT changes its attention to another process or the user switches applications.

Quick and Easy Disk Speedup

If you can place the paging file (your virtual memory) on a separate physical disk from your data, Windows NT will "apparently" speed up quite a bit. This is because there is simultaneous need to read/write both the paging file and the application data. In this instance, two heads (disk heads, that is) are better than one.

Really Fast Disks

Several third-party vendors have RAM or virtual disks available for Windows NT. These are areas of RAM that mimic a hard disk, but operate almost as fast as RAM itself. (There is some overhead making them marginally slower than RAM itself.) If you can spare the RAM and need something usually stored on hard disk to really fly, consider buying one of these.

Saving Performance Monitor Settings

You can save the state of the Performance Monitor into a file by choosing the menu selections File|Save As. Then, during a subsequent Performance Monitor session, opening the file (File|Open) will return the Performance Monitor to its previous state.

FIGURE 15.10.

Here are four counters, two
each for processor resources
and disk.

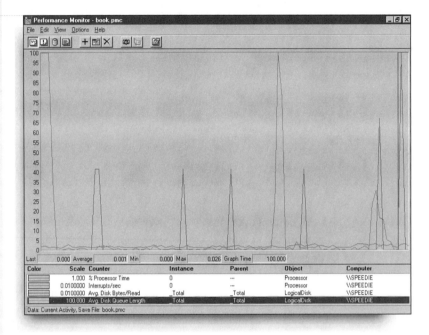

Figure 15.11 shows the Performance Monitor while a complex
Microsoft Access query is running. Note the greater density of
the previous spikes and (take my word for it) the addition of a
longer disk queue. In fact, the disk queue in Figure 15.10 is
almost zero, meaning that there is no delay in disk reads or
writes. As soon as Access started its query, Windows NT experienced a slight increase in the disk queue length.

So what does this tell you? Not surprisingly, adding a query to
the tasks that Windows NT must support dramatically increases
the burden on the entire system. The most dramatic increase in
burden, however, is in the disk queue—the length of the "line"
for data to be read from or written to disk.

You can interpret the results shown in Figures 15.10 and 15.11
two ways. The first way is to see that getting a faster disk will
speed up Access queries. The second way is to see that the
queues do spike and don't plateau, meaning that the system can
catch up with its disk read/write request. I interpret these
screens as saying that this system needs no changes to run the
type of query shown in Figure 15.11 (one million records with
60 fields in one table).

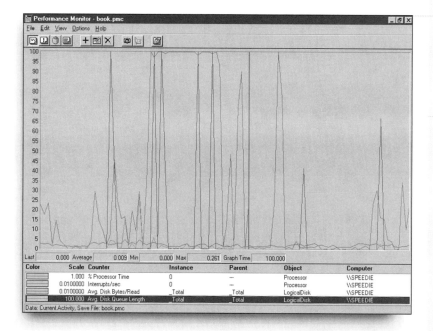

FIGURE 15.11.

Running a query increases the disk queue length from almost zero to a significant amount. It also calls on other system resources.

Figure 15.12 shows the same computer running the same applications and services, but with no user input or application operations. The two spikes you see are disk writes. A little spike is showing increased queue length and processor time within the large spikes. Details such as these are important to interpret the Performance Monitor display.

An idle computer will still write to the disk from time to time, flushing the cache or, in the case of some programs, doing an autosave.

Notice in Figure 15.12 that when the disk reads/writes go up dramatically, the length of the queue and the processor burden go up somewhat, too. That they didn't go up dramatically indicates the system is well within its desired performance metrics.

Say, for example, that the queue not only spikes when the system needs to do some reading or writing, but stays on a plateau for a while. This indicates that the system is delaying its reads or writes, and thus is adversely affecting system performance.

The Wasted Queue

Tasks waiting in queues for computer attention are the single greatest cause of performance penalties. Reducing all queues wherever they form is the path to fast computers.

FIGURE 15.12.

Notice the queue and processor spikes within the larger spike.

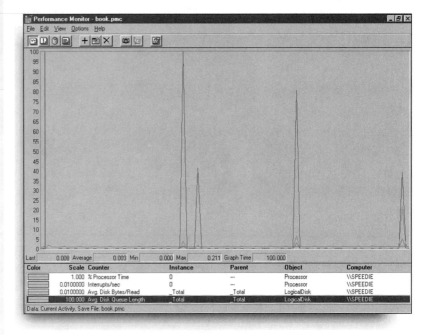

Figure 15.13 shows two different counters, both system ones relating to processor time and processor (not disk) queue length. I generated the spikes at the left of the figure by doing a blur on a large bitmap image. The display shows the spike and the processor usage time, as well as plateaus in the queue length. This indicates that, for this type of operation, the computer is "processor bound" and would be improved by increasing processor throughput. Whether this is practical depends on how much time you spend doing blurs or related operations.

By far the most prevalent performance problem is memory of some type or another. A good set of counters to check your memory's performance are as follows:

- Pages per second: need for the system to read data not in memory.

- Page faults per second: need to read data not in memory or virtual memory.

- Cache faults per second: need for the system to go out and find data not in the disk cache.

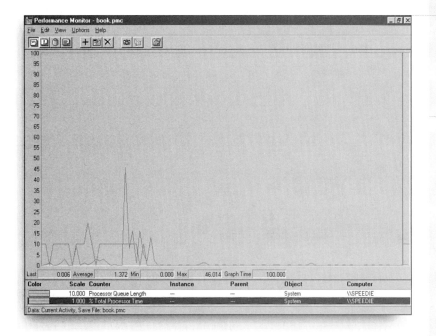

FIGURE 15.13.
Doing bitmap manipulations
are among the most processor-
intensive tasks. This computer
got behind itself when put to
such a task.

Keep in mind that most counters involve other counters or system processes. Ask yourself what other parts of your system might be involved when you find a suspicious counter in Performance Monitor. Always understand that the counter you're seeing might not be the source of the problem, but another symptom.

Quick System Summary—Task Manager

Windows NT has a shortcut system monitor within the Task Manager. To bring up the Task Manager, right-click on the taskbar and choose Task Manager from the context menu. The Task Manager has three tabs.

- *Applications*. The user applications running. You can switch between these applications or end (kill) by using the buttons on this tab. Figure 15.14 shows the Applications tab. The New Task button brings up a dialog box functionally identical to the Start | Run dialog box.

A Blur?

A "blur" process on a bitmap softens the image. Because a blur needs to be applied to all pixels, it's a very processor-intensive operation.

FIGURE 15.14.

The Applications tab of Task Manager enable you to switch between tasks or to kill a runaway program.

- *Processes*. The underlying processes, including those for application programs, currently running in your computer. These processes include various system services. You can end (kill) a process by highlighting it and pressing the End Process button. Be very careful doing this; many processes support the operating system itself.

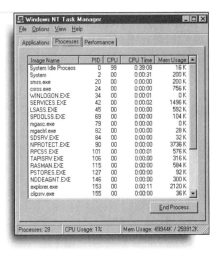

FIGURE 15.15.

Windows NT's Task Manager allows the ending (killing) of individual processes, but this power can lead to ruin.

- *Performance*. Shows some of the most important information for system health. Figure 15.16 shows this tab for the same computer used for the Performance Monitor figures earlier in the chapter.

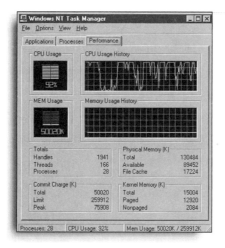

FIGURE 15.16.

The Performance tab is a mini-Performance Monitor, having the most often used counters permanently installed.

The Performance part of Task Manager shows metrics, or counters, for processor usage and memory. Most of the display is self-explanatory. The only non-obvious metric is Commit Charge (K) in the lower-left corner of the Performance tab. This is the total amount of memory committed to application programs. The Total, Limit, and Peak amounts might exceed the physical RAM in a system because of the use of virtual memory. This system has a paging file of roughly 130MB along with physical RAM of 128MB for a total (Limit) memory of roughly 258MB—the middle entry in the Commit Memory (K) section of Figure 15.17. If the memory demands of this system were to exceed 258MB, Windows NT would increase the paging file size to accommodate the demand.

Figure 15.17 shows the Task Manager after I opened several programs to run up the Commit Charge and then closed them to release memory again. Note that the current Total is higher than the one in Figure 15.16, although the applications are the same and the Peak is higher. This reflects that Windows NT's dynamic memory allocation hasn't released all the memory it

Specific Hardware

In Figure 15.15, the two services starting with "mga" are for the Matrox display adapter in this system. Ending either can bring down the display side of this session. Your Task Manager will vary its display, depending on your specific hardware.

allocated when opening the programs. This is normal because it is desirable to have some parts of commonly used elements remain in memory until that memory is demanded by another application and there's none available.

FIGURE 15.17.

Windows NT will release memory when you close applications or end processes, but will let itself have the luxury of keeping certain elements in memory just in case they're needed again during this computing session.

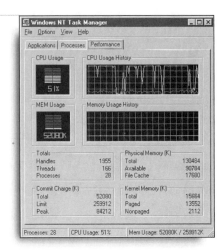

Task Manager at Your Service

You can launch the Task Manager by either right-clicking on the taskbar and then choosing Task Manager from the context menu or by pressing Control+Alt+Del and clicking the Task Manager button from the Windows NT Security dialog box. The program file for Task Manager is taskman.exe, located in the main Windows NT folder. You can create a shortcut to that file using the usual techniques (see the section titled "Creating a Desktop File Shortcut" in Chapter 1, "Using and Understanding Windows NT Workstation 4") if you wish to have a quick way to start the Task Manager from a folder or the desktop.

The Task Manager has menu options available to keep it on top (float) and to alter its sample rate. Remember, a high rate of sample will add to the burden your computer is carrying. Keep the Uncertainty Principle in mind whenever monitoring!

Disaster Prevention

Will It Hit Me?

We all know when we use computers that disasters, small or big, can and do strike. Whether it is a file we have accidentally deleted, a crash from which we cannot recover, or a power outage that causes us to lose hours and hours of work, most disasters can be prevented. This chapter outlines some of the features and techniques that will help you prevent disasters. We focus on protecting your hardware from power surges, power outages, how to back up information, and how to use Windows NT's Emergency Repair Disk. The Emergency Repair Disk (ERD) is a vital part of what a user must do to maintain Windows NT's integrity. You will find it mentioned in several places within this book.

Unfortunately, Windows NT has no mechanism to automatically create or update an ERD. You, the user/system administrator, must do this at a regular interval.

ERDs

The Emergency Repair Disk (ERD) is a vital Windows NT tool. Be sure to keep an updated one handy. ERDs are discussed in this chapter, as well as Chapter 1, "Using and Understanding Windows NT Workstation 4," Chapter 17, "When Problems Strike," and Chapter 19, "Setting Up Windows NT."

Basic Forms of Power Protection

At the very least, you should use a surge-protected power strip for your computer equipment. These devices can protect your PC against power spikes, which can burn out components of your computer. Many of these devices can also protect phone lines, lowering the risk of damaging your modem or fax machine. After having three modems go bad in as many years, I have become much more adamant about protecting my phone line. The better surge protectors carry insurance policies or guarantees against power-related damage. This is a sign of a serious surge protector and is well worth the outlay of a premium price.

Using and Configuring a UPS

The most common event that can leave your system unbootable or result in the loss of data on your computer is a power outage. Yet preventing a power outage from affecting your computer is as simple as obtaining a simple, relatively inexpensive piece of equipment called an uninterruptible power supply (UPS).

A UPS is essentially a battery that supplies electricity to your computer when there is a power outage. You connect the UPS into your a power outlet, and then plug your computer (or other piece of equipment) into the UPS. When the UPS is plugged in and powered up, power is passed through the UPS to the computer as the battery receives a charge. When there is a power outage, the UPS senses this and provides battery power to the computer until either the power is restored or the battery drains completely.

What to Connect to a UPS

How effective a UPS will be in protecting your computer against power outages depends on the power requirements of the equipment you plug into the UPS and the capacity of the UPS itself. As a general rule of thumb, put as little equipment as possible on the UPS: the main CPU and monitor. If you use external disk or CD-ROM drives, connect them as well—just as you should connect any peripheral whose disconnection would leave your computer unstable. Printers can be connected as well, but the power load will either shorten the number of minutes the battery can stay on or cause you to buy a larger, more expensive UPS.

How to Choose a UPS

The capacity of a UPS is usually expressed in watts. Some general sizing guidelines are as follows. Keep in mind, however, that the best way to size a UPS will be to follow the sizing guidelines for the manufacturer of the UPS. This chart is a very rough rule of thumb. To truly size a UPS for your needs, you must add up the wattage requirements for your particular system and then decide how much time you wish to run in the case of a power outage or brownout.

A typical modern Pentium II computer with a 17" monitor requires a minimum of a 650 watt UPS.

UPS Delivers

An uninterruptible power supply (UPS) is essentially a battery that supplies electricity to your computer when there is a power outage.

TABLE 16.1   **General sizing guidelines for a desktop computer's UPS**

Computer Type	Less Than 15 Minutes	Less Than ½ hour
Desktop PC	200–300 watts	600 watts
Desktop w/multimedia	300 watts	600+ watts
Tower PC	400 watts	800 watts
Large Tower PC	600 watts	1200 watts

Enabling UPS Monitoring

When a UPS is on battery, there is a limited amount of electricity to power the computer. Because the loss of power to the PC can compromise data on the computer, some UPS units can tell the computer to shut itself down gracefully when the UPS is on battery or low on power. This ensures that the system will not lose data when the UPS can no longer power the computer. For communication between the UPS and the computer to work, the UPS must have the capability to communicate with the computer. Windows NT comes with the necessary software to communicate with a UPS via a serial port; many UPSs come with software to serve the same purpose with additional features unique to the UPS.

You will need the following items to use UPS monitoring:

- UPS with serial port signaling or some other similar connection capability
- Unused serial port or other port (such as USB) on your computer
- A connection cable for your port if not supplied with UPS
- Any required adapters
- Vendor-supplied UPS software (optional)

Using the UPS Service

The software that comes with Windows NT to enable communication with a UPS is called the UPS service. The UPS service, shown in Figure 16.1, can both receive power status signals from the UPS and turn off the UPS if the UPS is on battery.

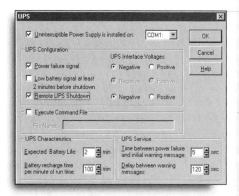

FIGURE 16.1.

The UPS service is used to communicate with a UPS to enable a smooth shutdown of Windows NT in the event of a power failure.

The UPS service is automatically installed with Windows NT; all you need to do is enable and configure the service.

Connecting a UPS and configuring the UPS service

1. Connect the UPS unit into a power outlet and connect the computer's plug into an open outlet on the UPS.

2. Connect the connection cable to the available communications port on your computer. If your UPS came with a cable, use that cable. If your UPS came with two similar but differently colored cables, you should use the cable indicated in your UPS documentation for "simple" or "basic" signaling. In other words, follow the instructions packed with your new UPS.

3. Connect the other end of the cable to the port on the UPS unit.

4. Open the Control Panel (Start | Settings | Control Panel) and double-click the icon labeled UPS. The UPS configuration window appears.

5. To enable the UPS service, check the UPS Is Installed On box, and select the serial port the UPS is connected to.

6. Check the boxes for the types of signaling your UPS supports. You need to check your UPS's documentation for what types of messages the UPS can exchange with the PC.

These messages can signal that the UPS is on battery (power-failure signal) and that the battery is running low on power (low-battery signal) and can also tell the UPS to turn itself off (remote-UPS shutdown).

7. For each of the signals, you can select the voltage polarity (negative or positive). The default settings (negative) usually work.

8. If you want a particular command launched when the Windows NT Workstation starts to shut down, put the command in here. You can use this feature to start a batch file by placing the batch file in the <winnt>\system32 directory and naming it in the text box.

9. If your UPS does not support sending low-battery signals, you have to tell the UPS service how long to wait while the UPS is on battery before the service can assume the battery is running low. You set this in the Expected Battery Life box. You can also set how quickly the battery recharges for each minute the UPS is on battery power.

10. When the UPS loses power, you will want to notify any users using your computer, either at the PC itself or using a shared resource of some kind. You would not want to warn users, however, if a power outage is brief and will be handled by the UPS without any noticeable disruption. Setting a delay in the Time Between Power Failure field sets how many minutes to wait before warning messages are sent to users. You can also specify how many minutes to wait between messages.

11. After you have filled out the UPS Setup dialog box, you are asked whether you want to start the UPS service. Selecting Yes starts the UPS service. Keep in mind that you're not protected until you start this service.

Testing the UPS Service

The simplest way to test the UPS service is to unplug the UPS from its wall outlet. You can observe messages from the UPS in the System log in the Event Viewer. You should test all the possible scenarios, such as a power failure that lasts a few moments, a few minutes, and until the power is totally drained or the UPS shuts down. I would make sure that no important applications are running while you run the tests until you are confident that the machine shuts down gracefully. Figure 16.2 shows the Windows NT dialog box that indicates a problem or problems with the UPS service.

FIGURE 16.2.

Communications problems with the UPS usually indicate the signaling or communications port settings are incorrect.

UPS Communication Problems

If the UPS service reports communications problems in the Event Viewer, or won't start after you have configured it, you must go through a diagnostic procedure.

Diagnosing UPS service problems

1. Ensure that you are using the right port. You can try various settings without too much trouble.

2. Uncheck some of the more sophisticated signaling types, such as the low-battery signal or the remote UPS shutdown.

3. Check the cable to ensure that it is the correct type. If your UPS came with a cable, try that cable. If you are using the UPS-supplied serial cable and having problems, you can try a standard serial cable or try using the software supplied with the UPS rather than the Windows NT UPS service.

4. Check the signaling polarity settings, particularly if you are getting incorrect messages from the UPS (for example, a low-power message when the UPS is plugged in fine).

Using Vendor-Supplied Software

If your UPS came with software, it may make sense to use that software rather than the Windows NT UPS service. The UPS service is basic, and vendor-supplied power software often has dramatically improved functionality, as illustrated by the following list and Figure 16.3.

- *Power voltage and line monitoring.* The capability to observe power quality, such as variations in amperage, wattage, and voltage. This can be important in troubleshooting intermittent hardware problems that may be power related.

- *Email or paging.* Some software can send you an email or page in the event of a power outage.

- *Capacity monitoring.* You can often see how much of the UPS's capacity you are using, and how many minutes of battery power you can expect to receive.

- *Power monitoring.* Some UPSs can monitor minor power fluctuations in the line, which are common and often unnoticed. Power monitoring can be useful to troubleshoot intermittent or hard-to-figure-out technical problems, such as workstation lockups, that can be caused by fluctuations in power.

- *Across the network shutdown.* If you have several computers on a single UPS, you can have one PC monitoring the UPS. This PC can send signals across the network to other machines connected to the UPS to initiate a shutdown. Although this saves on the need to have multiple UPSs or specialized expansion units for additional communications lines, this method is only effective if all the necessary network components are on a UPS as well (for example, the network hub that provides the physical connection between the workstations).

FIGURE 16.3.

The UPS software available from the UPS vendor offers additional functionality than the Windows NT UPS service, such as the capability to monitor power fluctuations.

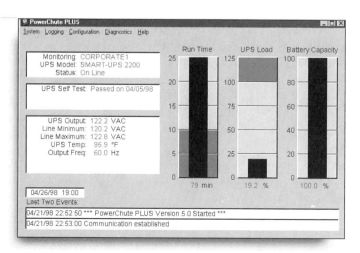

Backing Up Data

The best way to prevent a disaster is to minimize the damage and time spent recovering from a crashed system. Having a good backup of the data on your PC can make a crash an annoyance rather than a real disaster. Backing up your data on a regular basis is the best protection for your system.

Backup Devices

Windows NT supports several different devices to back up your data. Some of these devices were designed and intended for backing up and recovering data; others are intended for long-term storage.

Tape

The most common and popular backup device is a tape unit; Windows NT comes with a basic tape backup utility that supports a selection of popular tape units. The basic tape types are the following:

- *Cartridge* (assorted sizes and capacities). These tapes are typically either consumer-oriented or older devices that use a proprietary tape format. Capacities vary from 125MB to over 2GB. Many of these devices connect to the floppy disk controller or the system's parallel port and have extremely limited Windows NT device driver support. You should ensure that the manufacturer includes drivers for Windows NT before you buy this type of tape unit. For the most part, the people who make these often inexpensive units intend them for inexpensive workstations such as those using Windows 98. Also don't be fooled by the initial lack of expense for these units. The price of the cartridges, if you buy many, often make these units at least as expensive as the faster DATs.

- *Digital audio tape* (DAT). Similar to the consumer audio technology of the same name, DAT cartridges come in 4mm and 8mm sizes, with capacities from 2GB to 8GB without compression. Most DAT drives today offer hardware compression that can double a tape's capacity. The most prevalent size is 4mm; 4mm DAT has multiple uncompressed capacities based on tape length: DDS holds 2GB; DDS2 holds 4GB; and DDS3 holds 8GB. DAT is the most common tape format found in Windows NT Workstation; DAT units almost always connect to the computer via a SCSI interface and may require a SCSI adapter card if your main board lacks one. Now that faster IDE interfaces exist, the industry is seeing some IDE type DAT units, but SCSI still dominates.

- *Digital linear tape* (DLT). DLT is quickly becoming a mainstream technology for servers. With a capacity of up to 40GB, DLT makes an excellent server technology (but is overkill for the desktop).

Autoloaders

Both DAT and DLT units can come in a configuration called an autoloader. Autoloaders hold multiple tapes in a cartridge or special holder and allow the automatic switching of tapes. This feature saves you the necessity of changing tapes on a regular basis, or swapping tapes in mid-backup when your data can't fit on a single tape. Autoloaders are often seen in server environments and are rare in desktop settings, but they can be applicable if you feel you need the additional capacity or cannot reliably change tapes on your own.

The danger of autoloaders is that they store an entire week of backups internally. This is handy, but can lull you into a false sense of security. In the case of a fire, flood, or theft, a full magazine of backups won't help you restore because you will likely lose the magazine along with the computer.

Removable Media

The category *removable media* covers a variety of devices, which appear to Windows NT as a regular disk drive, but offer the convenience of a removable cartridge or floppy disk. The benefits of removable media include ease of use and speed; because they appear to Windows NT as disk drives, you just copy the files you want to back up to the drive. Examples of removable media drives include the Iomega Zip and Jaz drives, which hold

The Whole Cost

When costing a backup system, include the price of media, not just the unit. Also consider speed, because time is money. A slow unit that will take hours to restore data in the case of a loss will cost the time lost even if it fully restores the data.

Remember to Back Up!

Don't get lulled into a false sense of security by autoloaders: Nothing replaces vigilance and proper procedures when it comes to backing up!

100MB and up to 2GB, respectively. The entire area of removable media is expanding rapidly.

Removable media is usually faster than tape, but speed comes at a price. Some system files cannot be backed up to removable media without special utilities. Removable media also often lack the capacity to back up the entire system on a single cartridge, although there are systems with capacities of more than 4GB. Given the drawbacks, many consumers use removable media because of its ease of use and versatility beyond simple backups.

Windows NT support for removable media drives is good and getting better. Popular vendors have begun to write Windows NT device drivers for their SCSI and parallel-port interfaced products, although it still makes sense to research Windows NT support before you buy a piece of hardware.

CD-R and CD-RW

The increasing popularity and lowering cost of recordable and read/writable CD-ROM drives are making this technology a popular choice for backups. Some drawbacks to CD-R and CD-RW technology is the limited capacity (680MB) and the fact that you may need special utilities to back up system files that are in use by the system and cannot be just copied. Also, some drives will require you to have enough free disk space for staging the information you want to put on the CD-ROM. The advantage of CD-R and CD-RW is primarily the low cost of the media (less than $10) and the fact that you can read the CD-ROM in any computer, without any special equipment.

Choosing the Right Backup Device

Choosing the best backup device often comes down to three distinguishing criteria: capacity, cost, and speed.

- *Capacity*. The backup method should have enough capacity to back up the entire system, particularly if you want to back up the entire system on a regular basis. If you do not have enough capacity for the entire system, you will either have to back up Windows NT, your applications, and your data separately or switch media during each backup.

Watch for DVD Writable

Any day now, we will see DVD writable either in a WORM (Write Once, Read Many) or a true RAM (erasable) system. DVD has much more capacity than the CD-ROM (which just came into use in the 1990s). DVD is definitely a future option worth watching.

- *Cost*. The backup method you choose will often be constrained by cost, both for the device itself and for the media you use to hold the backups. Cost factors may drive the use of a multipurpose technology such as CD-RW or removable media over tape.

- *Speed*. The time it takes to perform each backup may influence how much data you back up at a particular time, or may just influence your consistency for performing regular backups. Speed is a consideration in ease of use, because some technologies (tape, for example) may take longer overall time to perform a backup but require less human interaction than quicker, more interactive backup methods.

Backup Software

Although backup devices provide the physical equipment necessary to perform backups, tape units in particular require software to perform basic backup and recovery functions. Windows NT comes with a basic backup utility called Windows NT Backup.

Installing the Necessary Components

Windows NT Backup comes pre-installed with Windows NT. However, you will likely need to install two components for Windows NT Backup to recognize the fact you have a tape unit. Although you should always consult the tape unit's documentation, these are some basic steps that work for most tape units and software packages.

Install the Adapter Driver

If your tape unit uses a SCSI or parallel port interface, it is likely that you will need to add a device driver to Windows NT's configuration. Follow these steps to install an adapter device driver.

Installing a SCSI device driver for backup hardware

1. Open Control Panel and double-click the SCSI Adapters icon. This brings up the tabbed dialog box shown in Figure 16.4.

What About Recovery?

A common mistake when thinking about backups is ignoring the real purpose of a backup: restoring data after a system crash. When considering backup methods, think about the steps necessary to restore the system. Plan a recovery strategy that includes mapping out the steps you will take to recover the system, such as fixing the hardware, re-installing Windows NT and tape unit, and restoring from a good backup. Another good practice is the creation of a rescue kit, a box or binder containing items critical to recovery: Windows NT media with Service Packs, ERD, MS-DOS boot disks, a recent and complete backup, and any special device drivers. Remember, the question is not *if* your system will fail, but *when*. Take steps to make recovery as hassle-free as it can be.

2. In the window that appears, click the Drivers tab. You should see a list of any drivers currently in use. If your tape unit is not attached to the devices listed, click the Add button.

3. A list of manufacturers and adapters appears in a new window. Select the appropriate manufacturer and adapter from the list shown. If the adapter is not listed and you have a vendor-supplied disk or CD-ROM that contains Windows NT device drivers, you can click the Have Disk button to browse for the driver.

4. Click OK until you close the SCSI Adapters window. Restart your computer and Windows NT.

NT Backup the Ultimate?

The backup utility bundled with Windows NT is decent, but not the cat's pajamas. Consider budgeting for third-party backup software, especially if you will be backing up more than your single computer. The time and effort you will save (especially during a restore) can be enormous.

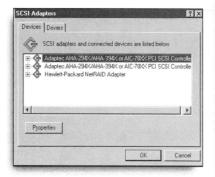

FIGURE 16.4.

The SCSI Devices Control Panel is used to add the device driver for your SCSI adapter.

Installing a Tape Driver

Windows NT Backup (as well as some other popular backup utilities) requires the installation of a Windows NT tape driver.

How to install a tape driver within Windows NT

1. Open the Control Panel and double-click the Tape Devices icon to bring up the tabbed dialog box shown in Figure 16.5.

2. You can have your tape unit autodetected by clicking the Detect button on the Devices page.

3. If Windows NT cannot detect your tape unit, you can select the appropriate driver by clicking the Drivers page and then clicking the Add button. The window that appears lists manufacturers and tape units. If your tape unit is one of the types shown under the Standard Tape Drives heading, select that type in the right-hand panel. Otherwise select the manufacturer and type of your unit.

4. Click OK to close the Tape Devices window. Restart your computer.

5. You can now use Windows NT Backup to back up and restore files to and from tape.

FIGURE 16.5.

The Tape Devices Control Panel is where you add the tape unit's device driver.

Performing a Backup

The icon for Windows NT Backup is in the Administrative Tools group. Windows NT Backup is a simple tool to use (see Figure 16.6). There are two main windows: a tape window, showing the tape in the tape drive; and a drives window, showing drives to be backed up. Either, both, or none may be shown at any given time.

Using NT Backup is fairly straightforward.

Using NT Backup

1. In the Drives window, select either entire drives or individual files to be backed up.

2. When you have all the files selected, click the Backup button to start a backup session.

3. A dialog box appears, as shown in Figure 16.7, outlining your backup options. These options include whether to overwrite (replace) or append any existing backups on the tape, whether to verify the backup after it is done, and what backup type to perform. Windows NT supports several types of backup:

Backups Are Where It's At

Remember you can use the command line interface's (CLI) AT command to schedule untended backups. See Appendix A, "Using the Command Line Interface," for more information on the command line interface.

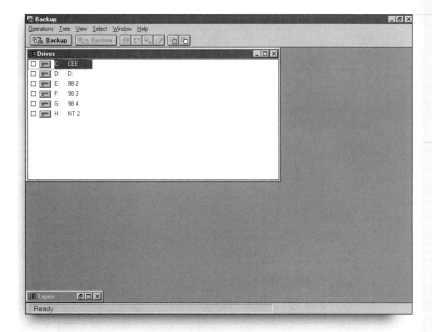

FIGURE 16.6.
Windows NT Backup performs tape backups and restores. The Drives window is where you select the files you want to back up; in the Tapes window, you can select your tape unit or backup sets on a tape.

- *Normal.* All files, directories, or drives selected are backed up to tape, and the files are marked as being backed up.

- *Copy.* All files, directories, or drives selected are backed up to tape, but the files are not marked as having been backed up.

- *Incremental.* Files that have changed since the last normal or incremental backup are backed up. The backed up files are marked as being backed up.

- *Differential.* Backs up files that have changed since the last normal or incremental backup, but they are not marked as having been backed up.

- *Daily copy.* Backs up the files that have changed on the date the daily backup is run, and does not mark them as having been backed up.

4. After you have selected all the backup options, click OK to start the backup. A backup status window appears, informing you of the backup's progress.

FIGURE 16.7.

Windows NT Backup supports several different backup options, such as how files are selected to be backed up and different logging levels.

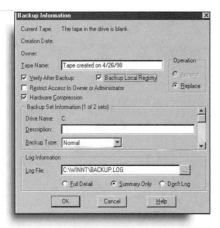

Choosing the Best Backup Method

The different backup methods (normal, copy, incremental, differential, daily copy) can be confusing. A normal backup (sometimes called a full backup) is the most common backup type. Normal backups take a greater amount of time and more tape capacity to create than other methods, but restoring is easy because only one tape needs to be restored. You can either use all normal backups if time and tape capacity are not an issue, or use a combination of normal and incremental or differential backups to balance the need for complete backups and the time it takes to perform each backup.

Restoring Files from Tape

Restoration of data is the opposite of backing up.

Using NT Backup to restore data

1. Load the tape in the tape drive and run Windows NT Backup. The Tapes window should show the tape name.

2. If the tape has multiple backup sets (you have appended multiple backup jobs to the tape), choose the Catalog option under the Operations menu bar. The tape will be cataloged and should show all the sets on the tape in the Tapes window.

3. In the Tape window, select the backup set and drill down until you find the directory or file you wish to restore. Figure 16.8 shows this process.

4. When you have selected all the files you wish to restore, click the Restore button along the top of the Windows NT Backup menu bar. This brings up the dialog box shown in Figure 16.9.

5. In the Restore Options window, you can enter an alternative location to restore the file; otherwise the file will be restored to its original location. You can set other restore options as well.

6. After you have selected all the appropriate options, click OK to start the restore operation.

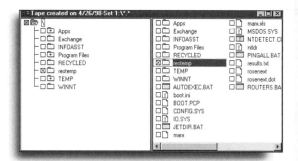

FIGURE 16.8.

Selecting files to be restored.

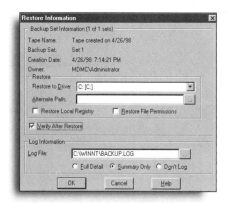

FIGURE 16.9.

Selecting Restore options.

Scheduling an Unattended Backup

You can run Windows NT Backup from the command line so that you can perform backups unattended, say from a batch file that is launched by the Schedule service. This enables you to have more time to perform normal (for example, full) backups in the evenings.

To schedule backups to run unattended, you need to configure the Schedule service and create the entry to launch the backup. Figure 16.10 shows the Service configuration dialog box.

Configuring the Schedule service

1. Open the Control Panel and double-click the Services icon. In the Services window, scroll down to the entry for the Schedule service.

2. Click the Startup button. The Service window for the Schedule service appears.

FIGURE 16.10.

Configuring the Schedule service to start automatically.

3. Set the Startup Type to Automatic. This starts the service each time Windows NT starts.

4. If you intend to back up network resources (for example, drives on other computers), change the Log On As settings in the This Account section to an account that has privileges on the remote computer. Make sure the password entered is correct.

5. Click OK to close the configuration window for the Schedule service.

6. In the main Services window, click the Start button to start the Schedule service. If any error messages appear, the most probable cause is an invalid username or password in the Log On settings for the service.

Windows NT Backup enables you to perform a backup from the command prompt without any intervention on your part. This is how you perform an unattended backup.

The AT command is used to add and remove commands to be run by the Schedule service at a predetermined time. In a Command Prompt window, type the following (this is an example for backing up the entire C: drive):

```
AT 23:00 /every:MF NTBACKUP.EXE backup c: /b
/l:c:\backlog.txt
```

This command schedules NTBACKUP.EXE to run at 11:00 p.m. (23:00) on every Monday and Friday. NTBACKUP will perform a backup of the C: drive, including the local Registry

(/b), and will log the results in a file called C:\backlog.txt
(/l c:\backlog.txt).

To find out more about the AT command, type AT /? at the command prompt. To learn about the command line options for Windows NT Backup, see the Help option within Windows NT Backup.

Third-Party Tools

Several companies offer backup software that is much more sophisticated than Windows NT Backup. These backup utilities enable you to do several things beyond simple backing up and restoring:

- *Back up across the network*. You can have a Windows NT or NetWare file server back up your workstation across the network to a tape unit attached to the file server. The advantage is that servers usually have higher-speed and bigger-capacity tape units, and file servers are usually backed up on a daily basis. A downside of this is that your workstation must be powered on and connected to the network, which must have the capacity and speed to make the backup practical. This approach works well in corporate environments with the tape and network resources to make it work.

- *Floppy disk disaster recovery*. The traditional method you use to recover from a catastrophic failure of some kind is to fix any hardware problems, re-install Windows NT, install the backup software, and restore from the last backup. This approach wastes a lot of time. Several companies, including Cheyenne and Seagate Software, provide products that enable you to fix the hardware, boot the backup software from a floppy disk, and restore the entire server, including Windows NT, from the last backup. This can save incredible amounts of time. Although this feature is more important for servers that impact many people, floppy disaster recovery and its associated software cost may make sense if you rely on your PC for critical, time-sensitive work.

Tape Rotation

One of the ways to manage your tapes is to use a technique called tape rotation. Tape rotation involves maintaining a library of tapes and a routine for which tape you use for each backup. Although a complex rotation scheme is rarely required for backing up a workstation, one of the benefits of switching tapes each time you perform a backup is that the wear and tear on the tapes is distributed across several tapes rather than one. Because tapes can (and will) fail over time, it makes sense to use a simple rotation scheme and proactively replace tapes after a year or more of use. Sometimes a backup will appear to work fine (even with Verify turned on) until you attempt to perform a restore and discover the tape is worn out or defective.

- *Emailed or printed notification*. You can have a log of your backup session either printed or emailed to you. This can be helpful for nightly backups when you don't wish to spend a lot of time ensuring a backup was performed properly.
- *Autoloader support*. Windows NT Backup supports basic tape hardware, but does not support the advanced functions of an autoloader, such as the capability to control which tape a particular backup goes on.

The Use of Cloning Software

System "cloning" or imaging software is becoming increasing popular as a method for quickly installing Windows NT on PCs in a bulk, assembly-line fashion. Cloning software creates a snapshot "image" of a computer's hard drive and stores that image on a recordable CD-ROM or a network server. That image can be applied to new workstations to quickly create multiple, identical installations of Windows NT on identical computers. Another use of cloning software is as a point-in-time recovery tool for your workstation. Although this is an unconventional use of this software (and is unsupported by hardware and software vendors), cloning CD-ROMs can provide a quick and dirty recovery tool that can be used to get a system up and running quickly.

Making and Maintaining ERDs

One of the methods Windows NT provides against an unbootable system is a Emergency Repair Disk, or ERD. An ERD maintains critical system information about the hardware and software you have on your computer, including the Registry, SAM (user account database), and the layout of your disk drives.

When to Use an ERD

You should use an ERD whenever the system is unbootable and performs a STOP error or blue screen (for example, the blue screen of death) at startup. These problems are often caused by corrupt or missing system files (such as the Windows NT kernel or the Registry), and the ERD helps in the process of recovering those system files.

Because the use of an ERD is a drastic step, use it with caution. Although the system may be recoverable with an ERD, it is likely that you will lose minor tweaks and system changes we all make to our PC to make it ours. The key to minimizing these changes is to occasionally update your ERD.

Creating and Maintaining an ERD

You should create an Emergency Repair Disk when you first install Windows NT. During the setup process, you will be prompted to create an ERD.

(((**Using RDISK (Repair Disk Utility) to make an ERD**

1. On the Start menu, go to the Run option.

2. In the Open text box, type RDISK and press Enter.

3. The Repair Disk Utility dialog box appears, as shown in Figure 16.11. You have two options: one to create an ERD, and the other to update an existing repair disk.

4. If you are creating a repair disk, select the Create button. Click the Update button if you are updating a disk.

5. When prompted, insert the floppy disk in your disk drive. The existing information on the disk will be overwritten, so make sure you don't have any files you want to keep on the disk.

6. The Emergency Repair Disk will then be created or updated.)))

FIGURE 16.11.

The RDISK utility enables you to create and maintain Emergency Repair Disks.

When to Update the Emergency Repair Disk

You should update your Emergency Repair Disk whenever you install any new system's software, such as a video, disk, or network card driver. Because the Emergency Repair Disk also includes disk drive information (particularly if you use Windows NT's disk striping or mirroring features), you should also update the ERD after any disk changes (such as the addition of a stripe set or new disk drive).

You should also update the ERD after applying a Windows NT Service Pack or installing Internet Explorer 4 or higher. This is critical because Service Packs can change the structure or values of keys in the Registry.

You cannot update the ERD too often, but remember to store the ERD (or multiple copies of the ERD) in a safe location where you can access it in the event of a system failure.

The Last Known Good
Configuration

Each time Windows NT boots, you
may have noticed a message men-
tioning that you can press the
Spacebar to load the Last Known
Good configuration. What is the
Last Known Good configuration?
Each time you log on successfully, a
copy of your current configuration is
copied into a separate part of the
Registry. If you make a system
change that leaves your system
unbootable, try loading the Last
Known Good configuration at
bootup by pressing the Spacebar
during the initial OS Loader message. If you boot successfully, you
may lose some minor system modifications (which you will have to
redo). If the Last Known Good configuration fails as well, you may
have to try the Emergency Repair
Disk.

The Repair Folder

The same information stored on the Emergency Repair Disk is
also stored in a directory under the <WINNT> called Repair,
and can sometimes be used in the event you have lost your
Emergency Repair Disk. Because this information is maintained
separately from the ERD, you will have to update it separately as
well.

Creating an ERD using the Repair folder

1. On the Start Bar, go to the Run option.

2. Enter the line RDISK /S and press Enter.

3. A progress window appears while the information is updated.

Using the Emergency Repair Disk or Repair Directory

When Windows NT does not boot because of a STOP or "blue
screen" error, and the Last Known Good configuration does not
work either, you should try to use the Emergency Repair Disk to
recover your system.

Using the ERD to restore your computer's system data

1. Boot the computer from the Windows NT setup disks.

2. Proceed to the point where you are asked whether you want
   to install Windows NT or repair a Windows NT installation. Press R to select Repair.

3. You will be given a list of options to select. How many of
   these options you choose depends on your estimation of the
   extent of the damage to the system. If you are unsure, you
   can check all the option.

4. If you checked Inspect Registry files, you will have to select
   which Registry files you want to verify. You can select all or
   none of them; if you are unsure, you can select all the
   options.

5. For the Verify Windows NT System files, you need to supply the Windows NT Workstation CD-ROM. This option

verifies the checksum information on the system files to ensure the files on your computer have not been corrupted. If the files on your PC are different from those on the CD-ROM, new files are copied to the computer. If you can start the system after this step, you will later need to reapply any Service Packs.

6. When prompted, put the Emergency Repair Disk in your A: drive.

7. If you do not have an ERD, you will be asked to select an installation of Windows NT on your computer. If you only have one installation, just select the option you are presented.

8. Restart the computer when the repair process is finished.

When Problems Strike

The Boot Process (Quick Tour)

The boot process in Windows NT is very different from that under MS-DOS, or other versions of Windows such as Windows 95/98 due to the architecture of Windows NT.

When you start up your computer, the following actions take place:

1. The Power On Self Test (POST) routine is run from the BIOS. This checks the integrity of the hardware and reports any errors.

2. The boot device (your A: or C: drive as recorded in the BIOS) is located and the Master Boot Record (MBR) loaded into memory. The MBR contains a program that is now executed.

3. The MBR program scans the Partition Boot Record (PBR), which indicates the location of the active partition—that is, the partition on your hard disk that contains the operating system loader. Once located, the boot sector from this partition is loaded into memory.

4. When Windows NT is installed on your computer, the boot sector is changed so that a file called NTLDR (NT Loader) is loaded automatically. This file then switches the processor into 32-bit (protected) mode and initializes mini-drivers to read the hard disk, whether FAT or NTFS formatted.

5. The BOOT.INI file is then loaded and displayed onscreen. This is where you see the Option screen to select the operating system with the countdown timer at the bottom.

6. If you select an alternative operating system such as Windows 98 at this point, the boot process loads a file called BOOTSECT.DOS into memory and passes control to that file. NTLDR exits and the other operating system starts. Windows NT has no further part in the boot process.

7. If NT is selected, NTLDR calls NTDETECT.COM. This carries out a hardware detection routine and writes information on all detected hardware into the Registry in the

HKEY_LOCAL_MACHINE\HARDWARE key. You can view this information by starting Windows NT Diagnostics from Start, Programs, Administrative Tools (Common) or by using the Registry Editor. This process is somewhat analogous to the initial POST mentioned in step 1.

8. After hardware detection has completed, NTLDR then looks at the path specified in BOOT.INI to load NTOSKRNL.EXE, HAL.DLL, and the Registry. These files then continue the boot sequence, load Windows NT, start the services, and finally present you with the Logon screen.

9. After you have logged on successfully, the current settings are written back into the Registry as the "Last Known Good" entry, indicating that your current configuration has correctly initialized the computer. The relevance of this process will be covered later.

10. The boot process is now complete.

Boot Failure—Prevention

As you can see from the preceding section, the process of initializing a computer is complex and depends not only on correctly functioning hardware but also on the presence of a number of different files in a variety of locations. Although diagnosing and correcting problems is not as difficult as you might suppose, a few precautionary measures taken after you have installed Windows NT can save you time should problems occur.

The measures add up to being prepared for disaster. To be so prepared, you need to create the following:

- An emergency repair disk
- A boot disk
- The NT setup disks

To do this, follow the steps as indicated for each of the following items. You will need a total of five floppy disks formatted under Windows NT to complete all the emergency recovery measures.

RDISK Utility

The RDISK utility will back up your Registry files and, optionally, your user account information to your hard disk and to floppy disk. This information is vital to repair your Windows NT installation.

If you just run RDISK without any switches, you will see the Repair Disk Utility screen. You can then select to Update Repair Info or Create Repair Disk. This will not back up your user account information, however; therefore you should use RDISK /S when creating emergency repair disks.

Creating an Emergency Repair Disk

You may already have created an emergency repair disk when you installed Windows NT. It is a good idea, however, to regenerate this on a regular basis, particularly before you add or remove hardware or add a significant number of users.

If you did not create the emergency repair disk on installation, you should do so without delay.

Creating an Emergency Repair Disk (ERD)

1. Make a backup of your security database by entering RDISK /S in the Start | Run dialog box, as shown in Figure 17.1. This copies all your Registry and account information into \systemroot\system32\repair and on to a floppy disk.

FIGURE 17.1.

RDISK is a computer-talk term for the Repair Disk utility.

2. When prompted, as shown in Figure 17.2, place a floppy disk into your A: drive and select OK. Make sure this disk does not contain any useful data because the RDISK program will destroy it.

FIGURE 17.2.

As usual, the utility will request confirmation before proceeding.

3. After the disk has been formatted and the configuration files copied across, a dialog box appears, as shown in Figure 17.3, reminding you to keep this disk in a safe place. This is because security account information has been saved to the disk, including a record of your user accounts. This disk is unique to your computer and must not be used to restore Registry information on another machine.

FIGURE 17.3.

Because Windows NT is a
secure operating system, you
need to keep close control of
any information allowing the
overriding of that security. The
information on an ERD is such
information.

An Emergency Repair Disk is only part of the tool suite you
need to be protected from disaster. You also need a way to start
your system in case the fixed (hard) disk becomes unbootable.
Although such occurrences are rare, they do happen and most
often to those without an ERD or boot disk.

Creating a Windows NT Boot Disk

Creating a Windows NT boot disk

1. Format a floppy disk under Windows NT. You can do this
with Explorer or from a command prompt. Place the disk
into the drive. With Explorer, click on the A: drive, and then
right-click and select Properties. Choose Format from the
menu. Do not double-click on the A: drive because that
would prevent you from formatting it. If using a command
prompt, type FORMAT A: and press Enter. Type Y to confirm
that you want to proceed with the format.

2. Copy the following files to the floppy disk. These files will
be on your C: drive in the root directory (folder).

NTLDR

NTDETECT.COM

BOOT.INI

NTBOOTDD.SYS

The last file exists only in SCSI setups, so don't be concerned if you can't locate it. If it's not there, you don't
need it.

3. If you can't see these files in Explorer, you need to make
your hidden and system files visible. From the View menu,

Windows NT Boot Disk

The Windows NT boot disk differs from the Emergency Repair
Disk in that it enables you to
restart your computer quickly
should a problem occur with
your selected boot device,
Master Boot Record, NTLDR,
NTDETECT.COM, or BOOT.INI
files. You can make the
Emergency Repair Disk
bootable, but the next time you
update the repair configuration
files you will have to copy
across the necessary files to
make it bootable again.

choose Options, and then select Display Hidden, System Files.

4. Test the disk by rebooting your computer with the disk in your A: drive. Your machine must be set in the BIOS to boot from the floppy drive first, which is usually the default setting. If you don't know how to do this, see the section on BIOS setup issues that follows later in this chapter.

5. If your computer boots successfully from the floppy disk, label this disk and keep it with your emergency repair disk. This disk may be used on another computer as long as Windows NT is on the same partition and directory as the machine the BOOT.INI file came from.

NT Setup Disks

As part of your Windows NT distribution, you should have received three setup floppy disks. These are the final part of your armory of preventative tools for use in solving boot problems.

If you do not have these disks, you can easily create them. The only tricky part of this next procedure is making sure you have a good supply of floppy disks on hand in case one or more prove to be unusable. For some reason, the setup disk creation routine in Windows NT is very fussy about floppy disks and will reject them more often than the format process.

Creating a set of setup floppy disks

1. Place your Windows NT CD into the CD drive. The Windows NT CD-ROM window will appear. *Do not* select the Windows NT Setup button, but click the Close button instead.

2. Select Start|Run from the taskbar.

3. Use the Browse button to change to the i386 folder on your CD-ROM. Select WINNT32.EXE and select OK. You should now see \i386\winnt32 in your Run dialog box. If you select WINNT, you will be reminded that WINNT does not run under Windows NT and that you need to use WINNT32.

4. Add the command line switch /OX to the end of the WINNT32 command and select OK. You can see the completed command line in Figure 17.4.

FIGURE 17.4.

This is the exact command line to make a setup disk set if your CD-ROM drive is the D: drive.

5. You will now see Windows NT setup process start. You will be prompted for the location of the Windows NT source files as you can see in Figure 17.5. Check that this is pointing to the i386 directory on your CD-ROM and select Continue.

FIGURE 17.5.

Before making much progress, you will need to remind Windows NT where its source files live.

6. A dialog box will appear, as shown in Figure 17.6, informing you that you need to provide three blank, formatted high-density (HD) disks. Note that you label these Setup Boot Disk, Disk #2, and Disk #3, and that you put Disk #3 in first. Select OK to continue.

FIGURE 17.6.

Although the procedure requests only three formatted disks, have a few extra on hand in case of disk rejection (a common occurrence).

7. You will be prompted to remove and replace the disks by the Setup program. Continue until all the disks have been created.

8. You can do this on a machine running DOS, but in this case you need to run WINNT /OX from the i386 directory. Then proceed as before. Windows NT setup disks are generic and can be used on any computer.

You have now created everything you need to repair your machine should you experience a missing file, a corrupted boot sector, or a damaged Registry.

Boot Failure–Diagnosis and Repair

So one morning the unthinkable happens. Your computer won't start. You switched it on, a message has appeared that you have not seen before, and the boot process stops. What now? And why does this always happen at the most inconvenient time?

Boot problems stem from a variety of causes, so first you need to identify what component is causing the problem. By careful analysis of the symptoms, it is usually possible to get your machine up and running again without wasting too much time.

POST Beep Codes

Problem: On switching on your computer, you hear a number of beeps in short succession.

Solution: The Power On Self Test (POST) routine on most systems will have beep codes built in that help you diagnose what is wrong with your system even if nothing is being shown on the screen. These are the POST beep codes and will be listed in your system documentation.

Hence if your machine beeps several times on startup, count the number of beeps. Consult your system documentation to discover what the error is. Some example errors are as follows:

- Memory refresh failure
- Memory parity error
- Microprocessor error
- Gate A20 failure

POST failures of this nature usually indicate a serious problem that is not caused by Windows NT and is beyond the scope of this book to solve. Your hardware documentation may be able to help, or you may need to contact your computer manufacturer's support line.

CMOS Setup Issues

Problem: A message reporting CMOS Battery State Low has appeared, or your machine seems unable to recognize its own hard disk.

Solution: Your BIOS keeps its firmware information (for example, hard disk size, RAM fitted, clock settings) in CMOS (Complimentary Metal Oxide Semiconductor) memory. This memory is preserved when the power is off by a battery (usually a rechargeable) that has a typical lifetime in the order of three years.

After this battery fails to recharge, you will see errors appearing reporting CMOS Battery State Low or CMOS Checksum Failure. Refer to your computer's documentation on how to replace the battery on the motherboard.

BIOS Setup Issues

Problem: The system reports Missing Operating System. On starting using the emergency boot disk, however, the following error is reported:

```
Windows NT could not start because the following file is
missing or corrupt:
<winnt root>\system32\ntoskrnl.exe
Please re-install a copy of the above file.
```

Solution: The problem here is that the system is not recognizing the hard disk. Most errors of this type are caused by failure of the backup battery, as previously described. This will lead to the system forgetting its settings, including the configuration of the hard disks. The hard disk and Master Boot Record will be unreadable, and the boot process will stop. Booting from the A: drive gets around the first problem (cannot find the Master Boot

Record), but falls over when it tries to load NTOSKRNL.EXE from the partition indicated in BOOT.INI.

Because different computers have different BIOS routines, no generic rules apply to all systems. Check that the CMOS battery is operational, and then reboot the machine, this time pressing either the Delete key or Ctrl+Alt+Esc to go to the BIOS setup screens. These text-based screens enable you to alter the configuration of the machine, including the type and size of the hard disk. If you have taken note of the hard disk configuration settings in the following sidenote, you can re-enter those, save the settings, and reboot your machine.

Changes to the BIOS are only made if you select Save and Exit. Choosing this option will write any modifications to the CMOS memory and reboot the computer.

Generally there is little reason to make changes to the BIOS, and any such actions should be undertaken with great care. Incorrect configuration can make your computer unworkable.

System Error Messages

Problem: You receive a message either during the boot process or when using the machine. Examples are as follows:

```
CH-2 Timer Error
Address Line Short!
CMOS Checksum Failure
```

Solution: Consult your technical documentation to find out what the problem is. With certain error messages, it may be possible to correct the malfunction. If not, you will need to contact your hardware support line.

Master Boot Record Failure

Problem: The system reports `Missing Operating System`. However, the system starts normally using the Windows NT boot disk.

Solution: This is caused by a corrupted Master Boot Record, Partition Boot Record, or active partition. Hence the system will

---

Keeping a Record of Your BIOS Settings

It is recommended that you find out the settings for your hard disk while the system is working correctly. Enter the BIOS routine as described opposite, and then select the option for Hard Disks.

Note the following information down:

Type: _____

Cylinders: _____

Heads: _____

Landing Zone (LZ): _____

Sectors: _____

Size: _____

After you have recorded this information, exit the BIOS without saving. If your system does fail, you can refer to this information to re-enter the correct information into the BIOS.

fail to load NTLDR and will therefore report `Missing Operating System`. When you reboot using the Windows NT boot disk, the system just carries out the boot from the floppy disk, which contains a valid Master Boot Record, Partition Boot Record, and active partition. NTLDR, NTDETECT.COM, and BOOT.INI are on the floppy disk, so they are loaded as normal. The BOOT.INI file still points to a valid copy of Windows NT, so the remainder of the boot continues as normal.

Although starting from the Windows NT boot disk will get you up and running, for a long-term solution you will need to re-create the Master Boot Record. This can be done in two ways. Either use the Emergency Repair process to repair the damaged files or install Windows NT again into the same directory. This preserves all your current accounts and settings.

For more information on installing Windows NT, see Chapter 19, "Setting Up Windows NT."

SEE ALSO
➤ *See Chapter 19, "Setting Up Windows NT," for more information on installation.*

If using the Emergency Repair process, select the following settings:

[ ] Inspect Registry Files

[X] Inspect Startup Environment

[ ] Verify Windows NT System Files

[X] Inspect Boot Sector

See the step-by-step guide at the end of this chapter for using the Emergency Repair process.

SEE ALSO
➤ *For more information on using the Emergency Repair process, see the step-by-step guide at the end of this chapter.*

Corrupted or Missing System Files

You may encounter problems from corrupted or missing system files, including bad or missing NTLDR, BOOT.INI, NTDE-TECT.COM, and NTOSKRNL.EXE files. Proposed solutions are provided in the following sections.

Bad or Missing NTLDR

Problem: You see the message `Cannot find NTLDR. Please insert another disk.`

Solution: This problem is most commonly caused by leaving a Windows NT-formatted floppy disk in the A: drive, so check this first. If there is a disk in the drive, remove it and reboot.

If there is no disk in the A: drive, the problem is a corrupt or missing NTLDR. Again the quick fix is to reboot with the Windows NT boot disk and then copy NTLDR across from the floppy disk to the C: drive. Alternatively, you can carry out the Emergency Repair process using the following settings:

[ ] Inspect Registry Files

[X] Inspect Startup Environment

[X] Verify Windows NT System Files

[ ] Inspect Boot Sector

See the step-by-step guide at the end of this chapter for using the Emergency Repair process.

SEE ALSO

➤ *For more information on using the Emergency Repair process, see the step-by-step guide at the end of this chapter.*

Bad or Missing BOOT.INI

Problem: Your computer misses the Boot menu and either goes straight into Windows NT or you see the following message:

```
Windows NT could not start because the following file is
missing or corrupt:
<winnt root>\system32\ntoskrnl.exe
Please re-install a copy of the above file.
```

Solution: This is usually caused by a missing or corrupt BOOT.INI file. If this file is missing, the computer may still start Windows NT, but only if Windows NT was installed in the \WINDOWS or \WINNT folder on the first partition of the first hard disk. This is what the line

```
multi(0)disk(0)rdisk(0)partition(1)\WINNT="Windows NT
Workstation 4.0"
```

in the sample BOOT.INI refers to. Figure 17.7 shows this boot initialization file.

This sample BOOT.INI file shows a standard installation of Windows NT into the \WINNT directory. The default ARC path points to the first partition on the first hard disk on the first controller card. See the following notes on ARC paths for more information on this rather obscure notation. There are two settings to boot in to Windows NT: a normal setting and the SOS setting. See the section titled "Corrupt File System Driver" for the significance of this setting. This system can also dual boot to MS-DOS, loading BOOTSECT.DOS in the process.

If your system boots normally, copy the BOOT.INI file from your Windows NT boot floppy disk to your system partition. If the system is not booting normally, reboot with the boot floppy disk in place and copy the file across as previously described. Alternatively, you can carry out the Emergency Repair process using the following settings:

[ ] Inspect Registry Files

[X] Inspect Startup Environment

[X] Verify Windows NT System Files

[ ] Inspect Boot Sector

SOS and Windows NT

If your computer seems to boot but won't bring up the usual user interface for Windows NT, try the VGA mode setting in BOOT.INI at the next boot. This bypasses all but the most vital startup activities, including all but the most basic video driver: VGA. It will often start an otherwise unbootable system.

Bad or Missing NTDETECT.COM

Problem: After selecting to start Windows NT, the following message is displayed:

```
NTDETECT V4.0 Checking Hardware
NTDETECT Failed
```

BOOT.INI and ARC Paths

The BOOT.INI file is a text file and contains information to enable the operating system to locate the NTOSKRNL.EXE file. This is represented as an ARC path (Advanced RISC Computing) and it enables reference to be made to any partition without the use of drive letters. For example,

multi(0)disk(0)rdisk
(0)partition(1)\WINNT="Windows
NT Workstation 4.0

indicates that NTOSKRNL.EXE is located on the first EIDE controller [Multi(0)], first physical drive [rdisk(0)]– the disk variable is ignored for EIDE drives, first partition [Partition(1)] in the \WINNT directory.

Solution: NTDETECT has been deleted, renamed, or moved. Either boot with the Windows NT boot floppy disk and copy NTDETECT.COM to your system partition as previously described or use the Emergency Repair process with the same settings as for a missing BOOT.INI file.

Bad or Missing NTOSKRNL.EXE

Problem: Booting up normally gives the message:

```
Windows NT could not start because the following file is
missing or corrupt:
<winnt root>\system32\ntoskrnl.exe
Please re-install a copy of the above file.
```

This time, however, the same message occurs when using the boot floppy disk.

Solution: This is usually caused because BOOT.INI is pointing to the wrong directory. The most common cause of this problem is adding partitions with Disk Administrator. Disk Administrator will prompt you if you need to change your BOOT.INI file.

To edit BOOT.INI, you need to make it no longer read-only. Select the file in Explorer, right-click it and choose Properties from the context menu. Uncheck the Read Only box, and then click OK. You can see the Properties dialog box with this check box in Figure 17.8.

Refer back to Figure 17.7 to see a sample BOOT.INI file.

FIGURE 17.8.

You can view a read-only file, but not write to it (edit). To do so, clear the Read-Only check box in this dialog box.

Double-click BOOT.INI to edit it and change the partition number. Usually if you have added a partition, you will have to increase the partition that Windows NT starts from by one.

For example,

```
multi(0)disk(0)rdisk(1)partition(3)\WINNT="Windows NT
Workstation 4.0
```

would need to be changed to

```
multi(0)disk(0)rdisk(1)partition(4)\WINNT="Windows NT
Workstation 4.0
```

Save the BOOT.INI file and restart the computer.

If your system partition is NTFS and you cannot access your hard drive under any other operating system, you can carry out the preceding process on the Windows NT boot floppy disk and restart the computer using that. Then edit the copy on your C: drive.

If this approach does not work, it is probably because the file itself is corrupt. Use the Emergency Recovery procedure with the following settings to restore this file.

[ ] Inspect Registry Files

[X] Inspect Startup Environment

[X] Verify Windows NT System Files

[ ] Inspect Boot Sector

Corruption of a System Driver File

Problem: During the boot process, the blue screen appears showing the amount of memory and number of processors. The procedure fails at this point, however, or takes a considerable amount of time.

Solution: This is usually caused by a failure of a driver such as the keyboard or mouse driver. To confirm this, restart the computer but select the VGA Mode setting. This starts Windows NT in with the /SOS and /BASEVIDEO modes. The /SOS setting will display each device driver as it loads up, enabling you to see which one is causing excessive delay or causing the process to fail. Use the Emergency Recovery procedure with the following settings:

[ ] Inspect Registry Files

[ ] Inspect Startup Environment

[X] Verify Windows NT System Files

[ ] Inspect Boot Sector

Using Last Known Good Option

Problem: You have just installed your new all-singing, all-dancing multimedia extravaganza card and are looking forward to getting your PC to make toast for you. Unfortunately, after installing the drivers and rebooting the machine, the system hangs.

Solution: Usually changes to your configuration that hang the machine on restart can be overcome by using the Last Known Good option.

Windows NT addresses this potential problem by a special feature in the startup process. The Registry contains not only the current settings used by Windows NT, but the previous settings as well. When you make a configuration change, the new settings overwrite the current ones and the current settings become the Last Known Good configuration.

The new current settings become the Last Known Good set after you have successfully logged on. The basis of this is that if you can log on, then your keyboard and monitor must be working properly.

If the new settings prevent you from logging on, however, you can reboot, activate the Last Known Good control set, and return to your previous configuration. This is carried out as follows:

Using the Last Known Good control set for the current control set

1. Reboot your computer and choose Windows NT on the Boot menu.

2. You will see the message

   ```
   OS Loader V4.01

   …

   Press spacebar NOW to invoke Hardware Profile/Last
   Known Good Menu
   ```

3. Take the system up on its offer. Upon pressing the Spacebar within five seconds of seeing the message, you will get a screen message and a prompt for action. The exact screen message and prompt will differ depending on the exact details of your Windows NT installation, but the following is a common one.

4. Press L to choose the Last Known Good configuration, and then press ENTER.

Your machine should now boot normally. It is possible that you may get a message warning you that a device or driver has failed to start. If you consult the System Event log, this will inform you as to the nature of the failure. Try removing and reinstalling the device, if possible. If not, a full emergency repair should solve the problem.

Note that any changes to your system since the last successful logon will be lost.

Whatever your message, the choices should be self evident to their results.

Performing an Emergency Repair

Recovery and Service Packs

If you carry out the Emergency Recovery procedure described in the next section, it is highly recommended that you reapply the latest Service Pack to your system.

See the hints on applying Service Pack 3 at the end of this chapter.

If all the previous suggestions do not work, you need to carry out an emergency repair. This will always be necessary if you have the following problems:

- Corrupt Master Boot Record or partition table
- Damaged Registry

To do this you require the following:

- The Windows NT Workstation CD-ROM or a copy of the i386 directory on your machine's local hard disk
- The three setup disks that came with Windows NT or ones created as previously described
- The emergency repair disk created as described previously and, hopefully, recently updated
- The distribution for Internet Explorer 4 (or higher) if you wish to restore that to your system
- The latest Service Pack (recommended)

Starting the Emergency Repair

The first step is to reboot your machine with the Windows NT Workstation boot disk—#1 from the set of 3—in the A: drive. Assuming your BIOS is not set to boot only from the C: drive, you will see a message informing you that Windows NT Setup is starting.

A blue screen will then appear with the following message:

```
Windows NT Setup
Setup is loading files (Windows NT Executive)…
Setup is loading files (Hardware Abstraction Layer)…
```

After you have pressed Enter, the following message appears:

```
Setup is loading files (Windows NT Setup)...
```

Various drivers are loaded—for example, video drivers, floppy disk driver, keyboard driver, FAT file system. These are required to initialise a limited text-based version of Windows NT so that the remainder of the setup can continue.

Initialization of Windows NT

The next stage is that this minimal version of Windows NT is loaded. This looks very similar to the blue screen that you see during a normal boot.

This is a good point to check that the configuration—that is, memory and processor—information matches what you know to be installed in the computer. If it does not—for example, the memory is not being reported correctly—you either have a BIOS configuration error or possibly a defective hardware component. In either case you need to reboot the machine and check the BIOS settings. Most PCs automatically configure themselves with the correct amount of RAM, but some (such as Compaq) require you to run the SmartStart utilities and change the settings manually.

At this point you want to press R to repair your Windows NT installation.

Unless you know that you have a non-standard CD-ROM or hard disk, it is best to allow Windows NT to detect the mass storage devices automatically.

If you do have a non-standard CD-ROM or hard disk, you will be prompted for a disk that contains the driver files for this device. A list will appear of the relevant driver files. Select the one that you want and press Enter to continue.

After you have replaced disk #2 with disk #3 from your set of three setup disks and have pressed Enter, the following message will appear at the bottom of your screen:

```
Loading device driver (Device type)...
```

Depending on what is attached to your system, you will see messages of the following format:

```
Found:  IDE CD-ROM (ATAPI 1.2)/PCI IDE Controller
```

After all the drivers have been loaded and mass detection has finished, the next screen displays.

Assuming the list represents all your mass storage devices (EIDE hard disks will not normally be listed here), you can proceed. If any devices have not been detected, press S and add the device drivers as previously described.

After continuing, the following messages will be displayed:

```
Loading Device Driver...
Windows NT File System (NTFS)
EIDE Hard Disk
CD-ROM File System
```

Now you will be prompted to select which repair operations you would like to carry out.

The word Continue is selected, as are all the tasks displayed. To deselect a task, use your * or * key to select the relevant task and press Enter to select or deselect it.

It is very important at this point to know which tasks to select. Only select Inspect Registry Files, for example, if you are attempting to restore user accounts. This is because your current user accounts and passwords will be overwritten with the ones in force when the emergency repair disk was created.

For each possible error scenario previously described, the recommended selection has been illustrated. If your problem is a bad or missing NTOSKRNL.EXE file, for example, there is no point in selecting the options to Inspect the Boot Sector or Inspect Registry Files.

After you have chosen which tasks you want to perform, move the highlight onto Continue and press Enter.

What is happening at this point is that the system is giving you the option to restore your system from the emergency repair disk or from the \WINNTROOT\SYSTEM32\REPAIR directory. Usually it is better to try and restore from the \REPAIR directory. This option is not available, however, if you are attempting to restore the database to another machine or if your hard disk has become corrupted.

If you select to restore from the emergency repair disk, you will see the following prompt:

```
The emergency repair disk will be read and the repair process
initialized.
```

The presence of the next few screens depend on which options you selected for the repair process. The next stage is that Setup checks the Master Boot Record and the system files against the files used for installation. This test requires access to the original source files.

An exhaustive check is now carried out on the hard disk. Generally this takes longer than the one that takes place during normal setup.

If you chose the Inspect Registry Files option, at the end of this process you will be prompted to select which items in the Registry you wish to repair. Microsoft recommends carrying out this practice in extreme cases only. Any changes that you made to your accounts database since the emergency disk was created will be lost. All passwords will be reset to their values when the repair disk was made.

System will restore items such as device driver configurations and settings such as TCP/IP addresses.

Software will restore software information such as program associations and user preferences. It will not restore the software itself.

Default will restore the default user profile. This is a set of folders found under \SYSTEM32\PROFILES.

Internet Explorer 4 and the ERD

An ERD made before the installation of Internet Explorer 4 will not work for an Active Desktop-enabled installation.

Make sure to make a new ERD after installing Internet Explorer 4 or after making any significant alterations to your system.

Applying Service Pack 3 for Windows NT 4.0

There are some undocumented command line switches that make installing Service Pack 3 for Windows NT 4.0 a little easier.

Instead of just running UPDATE.EXE, try running

UPDATE -u -f -n -q

This installs Service Pack 3 in Unattended Quiet mode without creating the uninstall directory and will force applications to close at reboot. After you have typed this in and selected OK, all you will see is some disk activity until your machine reboots with the Service Pack installed. For all the command line options, run UPDATE /?.

NTUSER.DAT is the set of initial Registry settings that applies to every new user.

Security covers all file and share permissions, including which groups can access which resources.

The SAM entry appears only if you ran RDISK with the /s option. This will restore the user and group accounts to the values and settings that were current when the emergency repair disk was created.

After the Registry is restored, the file compare process happens. The original image files are compared with the versions that exist on your Windows NT installation. You are prompted to replace any missing or corrupted files.

Upon restarting your computer, your system should be working again. If there still seems to be a problem, try running Setup again and this time instead of doing a repair, try re-installing Windows NT as an upgrade. This will preserve all your accounts, security information, and program registrations. After you have done this, apply the latest Service Pack as well. See Chapter 19, "Setting Up Windows NT." Finally, and again, don't forget to apply the latest Service Pack.

SEE ALSO
➤ *See Chapter 19, "Setting Up Windows NT," for more information on Windows NT setup.*

Full Backups

This chapter has concentrated on some rather technical aspects of Windows NT when it comes to recovering from some system-type disaster. Windows NT itself, when running on an NTFS partition (NT file system), is extremely robust, but disks are mechanical devices.

Not only can disks fail, but fires and earthquakes do occur. This chapter mostly assumes some odd occurrence that leaves your system and data mostly intact, but unreachable due to startup problems.

Unfortunately, most disk problems don't leave your data intact.

Repairing or recovering your Windows NT system only to find your data missing isn't a good experience—believe me! The only real protection is to make complete backups of not only your system, but also of your data. If you wish to truly be safe, you need to store a backup off premises. A fire, flood, or earthquake won't discriminate between your data and its backups.

The Tape Was Always Handy

I once got a call from a client who had been burglarized. He was frantically upset about his lost billing data. I told him to relax, that I could duplicate the hardware stolen in a day and then I would use his backup tapes to have him running that evening. Unfortunately for him, the only backup tape he had was left in the tape drive when the computer was stolen. The upshot for him was much lost revenue and goodwill as he tried to reconstruct his records from memory and guesses.

Don't let this happen to you. Have a backup off premises and away from danger.

Windows NT Workstation 4 Nuts and Bolts

Hardware Considerations

Buying the Computer

When you make the decision to purchase a computer to run Windows NT Workstation, or you are considering running Windows NT on an existing PC, hardware is a key area of concern and caution.

Because Windows NT is a distinct and different operating system from Windows 3.1 or Windows 95/98, hardware and software that may work under those operating systems may not work with Windows NT. Windows NT also requires more horsepower than Windows 95/98, such as RAM, disk space, and to some extent processing speed. This chapter discusses both performance and compatibility considerations for hardware when you run Windows NT Workstation.

Sizing Your Computer

Windows NT Workstation has minimum hardware requirements and a recommended configuration. That configuration produces acceptable performance. Although no one ever complains when a computer is too fast, speed comes at a price.

Minimum Hardware Requirements

The minimum Windows NT hardware requirements are designed to portray the absolute minimum hardware you need. Traditionally this minimum is understated by Microsoft to help dispel the notion that Windows NT requires more RAM and processing speed than Windows 95. The Microsoft-recommended minimum hardware requirements are as follows:

- Intel Pentium-class processor (or DEC Alpha AXP)
- 16 to 32MB of RAM
- 110MB of free disk space
- CD-ROM drive (or network access to a CD-ROM drive)
- Microsoft mouse or compatible pointing device
- VGA-compatible (or higher-resolution) graphics adapter

Fast Processors and NT

Actually Windows NT runs well on any CPU that will run Windows 98. The difference is the applications. For the most part, Windows NT Workstations tend toward heavier applications than those running Windows 98. That's what drives them toward faster CPUs.

Recommended Hardware Requirements

The more realistic requirements for Windows NT Workstation are as follows:

- Intel Pentium 166MHz processor or greater
- 32 to 64MB of RAM
- 250MB of free disk space
- CD-ROM drive
- Mouse
- Super VGA-compatible or greater graphics adapter

Processor Choices

Windows NT Workstation is supported on Intel i386-compatible and DEC Alpha processors. (Microsoft recently dropped ongoing support for MIPS and PowerPC processors after a lack of market acceptance.) Intel-compatible processors dominate the Windows NT marketplace; therefore, this discussion focuses primarily on your Intel brand and Intel-compatible processor options.

Processor Features

When you are selecting a processor, you should examine several characteristics:

- *Processor clock speed* (expressed in megahertz). This indicates the clock speed the processor uses to communicate internally. It is the most common method by which processor performance is measured.

- *Cache* (expressed in megabytes or kilobytes). The cache (pronounced like "cash") is a special, super-fast type of memory inside the processor that stores frequently used information. There are two types of cache: a small Level 1 cache and a larger, slower Level 2 cache. The machine's main memory outside the processor is relatively slower, so there is a performance hit when the processor needs to access memory outside the cache. A larger cache can offer some performance increases. Newer processors such as the

More than On

Windows NT, unlike other Windows, can use more than one CPU to great advantage. If you are planning on very heavy application use such as 3D rendering, consider using a workstation with two or four CPUs.

real Pentium II have a cache size of 512KB or more. Watch out for the cut-rate processor also marketed as a Pentium II, but without any cache; it is slower than the regular Pentium MMX version.

- *Instruction pipeline*. Traditional processors accept and execute a singe instruction at a time. Newer processors can execute multiple instructions at a time by using multiple instruction pipelines—the path instructions take through the processor.

- *System bus speed*. The processor is connected to the rest of the computer by a shared connection called a bus. Some processors use bus speeds of 66MHz. Intel is now offering high-performance processors with a bus speed of 100MHz.

Intel Processor Choices

You have the following choices for Intel processors:

- *Pentium II*. The Pentium II is designed for high-performance workstations and midrange servers, offering speeds from 266MHz and beyond. Intel is focusing large amounts of effort into enhancing the performance of the Pentium II by aggressively boosting its clock speed. The Pentium II has dual instruction pipelines, with newer processors offering a system bus speed of 100MHz. The Pentium II is currently limited to scaling to two processors in a single machine and includes MMX extensions (as discussed later in this list).

- *Pentium Pro*. The Pentium Pro is the processor positioned for the midrange and high-end server. Although its clock speed is slower than the Pentium II, the Pentium Pro sports a larger cache and supports the capability to scale to four processors. Some vendors have created proprietary systems allowing up to eight CPUs, but the performance of Windows NT on these system is quite variable. Going beyond four processors in Windows NT requires very careful research.

- *Pentium processor with MMX technology*. Intel's MMX technology (MMX stands for multimedia extensions) is an additional set of processor instructions designed to improve the performance of graphics and multimedia applications.

- *Pentium*. The Pentium is Intel's first "brand name" processor, abandoning the long-held tradition of numbering each successive processor generation (for example, 80286, 80386, 80486). Intel did this to prevent processor clones from using the same numbering scheme. This has not, however, slowed the pace of companies offering Intel processor clones.

Intel-Compatible Processor Clones

The success of Intel's microprocessors, combined with Intel's early use of cross-licensing deals to produce early generations of PC processors, created a market for processors that support the Intel instruction set. This means that applications and operating systems designed for Intel processors run on these processors as well, even though the processor's internal structures and mechanics differ.

The primary reason you would buy an Intel processor clone is price relative to performance. Intel processor clones offer similar processor performance at a dramatic price break. Because price is the large benefit of a compatible processor (even though the clone companies may have some legitimate claims of technical superiority), these processors are typically found in price-sensitive, consumer-oriented computers. The emergence of sub-$1000 PCs has in part been fueled by the eventual market acceptance of Intel processor clones, a trend noticed by Intel and addressed by the recent announcement of the Intel Celeron processor.

Several companies manufacture Intel-compatible processors, although the market leaders are AMD and Cyrix. Both companies have licensed MMX from Intel and offer MMX in their products. AMD, once an Intel-licensed manufacturer of 8088 and 80286 processors, markets the AMD K-5 and K-6 processors. Cyrix, along with a licensing agreement with IBM, makes the MII and 6x86MX processors. The AMD K-6 and Cyrix MII processors compete with the Pentium II; the AMD K-5 and Cyrix 6x86MX compete with the Pentium processor. (The 6x66MX also competes with the Pentium II, but the MII is a newer product.)

Those Intel Clones

Although most users' experiences with Intel clones from AMD and Cyrix have been mostly positive with Windows 98, the actual field use of these chips with Windows NT and its applications is less common than with that lesser operating system. If you go this route, you will likely be all right, but you will be somewhat of a pioneer too.

Windows NT Workstation and Intel Processor Clones

The processor clone manufacturers are quick to mention that Windows NT runs on their products. They are correct, but Windows NT will disable the write-back cache on some Cyrix processors to prevent serious system problems. This limits the performance of the processor. This problem is well publicized by proponents of Intel processors as an example of subtle incompatibilities introduced by straying from the Intel path. The general rule of thumb is to be cautious and investigate any known issues before purchasing a system with an Intel-compatible processor.

RAM

Memory, both the type and quantity, is one of the biggest considerations when buying a computer for Windows NT. Memory is the single most important component of a properly sized Windows NT computer; adding additional memory is usually the simplest and most effective way to improve performance.

How Much Memory Do I Need?

Determining how much memory you will need depends on several factors, such as the number and type of applications you run on a concurrent basis, as well as the number and type of Windows NT services you run (such as the Remote Access Service, Personal Web Server, and so on).

TABLE 18.1   **Minimum sizing guidelines for RAM**

Computer Role	Typical Amount of RAM
Word processing, general Internet	32–64MB
Moderate Web development, publishing	64+MB
Desktop and Web, print server	64MB
Desktop publishing, engineering, CAD	64–128MB
Video rendering, raster high-end CAD	128+MB

How Much Memory Applications Need

One way you can determine how much memory you need, or determine whether it may make sense to add memory, is to examine how much memory each process or application on your machine is using. The component that will give you this information is the Task Manager. For more information on the Task Manager, refer back to Chapter 15, "Optimizing."

SEE ALSO

➤ *See Chapter 15 for more information about the Task Manager and how to use it to determine how much memory each process or application on your machine is using.*

A less-scientific method for estimating memory requirements (which may be necessary if you don't have a computer to experiment with) is to estimate Windows NT Workstation's base memory requirements and then add memory load for each application that you intend to use. Although virtual memory enables you to run as many programs as you like, Table 18.2 helps you get a feel for the vast amounts of memory these applications use and the potential performance gains you could get by adding any amount of RAM.

TABLE 18.2   General memory usage for popular applications while open

Application	Estimated Memory Used
Windows NT Workstation	12–16MB
Microsoft Word 97	8–16MB
Microsoft Excel 97	6–8MB
Microsoft PowerPoint	3–10MB
Adobe Acrobat Reader	10MB
Visio Professional	12MB
Microsoft Fax Service	3MB
Dial-Up Networking	2MB
Internet Explorer	10–15MB
Microsoft Outlook	3–5MB

Types of Memory

Memory comes in several sizes, speeds, and flavors. This is a consideration when buying memory for your PC.

- *Size.* Typical memory used in desktop computers come in 8MB, 16MB, 32MB, and 64MB sizes. (Server RAM can come in much larger sizes.) Using a smaller memory module may save you the need to spend as much money, but the general rule is to buy the largest module you can afford. Most systems today require you to install memory in pairs of identical modules, so you may have to buy two 16MB modules rather than one 32MB module if you want an addi-tional 32MB of RAM.

- *Speed.* The speed of memory is measured in nanoseconds (ns), and is important because memory that is too slow for your processor may require you to physically slow down your system by adding "wait states," or processor pauses so that your memory can catch up. As a general rule, use memory of at least 60 ns or less, and when in doubt check your computer's manual for recommended speeds (or ask your vendor).

- *Type.* Memory modules come in several flavors, such as parity, non-parity, and EDO (Extended Data Output) RAM. EDO memory is faster than traditional (that is, parity and non-parity) RAM, and is what most new systems use. Parity and non-parity memory use chips in odd- and even-numbered sets, respectively; which memory your PC uses depends on its age and design.

Buyer Beware

People commonly make the mistake of purchasing the wrong type of memory for their PC when upgrading RAM. Although some companies can help you choose the right kind of memory for your computer, the best source of information is a combination of the computer's user manual and your own eyes. The manual can tell you what kinds of memory your computer accepts, and your eyes will tell you how many modules are already installed in your computer.

Hard Disks

Whether you are buying a new PC or upgrading your existing computer, the hard drive is an important consideration. Hard disks not only vary in capacity, they also vary in how the hard drive communicates with the rest of the computer.

Capacity

As with most things to do with computers, you can never have too much disk space. Although you may have no need for disk space today, applications and operating systems are using increasingly more disk space with each successive version. Because you can quickly fill a hard drive, and you may be limited in how many disk drives you can add to your system, purchasing a disk drive of at least 2GB in size makes more and more sense.

Hard Drive Interface Types

Hard drives use several different technologies to connect and communicate with computers. These vary in terms of speed, marketplace use, complexity, and required hardware. These technologies are as follows:

- *SCSI* (Small Computer Systems Interface). SCSI (pronounced "scuzzy") is a popular standard, traditionally in servers and Macintoshes but becoming increasingly popular in PCs. SCSI is known for supporting a wide variety of devices, including disk drives, tape units, CD-ROM drives, and scanners. SCSI supports up to seven devices on a single SCSI adapter, with each connected device requiring a unique, manually set SCSI ID. Newer versions of SCSI such as SCSI-2, Fast/Wide SCSI, and Ultra SCSI support higher speeds and additional devices. Because most computer mainboards do not include a SCSI adapter, you must purchase one; this makes SCSI more expensive than competing standards such as IDE, EIDE, or UIDE. However, recent price reductions in SCSI disks make them quite competitive with the faster IDE schemes such as UIDE. This leaves the price of the interface adapter as the single most costly difference in the two hard disk technologies. If, because of other considerations, you will be buying a SCSI adapter anyway, consider a SCSI hard disk very seriously: SCSI exhibits greater speed and dependability than IDE generally does. SCSI disks are also noisier and run hotter than IDE.

- *IDE* (Integrated Drive Electronics). IDE and its siblings are the most common drive standard found in desktop computers. IDE is different from traditional drive standards such as SCSI in that most of the controller (the hardware that manages the disk drive and how it operates) is integrated into the drive hardware itself, making the drive cheaper and requiring simpler hardware on the computer's side. IDE is

Adding RAM

A simple readout while your PC boots is not enough information; if your PC had 32MB of RAM, you could have two 16MB memory modules or four 8MB memory modules. The difference between the two is important, because most machines have four memory slots. If all are full, you will have to discard two modules to perform an upgrade (an important consideration when you are buying a new PC as well). On some systems, you can add a single memory module, although most require you to add memory in pairs of identical modules. Buying memory will require some research on your part, but will pay off in fewer headaches in the long run.

The Hardware Compatibility List (HCL)

Windows NT supports fewer hardware devices than Windows 95/98, which can make buying equipment difficult and frustrating. Many imaging, multimedia, and gaming products don't work with Windows NT. On its Web site, Microsoft publishes a list of PCs and peripherals known to work with Windows NT (`http://www.microsoft.com/hwtest/hcl`). This list is called the Hardware Compatibility List (HCL). Although the list is not exhaustive by any means, it is worth a look to find equipment or vendors that support Windows NT.

Not All Appear on the HCL

Also keep in mind that many devices and systems work perfectly well with Windows NT, but don't appear on the HCL. I'm writing this now using a computer that, other than the display adapter, doesn't have a single component on the HCL. The problems usually crop up not with the computer systems of today, but the peripherals such as scanners and printers. That's where you need to check carefully.

limited to two hard disks per IDE interface and supports slower transfer speeds than SCSI. Today, given the improvements in IDE technology, there is little justification for running the simple IDE technology disks. Avoid it if you can.

- *EIDE* (Enhanced IDE), *Fast ATA*, *Ultra IDE*, *Ultra ATA*. EIDE and the various flavors of enhanced IDE address many of the shortcomings of IDE, such as higher transfer speeds and the support for up to four devices in a single PC. Different vendors are supporting and advocating different standards, with Western Digital advocating EIDE while Seagate and others advocate Fast ATA. The differences are minor, and all the standards are backward compatible with IDE (but not with each other). Ultra IDE (UIDE) and Ultra ATA offer transfer speeds of up to 33Mbps, and are good choices for a new PC. You should check your PC's documentation to determine which advanced drive standards your PC supports and carefully choose the correct disk drive.

Graphics Cards

Windows NT supports VGA-compatible graphics adapters. Most of us will use Super VGA or more sophisticated graphics cards. When you are choosing a graphics adapter, you have several choices:

- *VGA and Super VGA*. Most of the computers on the market today support standard Super VGA (SVGA), which is up to 1024 across by 768 pixels down. Most SVGA cards have 1MB or more of video RAM; 1MB should be your minimum, and 2MB of video memory is a plus. Additional memory gets you a higher resolution, more colors, or both.

- *Graphics accelerator cards*. These cards speed up graphics performance by offloading some common display logic from the PC to the graphics card by way of a more powerful processor on the graphics card. Graphics accelerator cards make sense for engineering, CAD, or gaming environments. Some cards offer TV tuners, 3D graphics rendering, and a variety of other functions.

Monitors

When purchasing a monitor for any computer, you should consider both the size of the monitor, frequencies and interlacing, and the dot pitch:

- *Size*. This is expressed in inches and is measured diagonally. Popular sizes are 15", 17", and 21". One thing to consider is that the physical size is what you purchase by, but the viewable size is always smaller. The main question then is what the *viewable* size of the monitor is.

- *Dot pitch*. The dot pitch is the size of each pixel or dot on the monitor's screen. A lower dot pitch means a sharper picture, all other things being equal. One thing to look out for is a larger, higher-resolution monitor with a poor dot pitch. For example, 0.28 dot pitch is fine for a 15" monitor, but is somewhat mediocre for a 17" monitor unless the monitor is very well tuned.

- *Resolution*. This is the maximum number of dots the monitor supports both horizontally and vertically. Most Super VGA monitors support 1024×768; 17" and 21" monitors support higher resolutions.

- *Frequency support and interlacing*. Higher-quality monitors support higher signal frequencies, sending a full screen of data in less time and thereby resulting in less monitor flicker. Likewise, some monitors use interlacing, which is the practice of alternating lines on the screen to paint. Our eyes see a full screen, while we suffer eye strain and see some flicker. Use a noninterlaced monitor at its highest refresh frequency to get the best results.

Backup Devices

Windows NT supports a variety of tape and removable media devices, some with drivers that come with Windows NT and others with vendor-supplied drivers.

SEE ALSO

➤ *See Chapter 16, "Disaster Prevention," for information on how to configure and use these units.*

Graphics Chipsets

Many graphics cards from different companies share the same graphics chips, called a *chipset*. There are half a dozen popular chipsets on which many more products are designed. Windows NT may not support your graphics card explicitly, but may support the chipset on which the card was built. If this is the case, Windows NT will work fine, although you may lose some of the advanced features of the card such as a deeper color depth. Even if your card's chipset is supported, it makes sense to use a more specific driver available from your graphics card's manufacturer if it is available.

Worthless Product Reviews

Don't rely on product reviews for monitor selection. Monitors vary from unit to unit in many cases. A cheap monitor might test well–because the sample furnished might be in great tune, but the one you get likely won't be.

A Matter of Taste

Monitor appeal is quite subjective. I like the monitor I personally use because it has brilliant highly saturated colors. It also has a screen that handles glare poorly.

A person who prefers a subdued color scheme or who works in a high-glare situation won't like my monitor at all, although it gets rave reviews from me. Be your own judge here.

Tape Units

Windows NT natively supports mainstream, server-class tape units, such as 4mm DAT, 8mm DAT, and DLT units. Consumer-oriented tape units, such as those that operate via the parallel port, are rarely supported by Windows NT, although some companies offer support as an additional software package (for a fee). You should buy tape units carefully to ensure Windows NT support. A review of the tape vendor's Web site should give you the information you need. Some products that support Windows NT don't mention it on the box, but have drivers that can be downloaded from the Internet.

SEE ALSO
➤ *See Chapter 16, "Disaster Prevention," for instructions on installing SCSI adapter and tape drivers.*

Many Windows NT–supported tape units require a SCSI interface as well as a tape driver.

Removable Media

Most of the popular removable media drives today—such as the Iomega Zip and Jaz drives—support Windows NT, using both SCSI and parallel port interfaces. Although parallel port interfaces are popular and cheap, a SCSI interface will give you dramatically improved performance.

Scanners

Windows NT offers limited scanner support, but more and more new products entering the market offer Windows NT device drivers.

HP ScanJets and older Visioneer PaperPorts, among others, support Windows NT. You should always check for Windows NT support before purchasing a scanner.

Windows NT Workstation on a Laptop

Windows NT Workstation was not designed for use on a laptop computer. Nonetheless, many people use Windows NT on laptops, and some hardware vendors have made an effort to make running Windows NT Workstation on a laptop as easy as possible.

Windows NT lacks much of the functionality offered to laptop users by Windows 95/98. You should be aware, however, of the functionality that Windows NT does offer and some workarounds, including the following:

- *Support for power management.* Power management allows the powering down of system components during idle periods. The hard disk drive can be powered down while idle, for example, and the PCMCIA card slots can be powered off while not in use. For safe use, Windows NT requires that most power management features be disabled.

- *Support for Plug and Play and hot-swappable PC Cards.* Windows NT does not support the swapping of PC Cards while the system is running. You must shut down the computer to switch cards. Plug and Play is not supported fully (although some Plug and Play features do work); you must use hardware profiles for each of your different PC Card and docking station configurations. You can add most of the PnP features of other Windows by installing the Plug and Play Service for Windows NT.

Vendor Support and Third-Party Software

Some laptop vendors have embraced Windows NT on the laptop and offer proprietary drivers and software to address the laptop shortcomings of Windows NT. These vendors include IBM, Compaq, and DEC. Many bundle a third-party PC Card software product called CardWizard from SystemSoft, which enables you to swap PC Cards while the system is running; it also enables you to autoconfigure PC Cards.

Installing Plug and Play in Windows NT

Locate the PNPISA folder on the Windows NT distribution CD. This is usually under the DRVLIB folder. Choose the folder corresponding to your processor. In the case of Intel and Intel clone CPUs, this is i386. Locate the file PNPISA.INF within the folder. Right-click on the file and choose Install from the context menu. You will need to boot Windows NT to activate this service.

Future Considerations

Microsoft has promised a unified driver model for future versions of Windows NT and other Microsoft operating systems such as Windows 98. This model has already started to show in Windows 98, and might appear for Windows NT 4 as a Service Pack before being available, as some hope for, in the next version of NT.

Keep an eye on the Microsoft Web site to see whether such a Service Pack ever becomes available. After the driver model gets unified (if it ever does), the problem of locating hardware drivers should abate considerably.

Setting Up Windows NT

Getting Started

Considering the complexity and power of the operating system, installing Windows NT is surprisingly easy. Before you undertake this task, however, it is recommended that you take time to ensure that your system is ready for installation and that you know how you want your system to work.

Installing Windows NT can be split into three main phases:

- Preparation
- Installation
- Initialization

Preparation

First, some prerequisites before you start the actual installation process.

How Much Memory (RAM) Is Installed?

To install Windows NT, you need at least 12MB RAM; otherwise the install will not even start. With this sort of system, however, don't expect to be able to do any work. A good working minimum is 32MB, and anything more than that will really make Windows NT fly.

RAM for Graphics Software

If you are using graphic software, especially raster image manipulation programs such as Picture Publisher or PhotoShop, you may want to consider 128MB–the increase in working speed will make it a worthwhile investment. Windows NT is very efficient with its use of RAM: The more you give it, the better it works.

How Much Free Hard Disk Space Do You Have?

You need about 120MB to install NT Workstation. The general rule of thumb is that if you are concerned about hard disk space, you probably don't have enough.

See the section titled "Preparing your Hard Disk" later in this chapter.

Is This an Upgrade?

Your upgrade options on Windows NT depend on what operating system is currently installed and whether you want to dual boot your computer after installation (see Table 19.1). If you want to set up your computer as a dual-boot machine, see the section on dual booting.

TABLE 19.1   **Upgrading to Windows NT**

Current OS	New	Upgrade	Dual Boot Install
NT 3.5x	Yes	Yes	New install only
NT 3.1	Yes	Yes	New install only
Windows 3.x	Yes	Yes	Both
Windows 95	Mandatory	No	New install only

Windows 95 and Windows NT 4.0 have incompatible Registry structures, hence there is no upgrade path.

Is Your Hardware on the NT Hardware Compatibility List (HCL)?

To obtain the latest information on hardware compatibility, visit `http://www.microsoft.com/hwtest/hcl/`.

When checking the list, be sure that you check your network cards, CD-ROMs, SCSI controllers, and so forth for compatibility. If your machine is not listed as being compatible, Microsoft will not support your installation.

SEE ALSO

➤ See `http://www.microsoft.com/hwtest/hcl/` *for the latest information on hardware compatibility.*

Even if your system is not on the HCL, however, you will probably be able to get it to work with Windows NT. This chapter is being written on a Dell P166s under Windows NT, for example, which is listed as not supported. Additionally, most computers sold in the United States are local OEMs, none of which will appear on the HCL. Today just about any Intel-based (or clone of Intel) computer will run Windows NT. The only dicey items left are certain multimedia and other add-on hardware such as scanners. For some reason, vendors of these items have been rather slow releasing Windows NT drivers.

Dual-Boot Advantages

Remember you can always create a dual-boot system with Windows NT and MS-DOS or Windows 95/98. The easiest way to have it all is sometimes to sacrifice the disk space to another operating system instead of pounding a vendor to make needed drivers for Windows NT.

Microsoft's Support for
Windows NT

In March 1998, Microsoft
announced a change in its support
arrangements for Windows NT.
Previously no-charge support was
only offered for two incidents,
whereas now you get 90 days free
support from the date of your first
support call. To qualify for this support, however, all your equipment
must be listed as supported on the
Hardware Compatibility List.

See
http://www.microsoft.
com/corpinfo/press/
1998/Mar98/NTWpr.htm
for more information.

SEE ALSO
➤ *Microsoft's online support is at* http://www.microsoft.com/support/.

Have You Read the Latest Installation Information?

Finding the latest installation info

  1. Read the SETUP.TXT file that comes with Windows NT.

  2. Read the README.DOC file for any updates.

  3. Look at http://www.microsoft.com/windows/NTW/ for the
     latest information on installing and using NT Workstation.

Is Your Computer Going to Be Used in a Local Area Network Environment?

If not, you can skip this section. If so, you need to know the following information. Note that the following section is quite
technical in detail for much of its length. You will need to consult with your network administrator if you're in any doubt
about the following items.

Consult Your Network
Administrator

Consult with your network administrator if you're in doubt about any of
the topics discussed in this section.

Computer and Workgroup Names

You need to decide your computer's name (a maximum of 14
characters) and the name of the workgroup that it will join. If
you are using Windows NT Workstation in a domain environment with Windows NT Server, you will need the name of the
domain that you are joining. Your network administrator will be
able to tell you this.

What Type of Network Card Is It?

Windows NT can autodetect most common network cards. If
the autodetect feature does not work correctly, however, you will
need to install the network card drivers manually. Check that
you have the latest driver disk. Your network card manufacturer's
Web site should have the latest drivers.

Windows NT 4.0 does not support Plug and Play configuration
for dynamically assigning IRQ and Base Memory Addresses.

What Protocols Are to Be Used?

There are three networking protocols that may be used with Windows NT. Which one(s) you use will depend on your particular situation, as discussed below.

- *NetBEUI.* This is Microsoft's simple networking protocol. Use NetBEUI if you have a small workgroup with no connection to the Internet and want to implement file and printer sharing.

- *NWLink.* Use this protocol if you have Novell NetWare servers on your network and want to store files and send print jobs to them.

- *TCP/IP.* This is the default networking protocol on Windows NT 4.0 and is becoming the most popular protocol in the world because the Internet runs on TCP/IP. If you are using TCP/IP, however, you will have to know some more configuration information. The following sections identify the information you require.

Will You Be Using Dynamic Host Configuration Protocol (DHCP) with TCP/IP?

DHCP is a system that automatically hands out IP addresses to computers that request them. It is found only on networks that use Windows NT Server, so in a home/workgroup environment it is unlikely that DHCP will be used. Hence you will have to specify your own IP settings.

If You Are Not Using DHCP, What Are Your IP Settings?

Each computer must have a unique IP address (a 4-octet number separated by a dot) on its network. This address is used to identify nodes on an IP network. It takes the form a.b.c.d, where a, b, c, and d take values from 1–254 (for example, 131.107.2.200). You must also provide a subnet mask (a 32-bit value that divides an IP address into a network ID and host ID) for your system to work correctly.

The following settings are optional and apply only in routed LAN environments:

Unique IP Addresses

An IP address is a unique 4-octet number separated by a dot, used to identify nodes on an IP network.

Masks and Values

A subnet mask is a 32-bit value that divides an IP address into a network ID and host ID.

- Default gateway
- First WINS server
- Second WINS server
- DNS server

If you are using DNS, you need to specify a hostname (machine) and a DNS domain (for example, yourcompany.com).

Do You Have a Modem Attached to Your System?

If you have a modem attached to your system, you need to know the following information about the model:

- Modem type
- Speed (in bps)

Check the HCL for supported modems and the manufacturer's Web page for the latest drivers. Even if the modem is not supported or recognized by Windows NT, however, you may be able to install it as a Standard modem type.

Donít Forget the HCL

For a list of supported modems, check the Hardware Compatibility List and consult the manufacturer's Web page for the latest drivers.

Other Considerations for Setup Preparation

Even if you are not going to be on a corporate LAN, most people wish to connect to the Internet or other online services. For these people, a modem is a necessity.

Also, as Windows NT moves from a corporate heavy-duty-only operating system into the mainstream, multimedia hardware becomes common.

Are You Going to Use This Modem to Connect to the Internet?

If you are using your modem to connect to the Internet via an Internet service provider (ISP), you need to know information about the TCP/IP addressing for your modem.

Some ISPs dynamically assign IP addresses and DNS information when you connect, rather like DHCP. Others require you to have your own IP address. In the first case, you will not have to do any IP configuration because this will be done automatically by Windows NT.

If you have been allocated a fixed IP address, you need to enter that information into your Remote Access Service (RAS) dial-up connection. You will need to obtain the following information from your ISP:

■ Your IP address

■ Subnet mask

■ ISP's primary DNS server

■ ISP's secondary DNS server

Do You Have a Sound Card and Speakers Installed?

You need to know what type of sound card it is and, if it is one not directly supported by Windows NT, whether there is a driver for it. In addition, you need to know the following information:

■ I/O base address (normally 220)

■ Interrupt request (IRQ)

Some sound cards require special instructions to set them up under Windows NT. You need to consult the instructions that came with your card or the drivers in these cases. As Windows NT becomes more common as a general operating system, these issues will fade away.

Licensing

When you install Windows NT, you will be prompted for either a licence number or a Product ID, depending on whether you have the retail or the OEM version of Windows NT. If you cannot supply a valid license number or product ID, you will not be able to complete setup.

A license number is of the form 040-1234567, and is found on the box the Windows NT Workstation CD came in.

A Product ID is of the form 12345-oem-1234567-12345, and is usually found on the Certificate of Authority that comes with the OEM NT Workstation pack.

Write these down; you will require one of them during setup.

Do I Have the Correct Materials?

Finally, before you do anything, check to make sure you have the correct materials.

To install Windows NT, you need the following items:

- *Windows NT CD-ROM* (or access to a drive with a copy of the installation files on it).
- *The three Windows NT startup disks*. If you do not have the three startup disks, they can be created as described in Chapter 17, "When Problems Strike."
- *A formatted high-density (HD) floppy disk*. This will become your Emergency Repair Disk (ERD).

Preparing Your Hard Disk

Before you can install Windows NT, you have to initialize your hard disk. You don't need to do this if you already have a Microsoft operating system installed. Most existing operating systems use the FAT16 disk organization system. During setup, Windows NT will offer to change this to Windows NT's File System (NTFS).

If you have a late operating system such as Windows 98 that can use the FAT32 file system, you will need to prep your disk for Windows NT because Windows NT 4.0 and below can't recognize such file systems.

Disk Considerations

Before moving on, let's examine some of the situations you might encounter when setting up Windows NT.

How Many Hard Disks Do You Have?

You need to decide on which hard disk you want to install the Windows NT system files and where you want to put the paging file (sometimes referred to as "page file").

The *paging file* is an area of hard disk used to supplement physical RAM, like the swap file in Windows for Workgroups or

---

Fast Track to Those Disks

If you don't have the setup disks and are familiar with using a computer, you can jump directly to making the set by running the program WINNT32.EXE with the /OX parameter from the i386 folder in your distribution CD. See Chapter 17, "When Problems Strike," for details on this process. You will need an operating system existing on a computer to make the setup disks, but that system doesn't need to be Windows NT.

Windows 95/98. NT will automatically create a paging file on the root of your system partition.

For optimal performance, the paging file should be on a separate physical hard disk from your boot and system partitions and on the hard disk with the fastest access time. If you have only one physical hard disk, putting the paging file on a separate partition does not improve performance.

Partitioning Your Hard Disks

If you have one physical hard disk (assuming it is larger than 1GB), a common approach is to divide it so that you have a 500MB partition for Windows NT and the remainder is used for your applications.

You aren't restricted to this strategy. Some people prefer to have all their data on one logical disk (drive), some don't. Some like having their system on one partition, their programs on another, and data on yet a third. This is particularly handy for backing up.

Another consideration is if you will be dual booting. If you run a late version of Windows 95 or any version of Windows 98, you can run the new FAT32 file scheme. Windows NT can't see FAT32; on the other hand, neither Windows 95 or 98 can see NTFS.

One strategy that some use is to have discrete Windows. Here's how this might work. Install Windows 98 on the C: partition (boot partition), a FAT16 one. Install Windows NT on D:, an NTFS one. Create an additional partition for Windows 98 programs and format that as FAT32 (using the Convert utility supplied with Windows 98).

This gives both operating systems access to the C: drive; but the Windows 98 one can't see the NTFS one, and the Windows NT one can't see the FAT32 one. Therefore, both systems see only the C: and D: drives, but the information on D: differs depending on the system booted.

Supplements and RAM

A paging file is an area of hard disk used to supplement physical RAM.

Boot and System Partitions

Boot and system partitions have a somewhat different meaning under Windows NT than might be expected. The system partition is where NT boots from. The boot partition is where the NT system files are.

This arrangement enables you to install Windows NT on a different partition from the boot partition for your system. In many dual-boot situations, people put the lesser system (such as Windows 98) on the C: drive and Windows NT on D: or higher. However, the computer as a whole must boot from C:, and C: only.

Beware of New FAT Schemes

If you convert the FAT16 boot partition to FAT32 using the Windows 98
utility, you will no longer be able to
boot Windows NT from that computer.

Similarly, converting the boot parti-
tion on a dual-boot machine to
NTFS will disable Windows 98,
Windows 95, or MS-DOS.

Formatting Considerations

Windows NT supports two types of disk formatting: File
Allocation Table (FAT16) and Windows NT File System
(NTFS). The advantages and disadvantages are as follows:

- FAT gives universal compatibility, being recognized by MS-
  DOS, O/S2, and so forth. It is also more efficient on small
  volumes, less than 400MB. It becomes progressively less
  efficient with larger volumes, however, and you cannot apply
  security or compression to FAT volumes. The maximum
  FAT volume is 4GB, although only 2GB of this will be
  reported in Explorer.

- NTFS can be read by Windows NT only, and is more efficient at storing information on larger volumes. It supports
  file-level security, compression, auditing, and allows practical
  partition sizes of up to 2TB (terabytes), depending on your
  hardware.

Both FAT and NTFS support long file and folder names with
backward compatibility for older Windows or MS-DOS programs.

So which one to choose?

If you want to have a dual-boot computer, your system partition
must be FAT. Any NTFS partitions will not be visible to
DOS/Windows 95/98.

If you want to use Windows NT only, and your system partition
is in excess of 400MB, use NTFS. In fact, if you are Windows
NT only, use NTFS unless you have some overriding reason not
to. I can't think of one myself.

If you want to implement file-level security, compression, auditing, or your partition is larger than 4GB, you will have to use
NTFS.

Nonsupported Hard Disks

If you have an unsupported or SCSI hard disk, you may also
need drivers from your disk manufacturer. These have to be
added when installing Windows NT.

Volume Formats

NT supports IDE, EIDE, SCSI, and EDSI hard disk types using FAT and NTFS formats. Most modern hard disks are EIDE or UIDE.

Windows NT 4.0 does not support the following formats:

- Large Hard Disk or a volume in excess of the DOS/FAT16 2GB limit) support on Windows 95 OSR2, Windows 98 (FAT32)
- Novell NetWare volumes
- HPFS format on O/S2 machines

If your disk's existing format is not supported, you can either create a new partition on unpartitioned space or reformat your current partition. You will need to back up any data before you do this because formatting will completely remove any information stored on the partition.

You can reformat your hard disk as part of the Windows NT Setup routine. Alternatively you can carry out the following procedure (assuming Windows NT is not already installed).

Creating and using a bootable disk preparation floppy disk

1. Create a system disk under DOS. Place a floppy disk into your A: drive and from a command prompt, type in

   FORMAT A: /S

   The /S switch will create a system (bootable) DOS disk.

2. Change to your DOS directory and copy the following files to the boot floppy disk:

   FDISK.EXE

   FORMAT.COM

3. Reboot your computer with the new disk in the A: drive. Instead of going to the C: prompt or running Windows, the machine will present you with an A: prompt. If not, you may need to enable booting from your A: drive. See the section on changing the BIOS in Chapter 17, "When Problems Strike."

How Much Is Your Time And Data Worth?

Keep in mind the danger of using anything that doesn't easily work with Windows NT. If you so dare, however, be aware of the potential unreliability and be prepared for the hassle factor. Hardware is comparatively cheap today. When it doubt, throw it out or at least give it away and get something that works well with Windows NT.

FAT32 and You

Microsoft has announced that the next version of Windows NT will support FAT32 volumes. Although not announced, the company might release a Service Pack (SP) or Option Pack (OP) that will add this facility to Windows NT Workstation 4.0.

Not Setup and No Way to Boot

Prior to reformatting a drive that contains the drivers to access your CD-ROM, you must have the original three Windows NT setup disks or have created new ones. If you do not, you cannot install Windows NT. The only exception to this is if your CD-ROM is bootable. To check this, try putting the Windows NT Workstation CD-ROM into your CD-ROM drive and rebooting. If you see a blue Windows NT setup screen on reboot, your CD-ROM is bootable and you can reformat your hard disk.

Don't assume your CD is bootable. Check.

4. If you have FAT32, Novell NetWare volumes, or HPFS partitions on your disk or you want to rearrange your volumes, type FDISK at the A: prompt. The FDISK program will start. FDISK enables you to create and delete partitions on your hard drive. Select the option to Delete a Partition and choose the partition that you want to delete.

After you have deleted a partition, you need to create a new partition and mark it as active. For more assistance, type HELP FDISK at the MS-DOS prompt. You will now have to format your newly created partition, as in the following exercise.

If you completed the preceding exercise, start the next one at step 2. If you just want to reformat to clean up a disk, you don't need to run FDISK, but can start from here.

Using format to finish disk preparation

1. Following the instructions in the preceding exercise, create a bootable floppy disk. Copy the file FORMAT.EXE to this floppy disk. Use it to boot your computer.

2. Type FORMAT C: /S at the A: prompt. This formats your drive as a system (bootable) drive. You will be prompted to enter a volume label for the disk, but this can be blank.

3. You now have a blank drive ready on which to install Windows NT.

Setting Up Dual Boot

To set up a system that can boot into Windows NT as well as the preceding operating system, you need to format your drive as FAT and install it to a proper directory, as discussed below (I'm getting a bit repetitive here, but this stuff is important):

FAT File System

For compatibility with Windows 3.x and Windows 95, your C: drive must be formatted as FAT.

Although utilities on the market can dynamically manage disk partitions, their use under Windows NT is not supported by

Microsoft. I have used such utilities with varied success. In too many cases, I have been left with lost data (except for backups) or with an unbootable computer or both.

These utilities caution to use them only after a full backup. Take this warning seriously.

Essentially, installing Windows NT onto a computer with an existing operating system such as Windows 98 will automatically setup a dual-boot situation.

Installation Directory

With the exception of Windows NT 3.x, you must install Windows NT 4.0 into a different directory from the one that the previous version of Windows is installed to. Windows 95/98 does not allow you to carry out an upgrade into its directory because of incompatible Registry structures. Installing Windows NT 4.0 into a Windows NT 3.x directory will upgrade the Windows NT 3.x installation to 4.0. However, you will not be able to dual boot into the preceding version.

Hence to set up your system for dual boot, you must have a FAT formatted C: drive with at least 120MB free and install Windows NT into a separate directory. The only exception to this is with Windows 3.x (not Windows NT 3.x), which allows dual boot even if Windows NT is installed into the \WINDOWS directory.

Running Setup

To start the installation of Windows NT, either:

1. Put the Setup Boot disk into the A: drive and reboot the computer.

or

2. If you have a bootable CD-ROM, place that in the CD-ROM drive and reboot.

or

3. Under the preceding operating system, change to the drive with the installation files on and run the setup program manually. This requires you to run WINNT.EXE from a command prompt. The options for this program are discussed at the end of this chapter.

SEE ALSO

➤ *See the section titled "Command Line Switches" at the end of this chapter for more information on various command line switches for use with each version of WINNT.EXE.*

After setup has started, you see a blue screen with the following message:

```
Windows NT Setup


Setup is loading files (Windows NT Executive)
Setup is loading files (Hardware Abstraction Layer)
```

After you press Enter, this message appears:

```
"Setup is loading files (Windows NT Setup)..."
```

Various drivers are loaded—for example, video drivers, floppy disk drivers, keyboard drivers, FAT file system, and so on. These are required to initialize a limited text-based version of Windows NT so that the remainder of the setup can continue.

Initialization of NT

During the next stage, this minimal version of Windows NT is loaded. This looks very similar to the blue screen that you see during a normal boot.

This is a good point to check that the configuration—that is, memory and processor information—matches what you know to be installed in the computer. If it does not—for example, the memory is not being reported correctly—you either have a BIOS configuration error or possibly a defective hardware component. In either case, you need to reboot the machine and check the BIOS settings. Most PCs automatically configure themselves with the correct amount of RAM; some (like

Compaq), however, require you to run the SmartStart utilities
and change the settings manually.

Windows NT Setup

Windows NT Setup goes through the following four stages:

1. Gathering information about your computer

2. Network setup

3. Displaying setup

4. Finishing Setup

Gathering Information

Much of Setup is automated and beyond the control of the user.
Although Plug and Play isn't really integrated into Windows NT
4.0 (it's a poorly documented optional add-on), the detection and
configuration technology behind it is part of the operating system. Therefore, for the vast majority of people, the only thing
they need do in Setup is to run the program and follow the
rather simple onscreen prompts.

Remember, as mentioned earlier, if you have a previous operating system installed such Windows 98, Windows NT will default
to creating a dual-boot situation.

If you wish to add another operating system after installing
Windows NT on a clean machine (no previous operating system), see the final section of this chapter for a way to do this.

For the most part, running Windows NT Setup is a matter of
sitting back and relaxing as the program goes through its paces.

Network Setup

The only partly tricky part of Setup is the networking. That's because for most people the terms used in networking are somewhat vague or obscure.

Here you should consult with your network administrator for help in determining specifications you must tell Setup at this stage. If your network uses a domain name server (DNS), for example, there is no way for you to know this or its specification without asking. Similarly, you will need to know what protocols (NetBEUI, TCP/IP, and so forth) to install. You might also need to know the settings for your network adapter (IRQ, I/O).

Remember that you can always finish Setup without installing any networking and then gather the needed information and install networking afterward. There is no penalty for this, so feel free to skip over this step and come back to it after you have gathered the needed information.

SEE ALSO

➤ *Chapter 8, "Networking Fundamentals," delves into networking theory and practice, such as installing networking, in great detail. If you have any questions, or just want to know more about the technology, that's the place to get it.*

Display Setup

In the not too distant past, setup of a display adapter was an enormous chore. This has grown much easier lately with the winnowing down of operating system vendors to just about one (Microsoft) and the maturation of the video board business.

Still, the one place where downstream operational difficulties persist when they shouldn't boils down to video issues. Therefore, I have included this small section on how Windows NT handles video installation.

Setup, after the reboot, brings you to a video screen shown in Figure 19.1. You can also invoke this screen by right-clicking the desktop and choosing Properties|Settings. This is where you specify the display driver for your adapter, the resolution, and the color depth you wish to run.

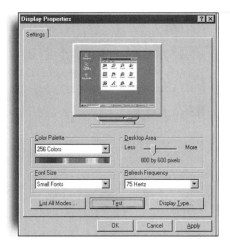

FIGURE 19.1.

This is the dialog box controlling the display Windows NT
will use for itself.

Windows NT will attempt to detect the display driver used on
your system. If a supported driver is detected, you are informed
via a dialog box. Otherwise the standard VGA driver will be used
instead. Select OK.

If you have the standard VGA driver detected, you can change
only the resolution from 640×480 to 800×600. If a Cirrus Logic,
S3, or other supported driver is selected, however, you can
change the color palette, font size, desktop area, and refresh
frequency.

The supported combinations depend on your video RAM and
monitor capability. Before you select OK, you need to click the
Test button to ensure that the monitor and video card will work
using your selected settings.

The screen will change to a test card showing color gradients,
horizontal and vertical lines, and sizing marks for the screen resolution. This screen should appear for about five seconds. You
will then be asked whether you saw the test screen. If the test
screen did not appear, was obviously not displayed properly, or
had noticeable flicker on the horizontal or vertical lines, you
should change the settings. Try reducing the color depth or
screen size. Whatever your settings, always try to keep your
refresh frequency as high as possible. The minimum refresh frequency that is recommended is 72Hz, meaning that the screen
should not show any detectable flicker.

If your card is VGA only, you are limited to a 60Hz vertical refresh rate. If you know the manufacturer of your video card, try searching their Web site for updated Windows NT drivers that can be installed after setup.

Finishing Up

Windows NT Setup must go through several boots and file copying sessions before it is fully done. The exact number of boots and instances of file copying differs, depending on the hardware (and drivers) as well as the Setup option (such as Custom).

The best thing to do during this process is to relax, perhaps reading a book on using Windows NT. From time to time, you might be asked a question or two, but Setup is patient. If you're not immediately available, it will wait until you get around to answering its queries.

Setup is an area that Microsoft has worked on very diligently to make it as foolproof as reasonable and as automated as its options allow. Here's a time for you to enjoy the fruits of Microsoft's labors in this area.

Command Line Switches

Here are the command line switches for running both WINNT.EXE and WINNT32.EXE. One of the more useful switches is the /T, allowing the installation of the rather voluminous temporary files to a drive other than the default C: drive. Use this if your C: drive is rather tight on space.

WINNT

Installs Windows NT.

```
WINNT [/S[:]sourcepath] [/T[:]tempdrive] [/I[:]inffile]
    [/O[X]] [/X ¦ [/F] [/C]] [/B] [/U[:scriptfile]]
    [/R[X]:directory] [/E:command]


/S[:]sourcepath
```

       Specifies the source location of Windows NT files.

       Must be a full path of the form x:\[path] or

       \\server\share[\path].

       The default is the current directory.

/T[:]tempdrive

       Specifies a drive to contain temporary setup files.

       If not specified, Setup will attempt to locate a drive
➥for you.

/I[:]inffile

       Specifies the filename (no path) of the setup
➥information file.

       The default is DOSNET.INF.

/OX   Create boot floppies for CD-ROM installation.

/X   Do not create the Setup boot floppies.

/F   Do not verify files as they are copied to the Setup
➥boot floppy disks.

/C   Skip free-space check on the Setup boot floppy disks
➥you provide.

/B   Floppyless operation (requires /s).

/U   Unattended operation and optional script file
(requires
➥/s).

/R   Specifies optional directory to be installed.

/RX   Specifies optional directory to be copied.

/E   Specifies command to be executed at the end of GUI
➥setup.

WINNT32

Performs an installation or upgrade of Windows NT 4.0.

```
winnt32 [/s:sourcepath] [/i:inf_file] [/t:drive_letter] [/x]
[/b] [/ox] [/u[:script] [/r:directory] [/e:command]
```

Parameters:

/s:sourcepath   Specifies the location of the Windows†NT
➥files.

/i:inf_file   Specifies the filename (no path) of the
setup
➥information file. The default is DOSNET.INF.

/t:drive_letter   Forces Setup to place temporary
➥files on the specified drive.

/x   Prevents Setup from creating Setup boot floppy
➥disks. Use this when you already have Setup boot floppy

```
↪disks (from your administrator, for example).
/b         Causes the boot files to be loaded on the system's
↪hard drive rather than on floppy disks so that
↪floppy disks do not need to be loaded or removed by the
user.
/ox          Specifies that Setup create boot floppy disks for
CD-
↪ROM installation.
/u         Upgrades your preceding version of Windows†NT in
↪Unattended mode. All user settings are taken from the
preceding installation, requiring no user intervention during
setup.

/u:script Similar to /u, but provides a script file for user
↪settings instead of using the settings from
the preceding installation.
/r:directory     Installs an additional directory within the
↪directory tree where the Windows†NT files are
installed. Use additional /r switches to install additional
directories.
/e:command                  Instructs Setup to execute a
↪specific command after installation is complete.
```

Post Setup Dual Boot

As mentioned earlier, you can install a second operating system after installing Windows NT, but the method isn't particularly obvious or simple. If you know prior to installing Windows NT that you will want a dual booter, by all means make your life easier and install the non-Windows NT system first and Windows NT on top of that to take advantage of its Setup's capability to automatically create a dual boot.

Even if you don't have the eventual system you wish, you can install something as a placeholder and then upgrade. If you wish to install Windows 98 and Windows NT as a dual boot, but don't have Windows 98 handy, for example, you can install Windows 95, and then Windows NT to a dual boot. After, when you upgrade 95 to 98 you will have the dual-boot aspect preserved, but with Windows 98 as the alternative to Windows NT, not Windows 95.

Well, let's say you didn't. Here's how to do an after-the-setup-fact dual boot. It uses a method to install MS-DOS first, and then you can upgrade to any Windows.

Using MS-DOS to create a dual boot

1. Back up your system fully, including making a new ERD. Don't say I didn't warn you: Things can, and will, go wrong here.

2. Use the Setup routine from MS-DOS to install that system on to your computer. This often means booting the computer with the Setup disk in the A: drive.

3. Run the Windows NT Setup program. Choose the option to run a Repair.

4. Tell Setup/Repair (by checking the appropriate check box) to examine (inspect) the boot sector and the setup environment.

5. Setup will grind away a while. It should detect the new operating system and add it to BOOT.INI. This establishes a dual-boot machine. The non-NT operating system can be upgraded as you wish.

Using the Command Line Interface

Why Bother with Commands?

Windows NT Workstation was designed from the outset to have a graphical user interface (GUI). Many people think of it as only having such an interface, but it also has integrated into it a command line interface (CLI).

The CLI for Windows NT Workstation is similar to late versions of MS-DOS, but without those commands that aren't appropriate. Additionally, Windows NT has many CLI commands exclusive to it and never found in previous Microsoft operating systems.

Although the CLI of Windows NT has less variety than other competing operating systems, such as various shells of UNIX, the most important commands are all there.

No UNIX Envy Here

The CLI for Windows NT isn't a patch on most UNIX versions—especially for those who like to write their own shell scripts. Several excellent add-ons for Windows NT give it the command-line power of UNIX, however, including the capability to create custom shell scripts.

Also many of the operations required from the command line in UNIX are possible through the GUI of Windows NT. Even so, some UNIX fans who enjoy playing stupid shell tricks find the subset of commands in Windows NT to be restrictive. Keep in mind that some add-ons from Microsoft, such as the Resource Kit, add some interesting utilities. The Resource Kit even has a Rexx interpreter for OS/2 immigrants.

What's In and Out of the CLI

Here is a list of the commands found in late versions of MS-DOS but deleted in Windows NT Workstation with an explanation and alternative if possible.

- Assign   Very dangerous in an NT environment
- Choice   A mysterious deletion. The reason for its deletion is a good topic to debate over Jolt colas.
- CTTY   You must issue commands from the console only.
- Dlbspace   This compression scheme is unrecognized by Windows NT Workstation due to security concerns. Use the file compression routine native to Windows NT in its stead.
- Defrag   Use third-party defraggers such as Disk Keeper or Norton Utilities.

- `Dosshell`   Windows NT Workstation uses explorer.exe as a shell.

- `Drvspace`   See `Dlbspace`.

- `EMM386`   Purposeless, given Windows NT Workstation's architecture.

- `Fdisk`   Use the Disk Administrator or make an MS-DOS boot disk specifically for disk initialization.

- `Include`   You have one DOS and only one DOS configuration.

- `Interlnk / Intersrv`   Purposeless with Windows NT Workstation inherently providing a superset of these services. MS-DOS clients can connect to Windows NT using a net start disk or RAS.

- `Join`   NTFS and DOS capacity to handle larger volumes makes this command obsolete.

- `Memmaker` and supporting files   Facilities automatically done in NTVDMs.

- `Menu[color][default][item]`   See `Include`.

- `Mirror`   Make and use an ERD.

- `Msav`   Use third-party utilities. DOS and similar virus checkers aren't effective under Windows NT

- `MSBackup`   Use the surviving and still unreliable `backup` and `restore` if you're masochistic and don't really care about your data anyway. Use `NTBackup` if you're normal or loss of your data will be troubling.

- `Mscdex`   Windows NT Workstation virtualizes the CD-ROM drive, eliminating the need for real-mode drivers it can't use anyway.

- `Msd`   Use Windows NT Workstation's Diagnostics utility.

- `Numlock`   You need to press the key yourself if you don't like the way things have turned out when turned on. Often this utility exists as part of your firmware's setup.

- `Power`   Windows NT Workstation doesn't support this utility. This doesn't mean it's `power`-less in any large sense.

Expect support for this or a similar utility in subsequent versions of Windows NT.

- Scandisk   NTFS volumes tend to be self healing. You can use the scandisk from Windows 95 or MS-DOS for FAT volumes by booting to DOS. Use third-party utilities.

- Smartdrv   Windows NT Workstation automatically and dynamically manages the disk cache. A Smartdrv for Windows NT would impinge on this hard-won sovereignty.

- Submenu   See Menu.

- Sys   Windows NT is too big to Sys from or to a floppy disk.

- Undelete   Files deleted from the Explorer are generally undelete-able. Files deleted from the CLI aren't unless a third-party utility protects your computer.

- Unformat   Don't format anything you don't want to stay good and formatted.

- Vsafe   See Msav.

Starting and Configuring the CLI

To start a command line interface (CLI) session, choose the Start-Command Prompt entry from the menu. This brings up a screen similar to Figure A.1.

FIGURE A.1.

The CLI should be familiar to anybody having seen MS-DOS, SCO UNIX, OS/2, or similar command-line operating systems.

The title bar tells you that you're at the command prompt and the command you executed is CMD. CMD is the command interpreter (shell) for Windows NT. Windows NT Workstation also contains a shell for DOS called, not surprisingly, Command. In most cases it doesn't make any difference which shell you launch. Keep in mind, however, that some DOS programs can become severely confused if launched under CMD—and Command is DOS-like, not NT-like.

You can configure the window for your CLI using the same tools as under later DOS versions with some interesting additions. To see a menu for configuring the CLI, click the MS-DOS icon in the upper-left corner of the CLI window or press Alt+Space. This will drop down the menu shown in Figure A.2.

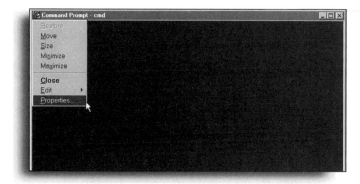

FIGURE A.2.

Configuring the CLI isn't as much fun as a holiday on ice, but you can't fall through and get wet either.

The Move and Size commands on this menu are real head-scratching bafflers. You can move the window by clicking its title bar and dragging just like any window. You can size it by clicking a border and dragging with the mouse.

The Maximize command will not really maximize the window, but only maximize it to its full size as a window. To make the window a real full-screen CLI, press Alt+Enter. This is a toggle. To get back to a window again, press Alt+Enter. This works only on Intel boxes because Alpha systems lack a full-screen mode.

The real action from this menu comes from the last entry, Properties. Click that and you will bring up the tabbed dialog box shown in Figure A.3.

FIGURE A.3.

No shocks here. The Properties entry brings up a tabbed dialog box.

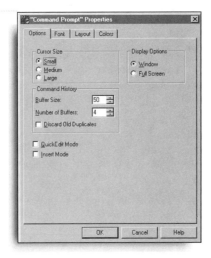

Here are the choices for the first and most useful tab, the Options tab.

- *Cursor Size.* This is how big the flashing "thingie" is, not how large the command prompt appears to be. Choose Large and the cursor becomes a block just about as big as a character box. If you change this option, the Properties dialog box enables you to make the modifications for all instances of this shortcut or only this session.

- *Display Options.* Start in window or full screen? This is whether you need to hammer the session down to a window with Alt+Enter or you need to blow it up with the same key sequence. This option is only for Intel boxes.

- *Command History.* Windows NT Workstation has the equivalent of DOSKEY built in to its command shell for recalling commands. This property controls how many commands it keeps in its buffer and how big that buffer is. The larger the buffer, the less room available for programs, but not by much.

- *Quick Edit Mode.* Enables use of the mouse to highlight, copy, and paste. If unselected, you need to use the Edit subcommands from the pull-down menu. To use the Quick Edit, highlight the area you wish to copy using the mouse, and then press Ctrl+C. Ctrl+V pastes at the cursor.

- *Insert Mode.* The default for the line editor in the shell is overtype. Check this box if you prefer to be in Insert mode. The Insert key (Ins) toggles this option in the editor.

The Fonts tab allows setting of the font type and size in either this session or all sessions. Figure A.4 shows the Fonts tab and the setting of the font for this session to a larger True Type rather than the default Raster.

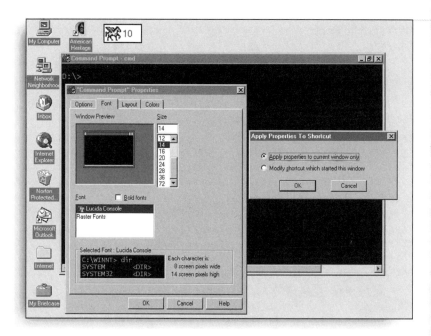

Changing the font size and type for a CLI session or shortcut will affect the size of the window the CLI occupies. Changes in this tab won't affect the full-screen (if available) mode of the CLI.

The Font tab will change the size and appearance of the prompt and any text displayed in the CLI window.

The command prompts aren't as flexible as the old DOS prompt with ANSI.SYS cocked and loaded, but you can still rock out if you feel so inclined. As in times of yore, you can alter the prompt by entering the Prompt command followed by a parameter. Here are some parameters:

- $A   & (Shift 7)
- $B | vertical line used for piping
- $C   (

- $D   System date
- $E   The ESC character
- $F   )
- $G   >
- $H   Backspace
- $L   <
- $N   drive
- $P   path
- $Q   =
- $S   Space or ASCII 32 (20h)
- $T   System time
- $V   Windows NT version
- $_   CRLF
- $$ $
- [Any Text]   Any text

So if you want to create a prompt that says

```
My Computer
Leave Alone
```

and shows the time, you enter

```
Prompt My Computer$_Leave Alone$_$t
```

at the prompt and press Enter or Return. Figure A.5 shows the command and the results.

Windows NT has the following two prompt commands that have no analogs in DOS.

- $+[more +'s]   Reflects pushed directories in the stack.
- $M   Displays the remote name associated with a network drive letter. This is null in a local drive.

In the Layout tab, you can configure how wide and how deep (in characters) your screen will be. It also enables you to set a default position for the CLI window. Figure A.6 shows this tab.

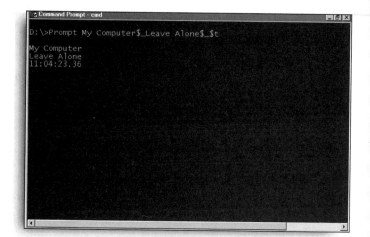

FIGURE A.5.

You can get just about as silly with CMD as you can with ANSI.SYS. To return to the default prompt, enter the command prompt with no parameters and then press Enter or Return.

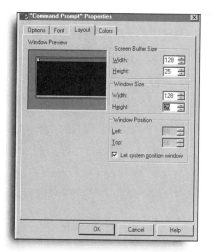

FIGURE A.6.

The Layout tab allows the setting of screen width, depth, and placement.

Figure A.7 shows the results of setting the Screen Buffer and Window Size to 128 characters. Because the Windows NT display is only 80 characters wide, the CLI session responds by placing scrollbars in the window.

The final tab in the Properties dialog box enables you to set the colors for the one where newbies tend to set the foreground and background colors for the regular screen and pop-up text. Figure A.8 shows this tab.

FIGURE A.7.

You can set the layout of the CLI window to be larger than 80 characters. Doing so has somewhat doubtful utility.

FIGURE A.8.

The Colors tab not only allows selection of colors, but also shows a preview of what you will get when you click OK.

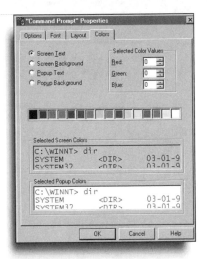

You can choose from the basic color bar in this dialog box or mix up your own colors using the RGB mixer at the upper right. For some reason, newbies tend to set the same colors for the screen text and screen background. This makes reading the CLI somewhat problematic.

You can also change the title in the title bar by entering the command

`title`

with some following text. Figure A.9 shows this command in action.

FIGURE A.9.

The title command enables you to title your CLI window to a text of your choosing.

Configuring the Shortcut or Program

The same options and more that are available to you from the CLI menu are available through the Properties tabbed dialog box of the program or shortcut itself. Figure A.10 shows this dialog box for a shortcut to the Windows NT CLI, CMD.EXE.

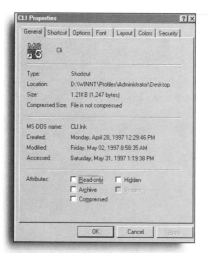

FIGURE A.10.

The Properties tabbed dialog box for a shortcut to the CLI has a superset of the options available from the menu within the CLI.

The three major differences between setting options at the shortcut level and the menu level are as follows:

- The shortcut options will affect all instances of the CLI unless explicitly canceled or countermanded by a menu configuration.

- The Shortcut dialog box has options for the shortcut itself just like other shortcuts.
- The Shortcut Properties dialog box contains a Security tab with buttons for Permissions, Auditing, and Ownership.

To get to the Properties tabbed dialog box, right-click the shortcut and choose Properties from the context menu.

Piping, Redirection, and Conditional Symbols

MS-DOS allows some piping and redirection of input and output. Windows NT takes this a bit further. Adding the following symbols to your commands or batch files can add considerable power and flexibility to them.

Here is a list of the command symbols you can use on your command line or in batch files.

- \> Redirection, usually from the console to a device or file. This works the same as DOS. The following:

  ```
  w.bat > myfile.txt
  ```

  redirects the output of the batch file w to a file, myfile.txt, rather than the console.

- \>\> Same as >, but will append output if the named file exists. This works the same as DOS. The following:

  ```
  v.bat >> myfile.txt
  ```

  creates myfile.txt and directs the output into that file. If myfile.txt exists, it will append the output of v.bat to the file.

- 2> Redirects only error output. This works the same as DOS. Therefore, the following:

  ```
  w.bat 2> error.fil
  ```

  directs any errors stemming from running w.bat to the file error.fil.

- < Places input from a source (usually a file) to a command capable of accepting the input. This works the same as DOS. The following:

  ```
  [command] < myfile.txt
  ```

  runs the file myfile.txt through the [command] program. To sort a file and dump the output to a new file, for example, enter the following:

  ```
  sort < myfile.txt > sorted.txt
  ```

- ¦ Pipes the output of one command to another command. This works the same as DOS. The following:

  ```
  dir ¦ sort
  ```

  runs the output of the DIR command through the Sort command.

- ¦¦ Executes the command to the right of the symbol if the command to the left failed. The following:

  ```
  Type myfile ¦¦ echo no type radio
  ```

  echoes "no type radio" if the Type command fails (if it can't find the file, for example).

- 2>> Same as 2>, but will append output if the file exists.

- ^ Interpret next character as a literal, not a command. This enables you to use command symbols in filenames or parameters. The following:

  ```
  Dir ^&file.txt
  ```

  allows the use of the DIR command with the file named &file.txt.

- ; or , Separates parameters feeding them individually to a command. The following:

  ```
  Dir myfile.txt;yourfile.txt
  ```

  executes DIR against the parameters myfile.txt and yourfile.txt sequentially.

- ( ) Groups multiple commands.
- & The AND of the CLI. Executes a series of commands sequentially from left to right. You can see an example of this in Figure A.11. The following:

  DIR A:&DIR B:

  runs DIR twice, once with the A: parameter and once with the B: parameter.

- && Executes the command to the right if the command to the left is successful. The inverse of the ¦¦ symbol. The following:

  DIR A:&& DIR B:

  runs DIR B: only if DIR A: worked.

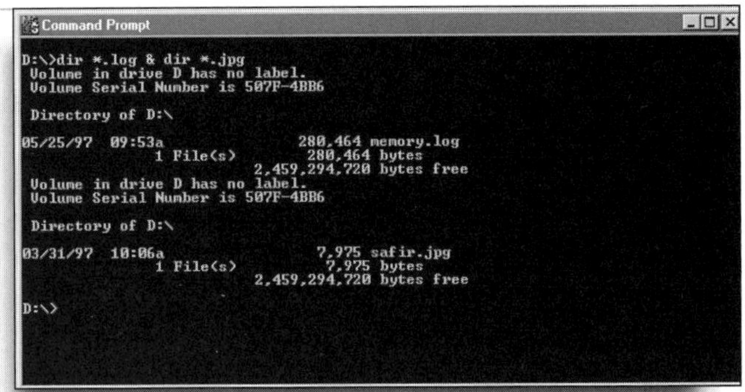

FIGURE A.11.

The ampersand is the AND symbol of the CLI. Here the command line dir *.log & dir *.jpg executed the DIR command first with the parameter *.log and then with the parameter *.jpg. The output is the console display showing files with both extensions. The command dir *.jpg & *.log will not yield the same output. Instead it will err on the *.log parameter.

```
D:\>dir *.log & dir *.jpg
 Volume in drive D has no label.
 Volume Serial Number is 507F-4BB6

 Directory of D:\

05/25/97  09:53a               280,464 memory.log
               1 File(s)        280,464 bytes
                             2,459,294,720 bytes free
 Volume in drive D has no label.
 Volume Serial Number is 507F-4BB6

 Directory of D:\

03/31/97  10:06a                 7,975 safir.jpg
               1 File(s)          7,975 bytes
                             2,459,294,720 bytes free

D:\>
```

Operating the CLI

If you have spent any time with MS-DOS, including the command line interface of Windows (that's DOS, too) or with a text-based UNIX system such as SCO UNIX or even Amiga DOS, you should be quite comfortable with the CLI of Windows NT Workstation. The basics of using a CLI are to enter a command with parameters (sometimes) and then press the Return or Enter key to tell the system to execute (or try to execute) the command. The subtleties of a CLI are enormous, however.

MS-DOS is a bone simple operating system that has been around in one form or another for more than 15 years. Even so, people are still discovering new twists or tricks with commands or batch files or both. This is partly because newer versions of DOS and DOS successors (like Windows 98) are slightly different in implementation, giving rise to a lore of DOS-dom similar to the nitpickers of *Star Trek*.

Throw in a more complex command set like that found in most UNIX shells (all today) and a language or two to interact with that shell (such as AWK or Rexx) and you end up with one of those almost infinite fields of study. If you want to delve into these complex but rewarding areas, you can use the native Windows NT shell or buy a shell extending the Windows NT command set. Two of such shells are the 4DOS type shell from J.P. Software and the Korn-like shell from MKS System. The latter especially is a real-time sync, but a lot of fun too.

Most people have all they can handle with the native Windows NT command set. Oddly enough, Microsoft has, for some reason, documented the command set fairly well.

Getting Information on the CLI

The Help command from the Start menu is the main entry to the GUI help system for Windows NT Workstation. Searching this system on the keyword

```
Command
```

brings up an alphabetic listing of most of the CLI commands. Although generally all right, this listing isn't perfect; nor is it right all the time. Figure A.12 is the GUI listing for the DISKPERF command. Note the command line parameters are as follows:

```
diskperf [-y¦-n] [\\computername]
```

This isn't entirely right. There is an e parameter, too, for use when the ftdisk service is running.

Figure A.13 shows the command-line help system for the DISKPERF command. This gives the proper and complete information for this command. Presumably, Microsoft is updating the help system at all times, so later versions of Windows NT

Workstation might have this and some other help anomalies sorted out by the time you get your copy. The DISKPERF help oddity appeared in a very early but commercial version of Windows NT Workstation.

FIGURE A.12.

The online help system for the CLI in Windows NT is a good idea and well implemented (although incomplete in some areas).

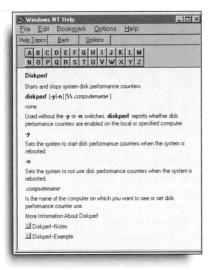

FIGURE A.13.

The command-line help for the DISKPERF command gives information about the missing parameter—missing from the GUI help system, that is.

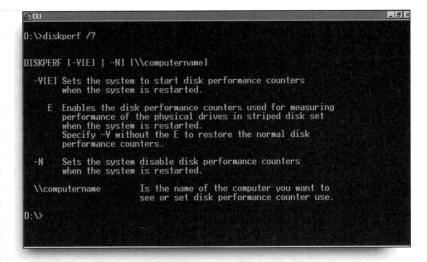

To see the command-line help text for any listed command, enter

```
[command] / ?
```

and press Return or Enter ([command] is any listed command).

Slashes and Dashes

Commands need some way to know what you mean by the entries following them on the command line. Consider the following simple Directory (dir) command, for example:

```
Dir d
```

This returns a display to the console of any files named d in the current directory. Figure A.14 shows the outcome of running this command.

FIGURE A.14.

Without any symbols, the DIR command takes the d in this command line to be a request to display any files named d.

Change this command line to

```
Dir /d
```

and the results will be the display shown in Figure A.15.

The difference between the two command lines is a simple slash. This tells the command interpreter (CMD.EXE in this case) that the following character or characters form a switch rather than a variable.

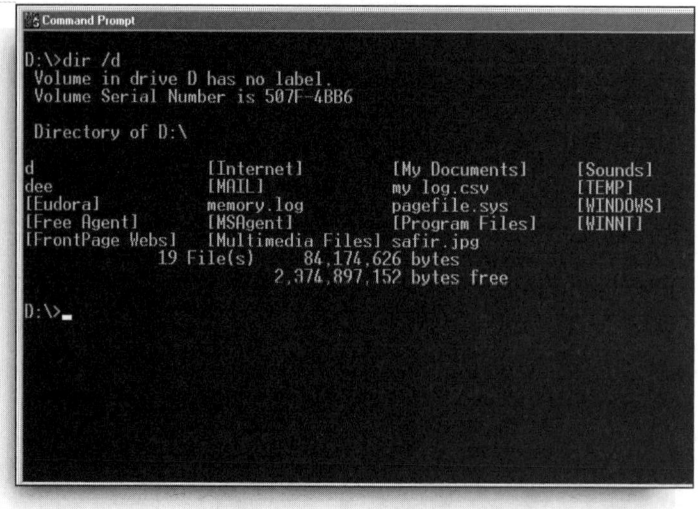

FIGURE A.15.

Add a slash to the d and the DIR command understands you mean a command-line switch rather than a file specification.

FIGURE A.15.

Add a slash to the d and the DIR command understands you mean a command-line switch rather than a file specification.

The vast majority of commands in the CLI take switches. Different commands require different switch symbols, however. As a general rule, the DOS-derived commands such as DIR, FORMAT, and FIND want forward slashes as a switch symbol. The TCP/IP commands need dashes and will often try to interpret the slash as a variable.

For example, if you enter

Help ping

on the command line, Windows NT Workstation will respond as shown in Figure A.16.

However, if you enter

Ping /?

on the command line, the command will try to Ping a computer named /?. Few networks have computers named /?; that's likely not what you were after anyway.

Figure A.17 shows the results of entering

Ping /?

on the command line. This screen shows the Ping command ended by a Ctrl+C.

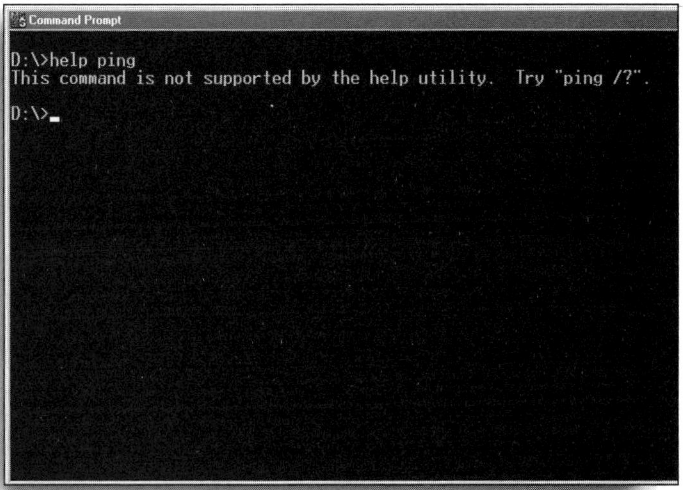

FIGURE A.16.

Seeking help on the Ping command will elicit a suggestion that you try the standard method to get help on an individual command.

FIGURE A.17.

Giving a slash rather than a dash to Ping confused the utility. Here it tried mightily to echo a Ping off a computer named /?. Although it's not apparent in this screen, Ping spent a lot of time trying to find the /?-named computer.

The problem is that Ping doesn't see the slash as a symbol to interpret the following string as a switch. Instead it sees the entire string /? as a variable. This is because in the land of Ping's origin, UNIX, the slash is a delimiter for directory navigation. A directory structure in UNIX, like other operating systems such as AmigaDOS, looks something like this on the command line:

`usr2/etc/med`

rather than the Windows NT (or DOS) look of

```
winnt\system32\user1
```

It works or fails to work the other way, too. If you want to see online help for Ping, you need to follow its UNIX conventions and enter

```
Ping -?
```

on the command line. Figure A.18 shows the results of entering this command line. If you tried to follow Help's suggestion of using the Ping /? rather than the Ping -?, you know how eternal optimists sometimes feel.

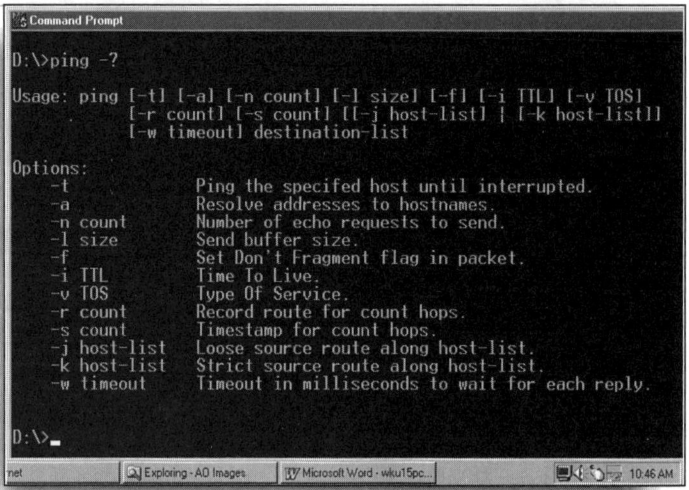

FIGURE A.18.

Ping and the other UNIX-derived commands will joyously give up their secrets if you have been initiated into the knowledge of how to coax them along. Note all Ping switches require a dash rather than a slash. If you use the slash rather than the dash, Ping will dash your hopes for success as it slashes your chances for a predicable outcome.

```
 Command Prompt

D:\>ping -?

Usage: ping [-t] [-a] [-n count] [-l size] [-f] [-i TTL] [-v TOS]
            [-r count] [-s count] [[-j host-list] | [-k host-list]]
            [-w timeout] destination-list

Options:
    -t              Ping the specifed host until interrupted.
    -a              Resolve addresses to hostnames.
    -n count        Number of echo requests to send.
    -l size         Send buffer size.
    -f              Set Don't Fragment flag in packet.
    -i TTL          Time To Live.
    -v TOS          Type Of Service.
    -r count        Record route for count hops.
    -s count        Timestamp for count hops.
    -j host-list    Loose source route along host-list.
    -k host-list    Strict source route along host-list.
    -w timeout      Timeout in milliseconds to wait for each reply.

D:\>_

net          Exploring - A0 Images     Microsoft Word - wku15pc...              10:46 AM
```

To add to the confusion, the DOS-derived commands won't accept dashes as switches, but will, like Ping's interpretation of the slash, interpret the dash as a variable. Figure A.19 shows one example of how DIR gets fooled by a dash. There are two files starting with the letter *d* in the directory shown in Figure A.19, but none named -d.

If there's a rule about when the slash will work or crash, or when the dash will prevail or bash, nobody seems to know what it is. Or they're not telling. If you have drifted through the UNIX or TCP/IP world, you can pretty well rely on any identically worded action-type command in Windows NT Workstation to need the dash.

Online help is a real saver here because it always gives the switches correctly within the specific help for a command.

The Batch Files

A batch file is a text file containing one or more commands that are executed upon the execution of the batch file itself. For example, the batch file containing the text

```
DIR d
DIR d*
```

first executes the DIR command with the variable d, and then with the variable d*. Batch files do have rudimentary flow control using primarily the FOR and GOTO commands. Virtually any command available on the command line can be run in a batch file. The FOR and GOTO commands, however, have no existence outside of these specialized files. Batch files require either the

.bat or the .cmd extension for Windows NT Workstation to recognize them as batch files.

Although you can use batch files for any purpose you can think of, under Windows NT Workstation most people use them for backups.

For example, the file mybackup.cmd containing

```
Ntbackup d:\winnt /a /b
Ntbackup d:\my documents /a
```

will, when executed, back up first the WINNT directory along with the local Registry, appending the backup to the existing tape; it will then back up the my documents directory and append that, too, to the tape.

Many users combine the AT command with a backup command set in batch files to start unattended backups after hours.

CMD, Commands, and Environments

You can launch a CLI either by starting the CMD.EXE or the Command.com applications supplied with Windows NT Workstation. CMD.EXE is a native Windows NT application just like any other Windows NT applet. Running Command.com will launch an NTVDM.

CMD.EXE will enable you to run native DOS programs under it. When you do so, however, you "convert" it from a native Windows NT application to an NTVDM.

There are two files, AUTOEXEC.NT and CONFIG.NT, that will enable you automatically to configure the CLI or DOS programs upon their launch. These files act just like the AUTOEXEC.BAT and CONFIG.SYS files from DOS and Windows days except for the limitations and extensions of running them under Windows NT.

Optimizing DOS

The simplest way to optimize a DOS program for use in Windows NT Workstation is to use the Properties dialog box. See Chapter 5 for more information on configuring MS-DOS programs for use under Windows NT.

If you are a masochist or just hate to let go of any once-useful knowledge set, you can also create those crazy old PIF files from Windows and Windows 95 heritage. Windows NT doesn't care.

Don't overlook the wealth of options Windows NT gives you when running these older-style programs. Most problems with business-oriented DOS programs under Windows NT stem from people not configuring them right or even not knowing that they can be configured. Figure A.20 shows the tabbed (surprise!) dialog box for a DOS program.

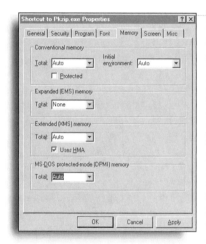

FIGURE **A.20.**

The tabbed Properties dialog box for DOS programs under Windows NT has a blizzard of useful options. Somewhere in there exists the combination to make just about anything run well.

The Properties of the program, PKZIP 2.04g, shown in Figure A.20 has had the XMS option altered from None to Auto. As you can see from the figure, the memory options for a DOS program are many and varied. They include the normally problematic DPMI type of memory.

Windows NT is pretty good about accommodating the often bizarre needs of DOS programs, but it can't do it all automatically. Properties is the place to show that you're smarter than Windows NT.

One greatly overlooked place to configure a DOS program is the Windows NT button on the Program tab. This enables you to specify two specific configuration files for this program. These files take the place of the DOS Config.sys and Autoexec.bat. By default, Windows NT will configure the

NTVDM using [%systemroot%]\system32\config.nt and [%systemroot%]\system32\Autoexec.nt. Click this button to change this default. You can specify different configuration files for every DOS program on your system. Figure A.21 shows the dialog box revealed when you click the Windows NT button on the Program tab of the Properties dialog box for an NTVDM.

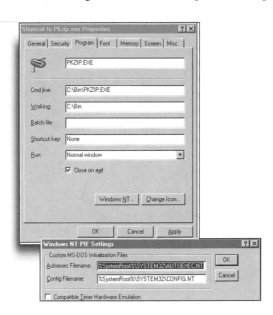

FIGURE A.21.

You can specify as many NTVDM configuration programs as you have or want to have NTVDMs. Within the world of Windows NT, you have the freedom to make your NTVDMs any way you want them. How you use that freedom depends on you.

If you experience trouble with a DOS program under Windows NT and can't get the configuration right, try these things:

- Under the Screen tab, try running in a full screen rather than a window.
- Under the Screen tab, uncheck the Fast ROM Emulation and the Dynamic Memory Allocation options.
- Check your documentation to see whether your program requires DPMI or XMS memory. If so, locate and select the appropriate settings under the Memory tab.
- Under the Memory tab, specify the amount of memory to assign to the program instead of leaving things to the Auto daemon-like routine.

- Under the Misc tab, deselect the Always Suspend and Screen Saver options one at a time.

- Under Misc, try selecting the Mouse - Exclusive mode option.

- Study the documentation for your program and configure files to replace the recommended Config.sys and Autoexec.bat files, and then use the Windows NT button on the Program tab to point at those files.

- If all fails, run the program in a DOS boot session.

Windows NT Command Reference

Starting the Command Line Interface

Getting Help on Commands

The Commands, Their Syntax, and Usage Examples

Obsolete Commands

Starting the Command Line Interface

You can start the command line interface for Windows NT Server by clicking Start | Run and then entering CMD (not case sensitive) in the Run dialog box. CMD is the Windows NT command processor similar in function to COMMAND.COM used in DOS and Windows 95/98 and still part of Windows NT Workstation. To make a shortcut for the CLI on your desktop, start the Windows Explorer, locate the file CMD.EXE in \[NT Location]\System32 and right-click it. Drag it to the desktop and release the right mouse button, choosing the Make Shortcut option when offered. Windows NT will, by default, place the MS-DOS icon for this shortcut. As with any shortcuts, you can change the icon or the title to one of your choosing.

Creating a shortcut gives you an easy way to modify the appearance of your command line interface. Figure B.1 shows the Options tab in the Properties sheet for such a shortcut. You can also reach the command line interface by clicking Start | Programs | MS-DOS Prompt.

The Buffers option button shown in Figure B.1 is where you can set how many commands the interface stores—similar to DOS's Doskey command. It has nothing to do with the Buffers statement used in CONFIG.SYS for DOS or Windows.

FIGURE B.1.

The Properties sheet for the CLI shortcut has many options, including the capability to run the interface in a window or in a full screen.

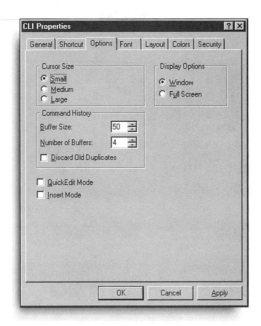

Note that this tab gives you the choice of running your CLI either in a window or in a full screen. The Colors tab is where you can set a color and font set for your interface. There is nothing stopping you from creating several shortcuts for the CLI, each with its own set of properties.

If you have used other command line interfaces, such as those in MS-DOS or UNIX, starting the CLI will put you in a comfortable place, as shown in Figure B.2.

FIGURE B.2.

MS-DOS users will be at home with the command line interface.

From here, entering commands is as simple as entering the command followed by its parameters, or switches, and pressing the Enter key.

Getting Help on Commands

Most commands respond to the *Command /?* convention used in Microsoft's other operating systems. Alternatively, you can see a list of some commands by entering Help after launching the CLI. The Help command, shown in Figure B.3, will bring up only a summary sheet for the most commonly used commands. If you want to see a complete listing of the commands along with some help text, choose Start | Help and select Windows NT Commands from the Contents tab.

The help system supplied by Microsoft is not as complete as the written documentation provided in some of the company's older operating systems. Especially missing are usage examples for some of the trickier commands that can yield unexpected results or a lot of frustration. So with that in mind, on to the commands.

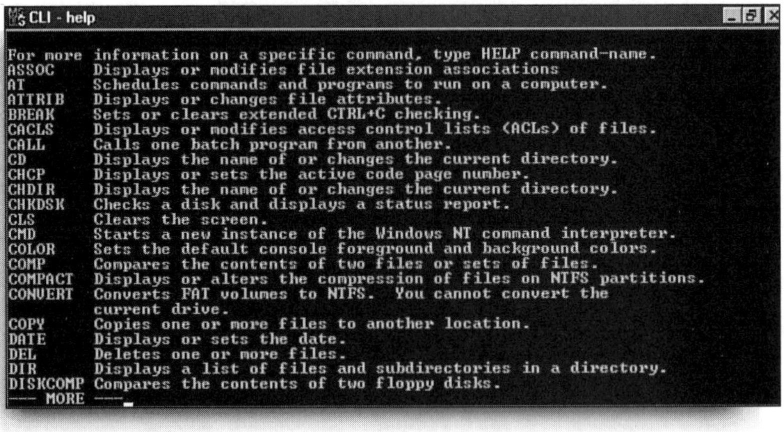

FIGURE B.3.

The Help command at the CLI will bring up a short summary of the most often-used commands.

```
CLI - help
For more information on a specific command, type HELP command-name.
ASSOC      Displays or modifies file extension associations
AT         Schedules commands and programs to run on a computer.
ATTRIB     Displays or changes file attributes.
BREAK      Sets or clears extended CTRL+C checking.
CACLS      Displays or modifies access control lists (ACLs) of files.
CALL       Calls one batch program from another.
CD         Displays the name of or changes the current directory.
CHCP       Displays or sets the active code page number.
CHDIR      Displays the name of or changes the current directory.
CHKDSK     Checks a disk and displays a status report.
CLS        Clears the screen.
CMD        Starts a new instance of the Windows NT command interpreter.
COLOR      Sets the default console foreground and background colors.
COMP       Compares the contents of two files or sets of files.
COMPACT    Displays or alters the compression of files on NTFS partitions.
CONVERT    Converts FAT volumes to NTFS.  You cannot convert the
           current drive.
COPY       Copies one or more files to another location.
DATE       Displays or sets the date.
DEL        Deletes one or more files.
DIR        Displays a list of files and subdirectories in a directory.
DISKCOMP   Compares the contents of two floppy disks.
--- MORE ---
```

The Commands, Their Syntax, and Usage Examples

The following section lists the most often-used commands exclusive to the CLI. They are classified by use. Some of these commands can and should be used within the file CONFIG.NT or AUTOEXEC.NT—both located in \[Windows NT] \System32. These files, similar to the DOS and Windows CONFIG.SYS and AUTOEXEC.BAT, respectively, control some environmental variables for command sessions within Windows NT Server. You can alter the contents of these files using any text editor such as EDIT or Notepad.

Many of the following commands will be familiar to those who have used DOS or Windows in the past. The reason for their inclusion is their unfamiliarity to those coming to Windows NT Workstation from other operating systems such as MacOS, UNIX, VMS, or MVS. The TCP/IP commands will be familiar to most UNIX users.

Unless noted, all commands and parameters are not case sensitive.

File and Disk Commands

Append: Allows programs to open data files in remote directories as if they were in the current directory. Syntax:

```
append [;] [[drive:]path[;...]] [/x:{on ¦ off}][/path:{
on ¦ off}] [/e]
```

/x tells the operating system to first search the current directory and then to extend its search to other specified directories; /e stores the append path in the environment.

Usage examples:

```
Append /x /e
Append c:\newpath
```

These two commands will instruct the application to first search the current directory for data and then c:\newpath. The /e switch tells the operating system to store the newpath information in the environment.

Assoc: Associates a file extension with an application. This command will also display and delete associations. Syntax:

```
Assoc [.ext[=[application]]]
```

Usage examples:

To show file extensions and their associations, enter

```
Assoc
```

To delete an association, enter

```
Assoc .ext =
```

where .ext is the three-letter extension.

To add an association, enter

```
Assoc .ext =application
```

where .ext is the three-letter extension and application is the name of the application.

Attrib: Sets certain attribute bits for a file. Syntax:

```
Attrib [+r¦-r] [+a¦-a] [+s¦-s] [+h¦-h] [path\file] /s
```

The parameters r, a, s, and h represent the bits for read-only, archive, system, and hidden, respectively. The /s switch tells the operating system to process similarly all files in downstream sub-directories.

Fast Associations

Using the **Assoc** command from the CLI is a much faster way to create file extension associations than going through the Windows Explorer. After you get the hang of using this command, you will never wish to go back to using Explorer.

Usage example:

```
Attrib -r -h \mypath\myfile
```

Will remove the read-only and hidden attributes from myfile located in mypath.

CD and Chdir: Change the working directory. These commands are interchangeable in all ways. Syntax:

```
CD or Chdir [\] path
```

Usage examples:

```
CD \
```

Changes to the root directory.

```
CD..
```

Moves up one entry in the tree.

```
CD \mypath
```

Changes the working directory to mypath.

Chkdsk: Checks a disk and a file for errors. Similar to Chkdsk in DOS or Windows. Note: Later versions of DOS and Windows have a similar utility, ScanDisk. This utility is not part of Windows NT Server. Syntax:

```
Chkdsk [path] [/f] [/v] [/r]
```

where

> /f tries to fix the problem(s) found.
>
> /v Verbose mode. Echoes filenames to the screen.
>
> /r tries to recover lost information from bad sectors. Chkdsk must have exclusive access to the volume for this switch.

Usage example:

```
Chkdsk c:\ /v /f
```

Checks the volume c: in Verbose mode and tries to fix problems encountered.

Comp: Compares the contents of two files or two sets of files. Syntax:

```
Comp [files1] [files2] [/d] [/a] [/l] [/n=number] [/c]
```

where

Back to UNIX

The directory commands **CD, MD,** and **RD** are very similar in UNIX and Windows NT.

NT's Chkdsk

The **CHKDSK** that ships with Windows NT works on both FAT and NTFS volumes.

files1 and files2 are the file sets for comparison.

/d yields a decimal display.

/a yields an alpha display.

/l shows the line numbers for differences rather than offset.

/n forces the line-by-line comparison for n lines even in different length files.

/c removes case sensitivity.

Usage example:

```
Comp \path1\myfiles \path2\myfiles /l
```

Will compare the files in \path1\myfiles with those in \path2\myfiles and show the line numbers of any discrepancies.

Compact: Applies, removes, or displays file compaction for NTFS systems. Compact can use standard wildcards. Syntax:

```
Compact [/c] [/u] [/s] [/i] [/f] [/a] [/q] filename(s)
```

where

/c compacts the file(s).

/u removes compaction from file(s).

/s processes subdirectories.

/i ignores errors.

/f forces compaction on files, even those already compressed.

/a forces compaction of system and hidden files. These are usually omitted from compaction.

/q Quiet mode (little echoed to screen).

Usage examples:

```
Compact
```

Shows the compaction state of the current directory. Figure B.4 shows this command run without parameters.

```
Compact g:\bitmaps /s
```

Will compact the bitmaps directory and all its subdirectories on the g: drive.

```
 Windows NT Server book                                              _ | 8 | X
C:\Program Files\Windows NT>compact

 Listing C:\Program Files\Windows NT\
 New files added to this directory will be compressed.

        0 :           0 = 1.0 to 1 C Accessories
    42256 :       26112 = 1.6 to 1 C dialer.exe
        0 :           0 = 1.0 to 1 C Windows Messaging

Of 3 files within 1 directories
3 are compressed and 0 are not compressed.
42,256 total bytes of data are stored in 26,112 bytes.
The compression ratio is 1.6 to 1.


C:\Program Files\Windows NT>
```

GUI Compacts

You can also compact a file, a folder, or a set of folders and files by highlighting them and then right-clicking and choosing Properties from the context menu. Selecting the Compress check box will, when you click OK in the dialog box, compress the selected items.

Convert: Alters FAT volumes to NTFS ones. When run, Convert will need to absolutely control (lock) the disk volume slated for conversion. If it cannot, it will offer to do the conversion on next bootup. Syntax:

```
Convert [volume:] /fs:ntfs [/v] [/nametable:myfile]
```

where

volume is the volume (drive) to be converted.

/fs:ntfs means to convert to the file system NTFS. This is an obvious switch now. Microsoft might have some future plans for more types of switches.

/v signifies Verbose mode.

/nametable:myfile creates a name table using the filename you specify. Use this if you encounter conversion problems due to having bizarre FAT filenames.

Usage example:

```
Convert d: /fs:ntfs /v
```

Will convert drive d: from FAT to NTFS, echoing messages to the console.

Copy: Copies files from one addressable device to another. Copy can use standard wildcards. Short syntax:

```
Copy [source][destination] /a /b /v /z /n
```

where

[source] is the location of the files to be copied.

[destination] is the target location of the files.

/a copies ASCII files that have a ^z character as their end of file marker.

/b copies binary files that can include the ^z character as part of their data.

/v attempts to verify the copy operation.

/z copies across networks.

/n forces the 8.3 DOS file-naming convention.

Usage example:

```
Copy c:\myfile a:\yourfile /v
```

Copies myfile in the root of c: to the root of a:, giving it the name yourfile, and then attempts to verify the write.

Del and Erase: Two commands doing exactly the same thing. These commands delete the directory entries for a file or files. They can accept the usual wildcards. Syntax:

```
Del (or erase) myfile
```

Usage example:

```
Del myfile
```

Deletes the file myfile from the current directory.

Dir: Gives a directory listing for the current or specified directory. Syntax:

```
Dir [path][filename] [/p] [/w] [/d] [/a: (attributes) /o:
(sortorder)" [/t: (time) [/s] [/b] [/l  [/x] [/n]
```

where

/p pauses the display.

/w shows a wide display without details.

/d shows a sorted wide display (in columns).

/a: shows files having attributes hidden, system, directory, archive, or read-only by using the first letter of the attribute with the switch. Also accepts the - for the inverse of the attribute.

Too Busy to Convert

Windows NT needs exclusive access to a volume about to be converted. If it doesn't have it, it will offer to convert on next bootup where the Convert utility will grab exclusive use and do the conversion.

/o: sort order, name, extension, date, size, grouped by directory by using the first letter of the order with the switch.

/t: time field using the following first letters of the field, creation, access (last), written to (last).

/s shows or searches subdirectories also.

/b bare display without headers or footers.

/l lowercase unsorted.

/x shows 8.3 filenames also.

/n long listing with filenames on right.

Usage examples:

```
Dir
```

A listing of the current directory.

```
Dir /s /x
```

A listing of the current directory, its subdirectories, and the 8.3 filenames for the files shown.

```
Dir /a:h
```

A listing of the hidden files.

Diskcomp: compares the contents of two disks. Syntax:

```
Diskcomp [driveA] [driveB]
```

where driveA and driveB are two disk drives. You can use one floppy disk drive with Diskcomp by specifying the same drive on both parameters.

Usage example:

```
Diskcomp a: a:
```

Will compare a disk in drive a: and then prompt you for the next disk to insert.

Diskcopy: Duplicates disks. Syntax:

```
Diskcopy [driveA] [driveB] /v
```

where

/v tries to verify writes.

Usage example:

```
Diskcopy a: a:
```

Will copy the disk in drive a: and then prompt you for a target disk to use for a duplicate.

Expand: Expands cabinet (.cab) files or compressed files (.ex) by nondestructive extraction. Cabinet files are files Microsoft uses to distribute many of its programs and operating systems. Compressed files with the .ex_ suffix are also widely used. Common expanders, such as those that work for .zip or .arc files, won't work with .cab files or .ex_ files. Syntax:

```
Expand [-r] cabfile [target]
```

where

-r renames the file.

Usage example:

```
Expand cab1.cab
```

Will expand the contents of the cab1.cab file to the current directory.

or if you have an .ex_ file,

```
Expand f:\user32.ex_ c:\winnt\system32\user32.exe
```

Will expand the contents of the user32.ex_ file to the user32.exe file located in the c:\winnt\system32\ directory.

FC: Compares two individual files for discrepancies. Syntax:

```
Fc[/a][/b][/c][/l][/lbx][/n][/t][/u][/w][file1][file2]
```

where

/a abbreviated display of discrepancies.

/b binary compare (ASCII is the default for files not having a binary extension).

/c not case sensitive.

/l ASCII compare for files having a binary extension (such as .exe).

/lbx buffer size (the x part) for how many discrepancies FC should tolerate before exiting.

> **Note**
>
> You will need to use a disk that is formatted the same as the one to be copied. Diskcopy requires identically formatted disks, otherwise it aborts the copy process.

/n shows line numbers during ASCII compare.

/t skips expanding tabs to spaces.

/u Unicode compare.

/w skips consecutive whitespace.

Usage example:

```
Fc myfile1 myfile2 /b
```

Compares and reports differences in the files myfile1 and myfile2 using a binary compare.

Files: Used like DOS and Windows to tell how many files a session can have open at the same time. Use in CONFIG.NT.

Usage example:

```
Files = 99
```

Findstr: This is a superior version of the older Find command, also included in Windows NT Server. Syntax of the most often used switches:

```
Findstr [/b] [/e] [/l] [/c:mystring] [/r] [/s] [/i] [/x] [/v]
[/n] [/m]
```

where

/b finds pattern at start of line.

/e finds pattern at end of line.

/l uses literal find pattern.

/c:mystring is the string to search for.

/r (default) searches for non-literal strings.

/s also searches subdirectories.

/i is not sensitive for case.

/x exact matching lines only.

/v opposite of /x—shows non-matching lines only.

/n prints line numbers.

/m shows matching files only.

Usage examples:

```
Findstr "A string"myfile.txt
```

Finds the string "A" and string "string" in the file myfile.txt.

```
Findstr /c:"A String"myfile.txt /i
```

Finds the string "A String" (not case sensitive) in the file myfile.txt.

Format: Formats disks. Usage is the same as DOS or Windows with the following extensions noted. Syntax for extensions:

```
Format drive1: [/fs:file system choice] [/a:unitsize]
```

where

/fs is FAT or NTFS.

/a is unit size for NTFS volumes.

Usage example:

```
Format e:/fs:ntfs /a:1024
```

Format drive e: as NTFS with a unit (similar to old cluster size in practice) size of 1024 bytes.

MD and Mkdir: Usage is the same as in DOS or Windows.

Move: Usage is the same as Copy in Default mode, but deletes source file.

Print: The print spooler from DOS and Windows. Usage is the same.

Usage example:

```
Print myfile
```

Prints a file to the default printer.

RD and Remdir: Identical expressions of the same command. Usage is the same as in DOS or Windows. This removes or deletes empty directories. Syntax:

```
RD (or Remdir) [/s]
```

where

/s means delete subdirectories also.

Usage example:

```
RD mydirectory
```

Removes the directory from the directory listing.

Ren and Rename: Rename files and directories. Usage is the same as later DOS and Windows.

Usage example:

Ren mine yours

Renames the directory (or file) mine as yours.

Xcopy: This is similar to the DOS or Windows XCOPY utility. It is an extended version of the internal COPY command. The chief differences are its intelligence and its capability to copy directory structures intact. Syntax of the basic command along with its more commonly used switches:

Xcopy source [target] [/c] [/v] [/q] [/f] [/l] [/d:] [/u]
[/s] [/e] [/t] [/r]" [/h] [/n] [/exclude:myfile.txt]

where

/c copies despite apparent errors.

/v attempts verification of copy.

/q Quiet mode (suppresses messages).

/f displays full source and destination filenames while copying.

/l lists filenames during copying process.

/d: with date after colon, copies only files with dates on or after specified date.

/u copies only files from source that already exist on target (update).

/s copies subdirectories. If used with the /e, copies empty directories.

/t copies the directory structure (tree), not the files. It will include empty directories if used with the /e switch.

/r copies over read-only files.

/h copies files with the system or hidden attribute bits set.

/n copies using the 8.3 naming convention.

/exclude:myfile.txt excludes files listed in the text file myfile from being copied.

Usage examples:

```
Xcopy c:\mypath d: /s
```

Copies the files in c:\mypath and its subdirectories to an identical directory structure on d:.

```
Xcopy r:\mypath\my long file a: /n
```

Copies a file with a long filename to the a: drive and excludes the long filename, instead using the 8.3 naming convention.

The Net Commands

Many of the Windows NT Workstation's CLI network commands start with the word Net followed by the command itself. These commands, where practicable, can be run from batch files. When run from either batch files or interactively, these commands will accept the /y and /n switches for a Yes or No response to the command's query without user intervention. The /y and /n switches are especially useful for batch file operations.

Many of these commands pertain to networking and were created for use by a network administrator. Most of them have some use for a workstation on a network, and because Windows NT can be used as a peer networking system, they can come in handy if it is your job to oversee such a system.

Keep in mind that Net commands have their analogs in the graphical user interface (GUI). Many administrators prefer to use the CLI version of a command because they are usually faster than navigating through the Start menu system or even locating the shortcut icon located in a handy program group on the desktop. What you choose is up to you. In some cases, the CLI method for running a command is superior to the GUI because you can call it from batch files, optionally running them using the AT command.

Following are the most commonly used Net commands, along with the most often-used switches, their syntax, and usage examples.

NBTStat: Displays the status of a network running NetBIOS over TCP/IP. Note that following UNIX standards (the origin of TCP/IP), the switches below are case sensitive and use a dash (-) not a slash (/). Syntax:

NBTStat [-a namedcomputer] [-A IP] [-R] [-r] [-S] [-s]

where

-a is the computer's name, such as tirilee (see Figure B.5).

-A is the IP, such as 100.101.100.100 (see Figure B.6).

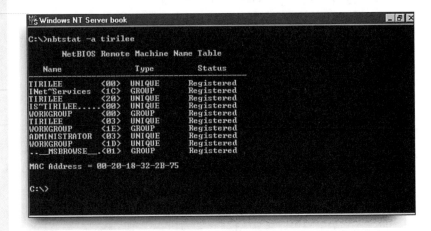

FIGURE B.5.

The -a switch for NBTStat uses the computer's name for parameter input.

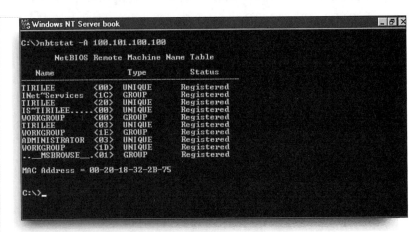

FIGURE B.6.

The -A switch for NBTStat gives the same information as the -a switch, but takes the IP address as an input parameter.

-R reloads the LMHOSTS file.

-r lists WINS name resolution. Requires WINS configuration to use.

-S attempts to list all clients and servers by IP.

-s same as -S, but attempts to list all by computer name using the LMHOSTS file.

Usage example:

```
NBTStat -A 100.101.100.100
```

Shows status for a computer with the IP address
`100.101.100.100`.

`Net Accounts`: A CLI version of the utility available in the GUI
User Manager. Most administrators prefer the GUI version for
administering accounts, but use the CLI version for a quick look
at account status because it's faster when lending interactive support over, say, the telephone. This command is also useful for
forcing user logoff. Syntax for the most often-used parameters:

```
Net Accounts [/forcelogoff:{timetologoff}]
```

where

> `/forcelogoff` takes the `timetologoff` and forces the user(s) off
> at that time.

When run without parameters, `Net Accounts` shows the current
settings for user profiles. Note: You must start this service before
the command will work. You can start this service either through
the Services GUI in Control Panel or the CLI Net Start.

Usage example:

```
Net Accounts
```

Shows the status of the user profile in effect.

`Net Config`: Shows a list of devices that you can configure and
allows modification of these devices. This command controls
either the Server or Workstation side of Windows NT. Syntax of
the most commonly used parameters:

```
Net Config server [/autodisconnect:time] [/hidden:]
```

or

```
Net Config workstation [/charcount:] [/chartime:]
[/charwait:]
```

where

> `/autodisconnect:time` is the time in minutes to automatically
> disconnect from an inactive client.

/hidden: is used with yes or no to hide the server from the list of servers. Does not affect permissions of the server.

/charcount: in bytes, the buffer Windows NT has for a communications device or port.

/chartime: in milliseconds. Same as /charcount, but in milliseconds.

/charwait: time in seconds Windows NT will wait on a communications device.

Usage example:

```
Net Config Server /hidden:yes
```

Run from the console, this hides the server from the list of available servers without affecting the permissions of the server.

`Net Continue, Pause, Start, Stop`: Continues, pauses, starts, and stops services, respectively. This is the CLI version of the Services applet available in Control Panel. Syntax:

```
Net [continue] [pause] [start] [stop] service
```

where

service is the service you want to continue, pause, start, or stop.

Usage examples:

```
Net stop alerter
```

Stops the alerter service.

```
Net start alerter
```

Starts the alerter service.

`Net File`: Displays a list of shared files and any file locks. Syntax:

```
Net File [/close]
```

where

/close will close a file, releasing any file locks.

Run without parameters, `Net File` will list open shared files.

Usage example:

```
Net File
```

Displays a list of open files.

`Net Helpmsg`: Displays help on an error message number. Syntax:

`Net Helpmsg messagenumber`

Usage example:

`Net Helpmsg 2000`

Tells you that error number 2000 means you have an invalid pixel format.

`Net Print`: Displays or manipulates a list of pending print jobs in queue. Similar to the Printers GUI applet in Control Panel; however, much faster if you have a CLI window open. Syntax most commonly used:

`Net Print \\computername\printername [/delete] [/hold]`
`[/release][/pause]`

where

　\\computername is the name of the computer hosting the shared printer.

　\printername is the name the printer is shared under.

　/delete purges print jobs.

　/hold pauses print jobs.

　/release restarts paused print jobs.

Usage example:

`Net Print \\tirilee\rainbow`

Shows a list of pending print jobs for the printer rainbow hosted on the server tirilee.

`Net Session`: When entered from the local console, gives information about computers located on the server. Syntax:

`Net Session \\anycomputername /delete`

where

　/delete ends the session with \\anycomputername.

Usage example:

`Net Session \\barbara /delete`

No Parameters

`Net Session` given without parameters gives information about the local computer.

Ends the session connection with the computer named barbara.

NetStat: Shows statistics for connections on a TCP/IP network only. This command requires the TCP/IP protocol to be installed and running. Note that like NBTStat, this command uses the UNIX-like dash (-) rather than the more common slash (/), and the parameters are not case sensitive. Syntax:

```
NetStat [-a] [-e] [-n] [-s] [-p] [-r] [time]
```

where

-a displays listening ports.

-e displays Ethernet statistics.

-n provides a numeric display of ports rather than the default names.

-s displays protocol. Can be combined with -e for comprehensive information.

-p is used with a protocol (such as TCP) to display only that protocol.

-r displays routing information.

[time] is the time in seconds to update the display. If omitted, it displays the instantaneous information.

Net Statistics: Displays statistics for the local computer. Syntax:

```
Net Statistics [server] [workstation]
```

Usage example:

```
Net Statistics server
```

Displays relevant statistics.

Net Time: Determines and can synchronize computer clocks. Syntax:

```
Net Time \\anycomputername /set /domain
```

where

/set sets the time on the local computer to that of the queried one.

/domain sets the time to a domain.

Usage examples:

```
Net Time \\tirilee
```

Displays the time on the computer named tirilee.

```
Net Time \\tirilee /set
```

Sets the time on the local machine to the same time as tirilee.

Net Use: Allows or disallows the use of a shared resource. This command also displays status information for shared resources. Syntax of the more often-used parameters:

```
Net Use  [\\computername\sharename] [password or *]
[/persistent:]
```

where

> \\computername\sharename is the computer and the share name of the device to use.
>
> password or *, where password is the actual password for the shared device. If you use the * (asterisk) in the place of the password, Windows NT will prompt the user for the password.
>
> /persistent:, when used with yes or no, will control whether the use persists from session to session.

Usage example:

```
Net Use \\tirilee\lily
```

Uses the shared resource lily on the computer tirilee.

Triggering the AT Command

Administrators often use this command within batch files triggered by the AT command to synchronize the clocks of all computers on a network or domain.

The TCP/IP Commands

Windows NT Workstation comes with several utilities commonly used in TCP/IP networks. Given the new visual tools for internetworking, few people use these CLI commands anymore, but in some cases they work well enough that they will be worthwhile tools for inclusion in your toolbox. The following are three of the most commonly used TCP/IP commands. You must have TCP/IP installed to have these commands, and the protocol must be functioning for them to work.

Ftp: A utility to transfer files (usually a binary file), using the File Transfer Protocol, to or from a computer running the Ftp daemon. As is common with the TCP/IP origin utility, Ftp uses the dash (-) rather than the slash (/) for switches. Note that the usual

```
ftp /?
```

for help will not work with Ftp because the Ftp utility will interpret the /? as a computer name and deliver an error message. Syntax for the most often used switches:

```
ftp [-i] [-d] [-g] [-s:myfile.txt] [daemoncomputer]
```

where

-i stops Interactive mode, which prompts you in cases of multiple file transfers.

-d enables Debug mode (echoing all messages).

-g disables wildcard use on local files (globbing in Ftp talk).

-s: used with a text file to script a series of Ftp commands. A batch file substitute.

Usage example:

```
ftp -d mack.rt66.com
```

Connects to a remote host running the daemon. When running the Ftp utility, your prompt will indicate this to avoid the problem of trying to execute commands remotely when you think you're local only. After you connect to the site, you navigate similarly to when you're on a local computer using the commands command, Dir, CD, and even MD or RD if you have permissions. When you find the file you want to transfer, use the Get command to transfer the file from the host to you or use Put to transfer the file from you to the host. Windows NT Help system has a complete listing of the 14 online Ftp commands.

When you install the TCP/IP protocol on Windows NT Server, you also get a shorthand version of Ftp called Tftp. This is less flexible, but also easier to use.

Ipconfig: Displays information about IPs, adapters, and Dynamic Host Configuration Protocol (DHCP). It's especially useful for the latter purposes. Syntax:

```
Ipconfig [/all OR /renew [adapter] OR /release [adapter]]
```

where

/all shows a complete listing.

The Joy of Ftp

Ftp (even Tftp) isn't one of those utilities that most people enjoy using interactively. Several visual utilities—at least one of which is freeware, FTP-32 Client For Windows, copyright John A. Junod—make Ftp a joy. You can find these utilities at all the usual online sources.

/renew renews DHCP information for a specified adapter.

/release releases or disables DHCP for a local computer.

Usage example:

```
Ipconfig /all
```

Displays complete information about a local computer.

Ping: A very useful command that's unfamiliar to those new to TCP/IP. Ping tries to echo a signal from a remote computer. This tests whether the remote computer (Internet or intranet) is responding. As with other utilities stemming from TCP/IP, Ping takes the dash (-) switch rather than the slash (/). Like Ftp and Telnet, Ping /? won't work because Ping will interpret the /? as a computer name. Syntax for the most commonly used switches:

```
ping [-t] [-n #] [-r #] [-w time] computers to ping
```

-t pings until told to stop with a ^c.

-n # pings # times.

-r # echoes the route up to # times. # can be from 1 to 9.

-w time milliseconds to time out.

computers to ping are the IPs or the names of the computers to ping.

Usage examples:

```
Ping -n 2 192.100.221.000
```

Pings the computer with an IP of 192.100.221.000 twice.

```
Ping tirilee.techtryx.com
```

Pings the computer named tirilee.techtryx.com once.

Telnet: This utility isn't included in the online help system. Instead, Windows NT Server treats it like its own program, complete with an included help system. It enables you to become a remote console on a host computer. What you can do with such a remote console depends on your permissions. As with Ftp and Ping, Telnet /? won't work. Syntax:

```
Telnet computer or IP
```

where

Sources of Ftp Utilities

Some of the more predominant sources of freeware and shareware on the Internet are as follows:

http://www.windows95.com

http://www.stroud.com

http://www.winntmag.com

http://www.shareware.com

Displaying Ipconfig

When run without parameters, Ipconfig displays a short information screen.

computer or IP is the computer name or the IP for the computer you want to be connected to. Figure B.7 shows the start of a Telnet session.

FIGURE B.7.

Starting a Telnet session requires logon just as if you were operating from the local console.

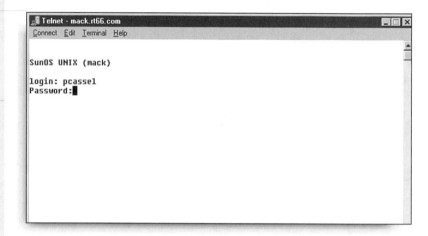

Commands to Control the CLI

The following are the most often-used commands to control the CLI environment.

Exit: Exits or quits a CMD or COMMAND instance. This command takes no parameters. It works identically to the Exit command from DOS or Windows.

Path: Same usage as in DOS or Windows. Can be used in AUTOEXEC.NT.

Usage example:

```
Path = newpath;%path%
```

Appends the path, newpath, to the existing path.

Popd and Pushd: Similar in usage to identically named utilities in DOS and Windows. The names come from programmers' use of the LIFO stack where program items are pushed (stored) then popped (returned). The concept comes from a stack of spring-loaded dishes in a cafeteria. Pushd stores a path; Popd restores the path.

Usage example:

`Pushd mypath`

Stores the path mypath. Now change directories and do some action.

`Popd`

Restores you to your former mypath.

`Prompt`: Alters the CLI prompt. Syntax of some of the more often-used switches (of many):

`Prompt [$t] [$d] [$g] [$p] [text]`

where

`$t` is the time.

`$d` is the date.

`$g` is the greater-than sign (>).

`$p` is the path (default).

`text` is the text you want to display.

Usage examples:

`Prompt $t $p`

Shows the system time and then the path as a command-line prompt.

`Prompt`

Returns to the default prompt.

`Subst`: Substitutes an addressable device letter for a path. Similar to the `Subst` in later DOS or Windows. Syntax:

`Subst [Drive1] [path] /d`

where

`/d` deletes the substituted drive.

Usage examples:

`Subst g: c:\mypath\mypath1`

Substitutes a "false" drive g: for the path c:\mypath\mypath1. When you enter `g:` on the command line or look for it in Explorer, the files contained will be those in c:\mypath\mypath1.

Subst g: /d

Eliminates the substitution.

Title: Changes the title of the CLI window. Syntax:

Title text

where

   text is the text you want to show in the CLI window.

Usage example:

Title Windows NT Rules

Displays the text Windows NT Rules as a title for the CLI window. Figure B.8 shows the results of entering this command.

FIGURE B.8.

The Title command alters the title of the CLI window.

Batch Files

Windows NT Server can use batch files just like DOS or Windows. A batch file is a text file containing a series of commands that execute in order unless the program control is altered by a GOTO command. Batch files under Windows NT Server can take the command line replaceable parameters %1 through %9. The following are the most often-used commands used in batch files, along with a concise usage example.

Call: Calls another batch file. Then after execution, returns control to the calling batch file.

```
Call mynew.cmd
```

Calls the batch file mynew.cmd from within another batch file, and then returns control to the calling file.

Echo: Echoes a line to the screen. By default, all batch file commands are echoed to the screen.

```
Echo off
```

Ends echoing of batch file commands to the screen.

```
Echo my line
```

Echoes my line to the screen after the Echo off command.

For: Applies a command to a set of files in a list. Uses the replaceable parameter %f to avoid confusion with the %1 through %9 used as replaceable parameters in batch file command lines.

```
For %f in (*.~mp) do del %f
```

Deletes files having the .~mp extension.

Goto: Branches to a label in a batch file. A label in a batch file is a line ending in a colon (:).

```
If exist r:\myfile goto quit
...
...
quit:
```

Will jump to the line below the last line shown if the file, myfile, at the root of drive r: exists.

If: Tests a condition. If used with the Not switch, tests for the inverse of a condition. Often used with the Goto command to change program flow within the batch file.

```
If not exist myfile Goto quit
```

Tests for the existence of the file, myfile, and if it doesn't exist, branches to the batch file label quit.

Rem: Remark. Tells the batch file not to process this line.

```
Rem Now test for existence of file and branch if it doesn't
exist
```

This line isn't evaluated, displayed, or executed by the batch file. Its only use is to inform. Note: If you want to display a line or lines, use the Echo command.

Batch File Extensions

Windows NT batch files can sport the extension .cmd or .bat.

Setlocal and Endlocal: Must be used in combination with each Setlocal having an Endlocal. Environmental settings run after Setlocal will expire on the Endlocal statement.

```
...
Setlocal
(set some environment variable here)
Endlocal
(environmental variable set above expires)
```

Shift: Rotates the replaceable parameters in a batch file. Given the following command line:

```
Mybatch file1 file2
```

The Shift command will replace the variable file1 with the variable file2 when encountered by the batch file processor. So with that command line in mind, the batch file

```
...
Goto FirstRun
Shift:
Shift
FirstRun:
Copy %1 a: goto shift
...
```

will jump to the label FirstRun:, copy file1, jump to the label Shift:, and copy file2.

Symbols Used in the CLI

Following are some symbols used to control the CLI. Some of these symbols will be familiar to DOS, Windows, or UNIX users. Window NT Workstation expands on the older DOS and Windows symbol set. Symbols don't have parameters. Each is shown with a short explanation and a usage example.

<: Redirects input to a program or utility.

```
Sort < myoutput.out
```

Sorts the file myoutput.out using the Sort utility.

>>: Appends output. Also 1>>.

```
Dir c:\*.* >> mylist.txt
```

Adds the output of Dir c:*.* to the end of the file mylist.txt.

>: Redirects output. Also 1>.

```
Dir c:\*.* > prn
```

Directs the output of Dir c:*.* to the default printer.

¦: Piping. Pipes the output of a command to another program, often the More utility.

```
Type myfile.txt ¦ More
```

Pipes the output of Type myfile.txt More, which will pause the display at each screen.

¦¦: A non-strict Or symbol. Used in batch files. Will execute the command to the left of the ¦¦ only, unless there is an error executing it. In that case, it will also execute the command to the right of ¦¦.

```
Error.exe ¦¦ Good.exe
```

Will try to execute Error.exe. Upon finding an error, it will execute Good.exe. If Error.exe doesn't error, Good.exe will be ignored.

2>>: Redirection of error display. Useful for making log files.

```
Mycommand 2>> error.log
```

Will redirect the error output of Mycommand to the file error.log.

, (comma): Separates command-line parameters. Also use ; (semicolon) for the same purposes.

```
Mycommand 1,2
```

Will feed the parameters 1 and 2 sequentially to Mycommand.

^: literal. Accepts the next symbol as a literal.

```
Mycommand ^>
```

Passes the > character as a literal parameter rather than a command-line symbol to Mycommand.

&: Used to separate commands on a command line.

```
Dir c: & Dir d:
```

Will execute first Dir c: and then Dir d:.

&&: The And symbol twice. Will execute the command to the left only if the command to the right succeeds.

```
Dir c: && Dir d:
```

Will execute `Dir c:` only if `Dir d:` completes successfully.

(): Groups commands together.

```
Command1 (Command2 && Command3)
```

Will execute `Command1` first, then `Command2`, and `Command3` only if `Command2` succeeds.

The *AT* Command

The AT command is so useful and so frequently used that it deserves its own section. In a nutshell, the AT command will execute a command or run a batch file at a given time of day. You need to have administrator rights to run AT. Also, Windows NT Workstation will not start the AT service by default. You must start it using the Net Start command or by using the Service applet in Control Panel. Because AT can start batch files, its use is only limited by imagination. The syntax for AT is

```
AT [\\anyconnectedcomputer] time [/interactive] [/every:]
[/next:]¨ command [[id] [/delete [/yes]]
```

where

\\anyconnectedcomputer is a computer where the command is to run.

time is the time to run the command or batch file.

/interactive means to run the called command or batch file interactively (involving human responses).

/every: runs on specified days of the week (M,T,W,Th,F,S,Su) or days of the month (1-31). If the parameter after /every: is omitted, AT will assume the current day.

/next: runs on the next day or date. If the parameter after /next: is omitted, AT will assume you mean the next occurrence of the current day of the week.

command is the command or batch file you want AT to run.

id is a job ID assigned sequentially by AT.

/delete removes the specified job ID from the queue. If no ID is specified, AT will remove all pending jobs from the local computer.

/yes runs the command or batch file, supplying a yes to all system queries rather than allowing the system to prompt for a yes or no.

Usage examples:

```
AT \\tirilee 18:00 /every:Th,S archive.exe
```

Runs the command archive.exe every Thursday and Saturday at 6:00 p.m. on the computer named tirilee. As with all Windows NT commands, you don't need the extension .exe as part of the command-line argument.

```
AT
```

Displays pending job information and job IDs.

```
AT 23:59 Net Time \\tirilee /set
```

Synchronizes the local system time with the computer tirilee at 11:59 p.m. today.

```
AT \\tirilee
```

Displays a list of jobs slated to run on the computer named tirilee.

```
AT 18:00 /every:1,10,20,30 back.cmd
```

Runs the batch file back.cmd every 1st, 10th, 20th, and 30th day of the month at 6:00 p.m. As with all Windows NT commands, you don't need the extension .cmd as part of the command-line argument.

```
AT 18:00 /next: back.cmd
```

Runs back.cmd at 6:00 p.m. on the next occurrence of the day of the week in which the command was entered.

Obsolete Commands

The following is a list of commands and utilities that have been part of DOS or Windows, but aren't included in Windows NT Workstation.

AT in Action

Most people use the AT command for unattended backups.

Storing AT Sequences

Windows NT Server stores all **AT** sequences in the Registry. To preserve your **AT** settings, create a Registry backup or a new emergency rescue disk (ERD) or both after setting up a series of **AT** commands.

Deleted Commands

These commands aren't part of Windows NT Workstation. There are some alternatives to these commands shown when applicable:

Assign, Choice, CTTY, Defrag (use third-party utilities), Deltree (use RD /s), Dosshell, Drvspace (replaced by Compact), Fasthelp (use Help), Fdisk (use the Disk Administrator), Join (NTFS makes this pointless), Interlnk, Intersrv, Keyb (Keyboard.sys is no more), Mirror (use NTBackup and an ERD), MSAV (use third-party anti-virus programs), MSBackup (use NTBackup), MSD (use Windows NT Diagnostics), Nlsfunc, Numlock, Power (Windows NT Server 4 doesn't support APM), Ramdisk (and the earlier Vdisk), ScanDisk, Smartdrv (NT Server does its own caching), Sys (NT system will not fit on a floppy), Undelete (use third-party utilities or the Recycle Bin), Unformat.

The following utilities and routines aren't in Windows NT Server because of its inability to support multiple DOS configurations: Include, Menucolor, Menudefault, Menuitem, Submenu.

The following commands aren't applicable to Windows NT Server because of its memory management, as opposed to DOS or Windows: Memmaker, EMM386, MSCDEX. (Real-mode drivers don't work under any Windows NT.)

Rump Commands

The following commands will not generate an error in Windows NT Workstation, but aren't a part of it either. Their inclusion is apparently to provide backward compatibility with old batch files: Break, Buffers, Driveparm, Lastdrive, Share, Verify.

Strange Stuff Still in Windows NT Workstation

The following commands and utilities are holdovers from DOS or Windows, but still function under Windows NT Workstation. Their actual value is questionable, however. Country, Command (use CMD), Debug (watch out), Edlin (old soldiers never die in Windowsland), Exe2bin, FCBS, Graphics, Mem (can be useful in rare instances), Setver.

Overview

The foregoing are the most commonly used commands for the command line interface (CLI) of Windows NT Workstation. The rare commands, including those used in command line OS/2 and retained in Windows NT Workstation for compatibility, have been passed over to allow for sufficient room for the ones used more often.

This is a case of one size not fitting all, however. If your situation uses OS/2 character-based applications or the old IPX protocol still found in NetWare, there are commands included in Windows NT Workstation that haven't been mentioned here. Instead, this appendix concentrates on commands a Windows NT Server administrator will use most often with or without the TCP/IP layer.

The final part of the appendix discusses commands either deleted or made obsolete in the migration from DOS or Windows to Windows NT. Some of these commands remain unchanged in function, but have lost their purpose as Windows NT takes over from previous Microsoft operating systems.

Glossary

Access Control List (ACL) A list of permit and deny conditions to a resource.

ActiveX An Internet version of Microsoft's Distributed Component Object Model (DCOM).

Administrator The account used to administer NT computers, domains, and workgroups.

Applet A Windows NT small program, usually a utility. Examples are applets to change the screen resolution and set multimedia properties. The Control Panel is comprised of applets.

AppleTalk protocol A protocol that allows Apple computers to use resources shared from an NT system.

Auditing The capability to record events and user actions while they are logged on to a Windows NT computer or domain.

Authentication Validation of a user through a username/password combination.

Backup domain controller (BDC) A Windows NT Server that holds a copy of the security database within a Windows NT domain and can authenticate users locally.

Binding The process of establishing communication between network protocols and a network hardware.

Boot partition A volume that contains the Windows NT operating system and enough support files to start a computer.

bps (bits per second) A measurement of the speed with which a device can transfer data.

Browser A program for displaying HTML (Web) pages.

Browser service A Windows NT service that displays a list of currently running Windows NT systems, domains, workgroups, file and print shares, and other shared resources on a network.

Cache A store of information containing the most recent or most frequently accessed data. In use, a cache generally refers to RAM used to store frequently accessed hard disk data.

Client Service for NetWare (CSNW)   A service that allows Windows NT connectivity to NetWare resources.

Command line interface (CLI)   The command shell of Windows NT, equivalent to UNIX shells such as the C shell or the MS-DOS command line.

Common Object Model (COM)   A standard that defines interfaces between objects to enable seamless integration of objects between applications.

Context menu   The menu resulting from a right-click (secondary button) of the mouse. The contents of the menu will change depending on the context of the click.

CSLIP (Compressed SLIP)   *See SLIP*

Default gateway   A router or computer that possesses routing capabilities and can direct traffic to its intended destination within or without the local network.

Device driver   Software that acts as a go-between for the operating system and accessory hardware, such as the display adapter or multimedia devices.

Dial-Up Networking (DUN)   The client side of Remote Access Service, enabling the client to connect to a network remotely over a phone line. Most often, DUN connects independent computers to the Internet or to corporate networks.

Domain   A collection of Windows NT systems defined to share a single security database.

Domain name service (DNS)   A service that has the capability of resolving an IP address, given an IP name, or vice versa.

Dynamic data exchange (DDE)   The capability to exchange data between two or more applications.

Dynamic Host Configuration Protocol (DHCP)   A Windows NT service that enables a client to lease an IP address from an IP pool maintained by a DHCP server.

Dynamic link library (DLL)   A file that contains routines and functions that are loaded when needed.

Email (or e-mail)   Electronic mail or messages sent over networks from one user to another (or many).

Emergency Repair Disk (ERD)   A disk created using the RDISK utility, which enables (along with Setup) the repair of a damaged installation of Windows NT.

Encryption   The process of protecting data by changing its contents so that it is decipherable only with a special key.

Extranet   An intranet running on private hardware (usually leased lines or satellites).

FAT   A file system dating back to version 2.x of MS-DOS. Now superceded by NTFS and FAT32.

File replication   The capability to replicate files and directories between two or more Windows NT machines.

File sharing   The capability to share files and directories over the network.

File Transfer Protocol (FTP)   A protocol to transfer binary files between remote machines using TCP/IP (Internet).

Fly-out menu   A submenu.

Folder   The name given to directories and subdirectories starting with Windows NT 4.0.

Group   A collection of users. Permissions granted at group level are inherited by its members.

Guest   A built-in Windows NT security account used by casual users connecting to the Windows NT network.

Hardware Compatibility List (HCL)   A list of devices, maintained by Microsoft, of hardware known to work well under Windows NT.

Host   A device on a TCP/IP network identified by an IP address.

Hypertext Markup Language (HTML)   A language used to create hypertext documents used for publishing on the World Wide Web.

Hypertext Transfer Protocol (HTTP)   An IP protocol used to transfer HTML data from a Web site to a user's desktop.

Integrated Services Digital Network (ISDN)   A digital communication service that has found popularity in providing WAN connectivity.

Internet   A network made up of a number of public networks tied using the same protocol, TCP/IP.

Internet service provider (ISP)   An independent business that provides access to the Internet as part of its product mix.

Internetwork Packet Exchange/Sequenced Packet Exchange (IPX/SPX)   A transport protocol used in a Novell NetWare network.

Interprocess communication (IPC)   The capability of two or more processes to communicate, independent of whether they reside on the same machine.

Interrupt request (IRQ)   A hardware signal used by a device to gain the attention of the processor.

Intranet A private version of the Internet, found primarily within corporations and businesses.

IP address A unique 4-octet number separated by a dot, used to identify nodes on an IP network.

Java A programming language developed by Sun Microsystems, designed for use in applet and agent applications, usually through a browser. Now mostly used for Web animations.

LMHOSTS file Used to resolve NetBIOS names to IP addresses.

Local area network (LAN) A collection of interconnected computers dispersed over a relatively small area, usually within a building.

Local Security Authority (LSA) The main component within the Windows NT security model. It is used to generate access tokens, maintain the system security and audit policies, and log audit alerts.

Media Access Control (MAC) The network layer that deals with network access and collision detection.

Modem An electronic device that converts binary data to analog tones and voltages that are suitable for transmission over standard dial-up or leased-line telephone lines.

MS-CHAP Microsoft implementation of Challenge Handshake Authentication Protocol, used to secure an encrypted connection between a RAS server and client.

Multihomed A machine that has more than one network interface card attached to separate physical networks.

Network Basic Input/Output System (NetBIOS) An IBM-developed standard software interface to a network adapter.

Network Basic Input/Output System Extended User Interface (NetBEUI) A nonroutable broadcast LAN protocol (an extension of NetBIOS).

Network interface card (NIC) An expansion card used to connect a computer to a network.

Newsgroup A public or private forum for exchange of text or binary messages.

Novell Directory Service (NDS) Novell's method of distributing resource information to LAN clients.

Novell NetWare A network operating system vended by Novell and that uses the IPX/SPX protocol.

NTFS A file system specifically designed for Windows NT.

OLE A Microsoft implementation of data transfer and sharing between applications.

Packet Assemblers/Disassemblers (PAD) A connectivity device to an X.25 network.

Paging file   A file used to store data temporarily swapped out from RAM.

Password Authentication Protocol (PAP)   An authentication protocol that uses clear-text passwords.

Permission   The level of access granted a user or user group.

Ping   A command-line utility used to verify connectivity within an IP network.

Plug and Play   An operating system's capability of identifying and configuring hardware.

Point-to-Point Protocol (PPP)   A standard framing and authentication protocol used within Microsoft's RAS.

Point-to-Point Tunneling Protocol (PPTP)   The ability to tunnel network protocols within a PPP connection. This can be used to create secure virtual private networks (VPNs).

Port   A location used to pass data in and out of a computing device.

Portable Operating System Interface (POSIX)   A standard that defines a set of operating-system services.

Post Office Protocol (POP3)   A protocol for the operation of a post office (delivery) of email.

Primary domain controller (PDC)   The Windows NT Server within a Windows NT domain that authenti-cates users and maintains the security account database.

Process   An executable program, a set of virtual memory addresses, and one or more threads. When a program runs, it is called a process.

Process identifier (PID)   A unique number assigned to a running process.

Protocol   A set of rules and con-ventions used to transfer information over a network.

Proxy   A machine that accepts incoming calls and validates them against an access list. A proxy oper-ates at a service level.

Registry   A database containing sys-tems configuration information stored in a hierarchical fashion.

Remote Access Service (RAS)   A Windows NT service that enables remote users to connect to a Windows NT network via a tele-phone connection.

Remote Procedure Call   Interprocess communication between processes residing on different machines.

Router   A piece of equipment that links networks. Routers find the best paths to destinations on the network and direct traffic via these best paths.

Routing Information Protocol (RIP)   The exchange of routing information between routers to build up a knowledge of the network. This information allows routers to decide on a best path.

Security Account Manager (SAM) A database containing account information such as passwords, account names, and policies.

Security ID (SID) A unique identifier to identify a user to a security system.

Services A process designed to execute specific system functions. Because services are RPC-based, they can be invoked remotely.

Simple Mail Transfer Protocol (SMTP) A TCP/IP suite of protocols the covers the transfer of electronic mail.

Simple Network Management Protocol A protocol used to monitor that state of a host on a TCP/IP network. Hosts can be monitored remotely via SNMP.

SLIP (Serial Line Internet Protocol) An old communication standard. It is still incorporated within RAS to ensure interoperability with third-party remote access software.

Small Computer System Interface (SCSI) A standard high-speed parallel interface for connecting computers to peripheral devices such as hard drives and printers.

Start A button on the taskbar containing the main menu for Windows NT.

Subnetmask A 32-bit value that divides an IP address into a network ID and host ID.

Taskbar The bar containing the System Tray and the Start button. By default, the taskbar lies at the bottom of your screen, but you can move it to any screen side.

TCP/IP A suite of networking protocols that provides connectivity across interconnected networks.

Uniform resource locator (URL) A pointer to, or name of, a unique resource on the Internet.

Uninterruptible power supply (UPS) A battery-operated source of power that automatically supports your computer if your main electricity supply fails.

Universal Naming Convention name (UNC) The full name of a shared resource on a Windows NT network—for example, `\\servername\sharename`.

User accounts A way of associating attributes to a user when logged on to a Windows NT domain or computer. These attributes include username, password, group membership, and so forth.

User Datagram Protocol (UDP) A complementing protocol to TCP that offers a connectionless datagram service that does not guarantee delivery or sequencing.

User Manager   A Windows NT tool used to maintain users, groups, and security policies within Windows NT.

User rights   A set of actions users can execute within a Windows NT computer or domain.

Virtual memory   A space on your hard drive used to hold data swapped out of memory temporarily.

Virtual Private Network (VPN) The capability to connect private LANs via a public network such as the Internet.

Wide area network (WAN)   A network connected over a large global area.

Windows Explorer (or just Explorer)   The main interface for Windows NT. This includes file and folder management services and, using the Start button on the taskbar, a graphical way to launch applications or services.

Windows Internet Naming Service (WINS)   Microsoft's name resolution service for NetBIOS names.

WINNT32   The program on the distribution CD that installs Windows NT.

Workgroup   A collection of computers grouped together for viewing purposes. Computers within a workgroup all have their own separate SAM databases.

WWW (World Wide Web)   An information service on the Internet whose content contains hypertext, graphics, and multimedia.

X.25   A packet-switching network.

Index

Symbols

& (ampersand), command separation, 555

^ (caret), literal characters, 555

, (comma), command-line parameters, 554

- (dash), CLI, 520-521

&& (double ampersand), commands, 555

>> (double greater than symbol)
appending output, 554
error display redirection, 554

> (greater than symbol), output redirection, 554

< (less than symbol), input redirection, 554

|| (non-strict OR), 554

( ) (parentheses), grouping commands, 555

| (pipe), piping output, 554

/ (slash), CLI, 517

A

Accessories folder, adding shortcuts, 60-61

account policies, 340

accounts, 367. *See also* **permissions; users**
guest, 368
disabling, 368-369
logons, 369

Active Channel site, 70

Active Desktop, 312-314. *See also* **IE4**
Active Elements, 85
adding, 85-87
giving focus to, 87
performance effects, 85
properties, 87
removing, 89
resizing, 87
saving, 89
channel bar, 313
Channels, 69-74
Active Channel site, 70
Channel Guide, 70
searching for, 71
subscribing to, 71
updating, 69
customizing, 90
disabling, 90
ERD, 69
folder options, 314
icons, hiding/displaying, 92
IE4, effects on, 89-91
installing, 64-69
interface, 74-75
OE, 140-141

options, 90-91
right-clicking, 74
SP3 (Service Pack 3)
downloading, 64
installing, 64-66
taskbar, 76
moving, 84
Quick Launch, 76-78
resizing, 83
toolbars, 79-83

Active Elements, 85
adding, 85-87
giving focus to, 87
performance effects, 85
properties, 87
removing, 89
resizing, 87
saving, 89

adapters. *See* **network adapters**

Add Permissions dialog box, 374-375

Add Printer Wizard, 97

Address Book, 156-157
adding/editing entries, 156
groups, creating, 156

addresses
IP, 194-195, 484
broadcast traffic, 194
computer names, 199-201